1998

THE
VICTORIAN UNDERWORLD

Other books by the author

The
Victorian Underworld

Donald Thomas

JOHN MURRAY
Albemarle Street, London

For Christopher Turk

First published in 1998
by John Murray (Publishers) Ltd,
50 Albemarle Street, London W1X 4BD

A catalogue record for this book is available from the British Library

ISBN 0-7195-5393-8

Typeset in 11/13½ Monotype Baskerville by Servis Filmsetting Ltd
Printed and bound in Great Britain by The University Press, Cambridge

Contents

Acknowledgements

It is a pleasure to record the assistance and support in writing this book of Mrs Caroline Knox, Mrs Gail Pirkis and Mr Michael Thomas. I am indebted to friends, family and colleagues, most of all to my wife, and to all those who may have felt that my deadlines too often seemed like their own.

Illustrations in the text are taken from *The Bank of England Forgery*, ed. George Dilnot, Geoffrey Bles, 1929; J. B. Booth, *'Master' and Men: Pink 'Un Yesterdays*, T. Werner Laurie, 1927; Charles Tempest Clarkson and J. Hall Richardson, *Police!*, 1889; *The Day's Doings* [1871]; Gustave Doré and Blanchard Jerrold, *London: A Pilgrimage*, 1872; *The Drunkard's Children* [1848]; *The Face of London* [1848]; *The Ferret* [1870]; *A Full Account of the Great Gold Robbery*, illustrated by Percy Cruikshank, H. Vickers, 1857; *Illustrated London News* [1848]; *Illustrated Times* [1848, 1863]; Henry Mayhew, *London Labour and the London Poor*, 1861–2; Henry Mayhew and John Binny, *The Criminal Prisons of London*, 1862; *Penny Illustrated Paper* [1869]; *Punch* [1850, 1852]; *The Trial of the Detectives*, ed. George Dilnot, Geoffrey Bles, 1928; *The Trial of Thomas Neill Cream*, ed. Teignmouth Shore, Notable British Trials, William Hodge, 1923; and *Working Man's Friend* [1852].

Darkest England

It was in June 1832 that *Fraser's Magazine* first warned its readers of the existence of a new and well-organized criminal class whose leaders acted as patrons of crime, arranging the disposal of stolen goods, and even regulating the admission of new members to their fraternity as if they had been nominating apprentices to an honourable craft. Such men thrived upon the certainties that the profits of the profession had grown large and that the chances of detection were remote. Carried away by its belief in this distinct sub-class of society, the magazine described its members as a criminal 'club', something to be known more commonly as an underworld.

The criminal class of the Victorian age, as distinct from the life of the underclass which usually sheltered it, was more easily recognized than defined. What was criminal often lay in the eye and the mind of the beholder. Begging, for example, was a last resort of poverty but also a traditional form of the trickster's art. The Society for the Suppression of Mendacity, founded in 1818, now required beggars to provide evidence of genuine distress and to face prosecution as impostors if they could not.

Even if prostitution were regarded as a facet of the criminal underworld, its practitioners seldom matched the stereotype of the diseased harpy weaving the nation's winding-sheet. There were many women who belonged to the profession when times were bad in the slop-shops of the tailoring trade, for example, and who left the streets again for their former employment when conditions improved. Most of the women on the streets regarded prostitution as a transition from maidenhood to marriage, rather than as membership of a class outside the law. Most were proved right.

Even the act of theft might be the work of a professional cracksman at one extreme and, at the other, the stealing of an apple from a barrow as an act of childish bravado. The act of the child who stole the apple shaded into the systematic thefts from Thames barges by gangs of little 'mudlarks', and thence into juvenile pickpocketing and professional house-breaking.

The underclass of the cities, hostile to the police and suspicious of the law, was a natural refuge of the habitual criminal. Yet many accomplished forgers and burglars of mid-Victorian England were sheltered within a professional class, their appearance and surroundings far removed from those of Bill Sikes and the Artful Dodger. Edward Agar, a man of business, led the Great Bullion Robbery in 1855; James Townshend Saward, barrister of the Inner Temple, was unmasked as 'Jem the Penman'; those who emptied the Bank of England of £100,000 in 1873 were habitués of the best hotels and travelled the world in considerable comfort, one reputedly having been a rebellious Harvard undergraduate; Harry Benson, who brought the Detective Police of Scotland Yard to ruin in 1877, had education and property, and a cosmopolitan persuasiveness equally effective in New York, Paris and London. A leavening of proletarian criminality by the cad and the bounder was never plainer than in the theft of the regalia known as 'The Irish Crown Jewels' from a closely guarded safe in Dublin Castle, six years after the end of Victoria's reign. This crime was the work of two officers and gentlemen, one of them brother to the polar explorer Sir Ernest Shackleton. His alibi witness was the late Queen's son-in-law, the Duke of Argyll.

Precise description and location of a criminal class were made no easier by a new mobility and a chameleon-like adaptation to new surroundings. On 17 January 1857, *The Times* lectured its readers on the manner in which professional burglars were travelling by railway, often in first-class carriages, moving from town to town with a speed that the police could scarcely match. London pickpockets travelled England and Continental Europe in search of opportunities, shadowing well-heeled tourists to the Irish lakes or the French spas and operating on the fringes of businessmen's gatherings at Manchester and in the North.

Crime shared the benefits of industrial progress. In 1839, a Report of the Royal Commission on a Constabulary Force revealed that burglars and safe-breakers in London were having tools made to the highest standards by the craftsmen of Birmingham, Sheffield and those other cities of the Midlands and the North that formed 'The Workshop of England'.

Such a professional underworld was largely synonymous in the public mind with the outcasts of London. The capital's population grew from 1,873,676 in 1841 to 4,232,118 in 1891, and the proportion of the nation's population which lived in the city rose by almost a quarter during those years. The 1851 census identified 13,120 criminals and 6,849 prostitutes in London. Other towns or cities might sometimes have more criminals proportionately but none could individually approach the number of offences committed in London nor offer such promising material for the study of criminality.

Indeed, figures for crime and criminals in the provinces appeared increasingly unreliable. As early as 1845, Friedrich Engels in *The Condition of the Working Class in England* had claimed a seven-fold increase in crime from 1805 to 1842, based on the number of suspects arrested. Yet a new form of policing had been introduced from 1829 onwards and the later figures revealed only that a greater number of offenders had been caught. By 1895, the Home Office Committee on Statistics complained that for many years the police forces in Birmingham, Liverpool, Bradford and Manchester had been unable to agree on what constituted either a known thief or a suspicious character. The committee dismissed the previously accepted figures as being of no value in trying to compare crime across the country. London, however, had enjoyed the advantage of being more intensively documented, the subject of such classic studies as Mayhew's *London Labour and the London Poor* and Dr William Acton's *Prostitution*.

In the English provinces during the early years of the Queen's reign habitual criminals were itinerant for good reasons. The Report of the Royal Commission on a Constabulary Force, which had deplored the trade in burglars' tools, also recorded the migration of suspects from those areas that were now policed to those which remained 'unprotected'. Any observer of the streets and race meetings of the 1850s might have noticed how the swindler who challenged passers-by to try their luck at the Three-Card Trick or Three-Thimbles-and-a-Pea was disappearing from city pavements, where a policeman on the beat might pass every twenty minutes, only to reappear on the safer ground of country fairs or racecourses.

According to Henry Worsley in *Juvenile Depravity* (1849) there was a difference in the quality of crime between the professionalism of London and the feckless offenders of the countryside. Poaching and petty larceny, rather than the metropolitan sophistication of forgery or house-breaking, characterized rural crime. Such acts scarcely represented the existence of a rural underworld. Most villagers, indeed, did not regard the stealing of game as morally wrong. In Worsley's view, the game laws themselves were as much a cause of crime as the beer shops and lodging-houses of the cities.

Even the metropolitan underworld was more elusive than the continued existence of the old criminal 'rookeries' might suggest. Working-class districts gave refuge to the humble dodgers, who lived by tricks and cheats, and to better-dressed burglars or swindlers of the swell mob. The best safe-breakers were found in the affluence of Russell Square and in quiet prosperity at addresses in Newington Causeway and the New Kent Road, looking like the successful businessmen they might otherwise have been.

Many who followed such crafts as forgery or coining chose the little streets of districts along the river, forming a community with coster-mongers and artisans. When there was trouble, the community was apt to take their side against the law. The costers sold fruit, vegetables, fish and other merchandise from their street barrows. They were naturally hostile to the police, whose duty it was to clear the streets of such obstructions as market barrows, hence depriving the traders of a livelihood. When the constabulary arrived to arrest a coiner, coster neighbours saw only an intrusion by a common enemy.

Those thieves or prostitutes who were precariously placed between crime and destitution might withdraw to the congested slums of the 'rookeries', the Devil's Acre in Westminster, Jacob's Island in Bermondsey, and the 'Holy Land', containing the adjacent rookeries of St Giles's and the Seven Dials, just east of the Charing Cross Road. These rotting tenements and taverns of an earlier century were not swept away by any single great act of social reform. They disappeared piecemeal from the landscape of London between the time when New Oxford Street was driven through part of St Giles's in the 1840s and the final redevelopment of Westminster half a century later. The crimes associated with them, as Superintendent Cornish of Scotland Yard remarked, were cleared from such areas and dispersed across London.

*

The Victorian criminal worked under three legacies of the recent past. The first of these, the gradual abolition of the so-called 'Bloody Code' of laws and punishments, followed the appointment of Sir Robert Peel as Home Secretary in 1822. In 1800, there had been more than 160 crimes for which the death penalty might be inflicted. At its worst, this code permitted the execution of children and prescribed hanging for trivial thefts. By the end of the 1830s, few capital offences remained apart from murder and treason. Hanging, however, continued to provide entertainment outside Newgate Gaol and other prisons until public executions were abolished in 1868.

A second change in the life of the criminal was less welcome. The penalty for professional failure was usually imprisonment. Until the 1830s, it was possible to live as well in gaol as it had been when gin shops had competed within the prison walls and the admission of women had enlivened the last hours of the condemned. The moralists of the new reign frowned upon such regimes as that under which prisoners with money were permitted to live in the Governor of Newgate's house with their own servants, their meals brought in from taverns or coffee houses. Time was passed by less influential inmates in drinking or in playing cards, tennis, skittles or billiards. In 1836, the new Prison Commissioners were outraged to see men in Newgate so drunk that they could not sit upright, let alone stand. Even though it was not as easy to import women into prison by this time, a male prisoner who claimed to be the relative of a female prisoner might be given free access to her.

To the 1840s, however, crime was a contagion. New prisons were built, dedicated to the proposition that each prisoner was to live in a species of solitary confinement, unable to communicate with any other convict, and that each should be masked by a Scotch cap, so that when prisoners saw one another identification was impossible. The provisions were known as the 'silent system' and the 'separate system'.

Resistance was to be broken by the crank, the tread-wheel, and shot drill, but most effectively by removal of food from a diet already meagre, until the rebel or malingerer wearied of near-starvation. As the system of transportation to penal colonies in Australia was progressively abolished in the 1850s and 1860s, some of the rigours of that system were incorporated in a new category of detention called 'penal servitude'. Though transportation ceased, convict hulks remained as floating prisons at locations like Woolwich, and at Portland until its prison was built.

The most novel deterrent to crime was a third legacy of the 1830s, the advent of the new police forces which had been initiated by Sir Robert Peel's 'Act for improving the police in and near the Metropolis' in June 1829. City watchmen had been ineffective and the Bow Street Runners, inaugurated by Henry Fielding and his half-brother Sir John Fielding in 1753, invited corruption and derision alike by recruiting former thieves and offering them rewards. Peel proposed London's first centralized and professional police. Within ten years, its officers were sufficiently well established to have drawn upon themselves the hostility of much of the working population and a suspicion that many of them had been corrupted by brothel-keepers, pornographers and others who wished to trade undisturbed.

On its creation, the Metropolitan Police contained no detective force, a concession to objections to 'police espionage' upon free citizens. It was only after two murder investigations, which the police were thought to have bungled, that a Detective Police division was created at Scotland Yard in 1842. This consisted of two inspectors and six sergeants. Yet the new detectives were hampered by rules that forbad any association with suspected criminals or underworld informants, rules that stemmed from a fear of police corruption and of espionage upon the innocent.

By 1869, the Detective Police at Scotland Yard had been increased from ten to twenty-seven, with 188 officers in the other Metropolitan divisions. Overall, Metropolitan Police manpower grew from 1,000 in 1829 to 9,000 forty years later. The installation of an electric telegraph in 1868 linked Scotland Yard with the divisions and in 1870 a Register of Habitual Criminals was set up. Criminals migrated to areas where work was easier. As late as 1856 some 40 per cent of counties still relied on the ancient system of law enforcement whereby a justice of the peace worked with a parish constable.

Setbacks to policing in London marked the latter half of the Victorian age. A successful prosecution for police perjury and a corruption trial which destroyed the entire system of detective policing at Scotland Yard resulted in the new Criminal Investigation Department with its Special Branch by 1884. Indeed, in the 1860s critics of police methods and evidence had already raised the issue of wrongful convictions through newspapers like the *Daily Telegraph* and the campaigns of senior lawyers like William Ballantine. Even incontrovertible scientific evidence proved to be nothing of the sort.

*

To a twentieth-century reader, the Victorian fight against crime may have a certain familiarity. England in the 1840s and 1850s, no less than in the 1940s and 1950s, was apt to believe that statistics proved crime to be out of control and to regret that harsher penalties had been abolished. This unease enabled Victorian documentary writers of the buccaneering genius of Henry Mayhew to excite middle-class interest in a self-portrayal of the poor and the dishonest. Edwin Chadwick had already brought to life the voices of young prostitutes and thieves in Manchester and Liverpool. Mayhew and his assistants spanned a dozen years in the life of the capital.

The 1860s, no less than the 1960s, seemed like a decade of release from years of sombre austerity. Prostitution and flamboyant sexuality were a source of scandal but also an emblem of the new nightlife of the West End with its lamplit pleasure-gardens, assembly rooms, parks and casinos. The rebellion of a younger and more Bohemian generation of Victorians against its elders found expression in pleasures and provocation, a subversion of propriety through pornography and bawdry.

As flamboyance faded, the 1870s like the 1970s called to account corruption at the heart of Scotland Yard. By the 1880s, mid-century hedonism was checked. Prostitution, which had appropriated the term 'gay' to describe itself twenty years earlier, became largely synonymous with child abuse and white slavery. Denunciation of such evils culminated in 1885 in the trials of Mary Jeffries, as a white slaver, and W. T. Stead, who had campaigned with ill-advised enthusiasm for a law to curb such outrages. Immoral publications, now including the novels, of Zola and Maupassant, fell under scrutiny and prosecution by the National Vigilance Association. Public decency was policed by an unappealing alliance of prudery and prurience. Libraries and booksellers, as the young novelist George Moore protested, demanded from authors and publishers a fiction of moral correctness intended for, even if not written by, what he called 'young unmarried women'. Prostitution withdrew to the shadows and pornography fled to Paris.

The underworld of the 1850s was eclipsed at the century's end by dramas of serial killers, the wraith of 'Jack the Ripper' or Dr Neill Cream, the Lambeth Poisoner. Serial killers were not new and crime itself had altered little, being one of the more conservative professions, where the penalty of failure discourages mere fashionable innovation. Yet the public appetite grew for tales of white slavery and multiple murder, the sensationalism of the *Pall Mall Gazette* prevailing over the social reality of *London Labour and the London Poor*.

*

Though fashions in the literature of true crime changed at the end of the Victorian period, it was Henry Mayhew and his assistants at mid-century who had opened the doors of their middle-class readers on the worlds of crime and deprivation. Photography and a new system of shorthand enabled them to bring the present alive to contemporaries and their successors with unparalleled vitality. From 1849 to 1862, Mayhew preserved word by word self-portraits of street-folk, lodging-house inmates, beggars, prostitutes, pickpockets, house-breakers and cracksmen who would have gone to their graves in silence at any earlier time. He gave to the world what Leslie Stephen, writing of the *State Trials* transcripts in 1892, described as 'the actual utterance of men struggling in the dire grip of unmitigated realities'.

Mayhew was to Victorian journalism what Dickens was to the novel. By contrast with the methodical approach of social investigators like Edwin Chadwick or the statistical exposition of the 1840s, his was a commercial and popular undertaking, written in the first place for the morning papers and then for those who would read his account of poverty and crime in penny parts. He was, after all, a dramatist and a former editor of *Punch*. In interviewing prostitutes, thieves and beggars, he relied upon the work of his assistants, 'Bracebridge Hemyng', alias Samuel Bracebridge, John Binny and Andrew Halliday, known in the theatres of London for his dramas of London's outcasts. A last volume, *The Criminal Prisons of London* (1862), was to be completed by John Binny, after financial problems forced Mayhew to retire abroad.

This present path through the underworld of the Victorian age begins in Mayhew's company.

Crime

Taking the census in the dark arches of the Adelphi, 1861

CHAPTER 1

Victoria's Other London

IN 1851, while London was trumpeted by the catalogue of the Great Exhibition as the showplace of 'the industrial triumphs of the whole world', Henry Mayhew concluded his Preface to *London Labour and the London Poor* by remarking that the extent of 'misery, ignorance, and vice, amidst all the wealth and great knowledge of "the first city in the world", is, to say the least, a national disgrace to us'. Mayhew, this 'clever and earnest-minded writer', as Thackeray called him, had been born in 1812. He became a dramatist and either composed or popularized 'Villikins and his Dinah', a comic song of doomed cockney lovers, introduced in his play *The Wandering Minstrel*. Like Charles Dickens, he was also a correspondent of the liberal *Morning Chronicle* before he began his survey, which he called in the Preface to his first volume a 'first attempt to publish the history of a people, from the lips of the people themselves'.[1]

Unlike Dickens, Mayhew had Mr Gradgrind's enthusiasm for facts and figures, though only so far as they demonstrated the curiosities of the city in which he lived. He wanted to know how many people slept in a room and how many to a bed in the 'low lodging-houses'. He calculated the earnings of costermongers and prostitutes, scavengers and flower-girls, the sizes of families and the rates of death. He listed the lives of beggars and burglars, how safes were opened and shopkeepers swindled. He tabled the daily and weekly income of sewer-hunters and showed that a sweep's boy could earn a shilling a day in street Harlequinades but was fed on sixpence halfpenny when he worked at his trade.

It was characteristic of Mayhew that he should include a careful analysis of 'Food Consumed by and Excretions of a Horse in Twenty-Four Hours'. With enthusiastic pedantry, he weighed the animal's food and excreta 'in their fresh state', and tabulated the figures to the last gramme – or to the last ounce for those who preferred a more homely unit of measurement. Neither his system nor its conclusions were comic in themselves. He calculated that each horse deposited over forty pounds of dung a day in London's streets, a ton in less than two months. Multiplied by the tens of thousands of working horses in a city crossed by 150,000 vehicles a day, this posed a formidable problem of health and civic cleanliness. Children, less winsome than Little Jo in *Bleak House*, owed their livelihoods and early deaths to the need to whisk a path across the insanitary streets with their brooms so that their betters might walk unsullied. More rebellious spirits were not sorry to see the 'aristocracy' sullied. As a scavenger who shovelled night-soil from the streets told Mayhew, laughing as he talked of it, someone might 'run off to complain that he's been splashed o' purpose' by the human 'slop' which was tipped into the scavengers' carts.[2]

The investigations of Mayhew and his colleagues, which eventually filled four volumes, were first published in twopenny parts. By no means all of those who told their stories in these pages were criminals, yet most remained a law unto themselves. An underclass, which nourished an underworld, was bred among the costermongers and the people of the city streets. Thanks to Mayhew's skill, the men and women of those streets still tell their stories through his survey, in words as clear and vigorous as if they had been spoken yesterday.

It was the first point in English history at which this could readily have been done. In recording the words of street-traders and beggars, thieves and prostitutes, entertainers and tricksters, Mayhew and his contemporaries relied upon shorthand. Though available in a more primitive form to Pepys two centuries earlier, it was not adequately systematized in England until Isaac Pitman's *Stenographic Sound Hand* in 1837.

By such means, Mayhew brought to his middle-class readership what Thackeray in 1850 called 'a picture of human life so wonderful, so awful, so piteous and pathetic, so exciting and terrible, that readers of romances own they never read anything like to it . . . these wonders have been lying by your door and mine ever since we had a door of our own. We had but to go a hundred yards off and see for ourselves, but we never did.'[3]

As far back as 1831, when the government began to investigate the conditions of the urban poor for fear of a cholera epidemic, Charles Greville, as Clerk to the Privy Council, noted that 'The reports from Sunderland exhibit a state of human misery, and necessarily of moral degradation, such as I hardly ever heard of.' Almost three hundred miles to the south, in Bethnal Green, 1,100 people were 'crammed into the poor-house, five and six in a bed; 6,000 receive parochial relief. The Parish is in debt . . . what can Government do?' Thereafter, blue books and Poor Law reports had contained a mass of information, telling the government what it could – and should – do for the deserving poor. Mayhew's achievement was to give reality and humanity to the findings of such investigations.[4]

He first drew a distinction between those who were destitute or starving and those who had chosen to live beyond the missionary reach of bourgeois society. An extensive population of the London streets consisted first of a self-confident coster community, numbering some 30,000 who traded in fruit, vegetables and fish from market barrows. With its familiar caps and carts, it traded upon its wits and usually in opposition to the newly constituted Metropolitan Police. Secondly, there was an army of outdoor workers, many of them like the garment-makers or the Spitalfields weavers earning starvation wages of a few shillings a week and living on a pauper diet of buttered bread and tea. The two groups were augmented by a third in the 1840s and the 1850s, a wandering tribe of hawkers, street-entertainers and beggars, drawn to London in the hope of better times than could be found in the new industrial cities or impoverished villages. Their prospects were reflected by Tennyson in two famous lines of 'Locksley Hall', as the farmer's boy turns his back upon his father's fields:

> And at night along the dusky highway, near and nearer drawn,
> Sees in heaven the light of London flaring like a dreary dawn.

The consequence of many such adventures was described no less poetically by an itinerant tin-ware seller in the 1850s. 'I resolved to go to London – the theatre of all my misery to come.'[5]

Between 1800 and 1850, the compact and familiar topography of London with its farm-carts and windmills had expanded from an eighteenth-century city of 865,000 people to a metropolis of some two and a half million. Those streets which had seen the harvest of nearby fields and orchards borne through them fifty years earlier were now crowded

Gustave Doré, A view from Brewery Bridge to St Paul's,
showing the interlinking of rookery tenements, 1872

by carts, cabs, twopenny buses, costers' barrows, coffee stalls and towering portable advertisements drawn slowly through the West End to publicize the latest waxwork show, or firework display, or *bal masqué* at the Holborn Assembly Rooms.

From Regent Street to the Ratcliffe Highway, from the criminal haunts of St Giles's rookery to the costers' 'penny gaffs' or the Lambeth street-markets on a Saturday night, Mayhew caught the life of the common people of mid-Victorian London with the precision of a tape-recording.

His was a city of coal-heavers and dock-labourers, dolly-mops and magsmen, cabinet-makers and seamstresses, bug-hunters and mudlarks. Above all, he immortalized the tribes of wandering street-folk, from beggars and ballad singers to running-patterers and the street fire-king.

The variety of street-traders and entertainers sounds as much in keeping with Elizabethan London as with the capital of Victoria's empire. In the streets of the 1850s, Mayhew recorded the lives of death-and-fire-hunters, chanters, second-edition sellers, reciters, conundrum-sellers, board-workers, strawers, sellers of sham-indecent publications, street-auctioneers, mountebanks, clowns, jugglers, conjurers, ring-sellers-for-wagers, sovereign-sellers, corn-curers, grease-removers, French-polishers, blacking-sellers, nostrum-vendors, fortune-tellers, oratorical beggars, turnpike sailors, various classes of 'lurkers', steno-graphic-card sellers and vendors of racecards or lists.

In the end, Mayhew's work was not to be remembered for its curious tables of figures but for a philosophy which put him on equal terms with the criminal and the dispossessed. 'A touch of nature', he wrote, 'makes all the world akin.'[6]

*

Mayhew's survey of London included fine set-piece descriptions, such as his panorama of the docks at Wapping and Shadwell or his progress through the Lambeth street-markets on Saturday night and Sunday morning. The drinking habits of the labouring class had made Sunday morning markets necessary to a wife who could not find her husband and his wages before the 'confusion and uproar' of the previous night's markets quietened. 'The system of paying the mechanic late on the Saturday night – and more particularly of paying a man his wages in a public house – when he is tired with his day's work – lures him to the tavern.' By the time his wife found him, a Sunday market was the only chance of getting their dinner. Drink remained a temptation to both sexes. Shoplifting on working days was frequently the result of the wife going out to buy food, meeting her friends and saying, 'I have not much to get the old man's dinner but we can have a quartern of gin.'

Despite last-minute Sunday purchases, however, the infernal glow of the Lambeth markets in the New Cut on Saturday nights in the 1850s was the true climax of the week's trading. It was also an introduction to the resilient and subversive world of the costers.

There are hundreds of stalls, and every stall has its one or two lights, either it is illuminated by the intense white light of the new self-generating gas-lamp, or else it is brightened up by the red smoky flame of the old-fashioned grease-lamp. One man shows off his yellow haddock with a candle stuck in a bundle of firewood; his neighbour makes a candlestick of a huge turnip, and the tallow gutters over its sides; whilst the boy shouting 'Eight a penny, stunning pears!' has rolled his dip in a thick coat of brown paper, that flares away with the candle.[7]

Some of the stalls were lit by a crimson glow from the holes in the baked-chestnut stove, while others boasted handsome octahedral lamps. A few costers were content with a candle shining through a sieve. From end to end of the street, the voices of the barrow boys merged into a salesman's raucous litany. 'Chestnuts all 'ot, a penny a score. . . . An 'aypenny a skin, blacking. . . . Three-a-penny Yarmouth bloat-ers. . . . Who'll buy a bonnet for fourpence?' In the background were the Lambeth shops, the sparkling ground-glass globes of the tea-dealers, and the butchers' gaslights streaming and fluttering in the wind like flags of flame. From a distance, the sky above the market suggested that the New Cut was on fire from end to end.

It was in markets like this that Mayhew's readers met the costers at first hand. If the two social groups converged again, it was probably in theatres south of the river such as the Coburg, which was later to abandon its official title in favour of the popular nickname of the 'Old Wick' or 'Old Vic'. Respectability and family occupied the stalls. The costers colonized the gallery, the largest in London, into which two thousand patrons could be packed. It extended so far backwards that, at the rear, coster boys took turns to sit on one another's shoulders for a view of the stage far below.

On Saturday nights a surging crowd waited in the streets and on the wooden gallery stairs for the earlier performance to end. After the later house had begun, little boys begged for the ticket stubs of those coming out in the course of it, which entitled the holders to return to the per-formance later. The stubs, unwanted by the original purchasers, could then be sold for a penny to those who would go in for the last part of the performance.

Classics of English drama were not popular with the coster audience. 'Of *Hamlet* we can make neither head nor side,' said one of the costers, suggesting that the play should be cut to the appearance of the ghost, the scene in the graveyard, and the 'killing off' at the end. '*Macbeth* would be better liked if it was only the witches and the fighting.' Plays were dull compared with the singers of flash songs and the dancing by lightly dressed girls in the so-called 'penny gaffs', the song and dance entertainments of the shabbier streets. Some of the costers' comments might have dismayed the white-chokered missionaries of the middle class. 'The "penny gaffs" is rather more in my style,' said one coster lad to Mayhew, 'the songs are out and out, and makes our gals laugh. The smuttier the better. I thinks, bless you, the gals likes it as much as we do.'

The theatrical diet of the Old Vic consisted of more respectable singing, dancing and melodrama. Its gallery was filled with men whose jackets were removed to reveal ragged shirts and braces, their women hanging bonnets over the gallery rail so that they would not obstruct the view of those behind.

> As you look up the vast slanting mass of heads from the upper boxes, each one appears on the move. The huge black heap, dotted with faces, and spotted with white shirt sleeves, almost pains the eye to look at, and should a clapping of hands commence, the twinkling nearly blinds you.

Small boys, arriving late at the back of the gallery and not able to find a view of the stage, would double themselves into a ball and roll down over the heads of those in front, causing a trail of confusion and retaliatory blows, until they came to rest at a better vantage point. Fights broke out constantly in the gallery and the din was such that the orchestra could only be heard in its louder passages. While the curtain remained down and the musicians played, the gallery bawled, 'Pull up that there winder blind!' or 'Now then you catgut scrapers! Let's have a ha'purth of liveliness!' With the raising of the curtain, the roars of 'Silence! Ord-a-ar! Ord-a-ar!' contributed to a continuing din.

> Whilst the pieces are going on, brown flat bottles are frequently raised to the mouth, and between the acts a man with a tin can, glittering in the gas-light, goes round crying, 'Port-a-a-a-r! Who's for port-a-a-a-r!' As the heat increased the faces grew bright red, every bonnet was taken off, and the ladies could be seen wiping the perspiration from their cheeks with the playbills.[8]

The educational effect of such dramas as were performed seemed questionable. A maiden of melodrama pleading for her father's life was greeted with shouts of 'Speak up, old girl!' or 'Change it to "Duck-Legged

Dick!"' A braver heroine fighting off her ravishers was urged on by yells of 'Go it, my tulip!'

Such theatrical experiences, combined with the street recitations of the running-patterer listing the contents of his pamphlets which retailed famous murders and sexual scandals, made up much of the formal education of the audiences at the 'Wick'. Beyond that, it seemed that neither education nor religion had penetrated far among the costers, either in the East End or south of the river. Mayhew persuaded a boy who had been in the theatre's gallery to give some account of his religious and general knowledge.

> Yes, he had 'eered of God, who made the world. Couldn't exactly recollec' when he'd heer'd on him. Didn't know when the world was made or how anybody could do it. It was afore his time, 'or yourn either, sir.' Knew there was a book called the Bible; didn't know what it was about; didn't mind to know; knew of such a book to a sartinty, because a young 'oman took one to pop (pawn) for an old 'oman what was on the spree − a bran new 'un − but the cove wouldn't have it, and the old 'oman said he might be damned. Never heer'd tell on the deluge; of the world having been drownded. . . . He weren't a going to fret hisself for such things as that. Didn't know what happened to people after death, only that they was buried. . . . Had heer'd on another world; wouldn't mind if he was there hisself, if he could do better, for things was often queer here. Had heered on it from a tailor − such a clever cove, a stunner − as went to 'Straliar, and heer'd him say he was going into another world.

From religion, they moved to geography and astronomy, and then back to religion again.

> Had never heer'd of France, but had heer'd of Frenchmen; there wasn't half a quarter so many on 'em as of Italians, with their ear-rings, like flash gals. . . . Had heer'd of Ireland. Didn't know where it was, but it couldn't be very far, or such lots wouldn't come from there to London. Should say they walked it, aye, every bit of the way. Had heer'd of people going to sea, and had seen the ships in the river, but didn't know nothing about it, for he was very seldom that way. The sun was made of fire or it wouldn't make you feel so warm. The stars was fire, too, or they wouldn't shine. . . . Didn't know how far they was off; a jolly sight higher than the gas lights, some on 'em was. Was never in a church; had heer'd they worship God there; didn't know how it was done; had heer'd singing and playing inside when he'd passed; never was there, for he hadn't no togs to go in, and wouldn't be let in among

such swells as he had seen coming out. Was a ignorant chap, for he'd never been to school, but was up to many a move and didn't do bad. Mother said he would make his fortin yet.

Finally, the boy was questioned about history and literature.

Had heer'd on the Duke of Wellington; he was Old Nosey; didn't think he ever seed him, but had seed his statty. Hadn't heer'd of the battle of Waterloo, nor who it was atween. Once lived in Webber-row, Waterloo Road. Thought he had heer'd speak of Bonaparte; didn't know what he was; thought he had heer'd of Shakespeare, but didn't know whether he was alive or dead, and didn't care. A man with something like that name kept a dolly and did stunning; but he was such a hard cove that if *he* was dead it wouldn't matter. Had seen the Queen but didn't recollec' her *name* just at the minute; oh! yes, Wictoria and Albert. Had no notion what the Queen had to do. Should think she hadn't such power as the Lord Mayor or as Mr Norton as was the Lambeth beak, and perhaps is still.[9]

This was typical of many more answers to Mayhew's questions and suggested that there were areas of London as uninstructed by Christianity as the remotest regions of the empire. When Mayhew asked one of the costers if he had heard of Jesus Christ as his Redeemer, the man thought only of his best clothes which were in pawn. 'Our Redeemer? Well, I only wish I could redeem my Sunday togs from my "uncle's".'[10]

The Christian doctrine of forgiving one's enemies was regarded with scepticism, if not scorn. One of the coster boys had been told something of such a religion and was unimpressed. 'I have heered a little about our Saviour – they seem to say he were a goodish kind of man; but if he says as how a cove's to forgive a feller as hits you, I should say he know'd nothing about it.' When a coster girl was hit by her boy, explanations seemed superfluous. 'In coorse the gals the lads goes and lives with thinks our walloping of 'em wery cruel of us, but we don't. Why don't we? – because we don't.' It was not uncommon for a boy to be living with a girl by fifteen, sometimes thirteen. This was not illegal, since the age of consent until 1875 was twelve. Moreover, the average age of death in the poorer areas was seventeen. Those who were to be the parents of the next generation were encouraged to begin adult life early. As Mayhew noted of a boy who took a girl at fifteen, 'It creates no disgust among this class, but seems rather to give him a position among such people.'[11]

From the coster girls of the East End, Mayhew recorded an interview with one who assured him that 'I daresay there ain't ten out of a hundred gals what's living with men, what's been married Church of England fashion. . . . Perhaps a man will have a few words with his gal, and he'll say, "Oh, I ain't obligated to keep her!" and he'll turn her out: and then where's that poor gal to go?' It might seem that, as the patrician order of Victorian England was too powerful to bow to Mrs Grundy, a playwright's creation as censor of sexual morals, the working class was too poor to afford the trappings of conformity. Among the costers, however, there was a more general alienation from the moral precepts of those who regarded themselves as their betters. In this case, whether the couple had words or the girl became pregnant, the result was much the same, according to this informant. 'When the gal is in the family way, the lads mostly sends them to the workhouse to lay in, and only goes sometimes to take them a bit of tea and shugger. . . . I've often heerd the boys boasting of having ruined gals, for all the world as if they was the finest noblemen in the land.'[12]

If coster boys beat their girls, it was perhaps because in childhood they themselves had been used to being beaten by their masters and mistresses. Moreover, marriage might be an exception but jealousy was the rule. 'If I seed my gal talking to another chap,' said a sixteen-year-old, 'I'd fetch her sich a punch of the nose as should plaguy quick stop the whole business.' Another lad told Mayhew 'with a knowing look', of a curiosity of coster life. He insisted 'that the gals – it was a rum thing now he come to think on it – axully liked a feller for walloping them. As long as the bruises hurted, she was always thinking on the cove as gived 'em her.'[13]

While the costers and their kind might excuse their own methods of settling domestic disputes, they were intolerant of such ill-treatment elsewhere. When Marshal Haynau of Austria visited England, he was known as the man who had ordered the whipping of women in northern Italy for their resistance to his army's occupation. On his English visit, the draymen of Barclay and Perkins brewery tried to knock him down and to drop a barrel on his head. Swag-shops supplying the street-traders encouraged this by showing his caricature in their windows with 'some implement of torture in his hand'.

Mayhew's coster girl readily conceded that she had been a fortunate exception to the usual fate of her kind. She was eighteen years old, one of six children. Her father had occasional employment, fitting and mending gas-pipes in the street. He was one of those 'costermongering mechanics', as they were called, who had been driven to such alien trades because they lacked the true coster's trading skill. The girl's mother sold apples and supplemented this by charring. Even though times were often hard, a certain amount of middle-class culture – including some ability to read – had found its way to the children of the family.

Unlike many coster girls, her parents had not turned her out into the street at twelve or thirteen to survive as best she could. Her mother insisted, however, that the girl must take on the trade of selling apples from a basket, while the mother herself went to look for more work as a charwoman. Mayhew reported that the girl's voice was 'husky from shouting apples'. She carried a basket on her head, covering it with a plaid shawl and protecting her hair from it with a badly crushed velvet bonnet. It was common for a girl to be put to work in this way at seven years old and to be punished by her mother if she failed to sell her basket of fruit.

'Yes mother's very fair that way. Ah! there's many a gal I know whose back has to suffer if she don't sell her stock well; but, thank God! I never get more than a blowing up. My parents is very fair to me.'[14]

Throughout the interview during which, as Mayhew described it, the girl dropped a curtsy each time he asked a question, the same theme recurred: 'My parents is very fair to me.'

Whatever the hardships of coster life, those who lived it were not the poorest of the poor. They could afford drink and entertainment. From the songs and dancing of the penny gaff they made their way to the pipe-smoking and card schools of the beer shops, of which there were some four hundred in London during the 1850s. 'In a full room of card-players, the groups are all shrouded in tobacco smoke, and from them are heard constant sounds . . . "I'm low, and Ped's high." "Tip and me's game." "Fifteen four and a flush of five." ' Bets were laid by the onlookers as well as the players. Other men in the room played shove halfpenny or skittles. Impromptu boxing matches were staged between coster boys for the prize of a pint of beer, the winner being he who first drew blood by giving his opponent a 'noser'. There were no other rules.[15]

Social occasions included 'twopenny hops', restricted to costers and attended by men and women from fourteen to forty-five. The dancing

Down Whitechapel Way, 1869

had little in common with the Victorian ballroom but consisted of 'vigorous, laborious capering'. Many costers went to a theatre or a dance three times a week. Others were happier at an evening's rat-killing or an illegal dog-fight. With their raucous entertainments, their holiday clothes and outings to race meetings, they saw themselves as rivals in leisure rather than as the subordinates of a law-abiding middle class.

An instinctive hostility to the police, who were regarded as being corrupt as well as vindictive, was central to the costers' view of crime and morality. Indeed the middle-class philanderer 'Walter', of *My Secret Life*, also thought that brothel-keepers paid the policemen on their beat to ensure that their trade was not interfered with. The costers showed a more active hostility. 'As for policemen, they're nothing to me, and I should like to pay 'em all off well,' said one sixteen-year-old boy. Costers did not forgive crimes committed against themselves, yet where others were the target of burglars or beggars, their dislike of the 'peelers' might prove stronger than their disapproval of the criminal. One who described the cause of this spoke for almost all his kin.

> Can you wonder at it, sir, that I hate the police? They drive us about, we must move on, we can't stand here, and we can't pitch there. But if we're cracked up, that is if we're forced to go into the Union (I've known it both at Clerkenwell and the City of London workhouses), why the parish gives us money to buy a barrow, or a shallow, or to hire them, and leave the house and start for ourselves; and what's the use of that if the police won't let us sell our goods? – Which is right, the parish or the police?

The parish might do something towards getting the costers back into business but when this man and his companions were reduced to seeking shelter in the workhouse, the authorities 'abuse us worse than dogs'.

There was 'continual warfare' against police action to clear vehicles from congested streets, a struggle in which the costers made common cause against any attempt to seize one of the barrows. While the officers went for help to move the obstruction, the costers would 'whip off a wheel'. The goods on the cart were passed to other traders in the area, who made it a point of honour to account for every item belonging to the man facing arrest. The policemen, on their return, would find a barrow that was empty and immobilized. It required a team of reinforcements to carry it away 'by main strength, amid the jeers of the populace'.[16]

As Mayhew noted of coster vengeance, 'To serve out a policeman is the bravest act by which a costermonger can distinguish himself.' Some of the younger lads were imprisoned repeatedly for this and were regarded as heroes by the others. 'When they leave prison, for such an act, a subscription is often got up for their benefit.' A coster with a grudge against a particular policeman would wait for his opportunity out of extreme 'love of revenge', watching and tracking his enemy, until he saw his chance. One of Mayhew's informants spent six months in this way until his quarry became involved in breaking up a fight outside a public house. Then he rushed into the fray and gave the policeman a savage kicking, shouting, 'Now, you bastard, I've got you at last.'

> When the boy heard that his persecutor was injured for life, his joy was very great and he declared the twelvemonths' imprisonment he was sentenced to for the offence to be 'dirt cheap'. The whole of the court where the lad resided sympathized with the boy, and vowed to a man, that had he escaped, they would have subscribed a pad or two of dry herrings, to send him into the country until the affair had blown over, for he had shown himself a 'plucky one'.[17]

According to the customs by which the costers lived, it was a common point of honour that they never stole from one another. In the courts leading off the New Cut, for example, costers' barrows and property worth more than £500 were left unattended every night. Nothing had ever been stolen by one from another. When a thief from outside their own community tried to steal from them, justice was invariably brief and bloody but never involved the police. 'At Billingsgate,' said one coster, 'the thieves will rob the salesmen far readier than they will us. They know we'd take it out of them readier if they were caught. It's Lynch law with us. We never give them in charge.'[18]

Such men and women took pride in being a clan united against the world and its laws, the members known often by nicknames alone, 'Rotten Herrings', 'Spuddy', 'The One-Eyed Buffer', 'Jawbreaker', 'Pineapple Jack', 'Lushy Bet', 'Dirty Sal', 'Blackwell Poll', 'Dancing Sue' and 'Cast-Iron Poll', the last of whom had been hit on the head with an iron cooking-pot and had suffered no apparent injury from it.

'Their ignorance and their impulsiveness makes them a dangerous class,' wrote Mayhew, after investigating the politics of the costers. They had no interest in political theories or programmes but were instinctively drawn to rebellion or revolution. Mayhew was assured that 'in case of a political riot every "coster" would seize his policeman'. They attended political meetings in groups of a dozen or so but played little part in the discussion. Many had supported the Chartists without understanding much about the Chartist demands. They were disappointed in the end because, as Mayhew was told, 'they could not understand why the Chartist leaders exhorted them to peace and quietness, when they might as well fight it out with the police at once'.[19]

If social investigators and governments were dismayed by the growth of criminality in Victorian London, they had only to reflect that the powerful and well-knit coster clan saw every policeman as a natural enemy and every beggar or burglar who preyed on the 'harristocrats' of other classes as a potential redistributor of wealth.

*

The most successful costers were said to be making thirty shillings a week and the average was put at ten shillings. They were the envy of the so-called 'garret-masters', who carried on their trades in the garrets of areas like Spitalfields or Shadwell where they and their families lived. Many outdoor workers or craftsmen were lucky to make five shillings and some less than half of that. 'Walter', the diarist of *My Secret Life*, encountered a girl of thirteen or fourteen, living in Southwark, who made sacks at the end of the 1840s for fourpence a day. Even the skills of cabinet-making, carpentry, weaving and sewing brought as little as five shillings or four and sixpence for six or seven days' work, usually for sixteen hours' labour each day. The income of many such craftsmen had gone down steadily in the new industrial age. A cabinet-maker described to the *Morning Chronicle* in August 1850 how his family lived on an income of between four and five shillings a week.

> I get up always at six. . . . My wife gets up after me . . . gets breakfast ready at eight. It's coffee and bread and butter. . . . She has dinner ready at one, and that's coffee and bread and butter three days at least in the week, and that's finished in ten minutes too. Then I've tea, not coffee, for a change about five, and I go to bed at ten without any supper – except on Sundays – after sixteen hours' labour, just with a few breaks, as I've told you.

The total meal-breaks in this sixteen-hour day were calculated at half or three-quarters of an hour. Some craftsmen worked sixteen hours on Sundays as well but not this man. 'I haven't strength for it,' he said simply. On Sundays, however, the diet of bread, butter, tea and coffee was varied a little. 'We have mostly half a bullock's head, which costs 10d to 1s. We have it boiled, with an onion and a potato to it; or when we're hard up we have it without either for dinner, and warm it up for supper. There's none left for Monday sometimes, and never much.'

In the coldest months, obliged to provide heat and light for his work, the cabinet-maker found that even this modest domestic economy was eroded. There had been times 'when we've had no butter to our bread, and hardly a crumb of sugar to our coffee. . . . The extra fire and candle in the winter takes every farthing, and more; and then we're forced to do without butter.'

His child, at five years old, was still too young to be put to work but the time would soon come. She was just learning to read and attending Sunday School. 'Children soon grow to be useful, that's one good thing,' said the cabinet-maker philosophically.[20]

The readers of the *Morning Chronicle* saw in this portrait a man who had once commanded a craftsman's place and wage in the society of his time. Even now, his daughter would grow up far better informed and more literate than the coster children. Her father described how he had served his apprenticeship, borrowed a little money from his mother, and set up as his own master, even as a potential employer of labour. But the economic depression of the 1840s had eaten away his trade and his energy. Competition had forced down the price of his labour. Now, as he confessed, he was almost too tired and famished to work. Those who read his story saw in him a man of honesty, industry and skill. If poverty could overwhelm him, how many readers of the *Morning Chronicle* could feel secure themselves?

Among the paper's other contributors, Charles Dickens wrote novels which described the rise of his heroes and heroines from straitened circumstances to financial security. As a journalist, however, he taught his middle-class readership a different truth, showing the ruin not only of garret-masters but also of modest hard-working shopkeepers and their class. *Sketches by Boz* contained the history of a shop near Marsh Gate, Southwark. It had been derelict for some time after the failure of a previous business. Unexpectedly, it was refurbished. Its new tenant announced 'an extensive stock of linen-drapery and haberdashery'. Dickens visited it soon after it opened and saw 'Such ribbons and shawls! and two such elegant young men behind the counter, each in a clean collar and white neckcloth, like the lover in a farce. As to the proprietor, he did nothing but walk up and down the shop, and hand seats to the ladies, and hold important conversations with the handsomest of the young men.'

The decay of the linen-draper's business was 'slow, but sure'. Tickets appeared in its windows, rolls of flannel on the pavement, an offer was advertised to let the first floor. 'The shop became dirty, broken panes of glass remained unmended, and the stock disappeared piecemeal. At last the company's man came to cut off the water, and then the linen-draper cut off himself, leaving the landlord his compliments and the key.'

A widower and his children tried to set up in the premises as a fancy stationer's. From the first their chances of avoiding ruin seemed precarious. The father began seeking work elsewhere while the children, in mourning for their mother, ran the shop. There was no kindly old gentleman of fiction – Mr Brownlow of *Oliver Twist* or a reformed Ebenezer Scrooge – to avert the small tragedy of the stationer's shop. The eldest daughter was soon visibly the victim of 'a slow, wasting consumption'. As the disease gained upon her, the rent was unpaid and the landlord evicted the family.

The premises passed to a tobacconist, 'a red-faced, impudent good-for-nothing dog' who smoked the greater part of his stock and then bolted, leaving the rent and his bills unpaid. As the building decayed, a series of small enterprises came and went, a brass plate on the door announcing it temporarily as a 'Ladies' School'. It became at last a broken-down dairy where 'a party of melancholy-looking fowls were amusing themselves by running in at the front-door, and out at the back one'.[21]

Death came early to the garret-masters and the daughters of the fancy stationer, as it did in the hovels of the slop-shops where the clothes of the middle class were made on starvation wages. The consciences of the slop-shops' customers were tweaked from time to time by such famous lines as Thomas Hood's 'Song of a Shirt':

> Oh! men with sisters dear!
>   Oh! men with mothers and wives!
> It is not linen you're wearing out,
>   But human creatures' lives!
>   Stitch, stitch, stitch,
>   In poverty, hunger, and dirt,
> Sewing at once with a double thread
>   A shroud as well as a shirt.

Charles Kingsley added a more sardonic comment on the social justice by which disease levelled the pampered daughters of the bourgeoisie with their working-class sisters. 'Cheap Clothes and Nasty', as he called them, united the comfortable middle class in a common doom with all that was most diseased in the tailoring hovels of Seven Dials or Monmouth Street with its open sewer, which ran down to Trafalgar Square. Monmouth Street was 'the only true and real emporium for secondhand wearing apparel', in Dickens' *Sketches by Boz*, 'the burial-place of the fashions'. The clothes of the dead and the dispossessed hung on rails outside the narrow shops, the dealers sitting on chairs and smoking their pipes, while their children, 'a happy group of infantine scavengers', played in the running contagion of the gutters. 'Slop' was the name given in common to the pauper trade of tailoring and to undrained sewage.[22]

Not only were the slaves of the slop-shops paid starvation wages by the 'sweaters', but they were also required to live on the premises. It was common for a sweater to charge more for board and lodging than could be earned. When the debt rose beyond sixpence, a sweater might with-hold food until the bill had been paid by additional labour. But the longer a man or woman worked, the greater the debt might grow.

By no means all the slop-workers waited until disease or starva-tion claimed them. If the subversive culture of the costers bred an antagonism to law and order, the slop-shops and the garrets supplied a breeding-ground of prostitution, begging, theft and casual crime. 'Oh, I'm a seduced milliner, anything you like,' said 'Lushing Loo', the Haymarket prostitute, in answer to Bracebridge Hemyng's question as to her origins.[23]

The clothes trade brought to the fashionable areas of Portman Square or Highgate all that was most diseased in the Seven Dials. Kingsley, contributing to *Politics for the People* in 1848, sketched the poverty of seamstresses and tailors and promised something akin to divine retribution on those who had reduced these men and women to such circumstances. His greatest anger is not for 'the blackguard gent . . . who flaunts at the Casinos and Cremorne Gardens in vulgar finery wrung out of the souls and bodies of the poor . . . the poor lawyer's clerk or reduced half-pay officer who has to struggle to look as respectable as his class commands him to look on a pittance often no larger than that of the day labourer'. It is the affluent and the self-satisfied, parading in the latest fashions, cut and sewn in the diseased hovels of the tailors and seamstresses, who are to be the true target of contagion's thunderbolt. Combining the rhetoric of the pulpit and the bitterness of social criticism, Kingsley visits Mammon with divine wrath:

> So Lord —'s coat has been covering a group of children blotched with small-pox. The Rev. D— finds himself unpresentable from a cutaneous disease, which it is not polite to mention on the south of the Tweed, little dreaming that the shivering dirty being who made his coat has been sitting with his arms in the sleeves for warmth while he stitched at the tails. The charming Miss C. is swept off by typhus or scarlatina, and her parents talk about 'God's heavy judgment and visitation'. – had they tracked the girl's new riding-habit back to the stifling undrained hovel where it served as a blanket to the fever-stricken slopworker, they would have seen *why* God had visited them.[24]

*

The nation's rulers were apt to doubt that crime and poverty were linked as fiction suggested. Charles Greville was one sceptic: 'To imagine a state of society in which everybody should be well off, or even tolerably well off, would be a mere vision, so long as there is a preponderance of vice and folly in the world.' In the disturbances of the 1830s, 'Distress is certainly not the cause of these commotions, for the people have patiently supported far greater privations than they had been exposed to before these riots, and the country was generally in an improving state.'[25]

It was not poverty alone, however, but poverty combined with the moral antagonism of groups like the costers towards their 'betters' that bred a culture in which the underworld thrived. As London grew, the population of the streets was augmented by wanderers who begged or sold or offered their services by day and lived at night in the moral and physical squalor of the common lodging-houses or 'padding-kens'. These lodgings of the homeless became the refuges and schools of crime. The running-patterer, the street-stationer, the bird-seller, the crossing-sweeper, the orphan flower-girl, the whistling man, the happy-family exhibitor lay in common wards of the lodging-houses as indiscriminately as corpses in a graveyard.

If they were fortunate, such wanderers had a place in a bed, though sharing it with men and women who might be strangers until that moment. Thirty lodgers were crammed into rooms which appeared incapable of holding more than a dozen. Sanitation consisted of what

A coster girl arrested for obstruction while selling apples, 1850

the Town Clerk of Morpeth in Northumberland described as 'a tub with vomit and natural evacuations'. The breath of the sleepers rose 'in one foul, choking steam of stench'. There was little ventilation except in such houses as a lodging in London's Drury Lane, where the tiles had gone from the roof and, as one of its occupants remarked, 'you could study the stars, if you were so minded'. The same man had prudently scraped a handful of bugs from the bedclothes and crushed them under a candlestick before attempting to sleep. Others found oblivion in drink.

> Why, in course, sir . . . you *must* get half-drunk, or your money for your bed is wasted. There's so much rest owing to you after a hard day; and bugs and bad air'll prevent its being paid, if you don't lay in some stock of beer, or liquor of some sort, to sleep on. It's a duty you owes yourself; but, if you haven't the browns, why, then, in course, you can't pay it.

A bed for a single person held three. In the narrow spaces between the beds were 'shake-downs', bundles of rags on the floor for those who could find no place elsewhere. If twopence was the price of a night's lodging, a wanderer might sleep in his clothes on the stone floor of the kitchen for a penny. Lodging-houses were at their worst on days preceding such events as Greenwich Fair or Epsom Races, filled by those

Victoria's Other London

31

who hoped to prosper by hawking their goods or entertainments or begging bowls among the sideshows.

The proponents of law and order who deplored the defiance of the police by the costers would have found little reassurance in the attitudes of the 'padding-ken'. As a patterer from a lodging-house remarked, 'A promiscuous robbery, even accompanied by murder – if it was "got up clever" and "done clean", so long as the parties escaped detection – might call forth a remark that "there was no great harm done", and perhaps some would applaud the perpetrators.'[26]

London was the prize that lured these wanderers and became the trap in which they perished. 'You see,' said the bootlace-seller, 'I heard people talk about London in North Shields, and I thought there was no poor people there at all – none but ladies and gentlemen, and sailors.' 'I came to London to beg,' said the begging-boy, 'thinking I could get more there than anywhere else, hearing that London was such a good place.' The litany of lost hope among these new arrivals in the city runs through mid-Victorian investigations. Some had imagined they would make their fortunes and others had wanted only to get away from home and parents. 'The young chap I first took up with was a carpenter. He was apprenticed to the trade,' said one of the girls sadly. 'He told me if I'd come to London with him, he'd do anything for me . . . but when I came over to London he ruined me, and then ran away and left me.'[27]

A few of the new citizens were sure that they had done better by coming to the capital. This group included a Haymarket prostitute, an inhabitant of the lodging-houses who called herself 'Swindling Sal'. She was a stout, florid young woman who relied upon the use of her fists against antagonists of either sex, being 'handy with me mauleys', as she put it. The life of a servant-girl in Birmingham was not for her, and her first attempts to sell herself to the regiment quartered at Coventry had been unrewarding. 'Soldiers is good, soldiers is – to walk with and that, but they don't pay; 'cos why, they ain't got no money; so I says to myself, I'll go to Lunnon, and I did.'[28]

Some men and women who lived in the padding-kens had not always been poor but claimed to have 'moved in good society'. One of them, fallen on hard times, commented philosophically, 'When a man's lost caste in society, he may as well go the whole hog, bristles and all, and a low lodging-house is the entire pig.'[29]

The 'low lodging-houses' of such areas as Whitechapel, Seven Dials and the Westminster slums were no more than communal dormitories often managed by the criminal class. Before Whitechapel's Cat-and-Wheel Alley became Commercial Street, its lodging-house then managed by a man called Shirley typified a hundred more. With a nod towards moral propriety, the owner had one side of the communal sleeping quarters for single men and women, the other for married couples. 'As these "couples" made frequent exchanges,' said one of his lodgers, 'it is scarcely probable that Mr Shirley ever "asked to see their marriage lines".'

Whatever trepidation Victorian mothers and fathers of middle-class families might feel about sexual impropriety, many of the casual lodgers of the padding-kens were untroubled by inhibition. 'I knew two brothers . . . who each brought a young woman out of service from the country,' said one inmate. 'After a while each became dissatisfied with his partner. The mistress of the house (an old procuress from Portsmouth) proposed that they should change wives. They did so, to the amusement of nine other couples sleeping on the same floor, and some of whom followed the example, and more than once during the night.'[30]

Part of Cat-and-Wheel Alley was pulled down but its lodging-house survived. On Shirley's death it passed to a Welshman with a wooden leg, whose name was Hughes but who was universally known as 'Taff'. Like Fagin in *Oliver Twist*, he was the organizer of a gang of child-thieves, though under cover of his lodging-house proprietorship. 'Taff was a notorious receiver of stolen goods,' said one of his lodgers. 'I knew two little boys who brought home six pairs of new Wellington boots, which this miscreant bought at 1s. per pair; and, when they had no luck, he would take the strap off his wooden leg, and beat them through the nakedness of their rags.'[31]

As surely as if they had lived in nineteenth-century India, the lodgers, like the costers, regarded themselves as forming a caste. They gave the lie to the smug legend of being poor but loyal subjects with a place in their hearts for the great sovereign who ruled over them. 'They hate the aristocracy,' said one of the running-patterers. 'Whenever there is a rumour or an announcement of an addition to the Royal Family, and the news reaches the padding-ken, the kitchen for half-an-hour becomes the scene of uproar – "Another expense coming on the bloody country!"'[32]

The politics of the dispossessed were unpredictable. Progressive-minded statesmen might have been disconcerted to hear that the beggars of the lodging-houses hated the Whig ministries, which had brought parliamentary reform. Their allegiance was liberal Tory. 'I know', said the patterer, 'that many a tear was shed in the hovels and cellars of London when Sir Robert Peel died. I know a publican, in Westminster, whose daily receipts are enormous, and whose only customers are soldiers, thieves, and prostitutes, who closed his house the day of the funeral, and put himself, his family, and even his beer-machines and gas-pipes, into mourning for the departed statesman.' It was not parliamentary reform but bread that the beggars and wanderers needed. Peel, by the abolition of the Corn Laws and their protectionist tariffs in 1846, had brought the promise of cheaper food.[33]

Many of those who moved from one lodging-house to another left carefully chalked fragments of autobiography on the walls. They mingled criminality and piety, sometimes embodying a poetry of Victoria's poorest subjects.

> Jemmy the Rake, bound to Bristol. Bad beds but no bugs. Thank God for all things.

> Razor George and his moll slept here the day afore Christmas. Just out of stir for muzzling a peeler.

> Scotch Mary, with 'driz' (lace), bound to Dover and back, please God.[34]

As the wanderers went their way, they also chalked signs on walls and woodwork for those who followed in search of customers. A diamond showed that a door was a good one to knock at. An inverted triangle indicated a good house spoilt by some other trader. A square meant that a caller was likely to be handed over to the police, while a circle with a dot at the centre was 'flummut', meaning that a hawker was likely to get a month in gaol.[35]

Among those of the Queen's subjects reduced to a level of deprivation scarcely imaginable a century later were some who showed a heroic refusal to be a 'victim' or an 'unfortunate', or to demand that their difficulties should be relieved by the support of others. Not the least remarkable were Victorian children. Two sisters, their ages fifteen and eleven, were orphan flower-sellers during the 1850s in Drury Lane, where they sat barefoot and thinly clad on a step, their thirteen-year-old brother earning threepence or fourpence a day as a coster's boy. His two sisters thought themselves lucky to make a shilling a day by selling flowers, usually it was sixpence. To have a shilling in reserve each day, as stock-money for the next morning, was essential. Without it, they could buy no stock and their livelihood would be gone.

The three orphans shared a bed, screened by an old curtain from a married couple who slept in the same hired room. The children had come from Ireland, had never known a father and were assumed to be illegitimate. When the elder sister was eight, their mother had died, having worked as a charwoman. Since then the elder girl had looked after the others and managed the trade upon which they lived. 'I've got myself, and my brother and sister a bit of bread ever since, and never had any help but from the neighbours. I never troubled the parish.'

At the same time, as the girl explained, 'I put myself and I put my brother and sister to a Roman Catholic School – and to a Ragged School.' All three children could read and the brother could write. They never missed mass on Sunday. Yet there were rainy days when they could not even earn enough in the empty street to replace their 'stock-money' for the next day's purchase of primroses or violets at Covent Garden or Farringdon Market.

> If it's bad weather, so bad that we can't sell flowers at all, and so if we've had to spend our stock-money for a bit of bread, *she* [the landlady] lends us 1s., if she has one, or she borrows one of a neighbour, if she hasn't, or if the neighbours hasn't it, she borrows it at a dolly-shop [the illegal pawnshop]. There's 2d. a week to pay for 1s. at a dolly, and perhaps an old rug left for it; if it's very hard weather, the rug must be taken at night time, or we are starved with the cold. It sometimes has to be put into the dolly again next morning, and then there's 2d. to pay for it for the day. We've had a frock in for 6d., and that's a penny a week, and the same for a day. We never pawned anything; we have nothing they would take in at the [licensed] pawnshop. We live on bread and tea, and sometimes a fresh herring of a night.

No less illuminating was the attitude of the well-dressed passers-by in Drury Lane.

> Gentlemen are our best customers. I've heard that they buy flowers to give to the ladies. Ladies have sometimes said: 'A penny, my poor girl, here's three halfpence for the bunch.' Or they've given me the price of two bunches for one. I never had a rude word said to me by a gentleman in my life.

Philanthropy had its limits, however, and the girl was positive that she had never been given as much as sixpence for a bunch of flowers.[36]

It was easy to see in the courage of the orphan flower-girl a determination and self-reliance which enabled early Victorian England to establish the world's greatest empire. Yet such qualities were not universal. Another flower-girl, nineteen years old, had had enough of her trade and had served a sentence of twelve months in prison for 'heaving her shoe at the Lord Mayor'. She confessed that she had done it 'to get a comfortable lodging, for she was tired of being about the streets'. On her release, she went into partnership with a beggar who traded on the girl's shabby appearance by standing in the middle of the street and intoning, 'My good kind Christians, me and my poor wife here is ashamed to appear before you in the state we are in.' When the partnership broke up, she smashed the lamps outside the Mansion House in order to get back into prison again. 'She was sick and tired, she said, of her life.'[37]

*

Beyond the recognizable trades of the costers, the destitute craftsmen or needlewomen, and the street-folk, were men who followed hidden and reclusive lives. They belonged to a class of scavengers who worked alone or in small groups and whose existence was generally unknown in the streets and squares of the city, though some of them clambered in darkness a few feet underground. There were, for example, dredgers of the river and the 'toshers' or sewer-hunters. The little boats of the dredgermen with their trawling-nets dragged the 'holes and furrows' of the river bed or raised the cargo of a sunken coal-barge. They also dragged for corpses and found that this usually paid well. Sometimes there was a reward for recovering the body of a missing person and sometimes there were pockets to be emptied. Much might depend on where the dead man or woman could be landed. 'There's 5s. 6d. inquest money at Rotherhithe, and on'y a shilling at Deptford,' said one disgruntled dredger. 'I can't make out how that is but that's all they give.'[38]

On the other hand, the authorities accepted that 'no body recovered by a dredgerman ever happens to have any money about it when brought to shore'. A watch would be left in the fob or the waistcoat pocket, since a watch might be traced. The purse or pocket-book would still be on the body, but it was invariably empty. 'The dredgers cannot by any reasoning or argument be made to comprehend that there is any-thing like dishonesty in emptying the pockets of a dead man. They say that any one who finds a body does precisely the same, and that if they did not do so the police would.'[39]

The dishonesty of the police was a truth evident to costers and scav-engers alike. Much of the dredgers' narrative sounds like a source for Charles Dickens. The autobiography of one man might serve as a parallel opening to *Our Mutual Friend*.

> Do you see them two marks there on the back of my hand? Well, one day – I was on'y young then – I was grabblin' for old rope in Church Hole, when I brings up a body, and just as I was fixing a rope on his leg to tow him ashore, two swells comes down in a skiff, and lays hold of the painter of my boat, and tows me ashore. The hook of my drag went right thro' the trousers of the drowned man and my hand, and I couldn't let go no how, and tho' I roared out like mad, the swells didn't care, but dragged me into the stairs. When I got there, my arm, and the corpse's shoe and trousers, was all kivered with my blood. What do you think the gents said? – why, they told me as how they had done me good, in towin' the body in, and ran away up the stairs.[40]

The dredgers were among the more affluent scavengers and might pay from ten shillings to twenty pounds for their little blunt-nosed boats. The toshers or sewer-hunters worked with their hands and arms in the deposits of sewage, which in some of London's ancient drains had grown to a depth of five feet. By the river's edge at Wapping and Shadwell it was possible to walk into the old sewers at low tide and to be drowned in them at high tide. Spring tides flooded the system, until such areas saw the gratings burst open and the sewage flood their streets. To check this, sluices and iron doors were installed in the rotting brick-work of the main tunnels. When they were opened at low tide, a tosher who could not escape into a branch sewer would be swept off his feet by the deluge and his body found on the river mud near the main outlet.

The state of the sewers had been investigated by the Board of Health in 1848 and 1849. In some places under Westminster the miasma was so thick that the glass of the spirit-levels used by the surveyors was covered by a thick scum within a few minutes of being wiped clear.

> At the outfall into the Dean Street sewer, it is 3 feet 6 inches by 2 feet 8 inches. From the end of this, a wide sewer branches in each direction at right

angles, 5 feet 8 inches by 5 feet 5 inches. Proceeding to the eastward about 30 feet, a chamber is reached about 30 feet in length, from the roof of which hangings of putrid matter *like stalactites* descend *three feet in length*. At the end of this chamber, the sewer passes under the public privies, the ceilings of which can be seen from it. Beyond this it is not possible to go.[41]

Under the most affluent areas of Mayfair, Grosvenor Square, Berkeley Square, and in Belgravia, the sewers were in the worst condition, so badly blocked that they had almost clogged the house drains. In the fashionable squares north of Oxford Street, the blockages were so bad and the sewers so decayed that any attempt to flush them might 'bring some of them down altogether'. In this hidden world, a few feet below the mansions of wealth and nobility, the toshers scavenged for coins and metal. For the most part they found discharges from breweries and gas-works, dead dogs, cats and kittens, offal and entrails from slaughter-houses, street and vegetable refuse, stable dung, the sweepings of pigsties, night-soil from the cesspools, kettles, pans, rags and broken stoneware.[42]

Henry Mayhew encountered a tosher in a court off Rosemary Lane, near the London docks. To enter the court, he passed through a dark archway, no wider than a door, which ran under the first floor of the houses on the street. The courtyard itself was about fifty yards long and only three yards wide. It was surrounded by 'tall wooden houses, with jutting abutments in many of the upper storeys that almost exclude the light, and give them the appearance of being about to tumble down upon the heads of the intruders'. None of the families who lived in this court occupied an entire house. They lived one or two families to each room.

At that moment the court was so packed with spectators, as two of the inhabitants prepared to fight one another in the course of a quarrel, that Mayhew could not get beyond the entrance. 'Labourers and street-folk with shaggy heads, and women with dirty caps and fuzzy hair, thronged every window above, and peered down anxiously at the affray.' Mayhew was astonished to calculate that in the thirty houses fronting on the court there were nine hundred and sixty people living. His conclusion caused amusement to one of the bystanders who knew the total to be higher. '"Well," continued my informant, chuckling and rubbing his hands in evident delight at the result, "you may as well just tack a couple a hundred on the tail o' them for make-weight, as we're not werry pertikler about a hundred or two one way or the other in these here places." '

In a garret, up three flights of narrow stairs that creaked and trembled at every footstep, Mayhew found his tosher. Like costers, the scavengers knew one another by their nicknames, Lanky Bill, Long Tom, One-Eyed George or Short-Armed Jack. It was a waste of time to ask for them by any other name.

Mayhew's tosher had come from Birmingham to London as a child. He had run away from home and had worked for twenty years in the treacherous mud and sewage of 'Cuckold's Point' on the south bank of the Thames, raking for rope and bones and iron. Sometimes he might find a coin. 'I know places where you'd go over head and ears in the mud, and jist alongside on 'em you may walk as safe as you can on this floor. But it don't do for a stranger to try it.' As a child, he was saved from sinking into the mud by an old man who scavenged the shore and the sewers. After that, they worked together in the sewers. 'I liked that well enough. I could git into small places where the old un couldn't, and when I'd got near the grating in the street, I'd search about in the bottom of the sewer; I'd put my arm to my shoulder in the mud and bring up shillings and half crowns, and lots of coppers, and plenty other things.' Once he had found a silver jug as big as a quart pot.

Such men were scornful of the dangers and diseases of the sewers. The packs of sewer-rats were the worst thing, the tosher thought. If a man was alone, it was said that they could overwhelm him and leave his bones picked clean. 'The rats is wery dangerous, that's sartin,' he insisted, 'but we always goes three or four on us together, and the varmint's too wide awake to take us then, for they know they'd git off second best.' As for the stench or the threat of cholera, 'Bless your heart, the smell's nothink; it's a roughish smell at first but nothing near so bad as you think.' There was always a danger of suffocation in some of the narrower tunnels but the toshers carried a hoe with them. Taking the candle from the lantern, they put it on the end of the hoe and ran it into the tunnel ahead of them. If the flame continued to burn, they knew that they were safe.[43]

*

Thackeray had scarcely overstated the truth when he wrote that there was a world almost at the doors of middle-class London, about which middle-class London knew nothing. What knowledge there was often came from reports of the police courts in *The Times*, the *Morning Chronicle* or the *Morning Post*. In a world that seemed otherwise hidden from this readership, the costers fought the police as their natural enemies. The dredgers robbed the dead because, if they did not, the police would do it anyway. The virtuous orphan flower-girl went to school and church. Her feckless rival broke the Mansion House street-lamps in order to get back into prison. The padding-kens bred a generation of thieves, beggars and prostitutes under the supervision of their criminal landlords. Scotch Mary trusted in God, while Razor George with his moll was as proud of muzzling a peeler as any coster boy might be. Most of his companions in the lodging-houses did not object to crime, according to the running-patterer, even if a robbery involved a murder. Instead they admired the skill and technique of the crime, as they were to admire Edward Agar's bullion robbery on the South-Eastern Railway.

Those who adopted such attitudes often saw themselves as belonging to a class that had been expropriated by progress. The costers were harried to clear the city streets for more important traffic. The cabinet-maker was starving through no fault of his own. Even the toshers and their kind were pessimistic about their survival in the new industrial age. As a cesspool sewerman complained, 'there's so many new dodges comes up, always some one of the working classes is a-being ruined. If it ain't steam it's something else as knocks the bread out of their mouths quite as quick.' The injustice of this seemed sufficient justification to those of Victoria's criminals who saw themselves as 'the poor who fought back'.[44]

In depicting the life of London's poor, Mayhew's genius combined art and economics as perhaps only an early Victorian commentator could have done. Few people who had experienced London at first hand would be in any danger of sentimentalizing it. Yet many of Mayhew's descriptions have a poetic quality, in the sense that Baudelaire in certain passages of 'Tableaux Parisiens' from *Les Fleurs du mal*, or Tennyson in *In Memoriam*, or Dickens in the opening of *Bleak House* rendered poetic the new urban monster that devoured its children. Even Dickens could scarcely have excelled Mayhew in one splendid description of a London night and morning, seen while the majority of consciences among the middle class slept as soundly as their bodies. It is worth quoting at length, as Mayhew abandons objective reporting to write with an emotional fluency that transforms prose into poetry.

> Again, at night it is that the strange anomalies of London life are best seen. As the hum of life ceases, and the shops darken, and the gaudy gin palaces thrust out their ragged and squalid crowds to pace the streets, London puts on its most solemn look of all. On the benches of the parks, in the niches of the bridges, and in the litter of the markets, are huddled together the homeless and the destitute. The only living things that haunt the streets are the poor wretched Magdalens, who stand shivering in their finery, waiting to catch the drunkard as he goes shouting homewards. There, on a doorstep, crouches some shoeless child, whose day's begging has not brought it enough to purchase even the penny night's lodging that his young companions in beggary have gone to. Where the stones are taken up and piled high in the road, while the mains are being mended, and the gas streams from a tall pipe, in a flag of flame, a ragged crowd are grouped round the glowing coke fire – some smoking, and others dozing beside it.
>
> Then, as the streets grow blue with the coming light, and the church spires and roof-tops stand out against the clear sky with a sharpness of outline that is seen only in London before its million chimneys cover the town with their smoke – then come sauntering forth the unwashed poor; some with greasy wallets on their backs to hunt over each dust-heap, and eke out life by seeking refuse bones, or stray rags and pieces of old iron; others, whilst on their way to work, are gathered at the corner of some street round the early breakfast stall, and blowing saucers of steaming coffee, drawn from tall tin cans that have the red-hot charcoal shining crimson through the holes in the fire-pan beneath them; whilst already the little slattern girl, with her basket slung before her, screams 'Water-*creases*!' through the sleeping streets.[45]

In such passages the raucous and opportunist world of Jemmy the Rake and Short-Armed Jack, Swindling Sal and Cast-Iron Poll seems closer to human experience than the blandness of any electronic image.

CHAPTER 2

The Dodgers and the Swell Mob

VICTORIAN ENGLAND was alerted by its press to a new self-confidence on the part of its criminal class. As early as June 1832, *Fraser's Magazine* had warned its readers against the new danger, which was represented by 'a distinct body of thieves, whose life and business it is to follow up a determined warfare against the constituted authorities, by living in idleness and on plunder'. Almost sixty years later, in 1891, a prison chaplain, W. D. Morrison, suggested that little had changed. 'There is a population of habitual criminals which forms a class by itself . . . to commit crime is their trade; they deliberately scoff at honest ways of earning a living, and must accordingly be looked upon as a class of a separate and distinct character from the rest of the community.'[1]

Whether such a criminal class was more firmly rooted and more numerous than in the past, rather than better documented, was open to question. The crisis of urban crime in the mid-eighteenth century had in 1753 impelled Henry Fielding and his half-brother Sir John Fielding to use their powers as London magistrates in founding the Bow Street Runners. They did so in response to the inability of the law to defeat organized 'gangs of villains and cut-throats', as Henry Fielding called them, or to combat what William Sharpe, Clerk to the Privy Council, termed 'that hydra of villains by which our streets and roads are infested'. Horace Walpole described a highway robbery of 1750 in the middle of Piccadilly, carried out while the public looked on and could do nothing. Men now travelled in London, he remarked, as if going into battle. Worse than any Victorian scandal of its kind were the so-called 'trading justices', like Justice Blackborough of Clerkenwell. Such men, holding office for money, regularly issued warrants for the arrest of scores of innocent people who happened to be on the streets, knowing that they could make two shillings and fourpence from each as the price of freedom on bail rather than immediate detention on some spurious charge.[2]

Few prosperous Victorians who became targets of villainy in their own time were likely to be reassured by the thought that crime was now more subtle and more professional in its methods than a century earlier. Yet a man in Piccadilly might now have his money taken from him in a spirit of amiability far removed from an assault by a Hanoverian highwayman.

In 1860, visitors from the provinces were readily drawn to the splendour of Oxford Street, London's newest emporium of fashion and manufacture. By the time that its construction was complete, the street ran from Hyde Park in the west almost as far as Holborn in the east, 'resounding with the din of vehicles, carts, cabs, hansoms, broughams, and omnibuses driving along'. Down its length many of the shops were 'spacious and crowded with costly goods, and the large windows of plate-glass, set in massive brass frames, . . . gaily furnished with their articles of merchandise'.

Gazing at the finery behind the plate glass, on certain mornings, was a man who might have been another country visitor, a jolly, red-faced farmer in appearance. He was better known to the police as a 'magsman', whose skills included card-sharping and fleecing the unwary at friendly games of skittles. The visitor from the provinces would be unlikely to notice that several other men were standing about in the vicinity, members of the magsman's gang who waited to play their parts.

In competition with these tricksters, the professionals of Oxford Street included a pair of well-dressed young men, 'bedecked with glittering watch-chains and gold rings'. They walked arm-in-arm, stopping occasionally to invite a lonely stranger to take a glass with them at a nearby gin palace. Closer inspection might show that the fingertips of the richly dressed pair had been curiously skinned. This enabled them to identify playing-cards by touch from a number of tiny pinprick holes made in the pasteboard. It was also noticeable, by those who bothered to notice, that only one of the two richly dressed men looked truly amiable. The other was more powerfully built and had a certain air of sullenness.

Among other prosperous passers-by in Oxford Street was a young man who had become a successful housebreaker. John Binny described him in 1861 as having 'an engaging appearance . . . very tasteful in his dress, unlike the rough burglars we met at Whitechapel, the Borough and Lambeth'.

As the visitor progressed on his journey through the West End, two 'tall gentlemanly men' crossed the Strand together and went into a restaurant. These were pickpockets, also well known to the police. 'They were attired in a suit of superfine black cloth, cut in fashionable style. They entered an elegant dining-room, and probably sat down to costly viands and wines.' If such men were not quite at the top of their profession, they were certainly a cut above Bill Sikes and the Artful Dodger and did not appear in the least like the criminal of the Victorian imagination.

A stop for refreshment at a beer shop near St Giles might reveal a pair of coiners having a drink, one a moulder of counterfeit, the other his look-out. Their techniques for putting false coinage into circulation were simple but usually effective. A favourite trick was 'ringing the changes'. The coiner would go into a shop, make a purchase, and offer a genuine sovereign in payment. The shopkeeper would chink the coin on his counter to make sure that it rang true. The customer would then ask for it back, saying that he believed he could pay in silver. The coin was returned but, having searched his pockets, the purchaser found he had not enough silver after all. A counterfeit sovereign replaced the genuine one in his hand by the slight movement of a finger. It was handed to the shopkeeper, who was quite sure that he had seen the same coin all the time.[3]

*

It was not remarkable that such men should be on display. Oxford Street and the Strand, as well as the most fashionable and prosperous residential areas of the West End, were natural targets for the criminal underworld. For despite the apparent divisions of class and wealth, these very areas were near neighbours of some of the most notorious criminal rookeries, among them St Giles's at the eastern end of Oxford Street, Seven Dials on the eastern side of the Charing Cross Road, and the Devil's Acre in Westminster.

Accounts of the Victorian underworld are threaded by references to the rookeries of London as citadels of crime. When the assault on St

St Giles's Rookery at the time of Sketches by Boz

Giles's began, as part of it was pulled down to make way for the building of New Oxford Street, Inspector Hunt of the Metropolitan Police
described his experiences of such thieves' dens as the Rose and Crown
within the rookery which were now yielding to demolition.

> The Rose and Crown public-house [was] resorted to by all classes of the
> light fingered gentry, from the mobsman and his 'Amelia' to the lowest of
> the street thieves and his 'Poll'. In the taproom might be seen Black Charlie
> the fiddler, with ten or a dozen lads and lasses enjoying the dance, and
> singing and smoking over glasses of gin and water, more or less plentiful
> according to the proceeds of the previous night – all apparently free from
> care in their wild carousals. The cheek waxed pale when the policeman
> opened the door and glanced round the room, but when he departed the
> merriment would be resumed with vigour.[4]

The decaying warrens of the rookeries had existed for centuries,
many of them the homes of seventeenth- or eighteenth-century
Londoners which had degenerated into verminous slums by the
Victorian period. In St Giles's Rookery, where the streets were often no
more than narrow alleyways and where, in a few places, a man had to
turn sideways to pass between the buildings, there was now an infamous
brothel on the corner of Church Street and Lawrence Street, where a

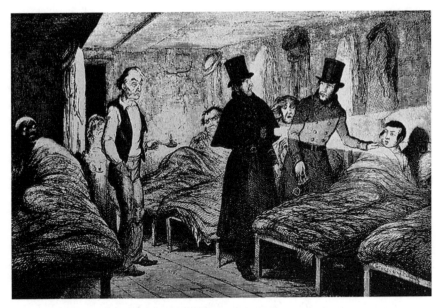

Taken in a Threepenny Lodging-house, 1848

handsome town house had once stood. Each floor consisted of several rooms connected by a gallery and rented by prostitutes.

Robbery, rather than sexual vice, was the stock-in-trade of such brothels in the rookeries. Their targets were drunken men picked up by the street-girls round Drury Lane or as far west as Regent Street. 'When they had plundered the poor dupe,' Inspector Hunt reported, 'he was ejected without ceremony by the others who resided in the room; often without a coat or hat, sometimes without his trousers, and occasionally left on the staircase naked as he was born.' In many cases, of course, the girls were as drunk as their customers and, said Hunt, 'In this house the grossest scenes of profligacy were transacted.' When the building was at last pulled down by Victorian town planners, it proved to be connected to a maze of escape routes through the rookery, by means of a hole in its wall which opened on to a timber-yard in another street.[5]

Such areas were the natural habitat of the coiner or the thief, given the difficulty of finding, let alone arresting, a fugitive. The narrow streets, combined with 'an almost endless intricacy of courts and yards', earned the policeman's cliché of a 'rabbit warren'. Interlinking back yards and low boundary walls made escape from one house to another as easy as crossing the road. Houses in one narrow street were 'connected by roof, yard, and cellar' with those in other streets. The buildings led into one another 'in such a manner that the apprehension of an inmate or refugee in one of them was almost a task of impossibility to a stranger'. In some there were traps set for the police which might prove lethal. In one cellar there lay a large cesspool, camouflaged so that the pursuing officer who put his foot on the covering would disappear into a vat of sewage. Other cellars boasted holes two feet square in their walls through which a wanted man could escape from one street to the next and then to another.

> These afforded a ready means of escape to a thief, but effectually stopped the pursuer, who would be put to the risk of creeping on his hands and knees through a hole two feet square in a dark cellar in St Giles's Rookery, entirely in the power of dangerous characters. Other houses were connected in a similar manner. In some instances there was a communication from one back window to another by means of large spike nails, one row to hold by and another for the feet to rest on.[6]

Through a gateway into Ivy Lane, the path led to what was regarded as the centre of St Giles's Rookery. Rats' Castle, 'a large dirty building', stood on the massive foundations of a leper hospital, built in the eleventh century by Queen Matilda, consort of Henry I. More recently, it had been the place where condemned felons, on their way from Newgate Gaol to be hanged at Tyburn, were allowed to stop for a bowl of ale. Like a latter-day Fagin's den, it was now occupied by 'thieves, prostitutes, and boys who live by plunder'.[7]

Dickens had been there one dull wet night, in company with Inspector Field and Constable Rogers from St Giles's police station, the latter with the 'eye' of a lantern clipped to the front of his belt.

> Saint Giles's Church strikes half-past ten. We stoop low, and creep down a precipitous flight of steps into a dark close cellar. There is a fire. There is a long deal table. There are benches. The cellar is full of company, chiefly very young men in various conditions of dirt and raggedness. Some are eating supper. There are no girls or women present. Welcome to Rats' Castle, gentlemen, and to this company of noted thieves![8]

The men of the rookery patronized a neighbouring gin palace when in funds and lounged against walls or posts when the money was spent.

In the background a pair of women who had passed the morning drinking gin and bitters were brawling and screaming abuse, fighting over a man whom one claimed as her husband. A large and enthusiastic crowd urged them to 'pitch into' one another, to put 'the kye-bosh on' and tear each other's eyes out. The gin palace itself was magnificent, 'in precise proportion to the dirt and poverty of the surrounding neighbourhood'.

> All is light and brilliancy. The hum of many voices issues from that splendid gin-shop which forms the commencement of the two streets opposite; and the gay building with the fantastically-ornamented parapet, the illuminated clock, the plate-glass windows surrounded by stucco rosettes, and its profusion of gaslights in richly-gilt burners, is perfectly dazzling when contrasted with the darkness and dirt we have just left.

The carved and polished mahogany of the bar, running the width of the building, a high-ceilinged saloon with a gallery beyond it, contrasted with the scene outside where, as Dickens wrote, girls of fourteen or fifteen walked barefoot with matted hair, their nakedness covered only by a white coat, begged or stolen. Yet the sham gentility of the gin palace was revealed as a fight broke out in the saloon. 'The landlord hits everybody, and everybody hits the landlord; the barmaids scream; the police come in; the rest is a confused mixture of arms, legs, staves, torn coats, shouting and struggling.' After a while, order returned to the gin palace, as violence broke out in the lodgings of the neighbourhood. 'Some of the party are borne off to the station-house, and the remainder slink home to beat their wives for complaining, and kick the children for daring to be hungry.'[9]

By no means all the patrons of the gin palace had homes. Indeed, there were children in the rookeries who no longer had parents to kick them. The young learnt early that crime was to be their profession, especially if they had been consigned to a lodging-house like Rats' Castle. Thieving, pickpocketing and prostitution were recommended to them by the mistresses of many padding-kens. The charge for a night's lodging was generally twopence, but smaller children might be admitted for a penny. If a boy or girl had no money to pay for that night's lodging, the 'mot of the ken', as the mistress of the house was called, would 'pack them off, telling them plainly that it will be no use their returning until they have stolen something worth 2d.'[10]

*

The Dram-drinker, 1848

The first resort of the criminal poor was begging – or 'cadging' as Inspector Hunt preferred to call it. Many who took to it perfected frauds of the greatest simplicity. A scene played up and down the land required a man made up as an African. The part was frequently taken by 'Chelsea George', an ex-convict whose travels had given him an unusually dark complexion. He was accompanied by two friends, one dressed as a clergyman. Confronted by such a scene the doubts of the unwary audience which gathered were quietened. The bogus clergyman introduced his 'African' to the crowd as a convert from paganism. The African would mumble a compound of French, Irish and gibberish. A 'pagan idol' would be produced for him to spit upon, which he would do. A hymn would then be sung, during which a 'school of pals' as they were known would take up a collection among the well-dressed audience. As much as £16 was collected at a single performance, more than many seamstresses or garret-masters might earn in a year.[11]

Of the same type as the 'African convert' and his friends were writers of begging-letters who represented themselves as various classes of unfortunate gentlefolk, including the decayed gentleman, the broken-down tradesman and the distressed scholar. Many of this class kept registers of their victims, noting the weaknesses of every donor and the stories that had already been told to each one. The characteristic mistake of less careful beggars was to tell the same story twice to the same person. One shabbily dressed man specialized in being a recently bereaved widower with infant children and no money to pay for his beloved wife's funeral. An old lady who had been duped by him saw him in a state of similar distress three months later. He 'gurgled' the same story, the conclusion of which was that 'owing to a series of unprecedented and unexpected misfortunes he had not sufficient money to defray the funeral expenses'. 'Oh, nonsense!' interrupted the old lady, 'You lost your wife a quarter of a year ago. You couldn't lose her twice; and as to marrying again, and losing again in that short time, it is quite impossible.'[12]

The more skilful beggars of this sort were capable of unblemished plausibility. Among the most accomplished were the members of the Kaggs family, whose efforts and ingenuity were handsomely rewarded in the 1850s. Mr Kaggs had begun his career as a lowly domestic servant, later a butler, who had run off with and married the daughter of his employer. They had several children. The elder girl, Betsey, attended by a servant (acted by her father), would call at the houses of philanthropic ladies. When the porter answered her knock, she would introduce herself as the daughter of a gallant but ailing army officer now reduced to poverty. To raise a little money, she was offering her few possessions for sale to ladies known for their charitable works.

Though Betsey Kaggs was not admitted to the house, she was invited to write to most of these charitable ladies. In some cases this led to a visit from the benefactress. Mr Kaggs was put to bed in the garret, his face made up to suggest mortal disease. The Kaggs family occupied the entire house but the tableau suggested that they were confined to the garret. Medicine bottles, a Bible and an army newspaper were placed by the bed. One daughter was dressed as a nurse. The visitor was treated to the story of this gallant officer, wounded at Barrosa in the Peninsular War and discharged from the army after Waterloo. An unworldly half-pay lieutenant, he had been persuaded to invest his small savings in railway shares, only to be left destitute by an absconding agent and a ruinous lawsuit. His old wound, received at Barrosa, had broken out again and laid the poor soldier low. The two youngest Kaggs children, who had been promised plums if they kept quiet, sat gloomily, dressed in black. When the visitor asked Betsey if these were her little brother and sister – which they were – she shook her head. They were the orphan children of her poor brother, a naval officer who had died on the Gold Coast, and of his delicate wife who had soon followed him to the grave.

The fact that the 'dead' brother and his family had not been mentioned earlier convinced the dupes that this was a genuine and deserving case. Mere beggars would surely not have shown such delicacy as to conceal so many of their other griefs. It was a first-rate performance and the Kaggs family prospered, until they became too widely known. Mr Kaggs decided that they must leave for Australia. He put advertisements in *The Times* and the *Morning Post*, informing the charitable and the humane that 'a poor but respectable family required a small sum to enable them to make up the amount of their passage to Australia, and that they could give the highest references as to character'. He did so well by this that he and his family remained in London for two more years before departing, at last, for Melbourne.[13]

A creative imagination was the basis of a successful career as a beggar. The streets of central London were a living theatre of those who posed as the victims of disaster. There were shipwrecked mariners who had never seen the sea, blown-up miners whose lives had been spent entirely above ground, and burnt-out tradesmen who knew nothing of any trade but this. In winter, as soon as frost and snow came, there were opportunist beggars who became impoverished gardeners, forced out of work by the harsh weather.

Among true artists were the 'Ashamed Beggars' whose general motto was 'To beg I am ashamed', but who did so with a fine technique and pertinacity. Such a man would have a regular beat in the West End and would stand silently with a tray of bootlaces or matches and a card round his neck.

Kind Friends and Christian Brethren!
I was once a
Respectable Tradesman,
doing a Good Business;
till Misfortune reduced me to
this Pass!
Be kind enough to buy
Some of the Articles I offer,
and you will confer a
Real Charity!

Andrew Halliday studied one of these men, in whom silence had become art. The beggar was dressed in seedy though well-brushed clothes, black and threadbare but scrupulously clean, and a white shirt that had seen better days.

> But the face of the beggar is a marvellous exhibition! His acting is admirable! Christian resignation and its consequent fortitude are written on his brow. His eyes roll imploringly but no sound escapes him. The expression of his features almost pronounces 'Christian friend, purchase my humble wares, for *I scorn to beg*. I am starving, but tortures shall not wring the humiliating secret from my lips.' He exercises a singular fascination over old ladies, who slide coppers into his hand quickly, as if afraid that they shall hurt his feelings. He pockets the money, heaves a sigh, and darts an abashed and grateful look at them that makes them feel how keenly he appreciates their delicacy. When the snow is on the ground he now and then introduces a little shiver, and with a well-worn pocket-handkerchief stifles a cough that, he intimates by a despairing dropping of the eyelids, is slowly killing him.[14]

The 'Shivering Dodge,' practised by 'Shallow Coves', was an alternative to the cough. On cold mornings, the lightly clad performer would stand shivering before warmly dressed pedestrians as they passed by, mutely or loudly imploring their charity. Yet the art of continued shivering had unwelcome consequences, as one beggar remarked. '"Shaking Jemmy" went on with his shivering so long that he couldn't help it at last. He shivered like a jelly – like a calf's foot with the ague – on the hottest day in summer.'[15]

Among the beggars' rivals were the so-called 'Lucifer Droppers'. These were groups of children, one of them a little girl, raggedly dressed. The girl would hold a box or two of matches, offering them for sale to the passing crowd. With a little practice, she would then contrive to get in the way of a passing gentleman and drop her matches. At a glance, it might appear that he had inadvertently walked into the child and had carelessly knocked the matches from her hand. At the sight of her pathetic stock of matches spilt in the mud, the girl would start howling with all the strength of her lungs. Either the man would give her money to quieten her or sympathizers in the crowd would contribute to make good her loss. When these benefactors had gone on their way, the children would gather the matches from the mud and prepare for the next encounter.

An easier trick, in which adults and children combined, was for a little girl to sit crying on a step with two packets containing some residue of tea and sugar. When asked what was the matter, she would sob that her mother had sent her out with a shilling to buy tea and sugar. On her way home, a nasty boy had snatched the change and thrown the tea and sugar in the gutter. The child's mother, posing as a mere bystander, would ask loudly, 'And was that your poor mother's last shilling, and daren't you go home, poor thing?' The onlookers, taking pity on the child, would organize a small collection. Small though it might seem, the income from this dodge was sometimes considerable, and the dodge could be repeated the moment the last benefactor was out of sight. Eighteen shillings might be made in a single morning, a fortnight's wages for most working men and women. A simple winter variation, described in *The Times* in 1862, required the little girl to stand shivering alone in the street, crying 'I'm so cold!' and – when the coast was clear – to carry her earnings round the corner to a gin shop, where her mother waited.[16]

A further class of beggars worked by horrifying passers-by at what they saw – or thought they saw. A number of London beggars in the 1850s had lost limbs or been born without them and the sight, for example, of a man without arms or legs moving crab-like at their feet had such an effect on mid-Victorian ladies that miscarriages were reported in consequence. This group of beggars also included those whom the police discovered to have simulated the loss of a limb by the amateurish device of keeping an arm strapped to the body or a leg doubled under at the knee.

In the past, beggars had often injured themselves to produce the appearance of ulcers or wounds. Now it was possible to work such tricks as 'The Scaldrum Dodge' painlessly. The Scaldrum Dodge consisted of simulating burns from an accident by covering the leg or the arm with a thick layer of soap. It was then saturated with vinegar. This would cause the soap to blister and give the appearance of a limb covered in running sores. Other beggars appeared with alarmingly swollen legs but this was produced by ligatures and might do permanent damage.

The Society for the Suppression of Mendacity had been instituted to set the law on those who imposed upon the public's sympathy. Before long, it had identified some of the more common abuses. There were beggars who simulated fits by observing reality until they could imitate 'the agitation of the muscles, the turning up of the whites of the eyes, the pallor of the face and the rigidity of the mouth and jaw'. Frothing at the mouth was produced by soap. Among the impostors was an old woman who staged her fits close to the door of a public house, in the hope of being revived by brandy. As one police officer remarked: 'I have known that old woman have so many fits in the course of the day that she has been found lying dead drunk in the gutter from the effect of repeated restoratives.' Others were known to fall purposely into the Serpentine in Hyde Park in order to be rescued and taken to the receiving-house of the Humane Society, where they were restored by brandy. After a while, some of them became so well known that the society's officer refused to go to their assistance. On being left to drown, they emerged from the lake unaided.[17]

The Choking Dodge required the beggar to sit on the doorstep of a house and gnaw at a piece of dry bread. In his feebleness and thirst he could not swallow. When he attempted to do so, he began to choke as if it would be the death of him, until he was given twopence to go to the public house and get himself a glass of beer. On being watched more closely, however, he turned away from the door of the public house at the last moment and slipped into another street. He was seen walking along it until he noticed a family at a first floor window. Then he sat down on an opposite doorstep and began his performance again.

The Offal-Eater was an elderly man who worked the area round Russell Square. He moved uneasily, as though his ancient clothes were verminous. His walk was listless and he looked about him in a vacant manner. In view of the windows of the houses, he would then pick up from the mud of the streets those scraps of bread that had been thrown out for the birds, wipe them on the lice-ridden velveteen of his ragged jacket,and begin to eat them. 'He will stand opposite your window for full ten minutes mumbling on that small piece of bread, but he never looks up to inspire compassion or charity, he trusts to his pitiful mumblings to produce the desired effect, and he is not disappointed.' Appalled at the man's silent desperation, the residents threw down coppers from every window so that he should not have to eat the soiled scraps of bread. The old man collected the coins and moved on, repeating his performance in street after street. Even when given fresh bread, he would still be found in the next street going through his usual routine. Later still, he was to be found in a beer shop in St Giles's Rookery with his feet up on the table, smoking a pipe and with a pint of beer before him.[18]

By no means all beggars were cheats nor did the affluent residents of areas like Russell Square hold a monopoly of charitable feelings. 'Chief Baron' Renton Nicholson, whose Judge and Jury Society was among the more scandalous entertainments of London in the 1850s, recalled being destitute as a young man. He had slept on a doorstep in St James's Square, having chosen the house belonging to the Bishop of London. By his account, it was the prostitutes of the Haymarket and Pall Mall from whom he received the readiest charity, 'the fallen sisterhood', as he called them.

> Their compassion and forced assistance to a destitute wretch will ever be remembered. It argues no merit in a man who has once been a homeless, hungry wayfarer over the sterile stones of this modern Babylon, gratefully to acknowledge help from any class, but more particularly that unhappy one against whom every hand is raised, and the hue and cry of false piety in starch, and pseudo-morals in silk brocade, hunt by persecutions even to the grave.[19]

'If none else gives prostitutes a good character, the very poor do,' wrote Andrew Halliday in 1862, '"I don't know what we should do but for them," said an old beggar-woman to me one day, "They are good-hearted souls – always kind to the poor. I hope God will forgive them."' Halliday observed how, when beggars entered a bar selling lace or buttons, the prostitutes would make their male companions buy something.

> I once saw an old woman kiss a bedizened prostitute's hand for a service of this kind. I don't know that I ever witnessed anything more touching in my life. The woman, who a few minutes before had been flaunting about the

bar in the reckless manner peculiar to her class, was quite moved by the old beggar's act, and I saw a tear mount in her eye and slowly trickle down her painted cheek, making a white channel through the rouge as it fell. But in a moment she dashed it away, and the next was flaunting and singing as before.[20]

*

Among the Victorian poor who begged in the streets and public houses of London, a great number did so out of necessity and desperation, while others made an art of it. The rivals of this latter group were men and women who made their livings more widely as cheats. Their accomplishments included coining, rather than forgery, the former a growing industry of the professional underworld by the 1850s.

Two decades earlier, with the disappearance of the Bloody Code of retribution in the criminal courts, coining and forgery had ceased to be capital offences though they still carried a maximum sentence of life imprisonment. Coining had also received a boost from Victorian technology, though the initial process of faking the currency remained much the same. A clean shilling or half-crown was greased with tallow or suet and a mould was made from it in plaster of Paris. The Britannia metal used for coining was usually obtained by melting down spoons, since pewter was too light and could be too easily detected. Though the two halves of the mould were held together by metal claws, great care had to be taken that the plaster itself was dry before the hot metal was poured in through the 'collar'. If there was moisture on the inner surface of the plaster, the entire structure would explode. When the mould was opened, the 'gat' or tag, where the molten metal had been poured in, could be pared off with scissors and the edge of the coin filed to perfect the 'knerling'.

> The coin is then considered finished, except the coating. At this time it is of a bluish colour. . . . You get a galvanic battery with nitric acid and sulphuric acid, a mixture of each diluted in water to a certain strength. You then get some cyanide and attach a copper wire to a screw of the battery. Immerse that in the cyanide of silver when the process of electro-plating commences.[21]

After plating, the coin required 'slumming' to dull its appearance and give an impression of age and previous use. This was done by rubbing it with a mixture of lamp-black and oil. Until an attempt was made to pass the fake, it would be kept individually wrapped in paper, so that its electro-plating should not be scratched by contact with any other coin.

A mould could generally be used twice and sometimes would produce as many as four coins before it became defaced. Coining was a skill in many working-class districts of London. Because the process had become so simple, it required only two people working together behind securely barred doors, usually a man and a woman. There was an advantage if they were husband and wife, since a woman might plead that she had acted under her husband's direction and therefore under the law of the time bore no criminal responsibility. A third person might be employed as a 'crow' or look-out to raise the alarm if the police came near.

Inspector James Brennan, 'a skilful and experienced public officer, who keeps a keen surveillance over this department of crime', was the scourge of coiners and pornographers alike in the court reports of the 1850s and 1860s. He was so familiar with the coiners' idiosyncrasies that he could even tell which teams had produced which fakes. When they had been identified, his raids on suspect premises were as unceremonious as any assault on a drugs baron a century and a half later. Unannounced, Brennan's chosen officers were trained to smash open the door of the building with a single blow from a sledge-hammer, hoping by this means to catch the suspects in the act of making their currency.

On these occasions, Brennan reported, the men who were coining endeavoured to destroy the moulds while the women threw the counterfeit into the fire or into the molten metal to make it unidentifiable. Alternatively, they held off the officers by throwing the molten metal at them, followed by the acids used in electro-plating. Finally, the coiners fought their adversaries with chairs and stools, 'until they are overpowered and secured'. This resistance was inspired by the knowledge that even a lenient sentence for coining might involve transportation to a penal colony for fourteen years.

In 1855, Brennan was rewarded with £10 by a trial judge following convictions at the Old Bailey. Five men, out of a gang of seven, had been arrested after a desperate fight at a coiners' in Kent Street, in the Borough of Southwark. The leader of the gang was a man named Green, also known as 'Charcoal'. His premises were on the third floor of the building, approached by a winding staircase. On the landing at the top, Brennan was confronted by three stalwarts, one of whom he recognized as Brown, a professional wrestler from Devon in regular demand as an underworld bodyguard. The three men tried to force their way down the stairs while Brennan attempted to hold them back. As he grappled with two of them, the third jumped over his head and disappeared towards ground level. A fourth man appeared from the upper room, hit Brennan on the head with an iron saucepan and forced him back against the staircase window. Inspector Bryant and Brennan's son, also a police officer, came to his assistance. The son struck his father's assailant on the arm with a crowbar. At this point, the staircase window gave way and the wanted man fell through it into the courtyard below. Another of the coiners jumped from a staircase window on to the roof of a shed, which gave way under him. He was arrested by Constable Neville who jumped after him. The men who had got past Brennan were also arrested in the yard below.

Two more of the coiners and two of their women were trapped in the upper room. 'Charcoal', who was one of them, began to smash the plaster moulds before he was overpowered. Enough of the larger fragments of plaster remained to provide the evidence for his conviction. Even so, two members of the gang had got clear of the *mêlée* and were never caught.

Brennan received his reward of £10 for 'the manly and efficient part he had acted on this trying occasion'. It was also the law's compensation for being hit on the head with an iron saucepan. He had been more severely wounded on a previous occasion, when he and Sergeant Cole raided a Shoreditch house in Old Street Road. In the struggle, Brennan caught the coiner by his leather apron and the two of them fell the entire length of the staircase. Brennan suffered injuries to the back of his head, as well as from having the coiner's knee driven into what was politely termed his stomach. Sergeant Cole, meantime, was in the room above trying to arrest the coiner's wife and his thirteen-year-old daughter. While Cole grappled with the pair, the family bulldog loyally joined in, seizing him by the leg of his trousers. A police constable outside heard the disturbance, entered, and decided the issue in favour of law and order. The coiner was committed to Newgate to await trial and was eventually transported for fifteen years. His daughter went to prison for two years 'for the exceedingly active part she had taken in the affair'. His wife was acquitted by virtue of the Victorian wife's defence that whatever she had done had been done under her husband's direction.[22]

Though coining was the more common art, there was also a brisk trade in forged Bank of England notes, frequently in denominations of £5 or £10. Yet forgeries were usually apparent at once to detectives or bank officials. A particular difficulty was attempting to copy the water-mark of genuine notes. Though forgers were able to reproduce it, the forged mark was said to vanish if the note was wetted.

A forger's first precaution was to make the counterfeit note as dirty as was practicable, so that imperfections would be less evident. It would also appear as if it had been in circulation a long time and must have been accepted as genuine on a number of occasions. Horse-fairs, markets, hotels and public houses were places where such notes were most likely to be put into circulation. Monday morning, while the banks were not yet open, was thought to be a good time for passing notes before they could be checked. A common trick was to send an accomplice, dressed as a servant, to buy goods with forged notes. The servant would claim to have been sent from a house whose owner's name was above suspicion in the locality.

Bills of exchange, issued by one bank and entitling the bearer to receive cash from another, might also be forged. However, these were often international and might involve very large sums of money. As such, their forgery was a matter for the true professionals.

*

Coining and forgery, though drawing on the technical advances of the Industrial Revolution, had a long history. For most Victorians, the more obvious forms of contemporary cheating were by-products of life in the new metropolis but also depended upon greater ease of travel, increased leisure, and national wealth more widely spread. Such improvements afforded chances of deception, practised by opportunists like the magsmen or the sharpers. The magsman, perhaps the best known of his kind, was dependent upon other members of a small gang but would himself be dressed as a gentleman or a country farmer visiting the capital. One gang of the 1860s used a liveried coachman to lure humbler victims and another had a magsman dressed as a clergyman with green spectacles. Though magsmen operated throughout central London, they made a point of visiting the British Museum, St Paul's

Cathedral, Westminster Abbey and the Crystal Palace, where trippers were most likely to be met with.

A common gambit by the magsman was to approach his dupe while passing a well-known public building, excusing himself by remarking what a noble building it appeared and asking what it was. The dupe thereupon felt that, as in his own case, this man must be a stranger to London. The magsman would confirm this by mentioning a country town where he had a good deal of property and hinting at his philanthropic activities there. He would also find some pretext for taking out his pocket-book and, as if by accident, letting his dupe see a bundle of banknotes, usually forged.

As the two men walked along, the magsman would ingratiate himself until he felt it was safe to invite his new friend to take a glass of ale or wine with him at a beer shop or gin palace. While they were at the bar, a second member of the gang would come in, pretending to be a stranger to the first. All the same, the two men would get into conversation and a wager of some kind would result between the magsman and his confederate. This usually led to a game of skittles being played for money between the two. The magsman was allowed to win, establishing his confederate as a very poor skittles player in the eyes of the dupe. Then the magsman retired to the bar and the dupe was allowed to play against the stranger. At first the dupe won a game or two for modest wagers. This made it difficult for him to quit without allowing the other to break even. Several bystanders, apparently strangers to one another but in fact members of the gang, might join in. Abruptly, the dupe's luck would change as opponents who had lost every game to him so far suddenly became possessed of remarkable proficiency. Honour would scarcely let him withdraw as he began to lose, and he lost with such rapidity that the final reckoning-up of the wagers would leave him almost penniless.

Having extracted all the money they could, the other players would allow the dupe to rejoin the magsman at the bar. The two companions would leave together, the magsman shaking his head at the misfortune of his new friend. After hearing the whole story of the skittles and the wagers, the magsman would say, 'I believe these men not to be honest. I'll go back and see where they have gone, and try and get your money back.' He would turn away on his errand and the dupe would wait patiently but never saw his well-wisher again. The same trick was worked with cards, rather than skittles, when the visitor from the provinces would be inveigled into playing with a gang of sharpers who pretended to be strangers to one another.[23]

Simpler forms of deception, set up in the streets or at fairs and race meetings, involved such well-established cheats as 'The Three-Card Trick' or 'Three-Thimbles-and-a-Pea'. The Three-Card Trick used one picture card and two plain. The sharp offered odds of two to one against a bystander being able to guess the picture card from the three dealt face-down on the ground. A first wager of a sovereign or ten shillings was put down by the sharp's man in the crowd. He, and he alone, would win. Other punters, though sure which was the picture card, found they had lost. This was not surprising. The secret of the trick was to abstract the picture card after the confederate had won and substitute a plain one from the pack.

Three-Thimbles-and-a-Pea was a variant of this trick. The sharp's man was allowed to win by guessing correctly under which of the three thimbles the pea was to be found. There was no chance of anyone else guessing correctly because the sharp had perfected the technique of hiding the pea under his rather long thumb-nail. The favourite pitch for these cheats by the 1860s was a fair or race meeting outside the Metropolitan Police area, within which the law had become too vigilant.

A characteristically mid-Victorian cheat was ring-dropping, a variation on the street trade in which rings or sovereigns were offered for wagers. The ring-dropper would buy brass rings that looked like gold at threepence a dozen from a swag-shop. Ring-dropping, known colloquially as 'fawney-dropping', was said by its practitioners to work best in country districts, at fairs and races. It had been profitable in London but by the 1860s it was as well known as the Three-Card Trick. In its simplest form, the ring-dropper would approach a dupe, showing a ring and saying that he had just found it on the ground. He would ask the dupe if it was worth anything. If the dupe took the bait, the ring-dropper would say that it was of no use to him but he might sell it. A conveniently placed 'bystander' would remark that it could be pawned for five shillings without even selling it. Sooner or later, the gullibility and greed of a victim would ensure a purchase.

An embellishment on this was to write a brief love-letter, said to have been found with the ring. One ring-dropper quoted the following:

My dear Anne,
I have sent you the ring and hope it will fit. – Excuse me not bringing it. John
will leave it with you. – I shall think every minute a year until the happy day
arrives.
Yours devotedly,
James Brown

Yet, said another man sadly, the public was now 'wide awake' to this
trick as well. The old dodge was 'coopered' and the ring-dropping 'lurk'
must be redesigned. One new routine required an approach to groups
of servant-girls by a female accomplice, 'made up so as to appear in the
family way – pretty far gone – and generally with a face as long as a boy's
kite'. She would confide in her dupes that she was pregnant, 'as you can
plainly see, young ladies'. It was important that she should call the
young servants 'ladies', the ring-dropper explained, because 'that prides
them, you know'. The usual 'tale of woe' on these occasions was the
well-worn tragedy of marriage, a series of pregnancies, and desertion
by her husband.

Servant-girls were easily moved by this recital from a poor young
woman reduced to offering her wedding-ring for sale, 'as she wants to
get back to her suffering kids to give them something to eat, poor things'.
She would offer it for half its alleged value or as security for a loan of a
few shillings. She could have pawned it but had not been 'in the habit
of pledging'. This was regarded as a masterstroke. 'The girls are taken
off their guard. She not being in the habit of pledging is a choker for
them.'

A consultation would follow among the girls, as they discussed which
of them might need a wedding-ring first. 'Oh, you'll want it, Mary, for
John. . . . No, you'll want it first, Sally, for William.' The trickster would
notice the girl who stood silently by and did not join in. Then the
'deserted wife' would say to the others, 'Oh, you don't want it; but
here . . . here's a young lady as does.' The silent girl might then giggle
and say, 'I don't want it, bless you, but I'll lend you a trifle, as you are in
this state, and have a family, and are left like this by your husband – ain't
he cruel, Sally?'

The success of the female ring-dropper might depend on the time of
year. If it was just after one of the four quarter-days, when servants were
paid, she might get four or five shillings for a ring that had probably cost
a farthing. Some of these women could take ten or twelve shillings a day.

An attic occupied by a family of ten, Bethnal Green, 1863

'The ring is made out of brass gilt buttons, and stunning well,' said one dropper, 'it's faked up to rights, and takes a good judge even at this day to detect it without a test.' The best of the fake rings were known as 'Belchers', with the crown and 'V.R.' stamped upon them, 'a good thick looking ring'. Though they would cost sevenpence a dozen from the swag-shop, a good 'fawney-dropper' might get several shillings for each of them.

Even so it had become a hard life, according to a seller who had fallen far since the days when he was 'a regular swell' with white kid gloves, choker, waistcoat and quizzing-glass. He now lived in the squalor of a Westminster padding-ken. With wistful optimism, he hoped that the second International Exhibition to be held at South Kensington in 1862 and the crowds attending it might mark a turn in his fortunes, as he looked back on his life.

> I never was saving, always spent my money as fast as I got it. I might have saved a goodish bit, and I wish I had now. I never had a wife, but I have had two or three broomstick matches, though they never turned out happy. I never got hold of one but that was fond of lush. . . . We expects to do great

things during the Exhibition. I think all of us ought to be allowed to sell in the parks. Foreigners are invited to witness specimens of British Industry, and it's my opinion they should see all, from the highest to the lowest.[24]

*

Though trickery might be the most common form of underworld trade, it was theft which more readily filled the columns of the police-court reports in the morning and evening press. While the crime of theft took innumerable forms, it was at its most disturbing when the thieves were children, their villainy an ill-omen for the future of society. John Binny spoke for his contemporaries in 1862 when he wrote that, 'Thousands of our felons are trained from their infancy in the bosom of crime; a large proportion of them are born in the homes of habitual thieves and other persons of bad character, and are familiarised with vice from their earliest years; frequently the first words they lisp are oaths and curses.' The 'little ragged urchin in St Giles's stealing a handkerchief at the tail of a gentleman's coat' was destined to become 'the elegantly dressed and expert pickpocket promenading in the West-end and attending fashionable assemblies'. In that example, it seemed that even the juvenile thief, in his own domain, was not immune to the Victorian virtue of self-improvement.[25]

Thousands of neglected children prowled the streets of Westminster, Whitechapel, Shoreditch, St Giles's, Lambeth and Southwark, 'begging and stealing for their daily bread'. Every morning, as John Binny observed them in the 1860s, they swarmed from the homes of their parents or from the padding-kens, 'in search of food and plunder . . . fluttering in rags and in the most motley attire'. That some might grow up to become honest and honourable citizens was little solace to the mid-Victorian constituency of *The Times* or the *Morning Chronicle*.[26]

Closer examination showed that the great majority of thefts by children were trivial enough. Even Binny conceded that the urchins who snatched fruit or nuts from barrows and ran off while cries of 'Stop, thief!' rang in their ears, acted 'from a love of mischief rather than from a desire for plunder'. Yet those who came out when the lamps were lit, in ragged trousers and tattered coats too big for them, barefoot and unwashed, were of a different kind. In areas like the Mile End Road, they would steal from stalls displaying brooches and bracelets, combs and looking-glasses, which were bought from them by a fence. If caught stealing by the police or by shopkeepers in areas like the New Cut or the Waterloo Road, they would lie down, screaming 'Let me go!' until onlookers came to their rescue. Such streets were said to be 'rookeries' of juvenile thieves.[27]

Thefts from the doors and windows of shops were common. Apart from the plate-glass constructions of Oxford Street, most shops in the 1860s still had windows with glazing-bars and domestic-sized panes. After dark, a group of boys would cluster admiringly at such a window, usually at one displaying sweets or tobacco. If a knife was inserted at the corner of a pane, it would produce a semi-circular, star-like crack in the glass. A sticking plaster pressed against the pane would enable the boys to pull the glass out. Within half a minute the window might be stripped of sweets or delicacies, pipes or tobacco. By the time the shopman woke up to what was happening the window would be half empty and the boys, known as 'star-glazers', would have disappeared down the street.

The more ambitious robbed clothes shops. One boy or girl would watch the shop from the other side of the street, while the second nimbly unbuttoned a coat from its display dummy outside the shop, stripped it off and sprinted away. If the owner gave chase, another child was usually posted to trip him up as he ran. When it was necessary to enter a shop, a boy would throw his cap in and then go after it, complaining that it had been thrown in by another child. Once inside, it was relatively easy to graduate to the robbing of tills, by crawling round the counter out of sight of the shopkeeper.

Girls grew up to be as adept at stealing as boys, though they generally worked with male accomplices. Their targets were goods displayed outside the shops of linen-drapers and brokers, including rolls of printed cotton, flannel, calico, tablecloths and individual fire-irons, all of which could be sold easily to fences and swag-shops. Though the readers of the middle-class press were the most dismayed by the criminality of which they read, the sufferers from such thefts were generally the struggling traders of the New Cut, Lambeth Walk, Petticoat Lane and Spitalfields.

Among the occupations of childhood which sounded engagingly innocent were the activities of those male and female mudlarks, ragged and mud-soaked urchins who scavenged on the foreshore of the river between Westminster and Southwark. Their occupation was to search for coal, timber or iron which might have fallen from the barges or, indeed, for anything else that might be saleable. When there was nothing to be found on the mud, they would climb quietly aboard the barges and knock overboard on to the mud lumps of coal, lengths of wood, rope, iron or 'anything else we can lay our hands on, and easily carry off'. If caught by the bargees, they were unceremoniously thrashed and thrown into the river, being left to 'swim ashore and then take off their wet clothes and dry them'. They breakfasted on bread and beer, being refused admittance to coffee shops because they stole the workmen's food. 'We are often chased by the Thames police and the watermen, as the mudlarks are generally known to be thieves,' said one boy. 'I take what I can get as well as the rest when I get an opportunity.'[28]

The Thames police, who had the legal powers of customs officers, kept watch on the river to curb the activities of the mudlarks but also in an attempt to prevent or restrict the smuggling of tobacco from the ships moored at Bermondsey or Shadwell. Sweeps, who swept the funnels of steam vessels, carried back contraband tobacco hidden in their bags of soot. Other men managed to carry sacks of it ashore in the middle of the night, when it was delivered to tobacconists' shops in the area.

Children were sometimes thieves but were by no means exempt from suffering theft in their turn. Child-stripping occurred even in the mews of the West End. Women, described by Binny as 'old debauched drunken hags', kept watch for a trusting and well-dressed child whom they would invite to come with them for the purchase of sweets or a treat of some kind. In a quiet place, the child would be given a sweet or a half-penny and told to take off its boots or other clothes and to remain there until the kindly old woman returned with some delicacy. The child waited as vainly for the return of its clothes as the magsman's dupe for the recovery of his money.

Small girls were robbed by a woman who would accost them when they were carrying a promising bundle or basket. A case was reported in 1861 at Marylebone Police Court in which a woman had accosted such a child and asked her if she knew where she must take her pur-chases. The child had innocently given the woman the address. 'You are a good girl and quite right,' the woman said. 'Mrs So-and-so sent me for them, as she is in a hurry and is going out.' The child, without doubt-ing this, had handed over the basket.[29]

The Victorian middle class was also conscious that its homes were constantly at risk from the dishonesty of servants and their followers. From time to time, there were such cautionary stories as that attending the trial and execution of Kate Webster in 1879. A single example of depravity on this scale was worth a thousand homilies. Kate Webster was a strongly built Irish servant who made a career of domestic theft. In the 1860s her profession was to rob the keepers and inmates of lodging-houses where she stayed. Then she moved on to domestic service, in Wandsworth, Notting Hill and Teddington, always with a view to robbery. Though she had served four prison sentences, her employers seemed to know nothing of her past. In 1879 she was dismissed by Julia Thomas of Richmond, a widow with whom she lived alone. Kate Webster responded by dispatching her mistress with a chopper. She then impersonated Mrs Thomas in order to sell the dead woman's jewels and furniture to strangers, while telling the neighbours that the widow had gone away. A good many other single men and women must have thought how easily they too might be eliminated by a resolute servant.

Kate Webster's fame was assured by the determination with which she first dismembered the body, then boiled the pieces in the copper and boned them. A foot was found at Twickenham. The torso was washed ashore in a hatbox at Barnes. Her downfall was her greed in trying to sell the dead widow's furniture, arousing suspicion in the area as to whether Julia Thomas would have gone away in such a sudden manner. The house was searched. A chopper and fragments of charred bones were found. The process of boiling the corpse had left a large deposit of fat in the copper. Most of this had been removed before Kate Webster fled. She had scooped it into two bowls and sold it round the neighbourhood as dripping. The feelings of those who consumed the dripping, said one witness, were not much to be envied.

By contrast with such domestic dramas, robbery in the full light of day seemed almost good-natured. Most thefts of the kind were carried out by pickpockets. This was usually a profession for men and women in their twenties but the apprenticeship began early. One sneak thief reported that most juvenile pickpockets lived in the padding-kens of Westminster and Southwark, not far removed from their West End targets.

> I have often seen the boys picking each other's pockets for diversion in the lodging-house, many of them from ten to eleven years of age. . . . I have seen young thieves encouraged by people who kept the lodging-houses, such

Kate Webster's effigy in Madame Tussaud's Chamber of Horrors, 1879

as at Keat Street, Whitechapel, and at the Mint. They would ask the boys if they had anything, and wish them to sell it to them, which was generally done at an under-price. In these lodging-houses some lived very well, and others were starving.[30]

Children who were destitute and could afford no place in the lodging-house might live and sleep by the river under the arches of the Adelphi. This was favoured as a convenient refuge for stealing handkerchiefs from the pockets of men who came ashore from the river ferries at the Adelphi Stairs.

Even in prison some of the most successful pickpockets lived extremely well, as the aristocrats of their profession. One boasted that during three months in Bridge Street Bridewell he had had no need to suffer the harsh prison diet. His food was provided by friends outside and brought in by bribing the turnkeys. 'I had tea of a morning and butter, and often cold meat. Meat and all kinds of pastry was sent to me from a cook-shop outside.' He was allowed to sit up later than the other prisoners and 'learned to smoke, as cigars were introduced to me'.[31]

In November 1862, the *Cornhill Magazine* assured its readers that pickpockets worked the cross-channel steamers, the lakes of Killarney, and the Manchester Exchange with equal skill and that they visited New York. It was a profession for those who wished to see the world. 'They generally go on the Continent in the spring, and remain there until the races and fairs are coming off in England. The London mobs go down to Manchester in December, there being a large number of commercial men about the town at that time.'

In London, the times and places chosen by such men to exercise their skill included Epsom Races for the Derby, Madame Tussaud's in Baker Street, the Crystal Palace, the Zoological Gardens, the evangelical preaching at Spurgeon's New Tabernacle, theatres where stealing purses at the rear of boxes was easily done as the performance ended, and Spitalfields Church, where pickpockets did well in taking ladies' purses as they came down the steps after morning service. 'I would rather rob the rich than the poor,' said one pickpocket piously, 'they miss it less.'

This same man might have been the despair of traditional penologists who believed in the deterrent effects of flogging and hanging. 'I've had four floggings; it was bad enough – a flogging was – while it lasted; but when I got out I soon forgot it. At a week's end I never thought again about it. If I had been better treated I should have been a better lad.' This man was present at one of the most famous public hangings of the century, that of Mr and Mrs Manning in 1847 for the murder of Patrick O'Connor. 'Mrs Manning was dressed beautiful when she came up. She screeched when Jack Ketch pulled the bolt away.' All the same, the thief had not been frightened by the spectacle and was certainly not deterred from his life of crime. 'I did 4s. 6d. at the hanging – two handkerchiefs, and a purse with 2s. in it – the best purse I ever had.'

When in prison, it was far better for a man to be known as a thief than as a beggar. 'The others say, "Begging! Oh, you cadger!" So a boy is partly forced to steal for his character.'[32]

The techniques of the pickpocket were necessary reading for the mid-Victorian bourgeoisie, some of the methods putting to shame the dexterity of stage magicians at the Egyptian Hall in Piccadilly. Gentlemen's scarf-pins might have seemed a difficult trophy but were not. An accomplished thief need only walk boldly towards his prey, taking an expensive handkerchief from his pocket as if to wipe his nose. This was done with a horizontal flourish and with the arm passing almost across the breast of his quarry. Under cover of the flourish, the pickpocket's other hand moved up unobserved to draw the pin clear of the scarf. Even if the victim suspected what had happened, the pin would have passed from the hand of the thief to that of an accomplice long before the first question could be asked.

Still more difficult, in appearance, was the removal of money from a trouser pocket. This was done by using a sharp knife to cut the cloth, 'lay open the pocket, and adroitly rifle the money from it'. Ladies' purses and watches were removed, even when fitted with a guard, by a man and a woman approaching and the woman asking for directions. Some time later, the lady would find that both her purse and her watch, which had been in a front pocket under a flounce, were missing. Only the guard remained with its ring broken.

Unlike other forms of theft, however, the pickpocket was usually seen by his victim or, indeed, by her victim. Women were particularly successful in picking the pockets of their own sex because their presence or proximity aroused far less suspicion than that of a man would have done. Yet the nature of the crime still heightened the chances of detection. However great their dexterity, pickpockets were apt to be remembered as the couple who had asked for directions or the man who had wiped his nose with a flourish and so were liable to be caught. Even the true professionals seldom operated beyond their mid-thirties. By that time, having been arrested and imprisoned several times, they had had 'the steel taken out of them'.[33]

*

The greatest prestige among thieves in the Victorian underworld attached to the professional burglar or cracksman. There were many more petty thieves or sneak thieves who stole from food-safes in base-ment areas or sought opportunities to lift windows or break glass and take what they could. However, they seemed mean spirits beside those who followed the hazardous professions of cracksman or cat burglar, men who gave time and skill to the meticulous planning of crimes, failure in which entailed a daunting prison sentence or death by mis-adventure. London cracksmen, according to John Binny, were the heroes of their class.

> They have the look of sharp businessmen. They commit burglaries at country mansions, and sometimes at shops and warehouses, often extensive, and generally contrive to get safely away with their booty. These crack bur-glars generally live in streets adjoining the New Kent Road and Newington Causeway, and groups of them are to be seen occasionally at the taverns beside the Elephant and Castle, where they regale themselves luxuriously on the choicest wines, and are lavish of their gold. From their superior manner and dress few would detect their real character. One might pass them daily in the street and not be able to recognize them.[34]

A number of the most successful jewel thieves had a single *modus operandi* which they used to great effect. These were the so-called 'attic thieves' or 'garret thieves', who were far more ambitious than their titles suggested. Their targets were substantial houses in fashionable West End areas such as Portman Square or Lowndes Square. Their method was to find a nearby house which was empty or at least had been closed up while the owners were out of town. If the thieves could enter this unoccupied building, they would make their way along the roofs or gutters or parapets from house to house towards their destination. The time chosen for the burglary was usually between seven and eight o'clock in the evening, so that they entered the garret windows of the house while the family was at dinner on the first floor and the servants were kept busy between that floor and the kitchen in the basement.

There was time for the thieves to go down to the second-floor bed-rooms, open the wardrobes and drawers with a short jemmy, and ransack the jewel cases without being disturbed. Though a burglar was unlikely to be discovered at this stage, the plan might easily go wrong. In 1861 a house in Lowndes Square was entered through the attic by burglars who made off with jewels worth £3,000, more than a hundred clerks or labourers would earn in a year. In order not to attract atten-tion in an area such as this, the men were well-dressed. In the windy night, they climbed back along the rooftop to the empty house by which they had gained access. As they did so, the hat of one of the men was blown off and landed on the slope of a roof belonging to another build-ing, which it was impossible to reach. The gang made its escape but the hat was found. It had recently been repaired and a slip of paper had been tucked inside the lining at the time, inscribed with the owner's name. He was arrested and sentenced to penal servitude for ten years.

Arrest followed by imprisonment was not the worst disaster that might overtake the garret thieves. In 1850, there had been a midnight drama at a furrier's on a corner of Regent Street, just to the south of the junction with Oxford Street. Three men had entered a public house between ten and eleven o'clock that night and two of them – Edward Blackwell and Henry Edgar – had concealed themselves in the privy, which was in the yard at the back of the building. They remained there undetected after the house closed and went up a fire-escape, from which they could reach the roof parapet of the furrier's premises. For some reason, they had not waited for the promised signal of their accomplice, the third man who had remained below, to tell them that the coast was clear.

Blackwell and Edgar began to cut out the panes of glass from a garret window, not realizing that there was a servant in the room preparing for bed in the dark. She went quietly downstairs and warned the furrier. Her master appeared at the garret window with two loaded pistols in his hands and told the men that he would shoot them if they tried to escape. Blackwell seemed to panic, lost his footing, fell three storeys into the yard below, and was killed outright. Edgar made a hazardous but successful leap to the roof of the next house in Regent Street, got down through a trap door and managed to find his way to a second-floor bedroom fronting on Argyle Street. The occupants awoke and saw him jump from their window into the street. By this time the alarm had been raised and the police were waiting for him. 'He was thereupon arrested, and conveyed in a cab, with the dead body of his "pal", to Vine Street police station.'[35]

But Henry Edgar was not yet defeated. The jump to Argyle Street had dislocated his ankle and he was taken to Middlesex Hospital under police guard. Eight hours later he escaped. His friends were waiting for him with a cab and got him safely to Blackfriars Road, then took him by another cab to Commercial Road, Whitechapel. A house was found for him in Corbett's Place, Spitalfields. In the meantime, however, the brother of one of his accomplices went to Vine Street police station and revealed his place of concealment. Before he could defend himself with the pistols which he kept to hand, Edgar was arrested and, on conviction, was sent to penal servitude.

Less resolute thieves were content to commit burglary on mansions in the West End by way of the front door and by the use of a confidence trick. The bell would be rung by a cabman who would inform the butler that a lady sitting outside in the vehicle wished to speak to the butler on important and confidential business. The butler, who was in effect the guardian of the house, would see the cab ten or twenty yards down the street. He would be kept in conversation by the lady inside it, his back to the house, while a well-dressed man slipped indoors. The plan usually worked but sometimes the intruder was spotted, traced to the bedrooms, and discovered to be in possession of a jemmy, wax tapers and 'silent lights', which were matches that struck without scraping.

Burglars of this sort lived well and dressed well, having 'a very gentleman-like appearance'. They employed servants, who were sometimes accomplices in the disposal of the stolen property. John Binny found one gang who lived in an expensively furnished house in Russell Square. The women connected with such gangs 'have an abundance of jewellery; they live in high style, with plenty of cash, but not displayed to any great extent at the time any robbery is committed, as it would excite suspicion'. Some of the most successful cracksmen, knowing that love and money might prove a combustible blend, 'are afraid to keep women, as the latter are frequently the cause of their being brought to justice'.[36]

Warehouses and shops, no less than the homes of the ruling class, were the targets of such gangs. Jewellers' shops might be entered through the attic of the building but a good many burglaries took place through the main door. This might depend on skeleton keys which were difficult to procure. More often the answer was provided by a circular 'cutter', which could cut out a hole including the lock, or an 'American augur', which would take out a panel of the door. The other essentials were a sheet of thick paper, painted the same colour as the door, and a young woman with a talent for amateur theatricals.

The advent of the Metropolitan Police had led to the systematic arrest in the streets of those suspected of carrying tools for house-breaking. By the 1850s, it was often the young woman, who was known in the trade as a 'canary' because she was required to 'sing' at the sight of danger, who took the carpet bag of tools to the premises. She appeared to those who saw her like a night traveller, hurrying on her way to or from one of the main railway termini. As in the coining trade, any man who played the part of look-out was known as a 'crow'.

The burglars who followed a look-out to the premises were empty-handed and seemed plainly innocent of any attempt at forcible entry. Once the coast was clear and the carpet bag had been handed over by the canary or the crow, one man would use the circular cutter – or the American augur – while another kept the instrument wet so that it would make very little noise. Once this had been done, the door could be opened, while the strip of identically coloured paper was pasted across it. At a casual glance there was no sign of a break-in.

The young woman's role was usually to parade as if she might be a prostitute and, if necessary, to monopolize the curiosity of any police-man on the beat. This was an essential part of the plan, since a policeman was likely to pass at intervals of between fifteen and twenty minutes. If necessary, the woman would either fall down in a fit, oblig-ing him to find a cab and take her to a doctor, or else pretend to be drunk and disorderly so that he had to arrest her and convey her to the police station.

Whichever the performance, the policeman was taken off his beat for half an hour or more. 'In the meanwhile the parties inside, with jemmy, chisel, saw, or other tools, and with silent lights and taper or dark lantern, break open the glass cases and boxes, and steal gold and silver watches, gold chains, brooches, pins and other jewellery, which they deposit in a small carpet-bag, as well as rifle money from the desk.'[37]

Warehouse robberies were equally common, their methods simple and well-rehearsed. One of the best-known crimes occurred in 1842,

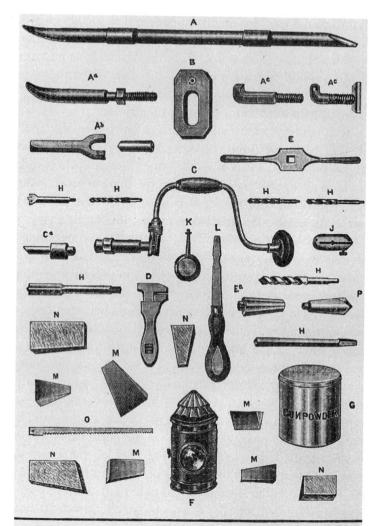

A SAFE-BURGLAR'S KIT.
(The whole were conveyed in a handbag.)

A Little Alderman, or Sectional Jemmy.	**F** Dark Lantern.
Aa Spare Section.	**G** Gunpowder.
Ab Cleaver end, to be screwed into **A**.	**H** Various Drills, "twist" drills.
Ac Prisers.	**J** Lock for Drills (to hold them fast).
B Persuasion Plate, for obtaining leverage.	**K** Oil-can.
C American Brace, or Drill.	**L** Screw-driver.
Ca Centre-bit.	**M** Steel Wedges, with razor-like edges.
D Adjustable Spanner.	**N** Wooden Wedges.
E Wrench.	**O** Saw for metal.
Ea Rimer for Wrench, to enlarge holes.	**P** Countersink.

p. 31

A cracksman's tools illustrated in 1889. Gunpowder has not yet been replaced by dynamite when goods valued at £1,500 to £2,000, as well as a banknote for £100, were taken from a silk warehouse in Cheapside. It happened over a weekend, when the burglars were admitted to the adjoining carpet warehouse by the foreman late on Saturday night. The gang had ample time to break through the nine-inch brickwork of the party wall and remove the silk by this route. It was carried away by hansom cab in the course of Sunday afternoon, during the intervals of the policeman's appearance on his beat. The robbery was not discovered until Monday morning because none of the policemen, seeing the padlock and fastenings intact on the door of the silk warehouse, had any cause for suspicion. By Monday morning, the foreman of the carpet warehouse had disappeared and twenty years later the police had still not found him.

The most proficient cracksmen of the 1850s showed an expertise which justified the cliché of a crime carried out like a military operation. Indeed, by comparison with the War Office's organization of the Crimean War in 1854–6 – potted meat that was poisoned and winter boots that proved to be exclusively for the left foot – the professionalism of such criminals seemed impeccable. A relatively routine warehouse robbery in the City involved premises that were impregnable at the front and had, at the rear, a stout door for letting the employees out, which was secured by three strong patent locks. The burglars had to make identical keys for these, as well as one key to fit a patent lock on the iron door to the counting-house, another for the safe, and yet another for the inner safe. As a precaution they needed a seventh key for a patent lock that barred the way to a second safe. They spent four months making and fitting the keys to the locks, never having the originals in their hands, while a succession of policemen on the beat passed the warehouse three or four times an hour and noticed nothing amiss. The cracksmen paid a visit one night and left with two iron boxes containing scrip, banknotes and bills of exchange to the value of £13,000, a sum worth roughly £2,000,000 a century and a half later.

The activities of such men initiated a running battle between the new techniques of safemakers like Chubb or Milner and the inspired improvisation of their adversaries. By 1860, Chubb's patent locks were proof against picking and the firm's safes were said to be resistant to any drill. In 1865, modern science enabled the first burglar alarms to be connected to a police station, as Adolphe Baab described in *The Times* on 12 April. Telegraph wires in the street 'can be placed in communication with the nearest police station, and . . . on the slightest attempt to tamper with any part of the safe will sound an alarm, and not only inform the police that a robbery is in progress, but acquaint them by means of a number, with the precise safe that is being attacked'.

Happily for the mid-Victorian cracksman, such devices were still regarded as newfangled or downright cranky. So long as robberies could be carried out by duplicate keys, there were men who seemed able to cut copies with disconcerting accuracy. A first-rate technician could cut a duplicate key without ever having the original in his hand. These men 'sometimes take a blank key without wards, cover it with wax, work it in the keyhole against the wards of the lock and by that means the impression is left in the wax'. It was little enough to work from but, as in the case of the warehouse with its seven patent locks, it proved to be sufficient.[38]

Removing a pane of glass from a window was reckoned to take fifteen seconds, enabling window catches to be unfastened from the inside. Shutters could be opened by a cutter, with two blades and a centre stock, making a hole large enough for the burglar's arm to go through and open them. Iron bars could be bent apart sufficiently for a man to get through by tying stout rope round two of them, inserting a piece of wood and twisting it until the tension bent the iron. If this failed, there was the Jack-in-the-Box, its brass stock wound by a steel bar until it brought to bear a pressure of several tons. When confronted by a pre-1860 safe, a cracksman might use a peter-cutter, which worked on the principle of a centre-bit into which drills might be fixed. The cutter was fastened into the keyhole of the lock with strong pressure on the outside. Elsewhere, an opening was cut just above the keyhole, enabling the cracksman to get his arm through, reach the wards of the lock, pull back the bolt of the lock and release the safe door.

> Expert burglars are generally equipped with good tools. They have a jemmy, a cutter, a dozen of betties, better known as picklocks, a jack to remove iron bars, a dark lantern or a taper and some lights, and a life-preserver, and sometimes have a cord or rope with them, which can be easily converted into a rope ladder. A knife is often used in place of a chisel

for opening locks, drawers, or desks. They often carry masks on their face, so that they might not be identified. . . . When they go out with their tools, they usually carry them wrapped up with lint so that they can throw them away without making a noise, should a policeman stop them, or attempt to arrest them.[39]

Behind such skills lurked the shadowy figures of the 'putters-up' of such robberies. With the patience of their trade, they watched houses at night to see the sequence in which rooms were lit or darkened, where the occupants slept, where the valuables might be kept, and what furniture appeared to be in which rooms. They courted servant-girls for information. They got on friendly terms, in public houses or elsewhere, with glaziers, painters, plumbers and other tradesmen who might be working in a house, drawing information from them. Some putters-up had been in business for thirteen or fourteen years. Though suspected by the police, nothing had been proved against them.

In the nature of the business, burglars were seldom heard from except when they were caught. As *Fraser's Magazine* remarked, the old-fashioned burglar, 'conspicuous and famed for daring acts of plunder', had been consigned to history in favour of his Victorian successor, 'famous for scheming, subtlety, and astuteness'. To have been conspicuous was almost a disqualification from the profession. 'Now a certificate must be brought of the man never having committed an indiscreet act in his calling.'[40]

However, in a dark side-lane of St Giles, John Binny talked one evening to a burglar who was at liberty and felt that he had nothing to hide. This man was thirty-two years old and had committed eighteen major burglaries, as well as other forms of theft, choosing shops and houses in the West End as his targets. Binny described him as fair-complexioned, about five feet two inches in height, slim and with a keen grey eye. His working clothes consisted of dark trousers, brown vest, a grey frock-coat buttoned up to the chin, and a cap drawn down over his eyes.

Binny at first doubted whether a man of such slight build could have carried out some of the burglaries he claimed. The burglar led him along the street to an adjoining back court. He took off his shoes and stockings and 'ran up a waterspout to the top of a lofty house, and slid down again with surprising agility'. Despite this agility, the young man had a number of convictions. His sentences served included two periods of transportation amounting to fourteen years, almost half his lifetime.

Binny's burglar and a friend had just pulled off a robbery at a large public house in the West End, choosing a time when there was cash on the premises to pay the brewers. This information was sold to them for the price of a drink by an out-of-work potman or barman. He assured them that the usual amount in the upstairs room was £200, a sum which many contemporaries might take eight or ten years to earn.

The two burglars entered the pub with several accomplices, knowing they would have to get past the bar and upstairs to the room where the money was kept. 'We found the lady of the house and her daughter serving at the bar.' Presently, the companions of the two burglars staged a 'row' in the tap-room. The landlady ran to see what was the matter and her daughter ran out for a policeman. The burglar slipped past the bar and up the stairs during the confusion, just before the daughter returned with the constable.

> The policeman knew one of my companions when he came in, and at once suspected there was some design. He asked if there had been any more besides these two. The landlady said there was another. I was coming down stairs with the cash-box when I heard this conversation. The constable asked leave to search the house. I ran with the cash-box up the staircase, and looked in the back room to see if there was any place to get away, but there was none. I took the cash-box up to the front garret, and was trying to break it open, but in the confusion I could not.
>
> I fled out of the garret window and got on the roof to hide from the policeman. My footsteps were observed on the carpet and on the gutters as I went out and slipped in the mud on the roof. I intended to throw the cash-box to my companions, but they gave me the signal to get away. I had just time to take my boots off when another constable came out of the garret window of the other house. I had no alternative but to get along the roof where they could not follow me, and besides I was much nimbler than they. I went to the end of the row of houses. . . . Seeing a water-spout leading to a stable-yard, I slipt down it, and climbed up another spout to the roof of the stable. I lay there for five hours till the police changed.
>
> I managed to get down and went into the stable-yard, when the stable man cried out, 'Hollo! here he is!' I saw there was no alternative but to fight for it. I had a jemmy in my pocket. He laid hold of me, when I struck him on the face with it, and he fell to the ground. I fled to the door, and came out into the main street, returned into Piccadilly, and passed through the

Park gates. On coming home to Westminster I found one of my comrades had not come home. We went to the police-station, and learned that he was there. We sent him some provisions, and he gave us notice in a piece of paper concealed in some bread that I should keep out of the way as the police were after me, which would aggravate his case.

The man arrested was sentenced to seven years' transportation. Binny's burglar had escaped for the moment and was lying low in the house of a cigar-maker at Whitechapel. Though he was cautious, the aftermath of crime was a time of gaiety and easy living. 'We spent the next three or four weeks very merrily along with our girls.' During hard times, other criminals came to his aid. This was just as well, since his next burglary, on a house in the West End, went badly wrong.

> The old gentleman came down stairs in his nightgown with a brace of pistols, just as we were going out of the window. He fired, but missed us. I jumped so hastily that I hurt my bowels, and was conveyed by my companions in a cab to Westminster, and lay there for six weeks in an enfeebled condition. My money was spent, and as my young woman could not get any, my companions said, 'You had better have a meeting of our "pals".' A meeting was held, and they collected about £8 to assist me.

The principle of the provident or friendly society was a characteristic of personal finance in Victorian England, as well-rooted among professional burglars as among their middle-class targets.

Despite his misfortunes, this burglar had, indirectly, scored a success in Victorian society. His first wife had died broken-hearted when he was transported. He was now married again. Between these two marriages he had met a beautiful Irish coster-girl, a 'good dancer' who was nineteen years old. She believed his story that he was 'a pianoforte maker' and they lived together for a little while until she began to pay attention to another man. The burglar told her to go home to her friends. 'I would not live with her any more.'

The girl's friends found her a job as a servant in a West End house, where she discovered that she was pregnant by her 'pianoforte maker'.

> She was not long in service before her young master fell in love with her, and kept her in fashionable style, which he has continued to do ever since. She now lives in elegant apartments in the West End, and her boy, my son, is getting a college education. I do not take any notice of them now.[41]

Despite the melancholy tone of the final comment, it seemed that even a rather unsuccessful burglar was not entirely immune to the virtues and benefits of Victorian progress. How many other sons and daughters of the Swell Mob were innocent of any knowledge of how their family had come by its modest fortune? This boy, with his college education and professional career ahead of him, perhaps as a clergyman or a lawyer, presumably grew up and prospered with a natural pride in his lost father, whom he spoke of as having been a piano manufacturer.

CHAPTER 3

Modern Babylon

DURING THE summer of 1885, England gave more attention to the 'great social evil' of prostitution than to any other political issue. The extent and nature of the profession had changed relatively little for many years but the 1880s combined a continued anxiety over venereal disease, unallayed by the compulsory examination of some prostitutes under the Contagious Diseases Acts of 1864–9, and alarm over the so-called 'white-slave trade', as it involved girls in their teens. Child prostitution, in the sense of prostitution involving girls under the age of consent, was not in question. That age had been raised from twelve to thirteen in 1875 and as the most famous of the campaigners against white slavery, W. T. Stead, wrote, it was very rare to find that a girl under the age of consent was involved in prostitution. In law, 'juvenile prostitution' referred specifically to 'girls under 21', which was the legal age of majority. What might sound like child prostitution could therefore refer equally to the conduct of a girl of thirteen or that of a young woman of twenty. When, in 1881, C. E. Howard Vincent, Director of Criminal Investigations at Scotland Yard, was asked by a Select Committee of the House of Lords what power the police had to stop a girl of thirteen from soliciting for immoral purposes, he replied, 'No power at all.'[1]

As for boys sent by middle-class families to take army or civil service examinations in London, their fate was hardly preferable to that of their female contemporaries. Howard Vincent described the seduction of the innocent.

I mean that everything centring in London, as it does in this country, all examinations are held in London; everybody sends their sons up to London necessarily for examination; and a boy must be a paragon of virtue, who, at 16 or 17, can walk from 11 o'clock at night till half-past 12 in the morning, from the top of the Haymarket to the top of Grosvenor-place, without being solicited to such an enormous extent, that he is almost certain to fall.

Moral corruption would be accompanied, in Vincent's opinion, by the further spread of contagious disease among the young. 'I was in the army, and had opportunities of knowing that this state of things does exist to this frightful extent with regard to boys of 16 or 17; there is scarcely a senior boy at Eton, a cadet at Sandhurst, or a subaltern in the army, who will not agree with me as to the enormous danger there is.' To the extent that this was true, it gave the lie to the myth of ignorance or innocence among Victorian youth as to the truths of urban life. Yet the panorama of vice, as Vincent portrayed it, owed everything to juvenile prostitution and the white slavery which supported it.[2]

Four years later, a scandal came to fruition. Before the autumn of 1885 was over, Bramwell Booth of the Salvation Army had been tried at the Old Bailey; W. T. Stead, editor of the *Pall Mall Gazette*, had gone to prison for abduction and indecent assault; Lewis Carroll had tried to persuade the Prime Minister, Lord Salisbury, to support prosecutions for obscenity against the campaigners; and the *doyenne* of the white-slave trade, Mrs Mary Jeffries, was back in business. The newspaper placards of July and August had filled the London streets with such headlines as THE LONDON SLAVE MARKET . . . WHY THE CRIES OF THE VICTIMS ARE NOT HEARD . . . STRAPPING GIRLS DOWN . . . I ORDER FIVE VIRGINS . . .

While no one could doubt the luridness of the allegations, the question debated with increasing intolerance was whether they had substance. Had prostitution assumed a more sinister and depraved character or was it much what it had been in the past? In the hands of the *Pall Mall Gazette* the evidence was, not surprisingly, a vivid tableau of debauchery and sadism. Stead made his career as a pioneer of sensational journalism in many other controversies, whether in his goading of the Gladstone government into attempting to rescue General Gordon from Khartoum, or in arguing the innocence of Israel Lipski who was waiting to be hanged for murder, or in denouncing the treason of governments who neglected to maintain Britain's naval supremacy. The story that he was to tell in the summer of 1885 was beyond question one of the most melodramatic ever seen in the British press. The issue was whether a new moral corruption had affected the decade of the 1880s or merely a new prurience and prudery.

*

Two views of prostitution had established themselves in the Victorian mind. Such icons as Dante Gabriel Rossetti's painting *Found* and William Holman Hunt's *The Awakened Conscience* presented the prostitute as the soiled dove or as the figure of a Magdalene ripe for redemption. A contrary opinion suggested that prostitutes had made their beds and should be left to lie on them. From Oxford, the voice of Benjamin Jowett, as Master of Balliol, described such women to Florence Nightingale as 'a class of sinners' best 'left to themselves'. 'Walter', the anonymous diarist of *My Secret Life*, was more forthright still in the 1880s, after his experience of hiring some 1,200 women over a period of forty years.

> The Priestesses of Venus, I am convinced, all like their occupation, and to talk over past frolics when they have quitted the life, whatever they may aver to the contrary. – When they are sick or plain in face or form, and unsuccessful, they are repentant and virtuous, are 'Magdalenes'. Repentance usually pays better *then* than fucking.[3]

At the end of the Queen's reign, however, Charles Booth in the final volume of his *Life and Labour of the People in London* (1902) concluded of prostitutes, 'However adopted, very few are happy in the life. Most would say they wished to quit it.' Perhaps they were hardly likely to say otherwise to a sympathetic missioner. There were certainly women who had taken to the profession from hunger or destitution or who had fled from the disgrace of seduction or pregnancy. Others had motives that were pragmatic or mercenary. In almost all cases, however, prostitution was not seen as a permanent way of life. To some, it was a temporary or occasional employment, as Booth described it for East End tailoresses or dressmakers 'who return to their trade in busy times'. To most, it was a transitory phase of full-time work which led to marriage – perhaps to being kept by one man – or to financial independence. Though disease and mortality would overtake the unfortunate, it was a less hazardous profession than many of its alternatives.

There was no such being, in social class or occupation, as the archetypal prostitute. Dr William Acton's comment in his book *Prostitution*

Considered in its Moral, Social and Sanitary Aspects in London, and Other Large Cities (1857) that 'the better inclined class of prostitutes become the wedded wives of men in every grade of society, from the peerage to the stable', is a match for the unlikely claim of a Victorian headmaster that 'a thoroughly conventional man in good society would sooner that his son should consort with prostitutes than that he should marry a respectable girl of a distinctly lower station than his own'.[4]

There were rare but striking examples of the prostitute's or courtesan's social mobility. Catherine Walters, 'Skittles', made a conquest of the Marquess of Hartington who succeeded his father as 8th Duke of Devonshire. Kate Cook passed as the Countess of Euston. Marguerite Steinheil survived the scandal of being rescued in 1899 from the bed of the President of France, Félix Faure, who had died of their mutual exertions. She also stood trial for murdering her mother and husband to make a better marriage. Narrowly acquitted, she lived until 1954, dying at the English seaside resort of Hove as the 6th Baroness Abinger.

As for those who promoted such success, some families succeeded in bringing their sons to heel, as when the Duke of Cleveland prevented the marriage of his heir to the prostitute 'Mabel Grey', who had begun life as Annie King, a Regent Street shop-girl in a mourning outfitter's. Other families were less successful: £60,000 and 170,000 words of reportage in *The Times* were spent on a lunacy case in December 1861 and January 1862 against William Frederick Windham. Known as 'Mad' Windham since his days at Eton, he had lately inherited Felbrigg Hall and the family estates in Norfolk. The cause of the trouble was that the young man had then bought Agnes Willoughby from her keeper, 'Bawdyhouse Bob' Roberts, in exchange for the timber on his estate. Worse still, he married her, though allowing Roberts to retain possession of her until the wedding-day.

The case for Windham's committal to an asylum was brought by his uncles: Lord Bristol, Lord Alfred Hervey and General Windham, known since the Crimean victory at Sebastopol as 'Windham of the Redan'. In their public attempt to show that the young man had not been sane at the time of the marriage, his family and the press brought to the breakfast tables of England reports of his gluttony, masturbation, lack of personal hygiene, a broad Norfolk accent despite years at Eton, and his enthusiasm for driving coaches and taking over the engines of passenger express trains without authority, as well as his propensity for patrolling the West End in police uniform as a means of 'arresting' those street-girls who took his fancy.

His uncles failed to persuade the jurors at the commission in lunacy that Windham was mad, however odd he might appear. Sir William Hardman, chairman of Surrey quarter sessions, thought that the weakness in the uncles' case was the private character of the victor of the Redan. General Windham was allegedly known for certain 'foul practices'. It would not look well if he appeared as a witness and if it was revealed in examination that this prosecutor 'was once accused of indecent exposure in Hyde Park, and was got off by his counsel on the plea of insanity'. Unable to risk cross-examination, the general stayed silent and the jurors found his nephew sane. Four years later, 'Mad' Windham died of an obstruction of a pulmonary artery at twenty-six. His bride and her infant son, of disputed paternity, remained in possession of his new estate at Hanworth, Norfolk, with a sum of £12,000 and rents of more than £5,000 a year.[5]

*

Despite the notoriety of such instances, prostitution generally had little to do with high society. Nor was it principally metropolitan. A walk through the centre of any Victorian industrial or commercial city was enough to convince most observers that neither chastity nor marriage had taken firm root among the urban poor nor, indeed, among many of the middle class. For every pavement 'courtesan' of London's West End, there were scores of shabbier women scattered throughout industrial England, in towns of flaring smoke-stacks and furnaces. Indeed, W. T. Stead's first observations on prostitution, dating from the 1870s, were based on his experiences as editor of a famous radical broadsheet, the *Northern Star*, in Darlington. 'Never do I walk the streets, but I see wretched ruins of humanity, women trampled and crushed into devils by society, and my heart has been racked with anguish for these victims of our juggernaut.'[6]

Victorian prostitution took root in manufacturing districts more than forty years before the white-slave scandals of 1885. In the 1840s, it had seemed a more attractive future to girls in their early teens than the dignity of honest toil. If they were exploited by female bawds, this appeared no worse than what they would suffer as servants at the hands of middle-class mistresses, whose meanness they must endure and whose excrement they slopped out each morning. Men who hired them for pleasure might be more humane than masters of labour who set them to work in such environments as the carding-room of a mill, where congestion of the lungs by specks of fluff and consequent early death were the rewards of honest toil.

Yet teenage prostitutes who were questioned in the areas of Liverpool and Manchester by Edwin Chadwick's workers early in the 1840s often gave the lie to the stereotype of the urban prostitute. Many of them were not victims of indifferent families or poverty. They had run away from homes where they remembered that 'great care' or the 'greatest care' had been shown them by hard-working parents. Many had been taken to church and some were sent there, though Jane Doyle admitted after her arrest that she and others played in the fields until church was over and then went home again. The youngest girls had run away to become thieves or prostitutes between the ages of twelve and fourteen, at a time when the age of consent was still twelve.

So far as there were common causes of their conduct, these were cited as the absence of fathers who were dead or serving abroad in the army; the girls being beyond the control of their mothers alone; drink enticing them into crime, and the hope of getting nice clothes. The road to prostitution often began when the death or absence of a father quickly obliged the mother to go out to work. When her father's authority was removed, Jane Doyle described how she and her brothers and sisters went their separate ways at the first opportunity, most of them taking to crime. Some girls of her kind grew to resent their mothers as figures of authority and when Mrs Reece boxed the ears of her thirteen-year-old daughter Ellen for some offence, Ellen decided to leave home. She was to become a prostitute in Manchester and Liverpool.

Parents searched for their runaways. Ellen Reece first lived in a cellar with a colony of child thieves for three days. Her mother found her, took her home and whipped her with a rod for a quarter of an hour. A month later, the girl ran off again and turned to prostitution, earning £4 from her first man. It took her mother twelve months to find her. She was then taken home and beaten severely with a rope. Her clothes were confiscated and she was locked in her room on a diet of bread and water for four days. This time she submitted to her mother by finding a job and working for six months. Then she ran off again. She was soon arrested for shoplifting and the prison chaplain arranged for her to be taken home once more. This time, her mother treated her kindly but Ellen remembered the twenty shillings a day she had made by thieving and the greater sums that had come from prostitution. She ran away for good, was caught stealing again and by the age of twenty-four had been sentenced to fourteen years' transportation for felony. Many of her contemporaries would have thought that she had enjoyed a comfortable childhood. Her parents were Welsh Congregationalists who attended chapel themselves and always took her to Sunday School. She had been educated for eight and a half years, the last three in a National School, and was one of a privileged minority who could read and write.

Jane Doyle agreed that she too had had plenty to eat and drink and a comfortable home, attending a dame school and Roman Catholic school until she was ten. She also took to a life of crime or vice in order to get drink and clothes. Apart from theft and prostitution, she worked with two men whose dupes she first accosted and who then knocked down the victims and robbed them. There were also tricks which involved a female accomplice. In the darkness of the street, the man she had solicited would hand her money. When he stood with his breeches down, the other girl would shout a loud warning, 'Watch!', as if a constabulary foot-patrol was approaching. The man's first thought was to dress himself and get away without stopping to argue over the money he had given her.

To Edwin Chadwick's missioners, Jane Doyle described how she and 'a deal of little girls' who had run away from their parents in the neighbourhood lived in the cellar of the George's Head in Garden Street, Liverpool, with a bawd who called herself 'Old Granny'. Their ages were between twelve and fourteen. Like Ellen Reece, she was found by her mother, taken home, beaten and locked in her bedroom without her clothes. Jane Doyle managed to run away again and this time worked the streets for Mrs Gaffery, under the tutelage of the eldest girl, Mary Ann Hammond, who was fifteen. Mary Ann 'showed them the town' and put Jane Doyle and Jane Shaw to work in Playhouse Square.

They were first picked up by a well-dressed man of about fifty. The two girls were both virgins, which pleased the client, presumably because he felt that there was no risk of infection from them. They refused to be separated, Jane Doyle remaining in the hired room with Jane Shaw and the man, who paid Jane Shaw ten shillings. When Jane Shaw cried out, Jane Doyle was frightened and told the customer that she had been with other men, so that he would be less likely to want her. She was given three shillings for waiting. Afterwards Jane Shaw said she would never go with another man if Jane Doyle refused to play her part. Jane Doyle was found by her mother again, beaten with a rope and kept without clothes on bread and water for a fortnight. But she ran away once more and at the age of nineteen was sentenced to ten years' transportation for theft.

The majority of the Manchester and Liverpool brothels were run by women. Mrs Matthews, owner of the house where Jane Doyle took men, catered for thirty women a night, only five or six of whom were full-time prostitutes, while the others worked casually at the profession.

Hiding money was important. A sure way for the police to prove that such girls were living by prostitution was to catch them with more coins in their pockets than they could have come by legitimately. There was also the risk of being robbed by a policeman. Yet the girls were less bothered about searches by a man, since these could not be the most intimate. Gold sovereigns might be hidden in secret pockets on the inside of garters or on the underside of corset stays towards the lower part. As many as thirty sovereigns might be hidden 'where decency forbids to name'. This usually succeeded, though Ellen Reece was caught once when the watchman and a female officer, the 'bad house woman', made her stand on a bed and jump off repeatedly until coins fell to the floor.

Manchester police matrons were less inhibited when searching female suspects. According to Ellen Reece, the young 'Deansgate beat' prostitutes would swallow the sovereigns they had earned before the search. Eleven sovereigns had been hidden in this way by one of the girls. The coins would pass through them while they were in the lock-up, and be retrieved from the floor. If the coins failed to appear within two or three days, the girl would complain of constipation and ask for 'opening medicine'. Ellen Reece had 'never heard of any one being injured' by this practice.[7]

*

Edwin Chadwick's girls represented a culture of casual and rather amateur prostitution. By the 1860s, the focus of pleasure was more sharply upon London in a decade of gaiety and greater affluence, its rebellion against the sobriety of an earlier generation by a more

Kate Hamilton's Night House in the 1850s

Bohemian culture. The symbols of that gaiety were its temples: the Cremorne Gardens, Highbury Barn, Kate Hamilton's Night House, the Argyll Rooms, the Alhambra, the Portland Rooms – 'Mott's', as they were known – and their kind. Night-life in the West End, once the preserve of those who attended gambling houses like Crockford's or Aldridge's, now seemed available to all.

The Cremorne Gardens in Chelsea had been opened by Charles Random de Berenger in 1830, for picnics, fireworks, concerts, dancing, galas and balloon ascents. The site extended along the northern shore of the Thames and survived the more famous and long-established gardens at Vauxhall, which closed in 1859. With a ballet theatre, oriental circus, menagerie, bowling gallery, pavilions, kiosks and ornamental lights, these were the true pleasure grounds of the Victorians. *Derby Night at the Cremorne* was a popular print, depicting young women in silks and furs, their patrons in silk hats and frock-coats, lounging with iced champagne at tables set in arbours of lamplit self-indulgence. Masquerades were also held at the Cremorne, the tickets including supper and wine.

As the *Saturday Review* pointed out, 'None but an idiot' could be

The Cremorne Gardens in 1857

unaware of the change that came over the gardens at dusk, when 'the female population of Cremorne is increased by a large accession of fallen characters'. Dr Acton described the gardens late at night, when respectable folk had gone home, 'leaving the massive elms, the grass-plots, the geranium beds, the kiosks, temples, "monster platforms" and "crystal lights" of Cremorne to flicker in the thousand gas-lights'. Instead of the families of innocent merrymakers who filled the grounds by day, 'on and around that platform waltzed, strolled, and fed some thousand souls – perhaps seven hundred of them men of the upper and middle class, the remainder prostitutes, more or less *prononcés*'. As the gaiety of the 1860s gave way to strengthening moral probity, the Cremorne lost its licence in 1871, after protests by the principal of the nearby St Mark's Training College, and finally closed six years later.[8]

The Cremorne would hardly do for winter. An all-weather rendez-vous was the Argyll Rooms in Great Windmill Street, established in the 1850s but flourishing a decade later. With its dance floor, gallery, alcoves and plush, it was advertised as an academy for dancing and generally regarded as a market-place for prostitutes and their clients. Despite its plush and glitter, however, it sold a good deal of beer or soda water and not much champagne. The Argyll lost its licence briefly at the end of the 1850s but soon regained it. The authorities judged it best to have the vices of these rooms gathered under one roof rather than scattered through the streets of the West End. Like the Cremorne Gardens, the fate of the Argyll was decided by the new prudery of late-century and it was closed in 1878. Among other rendezvous was the Alhambra in Leicester Square, with its ballets and promenade, which had opened as the Panoptican Exhibition Hall in 1854: behind Regent Street lay Kate Hamilton's Night House, and to the east the Holborn Assembly Rooms or Casino de Venise.

The streets of the West End too, from late afternoon until early morning, were a promenade of sexual opportunity to an extent that the capital had never known before. In vain did the shopkeepers of Regent Street tear down Nash's elegant colonnade to prevent the girls and young women sheltering from the rain. Lust appeared to flourish, whether in the crowded 'introducing houses' of hasty copulation behind the Haymarket or in the elegant villas of apple-cheeked maidens such as that in Circus Road, St John's Wood, where the poet Swinburne and his fellow enthusiasts whipped or were whipped according to taste.

'A stranger on his coming to London,' wrote John Binny in 1861, 'after visiting the Crystal Palace, British Museum, St James' Palace, and Buckingham Palace, amid other public buildings, seldom leaves the capital before he makes an evening visit to the Haymarket and Regent Street.' For every daughter of the working classes, several gentlemen from the upper and middle classes – and many from her own – were ready to patronize her.

> It is not only the architectural splendour of the aristocratic streets in that neighbourhood, but the brilliant illumination of the shops, cafés, Turkish divans, assembly halls, and concert rooms, and the troops of elegantly-dressed courtesans, rustling in silks and satins, and waving in laces, promenading along these superb streets among throngs of fashionable people, and persons apparently of every order and pursuit, from the ragged crossing-sweeper and tattered shoe-black to the high-bred gentleman of fashion and scion of nobility.[9]

By 1861, the population of greater London stood at 2,800,000. Allowing for the imbalance of the sexes and the fact that about a third of all males were too young to be likely clients, potential customers numbered around 850,000. In 1857 the Metropolitan Police reported knowledge of 8,600 prostitutes. This hardly seems an accurate total. For example, the return shows that – contrary to all experience – no prostitutes were to be found in Metropolitan Police 'A' Division, which included the parks. Bracebridge Hemyng, Henry Mayhew's colleague, wrote that the police had done little more than 'record the circulating harlotry of the Haymarket and Regent Street'. Henry Phillpotts, the Bishop of Exeter, and Hemyng put the true total at 80,000. Hemyng thought it might be higher. This figure no doubt included many casual or part-time prostitutes who were making up the wages of other employment. However, it would give a ratio of one woman living in some way by prostitution for every ten adult males in London.[10]

From the ranks of prostitutes, two interviewed by Hemyng stand out as clearly as any novelist's creations. They typify two groups. 'Swindling Sal', as she called herself, was a pugnacious representative of working-class prostitution, a member of a wider criminal network, an associate of magsmen or cheats, and of professional burglars. 'Lushing Loo' was the fallen daughter of the middle class, deserted by a military lover.

Swindling Sal, sitting with her inquirer in a bar, was vehement and vigorous.

> She changed places, she never stuck to one long; she never had no things for to be sold up, and, as she was handy with her mauleys, she got on pretty well. It took a considerable big man, she could tell me, to kick her out of a house, and then when he done it she always give him something for himself, by way of remembering her. Oh! they had a sweet recollection of her, some on 'em.

A tall stout woman of about twenty-seven with a round face and fat cheeks, she still had some of her youthful good looks but was more impressive for her powerful physique as she talked of 'rows' she had had. 'Been quodded no end of times. She knew every beak as sat on the cheer as well as she knew Joe the Magsman, who, she *might* say, wor a very perticaler friend of her'n.'

Hemyng asked her, 'What do you think you make a week?'

> Well, I'll tell yer, one week with another, I makes nearer on four pounds nor three – sometimes five. I 'ave done eight and ten. Now, Joe, as you 'eered me speak on, he does it 'ansome, he does: I mean, you know, when he's in luck. He give me a fiver once after cracking a crib, and a nice spree me an' Lushing Loo 'ad over it. Sometimes I gets three shillings, half-a-crown, five shillings, or ten occasionally, according to the sort of man.

He then asked her about Joe the Magsman. 'Who is this Joe as I talks about? Well, I likes your cheek, howsomever, he's a 'ousebreaker. I don't do anything in that way, never did, and shan't. It ain't safe, it ain't.'

As she left the bar, Swindling Sal reflected on her profession. 'I soon found my level here. It's a queer sort of life, the life I'm leading, and now I think I'll be off. Good night to yer. I hope we'll know more of one another when we two meets again.'[11]

When she had gone, Hemyng turned to the other young woman, 'Lushing Loo', with whom Swindling Sal claimed to have had 'a rumpus'. If Sal was a figure of proletarian self-reliance, Lushing Lucy appeared a study in genteel despair. Hemyng described her as 'lady-like in appearance, although haggard'. Her clothes were neat, though cheap, and showed taste in their selection. When he spoke to her, she looked up without giving him an answer, 'appearing much dejected'. Hemyng gave her a half-crown and told her to get what she liked with it. Lucy called the barmaid and ordered pale brandy, 'a drain of pale', as she called it. She drank steadily until the half-crown had been spent and then complained of her 'poor head'. Presently, she replied to his questions.

> My heart's broken. It has been broken since the twenty-first of May. I wish I was dead; I wish I was laid in my coffin. It won't be long first. I am doing it. I've just driven another nail in. 'Lushing Loo', as they call me, will be no loss to society. Cheer up; let's have a song!

As he watched her, she began to sing.

> The first I met a cornet was
>   In a regiment of dragoons.
> I gave him what *he* didn't like,
>   And stole his silver spoons.

Her story, when she finally told it, was of being the daughter of respectable parents. She had fallen in love with her cousin when she was very young and had been seduced by him. That was her 'ruin'. 'She had gone on from bad to worse after his desertion, and at last found herself among the number of low transpontine women.' Hemyng asked her why she did not try to save her life by entering a refuge. 'I don't wish to live. I shall soon get DT, and then I'll kill myself in a fit of madness.'[12]

*

Hemyng's survey swept the panorama of sexual opportunity which London offered at the beginning of the 1860s. It ran from the streets of

The Haymarket in the 1850s

brilliantly lit shops, cafés, cigar divans, dancing academies and pleasure gardens of the West End and Chelsea to the opium houses of Stepney, the tavern rooms of the White Swan in Shadwell and the dance halls of the Ratcliffe Highway. In a more limited description, John Binny listed the types of Haymarket prostitutes 'from the beautiful girl with fresh blooming cheek, newly arrived from the provinces, and the pale, elegant young lady from a milliner's shop in the aristocratic West End, to the old, bloated women who have grown grey in prostitution, or become invalid through venereal disease'.[13]

In 1857, Dr William Acton had divided the prostitutes of mid-century into three groups: the 'kept' women who had a single lover; prostitutes who sold themselves to the first comer and knew no other profession; and those for whom prostitution was 'a subsidiary calling' to some other way of making a living.[14]

Four years later, in a more detailed analysis, Hemyng divided London's prostitutes into classes of descending prosperity. First he categorized the 'seclusives', who were either mistresses kept by one man or 'prima donnas', who were able to live alone in a 'superior style'. They were the tenants of private houses or apartments. A second class consisted of 'board lodgers', who found a place in a brothel and gave the mistress of the house a portion of their earnings in exchange for board and lodging. A third group contained prostitutes who lived in 'low lodging houses'. Hemyng put both Swindling Sal and Lushing Loo into this class. There was a wide variation in the incomes of all these women, which he put at a minimum of £4 a week and a maximum of £30. Even £4, approximately what Swindling Sal claimed to make in a week, was a substantial income by comparison with the few shillings earned by most working men and women.

West End prostitutes whose beat was in the Haymarket or Regent Street were very often independent of a bully or a pimp. The superior brothels of the area employed no bullies, 'for it would not pay them to extort money from their customers, as they have a character and a reputation to support'. If a prostitute in this class had a fancy man of her own, he was usually good-looking, well-dressed and connected with the turf. He might cheat a gullible customer at tossing for bottles of champagne in the night-houses of the area but otherwise fancy men 'bet when they have money to bet with, and when they have not they endeavour, without scruple, to procure it from their mistresses, who never hesitate a moment in giving it them if they have it, or procuring it for them by some means, however degrading such means may be'.[15]

A curious sub-species of the prostitutes who worked such areas as the Strand and Drury Lane was that of the 'dress-lodgers'. They were usually still young and attractive but too poor to afford the clothes which might show them to their best advantage in the West End trade. Such girls were employed and dressed by women who ran brothels in these areas. Because of the value of the clothes, each dress-lodger had her 'watcher' in attendance, 'the badly-dressed old hag who follows at a short distance the fashionably attired young lady'. The watcher, an older woman who had very often been a prostitute herself, was paid a fixed wage and was never to lose sight of her charge.

> The dress-lodger probably lives at some distance from the immoral house by whose owner she is employed. She comes there in the afternoon badly dressed, and has good things lent her. Now if she were not watched she might decamp. She might waste her time in public-houses; she might take her dupes to other houses of ill-fame, or she might pawn the clothes she has

on; the keeper could not sue her for a debt contracted for immoral purposes.[16]

Hemyng interviewed a grey-haired woman of fifty, 'Old Stock', as she
called herself, who was a watcher or follower of a young dress-lodger
named Lizzie. The pair had come to the Strand at nine that evening and
it was now midnight. 'We have taken three men home, and Lizzie, who
is a clever little devil, got two pound five out of them for herself, which
ain't bad at all. I shall get something when we get back.' From long
experience the watcher knew who the best and most likely customers
were for her girl. 'Bilks', or cheats, were to be avoided, and 'dollymops',
or amateur prostitutes, were often their victims.

> Lizzie paints a bit too much for decent young fellows who've got lots of
> money. They aren't our little game. We go in more for tradesmen, shopboys,
> commercial travellers, and that sort, and men who are a little screwy, and
> although we mustn't mention it, we hooks a white choker [clergyman] now
> and then, coming from Exeter Hall. Medical students are sometimes sweet
> on Lizzie, but we ain't much in favour with the Bar. Oh! I know what a man
> is directly he opens his mouth. Dress too has a great deal to do with what a
> man is – tells you his position in life as it were. 'Meds' ain't good for much;
> they're larky young blokes, but they've never much money, and they're fond
> of dollymopping. But talk of dollymopping – lawyers are the fellows for that.
> Those chambers in the Inns of Court are the ruin of many a girl. And they
> are so convenient for bilking, you've no idea. There ain't a good woman in
> London who'd go with a man to the Temple, not one. . . . I've been at this
> sort of work for six or seven years, and I suppose I'll die at it. I don't care if
> I do. It suits me. I'm good for nothing else.[17]

Such groups as these were relatively easy to recognize and define.
Beyond them were classes of women who belonged to an ill-assorted
generality of poverty and crime. There were sailors' women in the slums
of Wapping or Whitechapel. Soldiers' women were to be found near the
principal barracks, in the Music Hall at Knightsbridge, or in the streets
round Wellington Barracks in Birdcage Walk. These barracks also provided the soldiers with access to the 'dollymops', the female servants and
nursemaids who took children to the parks, as well as the shop-girls and
milliners who could be picked up at 'dancing academies' in the area. As
Swindling Sal remarked, soldiers had very little money and even if they
did pay for their pleasures it was not to the tribes of what Hemyng called
'elegantly dressed courtesans, rustling in silk and satins, and waving in

laces', who occupied the pavements from Langham Place to Pall Mall. When the admiring dollymops went home, the soldiers resorted to the so-called 'park women' who came out at dusk. They had, as a rule, grown old in their profession and had nowhere else to carry it on. They would, wrote Hemyng, 'consent to any species of humiliation for the sake of acquiring a few shillings'.[18]

By 1864, the War Office and the Board of Admiralty were sufficiently alarmed by the spread of syphilis in the army and navy to advocate measures which were embodied in the Contagious Diseases Acts of 1864–9. This legislation authorized the detention and medical examination of suspected prostitutes in the neighbourhoods of barracks or dockyards. The statutes provoked opposition on behalf of women from Florence Nightingale, Josephine Butler and other campaigners. The operation of the acts was suspended in 1883 and they were repealed three years later. Hemyng's account acknowledged the danger of syphilis as 'very prevalent among soldiers', but thought 'the disease is not so virulent as it was formerly. That is, we do not see examples of the loss of the palate or part of the cranium, as specimens extant in our museums show us was formerly the case.'[19]

Yet there was evidence outside the museums which seemed less reassuring. Hemyng remarked that a woman had been pointed out to him, as she plied for hire in the Knightsbridge Music Hall, 'who my informant told me he was positively assured had only yesterday had two buboes lanced. . . . She was so well known that she obtained the soubriquet of "The Hospital", as she was so frequently an inmate of one, and as she had so often sent others to a similar involuntary confinement.'[20]

The commerce of soldiers and prostitutes was a feature of life in the West End, in its parks if not in its streets. Sailors and their women, a class often close to destitution, belonged to the East End districts of the docks. Hemyng accompanied Inspector Price and other officers through the worst areas of Stepney, Shadwell and Spitalfields. The public houses of the Ratcliffe Highway and its neighbourhood, including the Prussian Eagle, the Horse and Leaping Bar, and notably Shadwell's White Swan, known familiarly as 'Paddy's Goose', were fronts for prostitution and brothel-keeping. Hemyng also joined a raid led by Sergeant Prior of 'H' Division on a better class of brothel, in an area of the docks which was the first of several to be nicknamed 'Tiger

The Gin Palace, 1852

Bay'. Prior was looking for a woman named Harrington who was wanted for felony.

> The rooms occupied by the women and their sailors were more roomy than I expected to find them. The beds were what are called 'four-posters', and in some instances were surrounded with faded, dirty-looking, chintz curtains. There was the usual amount of cheap crockery on the mantelpieces, which were surmounted with a small looking-glass in a rosewood or gilt frame. When the magic word 'Police' was uttered, the door flew open, as the door of the robbers' cave swung back on its hinges when Ali Baba exclaimed 'Sesame'. A few seconds were allowed for the person who opened the door to retire to the couch, and then our visual circuit of the chamber took place. The sailors did not evince any signs of hostility at our somewhat unwarrantable intrusion, and we in every case made our exit peacefully.[21]

Elsewhere, in a tumbledown hovel, a table and a palliasse on the floor were the sole furnishings. There was 'a sickly smell' of opium that had just been smoked. A Lascar seaman, 'apparently stupefied', lay on the palliasse. His woman was beside him, 'half idiotically endeavouring to derive some stupefaction from the ashes he had left in his pipe'. In another room, unfurnished, an Irishwoman lay wrapped in a shawl on the bare floor. 'Her face was shrivelled and famine-stricken, her eyes bloodshot and glaring, her face disfigured slightly with disease, and her hair dishevelled, tangled, and matted.' She looked more like a beast in its lair, Hemyng reported, than a woman in her home. 'She cleaned out the water-closets in the daytime, and for these services she was given a lodging gratis.' Whatever hopeful gaiety attended prostitution at Chelsea's Cremorne Gardens or in the Argyll Rooms and the Alhambra, Shadwell and Whitechapel seemed to share very little of it.[22]

Apart from women who made their livings as prostitutes, there were also thieves' women who posed as prostitutes in order to rob or black-mail their dupes. There was little enough subtlety in their trade. In such areas as Golden Lane, near the Barbican, the woman would approach a man and solicit him. As he stood listening to her, the 'bully' would emerge from the shadows, knock the man down with a blow under the ear, then strip him of cash, watch and jewellery. A variation on this was for the woman to accost her 'mug', as he was now called, and then for the bully to approach with the demand, 'What are you talking to my wife for?' The respectable dupe would usually hand over his money and valuables without the necessity for violence, to avoid being implicated in scandal.[23]

Even in a brothel or the prostitute's room, the bully's role might be to appear as an outraged husband or simply as a robber, once the man picked up by the woman was thoroughly compromised. It was the oldest trick in the trade, difficult for the police to deal with when the victim dreaded publicity, and certainly not unique to London. James McLevy, an Edinburgh detective whose territory included the city's brothel district of 'The Happy Land', was at length successful in arresting Mary Wood, whose tenement accommodation included a room with a closet opening off it. She catered for voyeurs, as well as her more usual clients, by having 'one or two augur-bored holes' in the closet door, 'intended for gratifying any one taking up his station there by a look of what was going on in the room'.

On the night of her arrest, however, the closet was occupied by a pair of bullies.

Mary was to go out in her most seductive dress, and endeavour to entice in any gentleman likely to have a gold watch and money on him, and when she succeeded in this, the two bullies, as they have been called, who, on a signal of her approach, had previously betaken themselves to the closet, were, when they considered all matters ripe, to rush out, seize the victim, and rob him.

The victim on this occasion was a Londoner on a brief visit to Edinburgh. Perhaps because he was unknown in the city, he was one of the very few 'mugs' who did not submit to blackmail and go quietly home after a beating without his watch and purse. Though having suffered considerable bodily harm, he went to the police. Mary Wood and the two men were arrested by McLevy that night. Subsequently, all three were sentenced to seven years' transportation.[24]

If poverty obscured the division between crime and moral apathy, the frontiers of contemporary prostitution were equally hard to define among the more fortunate women, whom Hemyng describes as 'Clandestine prostitutes': 'Literally every woman who yields to her passions and loses her virtue is a prostitute, but many draw a distinction between those who live by promiscuous intercourse, and those who confine themselves to one man.'

On this basis, Hemyng added to his categories those who were amateur or part-time prostitutes plying for hire and who might otherwise work as seamstresses or in a comparable trade. Women who worked as domestic servants were as a rule lovers of one man, even though he might be a soldier in the park. There were 'ladies of intrigue' whose aim was to 'see men to gratify their passions' and women who kept 'houses of assignation' where such intrigues could be carried on. Once again, these assignations were usually affairs between lovers that could only be carried on by such means. Ladies of intrigue were seldom for hire, though John Binny suggested that they might not always bother to use a house of assignation.

Sometimes a fashionable young widow, or beautiful young married woman, will find her way in those dark evenings to meet with some rickety silver-headed old captain loitering about Pall Mall. Such things are not wondered at by those acquainted with high life in London.[25]

*

In the court reports of the morning and evening papers, the public was reminded of trades that went beyond the prostitution that Hemyng or

Mayhew described. From time to time, for example, a trial or a scandal revealed the existence of homosexual prostitution and the brothels which supported it. Organized prostitution of this kind had already been a feature of pre-Victorian London. In 1813, in *The Phoenix of Sodom: or, The Vere Street Coterie*, Robert Holloway publicized the activities of a homosexual brothel at the White Swan in Vere Street, running north from Oxford Street. A number of sentences, including death sentences, had been passed upon those frequenting the establishment. Unfortunately, Holloway also included false allegations against Jimmy Stewart, alias Moggy Stewart, and was gaoled for eighteen months on conviction of publishing a criminal libel.

Four years later, George Pritchard, Secretary to the Society for the Suppression of Vice, informed the Police Committee of the House of Commons that articles 'representing a crime which ought not to be named among Christians, which they termed *"the new fashion"*', were being made by convicts at Stapleton near Bristol. It was customary in indictments before a grand jury for the charge of 'a crime which ought not to be named among Christians' to be named none the less as sodomy.[26]

Individual prosecutions of this type occurred from time to time in the early nineteenth century. In 1833 two Members of Parliament faced separate trials. Charles Baring Wall was found not guilty on 12 May of indecency with a policeman, while W. J. Bankes was acquitted on 2 December of attempting to commit an unnatural crime in the grounds of Westminster Abbey. There was a certain amount of well-bred amusement in consequence of the latter verdict. 'Nobody can read the trial without being satisfied of his guilt,' wrote Charles Greville, Clerk to the Privy Council, in his diary. '"The Foreman said he left the court without a stain" – "on his shirt" said Alvanley, when he was told the verdict.'[27]

In 1871, newspaper readers were diverted by the trial of two young men of good family, Ernest Boulton and William Park, clerks respectively to a stockbroker and a solicitor. They had attracted the suspicion of the police by dressing as women and parading among the female prostitutes of the Burlington Arcade, the Alhambra in Leicester Square, and the Surrey Theatre, south of the river. The two men were arrested and charged with conspiring and inciting persons to commit an unnatural offence. Lord Chief Justice Cockburn, presiding over the trial, ruled that there was no case against two other defendants, and charges against three more men were not pursued. A further defendant, Lord Arthur Clinton, son of the Duke of Newcastle, had committed suicide before the case began.

There seemed little doubt that Boulton and Park had solicited men while dressed as women. In court, however, there was evidence only that they had worn women's clothes, which might have been done for 'a frolic', as Cockburn described it, and that they had written effeminate letters to other men. The police surgeon, who had examined them without authority, testified that he had found evidence of unnatural practices. Two other medical witnesses, including the surgeon of Newgate Gaol, contradicted him. The prosecution was further compromised by the discovery that the papers belonging to the two men had been seized illegally by the police without a warrant.

Less than an hour after retiring, the jury acquitted both defendants. The jurors may well have been influenced by the improper conduct of the police and the apparent incompetence of the police surgeon. Yet the 1870s were also a last decade of comparative innocence before the advent of psychopathology in the 1880s. However implausible it might seem to their successors, it was still possible for these jurors to believe that men who paraded the pavements of Leicester Square in women's clothes were doing nothing more sinister than 'larking about' in the style of pantomime dames.

The existence of homosexual brothels in the last years of the century was evident from the legal proceedings which they attracted. In 1889, the so-called Cleveland Street Scandal was precipitated when telegraph boys in central London were found to be in possession of an inexplicably large number of sovereigns with which they were playing pitch-and-toss. The owner of 18 Cleveland Street, Charles Hammond, fled to the Continent. So did Lord Arthur Somerset, a royal equerry and keeper of the Prince of Wales's stables. Two men were arrested at the house and were sentenced to several months' imprisonment. Ernest Parke, editor of the *North London Press*, was sentenced to a year's imprisonment for alleging that Lord Euston was involved in the scandal and then being unable to substantiate this statement in court.

Six years later, the first trial of Oscar Wilde revealed the existence of Alfred Taylor's homosexual brothel at 13 Little College Street, Westminster, 'these rooms, with their heavily draped windows, their candles burning on through the day, and their languorous atmosphere heavy with perfume', as Charles Gill described them in opening the case for the Crown.[28]

There was still sufficient public innocence of sado-masochism as an erotic indulgence for the brothels which specialized in it to escape undue attention. The erotic flagellation of a man going to 'solace with his whore' had appeared in English poetry at least as far back as Sir John Davies' *Epigrammes* of 1599. The principal brothels in London where men were whipped by women, or women by men, for sexual gratification were listed by Henry Spencer Ashbee in 1877 as being run by Mrs Emma Lee, *née* Richardson, of 50 Margaret Place, Regent Street; Mrs Phillips of 11 Upper Belgrave Place; Mrs Shepherd of 25 Gilbert Street and Mrs Sarah Potter of various addresses in Chelsea and Soho.[29]

The addresses of these establishments suggested a market superior to that of common prostitution. Ashbee remarks, 'were it not indiscreet, I might add the names of one or two other ladies who still carry on their calling'. Discretion also veiled the activities of such suburban villas as 7 Circus Road, St John's Wood, patronized by Algernon Charles Swinburne. The poet was introduced to it by one of its backers, John Thomson, found by Swinburne reciting *Paradise Lost* in the kitchen of a lodging-house. At Circus Road, as Edmund Gosse described it in an unpublished essay on Swinburne, 'two golden-haired and rouge-cheeked ladies received, in luxuriously furnished rooms, gentlemen whom they consented to chastise for large sums of money'. An elderly woman was in attendance to take the cash. Gosse concluded that 'Swinburne much impoverished himself in these games, which also must have been very bad for his health.'[30]

In other houses, women were whipped by male clients or in front of a paying audience. Among courtroom scandals attending this variant was the prosecution of Sarah Potter in 1863 on charges of assault, a case brought at the instigation of the Society for the Protection of Females and Young Women. *Lloyd's Weekly London Gazette* for 12 July 1863 reported the previous day's proceedings at length. The charges were dealt with summarily by the Westminster magistrates at the request of the prosecution, so that the details should not be more fully available to the press if the defendant were committed to the Central Criminal Court.

The complainant, Agnes Thompson, described herself as 'about fifteen', and therefore three years above the current age of consent. A year previously she had accompanied a man to a house where he had 'effected her ruin'. Since then she had been employed by Mrs Potter at 3 Albion Terrace, King's Road, Chelsea, and had solicited in the nearby Cremorne Gardens. Her complaint was that 'I was flogged by gentle-men with birch-rods. I was beaten on my naked flesh.' The defence pointed out that the girl had not left the house after the first occurrence, though she had been free to do so. The case had come about as a result of such further incidents as Agnes Thompson described, when 'I was on another occasion flogged by a man named "Sealskin", and by another known as "The Count".' All this had taken place in the drawing-room of 3 Albion Terrace, where she claimed that she had been fastened to a step ladder, an exhibit that was produced in court.

Similar ordeals were recounted in evidence to the court by Catherine Kennedy, who was seventeen, and Alice Smith, described by the press report as 'a young woman of considerable personal attractions'. Alice Smith underwent her ordeal without payment in what was called 'The Schoolroom'. Mrs Potter was convicted and sent to prison. An oddity of the case, according to Ashbee, was Agnes Thompson's subsequent behaviour. 'Certain it is that she returned to Mrs Potter after her release from prison, and lived with her a considerable time in Howland Street.' Sarah Potter died in 1873 and is commemorated by an imposing tomb-stone in Kensal Green Cemetery.[31]

The diarist of *My Secret Life*, writing of the 1870s, recorded a curious meeting in a brothel with a girl who described how she had been 'flogged by a woman for a lady's delectation. . . . No man was present, it was a lady's letch, and the lady was masked. This story I did not then believe, but do so now.' If true, it is a rare glimpse of the Victorian lady as brothel patron.[32]

*

Blackmail courted the prostitute's clients. Blackmail of the commonest sort occurred when a man who had been enticed into the shadows and robbed by a bully, or 'discovered' and robbed by a 'husband' in the woman's bedroom, found that he must choose between ruining his rep-utation in a public court or submitting to his loss and injuries – 'Traps for Jacks', as Dickens called it when a sailor was the victim.

None the less, blackmail or extortion defied class and type. When Earl Russell, grandson of a prime minister and elder brother of Bertrand

Russell, married Mabel Edith, daughter of Selina, Lady Scott, in 1890, he was embraced by two women whom he later described as having 'the morals of a pair of Choctaw Indians'. Lady Scott, who was already separated from Sir Claude Scott, first hoped to take the young man for herself. 'I have had plenty of good offers but must get riches,' she wrote to the elderly Countess of Cardigan.

By 1896, the Russell marriage had been trailed through the courts and the press on three occasions. Attempts to extort money from Russell by allegations of homosexuality and bestiality led to Lady Scott's imprisonment for criminal libel in 1896. Unsurprisingly, the plot against the young nobleman was matured at premises in Cranbourn Street, Leicester Square, where Lady Scott's sister still worked as a 'masseuse' and whose proprietor, Arthur Carrez, sold rubber goods and pornography on the ground floor. Russell's determination to escape Mabel Edith at any cost led to his being the last defendant convicted by his peers in the House of Lords, on a charge of bigamy in 1901.[33]

Blackmail had subtleties that might defy the law. Charles Augustus Howell, who was to be Conan Doyle's model for the blackmailer Charles Augustus Milverton, used subtlety to great effect in respect of Swinburne's sexual deviations and Dante Gabriel Rossetti's sensitivity over the exhumation of his wife. Howell had been the 'friend' who retrieved Rossetti's poems from the coffin. One of his techniques was to correspond affably with an intended victim, pretending to share sexual obsessions or anxieties. He was said to have accompanied Swinburne to Circus Road and similar destinations. Having acquired a series of indiscreet replies to his letters, he would paste them into an album.

His correspondent would next hear that Howell had fallen on hard times and had had to pawn the album for an amazingly large sum, obtainable only because of the fame of the author of the morally compromising letters. Howell himself had no money to redeem his pledge. If the victim did not do so quickly, the pawnbroker would presumably sell the album of letters at the best price. There was nothing plainly illegal in this. Yet the victim or his family could be relied upon to pay whatever was asked to prevent the letters being hawked round the London auction rooms. Howell would then share the proceeds with his confederate pawnbroker. He was cordially loathed by former friends and, as a defensive move, was apt to issue announcements of his own death and funeral when matters became difficult. He died in reality in

1890 of 'pneumonia'. Oscar Wilde and Swinburne's bibliographer, T. J. Wise, reported that, in truth, he was found dead in the gutter outside a Chelsea public house with his throat cut and a half-sovereign wedged between his teeth, the reward of a slanderer.[34]

Of Victorian blackmailers who emerged from the shadows of sexual vice, none seemed more detestable than 'Madame Rachel', alias Rachel Leverson of the Temple of Beauty in Bond Street. William Ballantine, who prosecuted Rachel Leverson successfully in 1868, described her business as 'extortion and robbery' and the woman herself as 'one of the most filthy and dangerous moral pests'.

Rachel Leverson was beyond the age for prostitution by the time that 'Beautiful For Ever' was painted on the sign above the door which invited gullible female customers into her premises in New Bond Street. From her shop she dispensed such cosmetics as Magnetic Rock Dew for removing wrinkles, Favourite of the Harem's Pearl White Powder for the skin, Indian Coal for the eyes, Mount Hymettus Soap and the Bridal Toilet Cabinet priced at between 25 and 250 guineas. This cabinet contained such treasures as 'Desert Water or Liquid Dew, purchased at an enormous outlay from the Government of Morocco'. The truly enormous outlay was by those who were caught in Rachel Leverson's web.

She knew the value of 'Houses of Assignation', as Mayhew and Hemyng called them. They opened a way to genteel prostitution and, hence, to blackmail. Adjoining her Bond Street shop were Madame Rachel's Arabian Baths, which offered beauty treatments and the facilities for discreet liaisons. Unfortunately, those who trusted to such discretion soon discovered that they had no secrets from Rachel Leverson, whose sympathy had a price. By 1867, she occupied a fine house in Maddox Street, between Bond Street and Regent Street, and a box at the opera for which she paid £400 each season.

Even those who visited her premises for innocent purposes were easily compromised. The wife of a stockbroker emerged from her Arabian Bath to find her diamond rings and earrings missing from the adjoining dressing-room. Madame Rachel informed her that if she tried to 'give herself airs' over the loss, her husband would be informed that she had been using the baths to meet a lover. The poor innocent informed her husband of the trick at once and a lawyer was consulted. Yet the couple decided against the ruin of their reputations and happiness which a court case would bring. The Victorian middle class consisted largely of those whom Serjeant Ballantine described as men and women 'who would sooner submit to felony and fraud than that their names should be exposed to the public'.

Madame Rachel's downfall was occasioned by Mary Tucker Borradaile, the foolish widow of an Indian Army major. She was first persuaded to part with £1,700, a third of her total capital, for preparations to repair the ravages of time and the tropics. From the shop, she progressed to the Arabian Baths where she saw in a passing a middle-aged bachelor, Lord Henry Ranelagh. After a while, Rachel Leverson made a winsome apology for her negligence, which had allowed Lord Ranelagh to peep at the widow in her Arabian Bath. The happy result, however, was that Ranelagh had been overcome by her beauty and was determined to marry her. Because Mrs Borradaile was of a lower social order, there would be opposition from his family. He would communicate with her by letter for the time being, through the good offices of 'Granny', as Rachel Leverson was now called.

Not only did Mrs Borradaile fall for this trick, she also responded to appeals for cash in 'Lord Ranelagh's' letters. He was to inherit a considerable sum but for the moment found himself short of ready money. Mrs Borradaile was worth about £5,000 in capital. It took Rachel Leverson and an unscrupulous attorney a mere three months to strip her of it. Then she was allowed to discover that Lord Ranelagh's letters had been written by Madame Rachel's minions. They had even got his Christian name wrong.

Mrs Borradaile might prosecute Rachel Leverson for obtaining money by false and fraudulent pretences. None of her other gulls had dared to do so, and Mrs Borradaile was reminded of the public humiliation and laughter which must greet her folly when she entered the witness box. To the dismay of her persecutor, however, she did what her predecessors had shrunk from. She sued Rachel Leverson in the Court of Queen's Bench, a trial overtaken by a prosecution for fraud in the Central Criminal Court in September 1868.

Mary Borradaile appeared in court, according to Ballantine, as 'a skeleton encased apparently in plaster of Paris, painted pink and white, and surmounted with a juvenile wig'. She 'tottered' into the witness box and so to her public martyrdom. Yet her ordeal procured the conviction of Rachel Leverson and an exposure of the frauds which the Temple of

Beauty represented. Madame Rachel was sent to penal servitude for five years. She served her time, went back to her old ways, was prosecuted again and received a long sentence of imprisonment, during which she died.[35]

*

As prostitutes and their hangers-on preyed upon the world through blackmail or extortion, so they themselves were preyed upon in turn. Perhaps such extortion or the discovery that he had caught venereal disease from one of the women provoked a murderous anger in the client against prostitutes as a class. Anger might turn to murder more often than was supposed. 'I am down on whores and I shan't quit ripping them till I do get buckled.' The first letter to be signed 'Jack the Ripper' was dated 25 September 1888 and summed up the philosophy of murderous vengeance. The police thought it was probably not the work of the killer but of a journalist with a grim sense of fun.

At first sight, the killing of prostitutes by a man or woman who was 'down' on them seemed a new phenomenon. Dr Cream in 1892 was a public example of it and, though a poisoner, he claimed on the gallows to be Jack the Ripper. A more reliable contemporary guide to the Whitechapel mystery was Sir Melville Macnaghten, Assistant Chief Constable at Scotland Yard. He named his first suspect as Montague Druitt, barrister of the Inner Temple, educated at Winchester and New College, Oxford, whose chambers were in King's Bench Walk. Macnaghten believed that five murders were committed by one man, ending when Druitt drowned himself in the Thames in December 1888. Though a barrister, he may have studied medicine for a year, after a Second in Classical Moderations and a Third in Greats in 1880. Macnaghten wrote, 'From private information I have little doubt but that his own family suspected this man of being the murderer: it was alleged that he was sexually insane.'[36] The case was complicated by letters purporting to be from the killer. Some, at least, were not. A memorable note was received on 16 October 1888. It accompanied part of a kidney alleged to be from a recent victim with the assurance, 'tother piece I fried and ate it was very nise'.

The poisoner Thomas Neill Cream was born in Glasgow in 1850. When he was four, his family emigrated to Canada. By 1881, he was practising medicine in Chicago where a number of his female patients

Dr Neill Cream,
The Lambeth Poisoner, 1892

died in curious circumstances, apparently as the result of chloroform or after taking medicines Cream had prescribed for them. He was assumed to be an abortionist. In 1881 he went to prison for life, convicted of the murder by poison of Daniel Stott, the husband of his mistress. It seemed that he had killed at least three young women before this. He was released in July 1891 and left for England. On 13 October that year, the murder of Lambeth prostitutes began.

His crimes were committed in or near the Waterloo Road. He would offer his victims capsules, which he promised as an aphrodisiac but which he had filled with strychnine. Within a short while the street-girls were in agony and, despite medical assistance, died in a few hours. Cream was known to have murdered four young women in this way in 1891–2 and attempted the murder of one other. The horror of the deaths was matched, as in the Whitechapel case, by the zany humour of his letters to the police. He wrote as a private detective, 'A. O'Brien', offering to solve the crimes if the police could not, 'No fee if not successful'. He wrote to Scotland Yard, accusing the young Earl Russell and

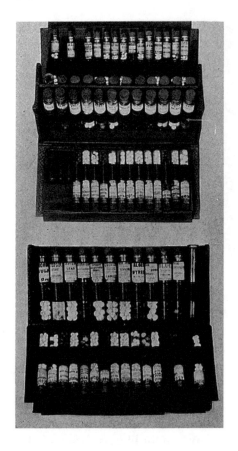

Dr Cream's sample case, top and side view. A white arrow, upper right, indicates an empty bottle which had contained strychnine pills

Frederick Smith, proprietor of W. H. Smith, of the first murder. He then wrote to Smith offering to defend him. He claimed to have murdered a girl, Matilda Clover, whom the police did not even know to be dead. On exhumation she proved to have died of strychnine, wrongly diagnosed as alcoholism. Cream emptied the Metropole Hotel in April 1892 by sending every guest a printed circular, announcing that the Lambeth poisoner was working in the hotel.

Cream was caught after eight months, only because he claimed in one letter to have killed Lou Harvey, who was still alive. She had secretly thrown her capsule away and, as the only survivor of his attentions, could identify him. Despite his claim to be Jack the Ripper, Cream was in prison in America during the Whitechapel killings, though a curious provision in the United States allowed a man to pay another to serve his

Ellen Donworth's Death

To the Guests,

of the Metropole Hotel.

Ladies and Gentlemen,

I hereby notify you that the person who poisoned Ellen Donworth on the 13th last October is to day in the employ of the Metropole Hotel and that your lives are in danger as long as you remain in this Hotel.

Yours respectfully,
W. H. MURRAY.

London April 1892

A serial killer's sense of fun: Dr Cream's bid to empty the Metropole Hotel. Ellen Donworth had been his first Lambeth victim sentence or part of it. Nevertheless, it seems unlikely to have included imprisonment for murder.

Both Cream and Druitt, if the latter committed the Whitechapel murders, belonged to a class of maniac who appeared unique to the last decades of the nineteenth century. Common sense connected their crimes with modern urbanization and the relative anonymity of the individual in metropolitan life. Historically, few communities had been big enough to shelter such a killer or perhaps to provide sufficient opportunity.

Richard von Krafft-Ebing's editions of *Psychopathia Sexualis* between 1886 and 1902 recorded multiple 'lust murders', including those in Whitechapel. Vacher the Ripper, as Krafft-Ebing called him, committed his crimes in France in 1894–6. Vincenz Verzeni, who confessed to 'an unspeakable delight in strangling women', went to life imprisonment in Italy in the 1870s. Cesare Lombroso, founder of the science of criminology, cited the case of a Spaniard, Gruyo, who strangled and mutilated six prostitutes in ten years. In 1895, Henry Holmes of Chicago was convicted after twenty-six murders over a period of nine years. Like the Whitechapel murders, a number of cases across Europe and America involved acts of cannibalism.[37]

In retrospect, some of England's earlier unsolved murders might have been the work of multiple killers. After Kate Webster's trial, in 1879, the press recalled certain outstanding cases. The Waterloo Bridge mystery of 1857 related to dismembered remains floating in a carpet bag. More recent victims, including Mrs Samuel of Burton Crescent, Eliza Grimwood, Harriet Buswell, Emma Jackson and Mrs Squire, exercised newspapers and readers. An earlier Dr Cream might not even have been suspected. Sir Henry Hawkins, who presided over the trial of Dr George Lamson in 1882, wrote that even then 'no chemical test could be applied to aconitine, any more than it could to strychnine in the time of Palmer'. The arrival of chemical tests did not prevent Matilda Clover's death in 1891 being attributed to alcoholism. Only Dr Cream's boast of murder alerted the police to the crime.[38]

How many dismembered victims of the 1840s rookeries were lost in the detritus of crumbling sewers and river bed or among the hastily buried victims of annual cholera epidemics in the summers of mid-century? Mayhew was probably right in believing that the murder of most street-girls in early Victorian rookeries would go unreported. The last face that the denizens of the Devil's Acre or the Seven Dials wanted to see was that of an investigating police officer. Were the deaths of drunken prostitutes attributed to gin or brandy, when the truth was poison? The serial poisoner was certainly not unknown by 1862, when Catherine Wilson was discovered to have poisoned at least two lovers and two other women and to have attempted the murder of a fifth victim. Dr Alfred Taylor, a leading toxicologist, 'fairly electrified the court', as the *Chronicles of Newgate* described it, when he announced at the trial that 'many deaths, supposed to be from cholera, were really due to poisoning'. The trial judge added that what he called 'secret poisoning' was 'rife' in London.[39]

Both Jack the Ripper and Neill Cream advertised their crimes. Had they merely killed for gratification, however, was it not possible that Cream who was hanged in 1892 might have escaped suspicion in 1862? By the time such questions were asked, the old rookeries, sewers and common graves of London had gone and had taken their secrets with them.

*

An alarm at moral decay made the 1880s and their successors more prudent or prudish, more determined to establish a culture which would put respect for women and children first. Within a dozen years, the English publisher of Maupassant and Zola had gone to prison for daring to disseminate the obscenity of such authors. Henry James had been reprimanded for suggesting that Zola was a social moralist. George Moore had denounced a new philistinism, whose principal concern was, 'Can my daughter of eighteen read this book?' Yet the appeal of moral reform was undeniable. The Slander of Women Act 1891 made words which imputed 'unchastity or adultery to any woman or girl' actionable without proof of damage. A National Vigilance Association was founded in 1886 and the broad-shouldered theologians of the Church of England Purity Society advertised their services in the weekly press. W. T. Stead of the *Pall Mall Gazette* urged his fellow-citizens to flog any man seen offering unwelcome sexual advances to a woman, 'young fellows chivalrous enough to take the chance – which, after all, would be very remote – of going to gaol for horsewhipping a scoundrel who habitually made improper proposals to virtuous girls'.[40]

Europeans might see a curiously English character in the way that the pleasurable indulgences of the 'sixties gave way to an almost sensual enthusiasm for repentance and moral renewal by the 'eighties. Yet the new mood was not exclusively English. When Krafft-Ebing surveyed Europe in the juridical section of his *Psychopathia Sexualis*, he did so without complacency. Statistics convinced him that sexual crimes, particularly against children, had increased to an extent that required medical men to invoke the law. Though the promenades of prostitution suggested that men played a major part in the fate of juveniles, Krafft-Ebing cited European and American evidence that many crimes of what was newly termed paedophilia were committed by women. 'A large percentage of cases is represented by lewd servant girls, governesses and nursemaids, not to speak of female relatives, who abuse little boys entrusted to their care, for sexual purposes and often even infect them with the gonorrheal poison.' The suggestion was not new. The diarist of *My Secret Life* recalled eavesdropping as a child while his mother was advising her cousin on the employment of nursemaids. '"When Walter was a little fellow she had dismissed a filthy creature whom she had detected in abominable practices with one of her children"; what they were my mother never disclosed.'[41]

Among European warnings of growing criminality, the German alienist Johann Ludwig Casper concluded from his experience of treating patients that sexual crime in Berlin had more than doubled between 1842 and 1861. Such offences amounted to only 20 per cent of crimes heard by French courts in 1826–40. By 1856–60 they had risen to 53 per cent. In 1826 there were 126 cases of child rape in France. By 1867 there were 805. A rival survey found 682 'immoral attacks' on children reported in France in 1872, increasing to 875 in 1876. In England there had been 167 sexual assaults on children in 1830–4 and 1,395 in 1855–7. Krafft-Ebing concluded,

> The moralist sees in these sad facts nothing but the decay of general morality, and in some instances comes to the conclusion that the present mildness of the laws punishing sexual crimes, in comparison with their severity in past centuries, is in part responsible for this. The medical investigator is driven to the conclusion that this manifestation of modern social life stands in relation to the predominating nervous condition of later generations, in that it begets defective individuals, excites the sexual instinct, leads to sexual abuse, and, with continuance of lasciviousness associated with diminished sexual power, induces perverse sexual acts.

However patchwork Krafft-Ebing's statistics might be and however open to the reservation that they might reflect greater accuracy in reporting rather than greater criminality, his condemnation of modern life was one that might have appealed strongly to English readers who surveyed the state of their own society in late-century.[42]

Even twenty years earlier, English prostitution had shocked Dostoevsky. In an account of the Haymarket written for *Vreyma* in April 1863, he recounted:

> Little girls of about twelve seize you by the hand and ask you to go with them. Once I remember seeing among the crowd of people in the street a little girl who could not have been more than six years old. Her clothes were in tatters. She was dirty, barefoot and beaten black and blue. Her body, which could be seen through the holes in her clothes, was all bruised. She was walking about aimlessly, hardly knowing where she was . . . she looked so wretched and unhappy. . . . I went back and gave her sixpence. She seized the small silver coin, gave me a look of startled surprise, and suddenly began running in the opposite direction as fast as her little legs would carry her, as though terrified that I should take the money away from her.

The sight of such children was so distressing that it was hard to find comfort in any kind of explanation. So far as hope existed, it amounted to a probability that the child seen by Dostoevsky was not in the Haymarket for the purposes of her own prostitution. Ragged children, perhaps beggars or dependants of prostitutes, were there in abundance. If they had any further purpose, their usual role was to act as a cover by accompanying their mothers or older women who were soliciting. Children were used by prostitutes, as they were by thieves, to suggest the respectability of a mother and daughter, diverting suspicion or the glance of a policeman.

The need to control prostitution on such a scale as the Haymarket presented soon acquired a more precise focus. Both W. T. Stead and the diarist of *My Secret Life* were agreed that it very rarely involved girls who were under the age of consent. 'Walter' encountered only one such girl among the 1,200 women and girls in his diary. There were, as Stead wrote in *The Maiden Tribute of Modern Babylon* (1885), 'children, many children, who are ruined before they are thirteen; but the crime is one phase of the incest which, as the Report of the Dwellings Commission shows, is inseparable from overcrowding'. Even at the worst times and in the worst places, he found the number of girls under age on the streets in any capacity to be 'very small'.[43]

Governments, however, were apt to let prostitution appear as the cause of such ruin among the very young rather than acknowledge a wider social evil of slum housing. Moral homilies on sexual vice were less costly than a general attempt to improve conditions in which two families commonly lived, procreated and died in a single room. This, rather than the Haymarket, was the scene of childhood ruin at the hands of other children. As Stead pointed out, when five-year-old Anne Bryant was 'outraged', it was not by a Regent Street swell in a silk hat but by young William Hemmings and a fellow-lodger who enticed the child with a penny cake.[44]

Yet the obstacle to protecting girls in their early teens was apparently the reluctance or inertia which had kept the age of consent at twelve until 1875 and at thirteen after that. There had been opposition in 1875 to raising the age to thirteen because, as Lord Chief Justice Coleridge pointed out, there might be an anomalous situation in which a girl had married at twelve but could not give her consent to sexual intercourse. The law was changed none the less. Prior to that, those girls of twelve who took Dostoevsky by the hand in 1863 broke no law that the police would enforce. They might have had protection, had they or their families chosen it. Under Section 55 of the Offences Against the Person Act 1861, it had become a criminal offence to take an unmarried girl under sixteen years of age out of her father's possession without his consent. The case of *R* v. *Prince* (1875) made this an offence of strict liability, so that it was no defence for a man to say that the girl looked or acted as though she might have been older than sixteen. Unfortunately, such a provision had little effect on those Haymarket girls whose mothers and, indeed, often their fathers were the instigators of their daughters' prostitution. Howard Vincent described the difficulty to the House of Lords Select Committee in 1881.

> Now it constantly happens, and I believe in the generality of cases it is so, that these children live at home; this prostitution actually takes place with the knowledge and connivance of the mother and to the profit of the household. . . . These procuresses, or whatever you may call them, have an understanding with the mother of the girl that she shall come to that house at a certain hour, and the mother perfectly well knows for what purpose she goes there, and it is with her knowledge and connivance, and with her consent that the girl goes.[45]

The juveniles to whom Vincent referred were a minority between fourteen and sixteen years old. The truth of this was qualified by the admission that the ages given by the girls who came into the hands of the police were often falsified. A girl of fourteen or fifteen might claim to be sixteen so that she would go to prison for a determinate time rather than through the indefinite rigours of a reformatory. She might also increase her age to escape being sent to an industrial school under the Industrial Schools Act 1857.

To most observers, it seemed that the Haymarket by 1881 had changed only for the worse since Dostoevsky saw it almost twenty years before. A recent calculation had found five hundred prostitutes at 12.30 a.m. in the few hundred yards 'between Piccadilly Circus and the bottom of Waterloo Place'. The centre of the nation's capital was such, in Vincent's words,

> that from four o'clock, or one may say from three o'clock in the afternoon, it is impossible for any respectable woman to walk from the top of the Haymarket to Wellington Street, Strand. From three or four o'clock in the afternoon, Villiers Street, and Charing Cross Station, and the Strand, are crowded with prostitutes, who are openly soliciting prostitution in broad daylight.[46]

To those campaigning for an end to juvenile prostitution, at least as it involved girls under the age of sixteen, were now added many more whose simpler purpose was to make the streets safe for respectable women.

There was little novelty in revealing that the mothers of a feckless underclass were instigating the prostitution of their daughters, since that had long been a cliché of the profession. In order that the nation might be roused, Stead and his campaigners needed a story to chill the blood of every family in the land. They found it in the drama of innocent English girls, in the bloom of maidenhood, being kidnapped by foreign criminals. The victims were shipped abroad under duress to imprisonment in white-slave brothels, where their young lives too often ended after they had been subject to the vilest and darkest sexual acts. Let the newspaper readers of England ignore that, if they dared.

Most of those who read such stories were readily convinced. Lewis Carroll, as the Reverend Charles Lutwidge Dodgson, was concerned that a favourite child model, thirteen-year-old Isy Watson, might be

A mission to prostitutes: The Reverend Baptist Noel's midnight meetings, 1862

'stolen' because she travelled alone by railway. 'I fear such beauty among the poor is a very dangerous possession.' Margaret Bradley, daughter of the Master of University College, Oxford, and a child in the 1870s, realized as the revelations of the 1880s gathered pace that 'there were traps set for young girls on journeys, of which my innocent mother was as ignorant as myself'.[47]

Neither innocence nor ignorance would last much longer. In 1880, the London Committee for the Exposure and Suppression of the Traffic in English Girls for the Purposes of Continental Prostitution was set up. Its chairman was an elderly and well-known supporter of good causes, Benjamin Scott, Chamberlain of the City of London. The committee had been formed by Alfred Dyer, a publisher of religious tracts, who heard that English girls were being held as what were now called 'white slaves' in Belgian brothels. Dyer had been to Brussels, visited a brothel and found such a girl in captivity. The Chief of the Brussels Police denied the truth of it. No woman was admitted to work in a brothel, under Belgian law, unless she first declared to a police officer that she did so voluntarily. She must be questioned further in her own language. At no point was the brothel-keeper or anyone else allowed to be present at the interview. The British Pro-Consul in Brussels, Thomas Edward Jeffes, also gave an assurance to 'parents of really virtuous girls that there is no fear whatever of their finding their children in the same position as the girls referred to by Mr Dyer'.[48]

With the support of Lord Shaftesbury, however, the campaigners pressed for the appointment of a Select Committee of the House of Lords on the Law Relating to the Protection of Young Girls. The Select Committee was appointed on 14 June 1881 and reported on 25 August. By then it had heard sufficient evidence to persuade it that a change in the law was needed and its report was formally presented to the House of Lords on 10 July 1882.

Those who appeared before the committee had no difficulty in persuading it that prostitution was thriving from Langham Place down to the Strand, nor in showing that girls as young as thirteen might solicit legally. The more contentious issue was whether white slavers were making off with English girls in their childhood and locking them away in foreign brothels.

There was ample evidence of an international exchange of prostitutes, which was already a feature of Victorian life when 'Walter' met Camille and other European women in London in the 1840s. In 1862, in the fourth volume of *London Labour and the London Poor*, Bracebridge Hemyng devoted a section to 'Traffic in Foreign Women'. French, Italian, Spanish and, particularly, Belgian prostitutes were common in London. Given the proximity of major ports like Boulogne, Antwerp and Amsterdam, this was scarcely surprising. Most of the women seemed to be in England 'of their own free will, and not upon false pretences or compulsion'. Their greatest complaint was that they had been lured to England by promises of easy living and wealth, which had not materialized. Hemyng also reported that English prostitutes were induced to go to Ostend, Boulogne, Dieppe and Le Havre because of the English colonies in those towns.[49]

Though the trade in prostitutes who moved between England and the Continent had continued, there was less conclusive evidence of the type of white slavery which Dyer alleged. One victim whose experience was presented to the Select Committee was Eliza Bond. She was twenty-two years old and had been a servant when she and her friend Ellen May were persuaded to go into service in France. Eliza Bond admitted that she had 'been with a man' in London but insisted that she had not been 'walking the streets'. However, she knew that the house in Lille was a brothel before she agreed, in the presence of a magistrate, that she wished to work there as a prostitute. It was some months later that she decided the life was not to her liking. She wrote a letter which reached the Society for the Suppression of Vice in London and she was brought home. The question, which all the assertions of the 1880s were not destined to resolve, was whether her experience amounted to white slavery.[50]

A table was presented to the Select Committee of 'English Women who have been enrolled as Inmates of the Licensed *Maisons de Débauche* at Brussels' for the three years 1878–1880 inclusive. It gave some indication of the extent of the problem. There were eight women listed in 1878, twenty-four in 1879, and two in 1880. Another table gave the names and ages of those registered in northern France, Belgium and Holland for the nine years 1871–9, listing the great majority as between eighteen and twenty. There was one girl of fourteen, three of fifteen, and two of sixteen. Whether they were twenty or fourteen, of course, they were juveniles in English law.[51]

As the evidence mounted, it became clear that these juveniles did not need to be rescued from abduction and slavery, rather that they should be rescued from what they had voluntarily decided to do. Eliza Bond was a disillusioned employee of the brothel rather than a reluctant conscript. She was disgruntled at having to pay for wine 'out of our own pockets, half a franc per glass', being charged at too high a rate for heat and lodging, and having to 'pay all expenses' for herself if Madame Raffael took her girls out. Mary McLean felt let down by her brothel in Brussels. 'I was led to believe I should lead a jolly life, but I was much disappointed.' Before going to the brothel, she said, 'I went to the Consulate, and the English Consul gave me good advice not to go into the house, and said he would find means to get me back to England, or find me a situation. This I refused.' Even Louisa H—y, whose narrative of her time in a house in Brussels was one of poor health and being a 'close prisoner', as she called it, had altered her age from nineteen to twenty-one to qualify for residence there.[52]

Such a conflict of evidence also set campaigners like Alfred Dyer against the British Consul. Adelaide Tanner, who was twenty, told a story of being plied with drink in London and taken to Belgium. Her medical condition required an operation to facilitate sexual intercourse. She alleged that she had been operated upon without anaesthetic in a Brussels hospital. The doctor she described might have been Sade's physician Rodin from the pages of *Justine*, for 'if I had not soon escaped from his hands, he would have tortured me to death or madness'. She did not need to escape, however, since she was removed by the police. They had come to arrest her for having given a false name, and committed her to prison. When the British Consulate was notified, she was visited by the Pro-Consul with the good news that her troubles were at an end. She was to go home to her sister and family in Bristol. To his dismay, Adelaide Tanner replied, 'Oh, that sort of thing won't suit me. She is a poor woman and has a small house. I have been living in a very different style, so that I do not want to go back, and in fact I shall not go.'[53]

The Select Committee had to decide whether the Pro-Consul was making up a story or whether Adelaide Tanner was telling the truth in her statement that her family would 'rescue me from my most horrible slavery; and to my unspeakable joy, when my imprisonment was over, instead of going back to the hospital or brothel, where death was the only thing I prayed for, I was claimed by my friends and brought once again to my native land'.[54]

At the very least, this did not sound much like Adelaide Tanner's unaided prose style. Nor was it, according to the Pro-Consul Thomas Edward Jeffes, who remarked sourly to the Select Committee that a good many of the so-called white-slave victims were downright unhelpful when he suggested rescue and a return to England. 'I have had to frighten them with the police to get them out of the country. They did not seem at all anxious to go.'[55]

The division of evidence and opinion was so complete that it seemed the drama of white slavery in the 1880s might do more for the titillation of the reading public than for social reform. The question of whether Adelaide Tanner and her kind were martyred innocents or seasoned opportunists was not to be answered. That difficulty did not, of course, prevent both sides in the debate believing that they knew the answer.

*

After the revelations of the House of Lords Select Committee in 1881, their lordships passed a Criminal Law Amendment Bill which, among other provisions, raised the age of consent to sixteen. The bill was referred to the Commons, where it was dropped. Lord Dalhousie introduced it again in the Lords in 1884 but it was sacrificed in the Commons to the passing of the Third Reform Bill. It was introduced again in 1885, though it was felt prudent to make the age of consent fifteen rather than sixteen. It came before the Commons on 22 May, the night when the house adjourned for the Whitsun recess. Only twenty members were in the chamber when the second reading was moved. Conservative members present were hostile and it was talked out, 'much to his own satisfaction' as Stead reported, by Cavendish Bentinck, the Member for Whitehaven. Bentinck was suspected of acting on behalf of Mary Jeffries, owner of eight London brothels and a flagellation house at Rose Cottage, Hampstead. Her clients included the King of the Belgians and 'patrons of the highest social order', as she termed them. Mrs Jeffries was tried at Middlesex Sessions for her activities and Bentinck's suspected allegiance to her was greeted from the opposite benches of the Commons by cries of 'Pity the poor fornicator!'

There could be no further compromise by the campaigners. On 4 July, in the *Pall Mall Gazette*, Stead announced that his next two issues were not intended for 'all those who are squeamish, and all those who are prudish, and all those who prefer to live in a fool's paradise of imaginary innocence or purity'. The truth of juvenile prostitution was now to be revealed in a serialization of *The Maiden Tribute of Modern Babylon*. Public opinion, informed by this investigation of the *Pall Mall Gazette*'s 'Secret Commission', would surely demand the passage of the Criminal Law Amendment Bill in its original form with the age of consent at sixteen.

Stead had the support of the Archbishop of Canterbury, Edward Benson; the Bishop of London, Frederick Temple; Cardinal Manning, Archbishop of Westminster; the Congregational Union; the Salvation Army; and a good many public figures. *The Maiden Tribute of Modern Babylon* mingled sermon and striptease in a classic of sensational journalism. The articles also appeared as a pamphlet and adorned the newsboys' placards in the London streets.

Anyone who expected to find what Charles Lutwidge Dodgson denounced as 'highly-coloured pictures of vice' in Stead's articles was likely to be disappointed. His technique was to set the scene in the prose style of such contemporary erotic fiction as *The Yellow Room: or, Alice Darvell's Subjection* and prompt the reader to imagine the rest.

> 'Here,' said the keeper of a fashionable villa, where in days bygone a prince of the blood is said to have kept for some months one of his innumerable sultanas, as she showed her visitor over the well-appointed rooms, 'Here is a room where you can be perfectly secure. The walls are thick, there is a double carpet on the floor. The window, which fronts upon the back garden, is doubly secured, first with shutters, then with heavy curtains. You lock the door and then you do as you please. The girl may scream blue murder, but not a sound will be heard. The servants will be far away at the other end of the house. I only will be about seeing that all is snug.'[56]

The overblown style of such revelations was reminiscent of old-fashioned gothic fiction and *fin-de-siècle* sado-erotic fantasy. Yet the tone changed to earnest social moralizing with the appearance of individual victims. If the headlines and the suggestive locales snared his readers, Stead had done his job as a journalist. Cavendish Bentinck, in the House of Commons, demanded to know why Stead was not being prosecuted for obscene libel. The Home Secretary was said to be consulting the law officers of the Crown upon this point. He was informed that Stead had evidence against Mrs Jeffries' most illustrious clients, including the King of the Belgians. If Stead were prosecuted, he would have them sub-poenaed and cross-examined as hostile witnesses. Cavendish Bentinck would be among them. The revelations would encompass visitors to Mrs Jeffries' three fashionable brothels in Church Street, Kensington, and her chamber of horrors in the Gray's Inn Road. Stead claimed to have 'Princes and dukes, Ministers of the Crown and members of Parliament' on the list of customers. Crown and Parliament might have felt that what had begun as a campaign for social reform was now dangerously beyond control.

Stead and his paper remained the focus of official hostility. The City of London solicitor prosecuted twenty-three newsboys who had sold the *Pall Mall Gazette*. The Lord Mayor, however, praised Stead's 'high and honourable views', and dismissed the charges. If the government refused to prosecute, 'I simply decline to go on with the case.'[57]

The attack on Stead was interrupted by a change of government on 25 June. Gladstone, as Prime Minister, was defeated on a Finance Bill amendment and Lord Salisbury now formed a minority Conservative administration. On 10 July, in the third and last of his articles, Stead reported cases of white slaves being dispatched from England to the Continent only two weeks earlier. He also accused the police of complicity, citing one brothel in the East End which paid Metropolitan Police officers £500 a year for protection. In the wake of this, the Criminal Law Amendment Bill received a third reading in the Commons on 7 August. It provided for 'the protection of women and children, the suppression of brothels, and other purposes'. Among the other purposes was the raising of the age of consent to sixteen and the criminalizing by statute of indecent acts between men. It was carried by 179 votes to 71 and received the royal assent.

In the 1860s, Sir William Hardman, presiding at Surrey quarter sessions, had thought twelve months' imprisonment enough for an old cats'-meat man who had intercourse with a girl under twelve. From 1885, intercourse with a girl under sixteen was punishable by two years' imprisonment or, where she was under thirteen, by penal servitude for life. Public policy, if not public opinion, had undergone a memorable change in its view of childhood and sexuality.[58]

The final act of the drama was the prosecution of Stead, as if to show that a man who had caused so much trouble must not expect to get away scot free. He was not prosecuted for obscenity, however, but for his part in taking from her parents a child of the slums, thirteen-year-old Eliza Armstrong. The girl was never put in the least moral danger. It was a stunt, intended to show how a pubescent girl might be purchased and shipped overseas.

Stead had gone first to Edward Benson, the Archbishop of Canterbury, who praised his motives but warned him of the risk. Cardinal Manning, Archbishop of Westminster, gave him his unreserved backing. With the aid of Bramwell Booth of the Salvation Army and a reformed prostitute, Rebecca Jarrett, Stead bought the girl from her drunken mother and violent father in the slum area of Lisson Grove, Marylebone. Mrs Armstrong agreed to sell her daughter, £5 being divided between her and a friend who acted as a procuress. On 3 June 1885, Eliza Armstrong went with Stead and Rebecca Jarrett to a London brothel where her virginity was confirmed by a midwife. She was escorted to safety in Paris by a Swiss Salvationist, Madame Combe. For the purposes of journalism, Stead's demonstration was complete.

None the less, whatever his motives and however careful he might have been that the girl should be unharmed, Stead had committed a criminal offence. He, Rebecca Jarrett, Bramwell Booth, Madame Combe and two others were charged under the Offences Against the Person Act 1861 with having taken Eliza Armstrong out of the possession of her parents while she was under sixteen and with indecent assault, which related to the midwife's examination. Booth and Madame Combe were acquitted, the others convicted. Stead was sentenced to three months' imprisonment, the judge taking the opportunity to add that the 'Maiden Tribute' articles – for which Stead was not on trial – had 'deluged' the country with filth. Their publication, 'had been – and I don't hesitate to say ever will be – a disgrace to journalism'.[59]

The public debate and the new law did not banish prostitution from the London streets nor did it suppress brothels. Yet it gave protection to adolescent girls by raising the age of consent. It was impossible to say that there would be no more Jane Doyles or Ellen Reeces but there were many fewer in the public eye. The white-slave trade in such girls was not much affected by the new law since, as Stead discovered to his cost, that was punishable by the Offences Against the Person Act which had already been in existence for thirty-four years, if anyone had cared to use it.

Mary Jeffries, doyenne of the scandal, the one figure identified publicly as a white-slaver, had pleaded guilty and escaped with a fine. Benjamin Scott and his committee had tried for more than a year to prosecute her. Among other stories was that of her 'white-slave house' by the river at Kew, from which drugged victims were exported abroad in closed coffins drilled with air-holes. The allegation had no substance in itself and the Assistant Commissioner at Scotland Yard declined to act upon Scott's other charge that Mrs Jeffries kept 'brothels for the nobility', a suggestion which he thought 'highly improper'. It was not until 16 April 1885 that she was committed to Middlesex Sessions on a charge of keeping a disorderly house, a case heard on 5–10 May.

Mrs Jeffries arrived at court in a brougham presented to her by a member of the House of Lords. She pleaded guilty after a preliminary consultation between judge and counsel, was fined £200 and ordered to find a further £200 as surety. Stead, at his own trial, accused the authorities of conspiring in this plea of guilty so that evidence would not be given in court. 'The White-Slave Widow', as she was called, paid the fine at once and in cash. A titled Guards officer stood surety for her. Before the day was over, she had gone back to business.[60]

Mary Jeffries was later seen handing out rotten fruit in the street for the crowd to throw at Stead and his co-defendants as they arrived for their trial in October of the same year. She had had her difficulties that summer but they had nothing to do with Stead's campaign. Following the fall of Khartoum at the end of the previous year, military reinforcements were sent out to defend Egypt against invasion by the Mahdi. 'Business is very bad,' said Mrs Jeffries mournfully. 'I have been very slack since the Guards went to Egypt.'[61]

CHAPTER 4

The Unknown Victorian

EDWIN CHADWICK, Henry Mayhew, William Acton, Josephine Butler, W. T. Stead and a hundred lesser names had not the least difficulty in persuading the prostitutes of Victorian England to tell their stories. The ratio of truth to falsehood or exaggeration in those reminiscences was open to question but there was enough corroboration of general experience. More difficult was the investigation of the hundreds of thousands of men who were the clients of these street-girls. They included a large proportion of soldiers and sailors in the garrison and dockyard towns, as well as young men in the great cities who were forced by meagre incomes to spend the first ten or fifteen years of adult life as bachelors.

Whatever might be the topics of conversation, reminiscences by the clients or casual lovers of such women are rare in Victorian writing. Here and there, a comment or an insight survives, as in a confidence made to Sir William Hardman by Thackeray. The famous novelist recalled meeting a polite and helpful Guards officer at his club, a man who was otherwise unknown to him. It happened that they left the club together and were walking down Pall Mall. They passed an attractive young woman. 'That's a nice-looking girl,' Thackeray said. After a pause the guardsman replied with the preliminary throaty sound that was supposed to be characteristic of the military aristocrat, 'Haw, yes, I have had her.' There was a longer pause and the soldier went on, 'Haw, my brother has had her.' There was a still longer pause and then, 'Haw, haw, in fact we have both had her.' Thackeray recalled that this was the entire extent of their conversation.[1]

Among the shadowy figures who went silent to their graves, none in Victorian England, nor indeed in any other country at any other time, kept such an extensive account of his sexual relations with women as the diarist who called himself 'Walter'. His diary, published as *My Secret Life*, runs to eleven volumes. It contains a social and physiological chronicle of his activities with a series of 1,200 women over a period of about forty years. The great majority of his partners were prostitutes and most of the rest were working-class girls known only casually, field-girls and domestic servants among them. As a rule his encounters were brief but he knew some of the younger girls for several years.

Walter's unique view of the age in which he lived is neither erotic nor pornographic, though it might be found repellent. The social underworld in which the events of his life occurred is depicted with candour and vivid detail, as is the public panorama of the age. That he should list his experiences with so many women is not as remarkable as it might seem. Bracebridge Hemyng thought there were 80,000 London prostitutes in 1862. During his career, Walter seems to have a hired a different girl about once a fortnight. Like so much else in his diary, this seems entirely probable.

Who was Walter? In his catalogue *Forbidden Books: Notes and Gossip on Tabooed Literature* (1902), the Paris publisher of English-language erotica, Charles Carrington, described how the first publication of the diary had taken place.

> About the year 1888, a well-known publisher and bookseller of Amsterdam, whose speciality was literature of an incandescent kind, was summoned to London by one of his customers, a rich old Englishman, who desired to have privately printed for his own enjoyment an enormous MS., containing in the fullest detail all the secret venereal thoughts of his existence. He defrayed all costs of printing, on condition that no more than six copies should be struck off. A few years afterwards, this eccentric amateur shuffled off the mortal coil; and a few copies of the extraordinary work made a timid appearance on the market, being quoted at the high figure of £100. It is evident that many more than the half-dozen copies stipulated must have been printed – let us say about twenty-five or so – as I have unfrequently seen a complete series, and I should say that at the time I am writing the book may be obtained by carefully searching for about £60 to £75 according to the condition.[2]

The only name to be put forward as the diary's author is that of Henry Spencer Ashbee (1834–1900). He was head of the international oil company Charles Lavy & Co, of Coleman Street in the City of London, with a town house in Bedford Square, a country seat at Hawkhurst in Kent, and an apartment in Paris. He was a book collector of more than usual wealth and compiled the first major English bibliography of erotic and pornographic writing in his *Index Librorum Prohibitorum* (1877) and two further volumes. By his will, he proposed to leave his unrivalled collection of erotica to the British Museum, which was not best pleased by the offer. However, Ashbee also possessed a fine library of Spanish literature, notably of Cervantes, which the museum was keen to have. The trustees were offered both – or neither. Ashbee's erotica was accepted and proved extensive enough to form the original 'Private Case' of the museum's forbidden books.

Yet Ashbee's dates do not match Walter's; neither do the events of his life or his style. Ashbee was more probably the man who arranged for the publication of the diary which, with his clandestine contacts in the book trade of Holland and Belgium, he was well placed to do. According to *My Secret Life*, its author was born about 1820, fourteen years earlier than Ashbee. He was educated at home by a governess, then went as a day-boy to a public school. The death of his father brought genteel poverty. Yet there is much about him and his family that sounds military and patrician. He was found a place at the War Office, after leaving school, but never joined a regiment.

His first encounter with a prostitute was apparently in the village on the eastern edge of London where his family lived. The year was probably 1836 and Walter, known familiarly as 'Wattie', was in company with Cousin Fred, 'a very devil from his cradle'. It was dark, about nine o'clock at night, and the woman was standing by a wall.

'She is a whore,' said Fred, 'and will let us feel her if we pay her.' 'You go and ask her.' 'No you.' 'I don't like.' 'How much money have you got?' We ascertained what we had, and after a little hesitation, walked on, passed her, and then turned round and stopped. 'What are you staring at, kiddy?' said the woman. I was timid and walked away, Fred stopped with her. 'Wattie, come here,' said he in a half whisper. I walked back. 'How much have you got?' the woman said. We both gave her money. 'You'll let us both feel?' said Fred. 'Why of, course, have you felt a woman before?' Both of us said we had, feeling bolder. 'Was it a woman about here?' 'No.' 'Did you both feel the same woman?' 'No.' 'Give me another shilling then, and you shall both feel my cunt well, I've such a lot of hair on it.' We gave what we had, and then she walked off without letting us. 'I'll tell your mothers, if you come after me,' she cried out. We were sold; I was once sold again in a similar manner afterwards, when by myself.[3]

'Kiddy' did not refer to their ages but was 1830s slang for 'smartly dressed'. In this case, however, fear of what the woman might say to his mother was matched by the threats of his godfather, a surgeon-major who gave Walter pocket-money after his father's death. Walter, in adolescence, grew terrified at these encounters.

He stared hard at me. 'You look ill.' 'No, I am not.' 'Yes, you are, look me full in the face, you've been frigging yourself,' said he just in so many words. He had never used an improper word to me before. I denied it. He raved out 'No denial, sir, no lies, sir, you have sir; don't add lying to your bestiality, you've been at that filthy trick, I can see it in your face, you'll die in a madhouse, or of consumption, you shall never have a farthing more pocket-money from me, and I won't buy your commission, nor leave you any money at my death.' I kept denying it, brazening it out. 'Hold your tongue, you young beast, or I'll write to your mother.'[4]

Within a year or two his godfather was dead, replaced as Walter's mentor by 'a middle-aged man with whom I chummed much at my Club, a major retired, and a most debauched individual. He borrowed money from me and did not repay it. His freedom of talk about women made him much liked by the younger men; the older said it was discreditable to help younger men to their ruin.' From this military philanderer, Walter learnt the lore of prostitution, the art of pleasing a girl whom he hired by feeding her well to begin with, the craft whereby he might be sold a virgin who had been a virgin a dozen times before.[5]

Despite this, Walter became the keeper rather than the casual customer of several of the girls whom he met. At twenty-one, he describes his affair with a French prostitute Camille, whom he picked up in Waterloo Place, facing Lower Regent Street. From Camille, he learnt about lesbianism and heterosexual sodomy, being a spectator at the first and a participant in the second. It was a period in his life when his pleasures were also provided by casual encounters with street-girls. His descriptions of early Victorian London ring clear and true, city landscapes as sharp as the drawings of Gustave Doré and as evocative as the later paintings of John Atkinson Grimshaw. Like Mayhew, he had an eye for the manifestations of change and decay, noting the run-down state of Waterloo Road and Granby Street, the groups of half-naked women for hire in ground-floor windows. The decline of this residential district was everywhere apparent, as the South-Western Railway advanced from Nine Elms to construct its new and ugly terminus at Waterloo.

Walter's account of early Victorian London scarcely suggests a city of great propriety, willing and waiting to be shocked. Its common people seemed as easy-going as in Regency or Elizabethan England. At the beginning of the 1840s, he was riding in a cab with Camille after buying her a bonnet, white silk stockings, gloves and garters. As they were being driven through the busy thoroughfares near Piccadilly and Regent Street, Walter believed that she would be excited or amused by seeing his erection, which he had prudently covered for the time being with a handkerchief. He removed this covering at just the wrong moment. ' "The omnibus, the omnibus," she cried out suddenly. Forgetting myself and all but my wants, I had exposed my randy doodle just as an omnibus passed, and as I looked up, there was the conductor laughing at me.'[6]

The portraits in the diary give life and depth to many of the girls whom he picked up as well as to the great city in which his sexual dramas were rooted. Several years after Camille, his first encounter with a fifteen-year-old, Yellow-Haired Kitty as he called her, might almost be a scene from Dickens or Mayhew. It was, Walter says, a blazing after-noon in June when he saw two girls, one tall, stout and in black, idling in the Strand and gazing at the shop windows. 'They were not got up in any showy way, but looked like the children of decent mechanics.' At first they did not respond to his offer of money. He walked towards a brothel in the little streets north of the Strand. The taller girl followed, pulling and cajoling the other. 'You are a foole,' Walter heard, spelling the elder girl's words as they sounded to him. 'You *are a foole.* Oh! you *foole.* Come he wants us. You *foole.*'

The elder girl alone accepted his offer of three shillings and sixpence, going with him to the top floor of the nearby house, kept by a red-cheeked woman in a white apron. It was the beginning of Walter's affair with Kitty, which lasted for several years. She lived with her mother and two younger children in the slums that lay south of the river. Though she was still fifteen, he wrote that 'a girl of twelve years of age is competent to judge of her own fitness for fucking'. In politer terms, the English law of the 1840s said the same.

In scrupulous detail, Walter documents the girl's life. As self-consciously as any missionary or social investigator, though still in bed with her, he asks Kitty about being 'gay', which was the common Victorian term for being a prostitute. Kitty, as a character, would not have done for the family-orientated entertainment of Victorian fiction, yet given the strength of her characterization and dialogue, she might otherwise have stepped from the pages of *Bleak House* or *Our Mutual Friend*. The vividness of her response, compared with the charts and tables of social analysis in the 1840s, gives meaning to Disraeli's comment on 'the imposture of statistics'.

'I ain't gay,' said she astonished. 'Yes you are.' 'No I ain't.' 'You let men fuck you, don't you?' 'Yes, but I ain't gay.' 'What do you call gay?' 'Why the gals who come out regular of a night dressed up, and gets their livings by it.' I was amused.

'Don't you?' 'No, Mother keeps me.' 'What is your father?' 'Got none, he's dead three months back. – Mother works and keeps us. – She is a char-woman and goes out on odd jobs.' 'Don't you work?' 'Not now,' said she in a confused way. 'Mother does not want me to, I takes care of the others.' 'What others?' 'The young ones.' 'How many?' 'Two – one's a boy, and one's a gal.' 'How old?' 'Sister's about six, and brother's nearly eight, – but what do you ask me all this for?' 'Only for amusement. – Then you are in mourning for your father?' 'Yes, it's shabby, ain't it? – I wish I could have nice clothes, I've got nice boots, – ain't they?' cocking up one leg – 'a lady gived 'em me when father died, – they are my best.'

'Are you often in the Strand?' 'When I gets out I likes walking in it, and looking at the shops. I do if Mother's out for the day.' 'Does she know you are out?' The girl who had been lying on her back with her head full towards me, turned on her side, and giggling said in a sort of confidential way, 'Bless you, no – she'd beat me if she knew, – when she be out, I locks them up, and takes the key, and then I goes back to them, – I've got the key in my pocket, and shall be home before Mother, – she is out for the whole day.'

'Do the children know you're out?' 'No, I says to them, "You be quiet now, I'm going to the yard."' 'What's the yard?' Suddenly it struck me, 'Going to the privy?' She burst out laughing. 'Yes that's it, I say I'm going to the privy, and then I comes out with her, and they can't get out, so they are all right, and we go back together if she's with me; if she ain't I go back by myself – there,' – and she stopped satisfied with her explanation. 'They may set fire to themselves,' said I. 'There ain't no fire after we have had break-fast, I puts it out and lights it at night if Mother wants hot water.'

'What do you do with yourself all day?' 'I washes both of them. I gives them food if we've got any, then washes the floor and everything, and then washes myself, then I looks out of the winder.' 'Wash yourself?' 'Yes, I washes from head to foot allus.' 'Have you a tub?' 'No we've only got a pail and a bowl, but I'm beautiful clean, – Mother tells everyone I'm the beautifullest clean gal a mother ever had. – I wash everything, Mother's too tired. Sometimes we all go out and walk, but that's at night; sometimes I lays abed nearly all day.'

Alone with him, Kitty asked Walter to give her friend a shilling, 'if you don't I shall give her a shilling of mine, and give her some of mine anyhow'. The other girl, the younger of the two, worked at home making sacks for sixpence a day. 'Oh! isn't it hard! – and her hands if you seed 'em, are hard and brown, stained with the string, and what they works with, – Mother wants me to work at them at home, but I won't – I tells her I'd run away first.' The friend was too little to carry sacks home on her head like the older women. She must pay another woman twopence of her sixpence to carry them for her. At this rate, Walter's shilling was three days' wages. His three shillings and sixpence for an hour with Kitty would have taken her friend ten days to earn. Hemyng's Swindling Sal had made ten shillings at a time from one client, more than Kitty's friend could earn in a month from making sacks.[7]

Walter's adolescent mistress was determined on her choice of career. She wanted what seemed to her luxuries and knew that there was only one way to earn them. Yet she was a careful girl, walking round by Westminster Bridge, saving the penny toll levied on Waterloo Bridge which would have led her more directly to the Strand. Walter asked what she did with the money that she earned.

I buy things to eat, I can't eat what Mother gives us, she is poor, and works very hard, she'd give us more but she can't; so I buys food, and gives the others what Mother gives me, they don't know better, – if Mother's there I eat some, sometimes we have only gruel and salt; if we 'ave a fire we toast the bread, but I can't eat it if I am not dreadful hungry.' 'What do you like?' 'Pies and sausage-rolls,' said the girl, smacking her lips and laughing, 'Oh! my eye, ain't they prime – oh!' 'That's what you went gay for?' 'I'm not gay,' said she sulkily. 'Well, what you let men fuck you for? Sausage-rolls?' 'Yes. Meat-pies and pastry too.'[8]

If *My Secret Life* contained nothing of value but these exchanges, it would deserve to survive. No pornographer would bother to fabricate such dialogue. It rings with authenticity and suggests a Victorian resilience of character. Not for a moment does Kitty feel a 'victim' of the kind fashionable a century and a half later. She does not see her situation as a social problem or demand that someone should be 'supportive'. The only favour she asks is on behalf of someone else. With almost nothing in her favour, she is resilient, resolute and, in a curious way, optimistic.

Though Kitty was over the age of consent, she was young to be a prostitute and there were those who regarded Walter's activities with distaste. When the girl was still fifteen, she could not leave home if it rained because she had no umbrella. If she bought one, her mother would want to know where she had got the money. Walter hired a cab and went to fetch her, taking her to their rented room. One cabby charged him five times the proper fare and said, 'Yer haught to be glad to be let orf with ten bob. Think yerself lucky a peeler don't drop on you for taking a young girl like that, – yah! you're a swell, ain't yer? – yah! – yah! – poop!' The final yahs and poop came as an encouragement to the horse as the cab drove off, rather than to Walter.[9]

The affair between them cooled. Walter went abroad and, on his return, met Kitty again, looking better-dressed and prosperous. By now she had met a man to whom she had promised to be faithful for the rest of her life, though she made an exception on this particular evening for old times' sake.

*

By no means all the encounters recorded in the diary were as good-natured. It was also in the Strand that Walter picked up a well-dressed girl with whom he went to a brothel for ten shillings. The house was in a court near Drury Lane Theatre and the room, on the top floor at the front of the building, was furnished with some elegance. As he was about to leave, he gave the girl the ten shillings agreed upon. Pretending to be astonished and offended, she insisted that he had promised her five pounds. 'Look at this room, look at my dress, – do you expect me to let a man come here with me for ten shillings?' She went to the door and called for the bawd, an old woman named Mrs Smith, 'a shortish, thick, hook nosed, tawney-coloured, evil-looking woman'. When Mrs Smith heard the girl's story, she was incensed, as Walter recalled.

Was I a gent? she was sure I was, why not pay properly then? – a beautiful young girl like that, – just out, – look at her shape, and her face, – she had written to a dozen gents who knew her house, and they had all come to see this beauty, – all had given her five pounds, some ten pounds, they were so delighted with her, – and much of the same talk. The girl began to whimper, saying she never had been so insulted in her life before.

Five pounds would have been an astonishing price for a prostitute who walked the pavements of the Strand. Bracebridge Hemyng's dress-lodger Lizzie had received a total of forty-five shillings in the Strand from three men, by being what her watcher called 'a clever little devil'. On that basis, the initial price which Walter agreed seems far more likely to have been ten shillings than five pounds. However, the trap had been baited and the attempted extortion began. He insisted, truthfully, that he had not five pounds in his pocket. The bawd was ready for this. 'Well if you have not money give us your watch and chain, we will pawn it, and give you the ticket, and you can get it out of pawn.' Walter had hidden his watch and swore he had not got one, 'and if I had I would see her damned first, before I gave it up'.

The quarrel grew louder, the bawd declaring that 'we don't allow a poor girl to be robbed by chaps like you in this house'. Presently the bawd was shouting for Bill to come up and a loud male voice from downstairs shouted 'Halloh!' although no one appeared. Walter was alarmed enough to throw up the window, stick his head out, and begin shouting, 'Police! – police! – murder! – murder! – police! – police!' He saw a policeman walking across the court below and recalled with dismay that the man would probably be one of those officers bribed to ensure the protection of brothels on his beat.

The bawd, frightened by the shouts, began whining for three pounds, then two. Walter seized a poker and shattered a window. He raised it against the looking-glass. 'Get out, or I'll smash this, and you, and every-thing else in this room.' He struck a chair, breaking it. By this time, the bawd was begging him to leave. He ordered the two women out first and made a cautious exit from the house, throwing down the poker on the mat. It was one of the very few occasions when he showed the least vindictiveness towards the women whom he hired and of whom he spoke collectively with affection. 'Look at me well, if you meet me in the Strand again, cut away at once, get out of my sight, or I'll give you in charge for annoying me, or robbing me, you bloody bitch, look out for yourself.'

He heard later of a fight in the house and a man being picked up dead on the stairs. The owner, Bill perhaps, had been transported for felony.[10]

By the 1860s, the diary is signposted with references to familiar pleasures of mid-Victorian London, notably the Argyll Rooms and the Cremorne Gardens. In the 1870s he met a prostitute at the Alhambra in Leicester Square, apparently for the first time on those premises. He encountered one of his more memorable girls, whom he called Amelia German, at the Cremorne Gardens. In such rendezvous, he became the client of women well-known in their trade, including Irish Kate, Brighton Bessie and the Great Eastern, nicknamed in tribute to Brunel's famous ocean liner. Then his interest turned to Europe, the Middle East, and the Atlantic seaboard of the United States. The extent to which he travelled abroad in the 1870s and 1880s may perhaps have reflected his own dislike of late Victorian mores, that sterner creed of sexual morality often coupled with an intransigent philistinism. As Walter says, he never much cared for 'uprighters'.

In the course of forty years, Walter expressed a piecemeal philosophy on sexuality and prostitution. During his middle years, he wrote intermittently of prostitutes in general, suggesting a humanity which complemented that recorded by observers such as William Acton, Josephine Butler and W. T. Stead.

> To their class I owe a debt of gratitude, and say again what I think I have said elsewhere: that they have been my refuge in sorrow, an unfailing relief in all my miseries, have saved me from drinking, gambling, and perhaps worse. I shall never throw stones at them, nor speak harshly to them, nor of them. They are much what society has made them, and society uses them, enjoys them, even loves them; yet denies them, spurns, damns, and crushes them even whilst frequenting them and enjoying them. In short, it shamefully ill-treats them in most Christian countries, and more so in protestant England than in any others that I know.[11]

His view of Victorian womankind was the contrary of the prudent Dr Acton, who wrote that a newly married man 'need not fear that his wife will require the excitement, or in any respect imitate the ways of a courtezan', and that, in any case, 'the majority of women (happily for them) are not very much troubled with sexual feeling of any kind'. In Walter's observation of his female contemporaries, 'Women who give themselves up to sexual pleasure have infinitely more enjoyment of life for a time than virtuous women have.'[12]

His own marriage had brought unhappiness to both parties and his view of the married state was unflattering. 'Women are all bought in the market – from the whore to the princess. The price alone is different, and the highest price in money or rank obtains the woman.' The whore was thus raised to the rank of the princess. Nor did he believe in the common assurance of the moralist that women who had fallen from virtue hated their profession and longed to repent. 'Some say that harlots are sick of their business, and hate the erotic whims and fanciers to whom they minister. Such is not my experience.' The figure of the Penitent Magdalene was not a symbol of virtue reclaimed but of professional failure.[13]

As time passed, he wrote of his own career with a weary self-criticism. In a later gloss on the second volume, he concludes, as if in a moment of revulsion from the life he has led, 'Fucking is a commonplace thing, the prince and the beggar do it the same way, it is only the incidents connected with it that are exciting. Voluptuous, reckless, youth and beauty together, make the vulgar, shoving, arse-wagging business poetical for a while, but it is animalism.' More often, he sees himself and his companions as participants in that struggle for survival which characterized the lives of a multitude of men and women in the great Victorian cities. As he writes in his second Preface to *My Secret Life*, 'Whatever society may say, it is but a narrative of human life, perhaps the every day life of thousands, if the confession could be had.'[14]

Gordon Grimley's characteristically perceptive comment in his edition of the diary reflects its portrait of a moral underworld that was the inevitable accompaniment to industrial development and material improvement. 'There must remain indeed from a reading of *My Secret Life* a final sense of compassion: a comprehension reborn . . . of the brevity of lives: the gaslit rooms long vanished under demolition, the fields built over under the striding of the suburbs; the vanished voices, emotions, lust, regrets, and laughter of the country women, the town women among whom Walter took his pleasure.'

The diary ends when Walter, a widower for many years, was probably in his sixties and may perhaps have acquired another wife or obligations of some kind.

I break with the past, my amatory career is over, my secret life finished. My philosophy remains the same. My deeds leave me no regret – with the exception perhaps of a very few. – Would that I were young enough to continue in the same course – that all might happen to me over again. – But age forbids, duty forbids, affection forbids – Eros adieu.[15]

No revelation of the moral underworld of England in the nineteenth century had ever been detailed with such self-conscious precision and yet with such affection. The scale is heroic, although the hero is not Walter but Victorian humanity at large. From the catalogue of hasty copulations, such figures as Kitty and Cousin Fred, Brighton Bessie and the choleric surgeon-major stand apart. But a sense of the teeming, struggling life of the Victorian city hangs over the narrative, dense and close, like the fog of a 'London particular'. As Walter noted, 'Foggy weather is propitious to amorous caprices.'[16]

CHAPTER 5

'More deadly than prussic acid'

THE REALITY of such experiences as Walter's was complemented in the Victorian period by a literature of sexual fantasy and moral subversion. On 13 May 1857, Lord Chief Justice Campbell rose to intervene in the House of Lords during a debate on the sale of poisons. It was a subject of public interest following the notoriety of Dr William Palmer, 'The Rugeley Poisoner', who had been hanged the year before. 'I am happy to say', Campbell told the peers, 'that I believe the administration of poison by design has received a check. But, from a trial which took place before me on Saturday, I have learnt with horror and alarm that a sale of poison more deadly than prussic acid, strychnine or arsenic – the sale of obscene publications and indecent books – is openly going on.' Campbell was seventy-eight. He had been Attorney-General, Chief Justice of the Court of Queen's Bench, was Lord Chief Justice in 1857, and soon became Lord Chancellor. If he had only just learnt of an active trade in such publications in central London, his must have been a uniquely sheltered life.[1]

Lord Campbell's purpose was to introduce the first Obscene Publications Bill in parliamentary history. Obscenity had been routinely prosecuted for a hundred and thirty years but that was the result of a judicial ruling, in the case of Edmund Curll in 1727, that there was such an offence as obscene libel, which the Common Law courts had not recognized before. 'Obscene libel' did not require defamation but was the common law term which described any obscene publication.

Since 1802, the efforts of the magistrates and the law officers had drawn support from private prosecutions by the Society for the

Suppression of Vice, known familiarly as 'The Vice Society'. The records of the Court of Queen's Bench contained indictments and convictions for such publications as the Marquis de Sade's *Juliette* in 1830, *Fanny Hill* repeatedly, and *The History of Dom B . . .*, and prosecutions of such periodicals as the *Town* in 1838, and the *New Rambler's Magazine*. The dates of the indictments suggest that more vigorous efforts were made to cleanse the London shops of these publications shortly before such major events as Queen Victoria's coronation in 1838 or the Great Exhibition of 1851.[2]

So far, it seemed that the police and the Vice Society had been losing the battle. Two days before he raised the matter in the House of Lords, Campbell had been confronted by two booksellers who were found guilty of obscene libel for selling a couple of periodicals, *Paul Pry* and *Women of London*, as well as a number of obscene prints. William Dugdale (1800–68), who had been in business as a publisher and bookseller for thirty years in the little streets north of the Strand, was sent to prison for twelve months. William Strange, who had sold the two periodicals, was sentenced to three months. Dugdale had already served at least nine prison sentences as a publisher of pornographic fiction printed under his own name from premises in Drury Lane as well as in nearby Holywell Street and Wych Street. He also issued books under the imprints of Smith, Turner and Brown. On being convicted before Lord Campbell, he produced a knife and was hastily restrained before he could use it on a representative of the Vice Society standing nearby.

Paul Pry was the more famous of the two papers in the 1857 case, first issued in 1856 by Robert Martin, who had been sentenced to imprisonment at a previous hearing. It followed the example of that other Victorian creation, the *News of the World* (1843), in its judicious mixture of titillation and moral outrage. Unfortunately for Robert Martin, his advertisers were less subtle in promoting their wares.

Just received from Paris

STEREOSCOPIC GEMS

A. J. begs to inform his subscribers, and the public generally, that he has just received from Paris an entirely new assortment of Stereoscopic Slides, depicting some of the fastest, and richest scenes, in the Bagnios of the French capital, all taken from life. They have only to be seen to be appreciated; in consequence of the late seizure in Paris (see daily papers) by the gendarmes of these warm gems, he has the greatest difficulty in obtaining as many as he wants of the right sort.

Single slide 5s. Set of twenty, £4 4s. Highly coloured, 2s. per slide extra. A. J. 4 Harpur St., Red Lion Square, London.

N. B. – A Catalogue, descriptive of these warm gems, sent on receipt of six stamps and a stamped envelope.

The talk of gendarmes, police seizure and shortage of stock was pure invention, a preliminary to jacking up the price. The photographs had never been nearer to Paris than the rooms east of Drury Lane where they were taken. At five shillings, a single print of one of these 'gems' cost as much as many working people would earn in a week during the 1850s. Apart from such advertisements, the downfall of the magazine's editor and his booksellers was precipitated by a story in *Paul Pry* describing graphically how a servant-girl, Susan, was seduced in the bedroom of the Right Honourable Filthy Lucre. Like *Women of London*, the magazine also included prints of what were later called 'bathing beauties' in the costumes of the day, though these were not apparently the cause of trouble in 1856–7.

When the Obscene Publications Bill received its second reading in the House of Lords, during June 1857, Lord Campbell found that he had less than wholehearted support from his brother peers. The former Lord Chancellor Henry Brougham, with the laconic scepticism of a Regency survivor, regarded the proposals as a mixture of humbug and tosh. There were passages in 'some of our most eminent poets' far more objectionable than anything in *Paul Pry* or its competitors. Lord Lyndhurst demanded to know what would happen if the police raided a shop and seized a print of a couple making love, which proved to be Correggio's painting *Jupiter and Antiope*. But Lyndhurst's well-bred contempt for the philistinism of popular morality was swept aside as England indulged in one of its periodic spasms of moral self-loathing and hasty legislation.[3]

The bill was passed into law. In July, the Vice Society announced the good news that it had seized a total of thousands of prints, hundreds of books and copperplate engravings, and hundredweights of letterpress. It was certainly true – and it made very little difference. Eleven years later, the state of cultural morality seemed as bad as ever, according to the society's report for 1868. Indeed there was 'a new phase developed in the history of vice' by the use of the stereoscope and through the 'secret trading' offered by an improved postal service.[4]

Worst of all, the new statute of 1857 had not even laid down the meaning of obscenity, 'pornography' being a word that the law had never used. In 1868, in *Regina* v. *Hicklin*, Sir Alexander Cockburn ruled that the test of obscenity was to be its capacity to deprave and corrupt those into whose hands it might fall and who might be open to its influence. Neither he nor anyone else could say how this was to be judged or measured.

To the pornographers, of course, the form of the law was irrelevant. They had always stood outside it and when necessary suffered the consequences. None of them would waste time publishing a work unless the law's prohibition made it profitable to do so.

*

The trade in pornography had been established in London for almost two centuries before Lord Campbell turned his attention to it. However, there was no doubt that the invention of photography and steel engraving, as well as the mass production of the printed word, had given it an unprecedented impetus. In addition to books, magazines and pictures, a trade in artefacts from Europe had developed since the end of the Napoleonic Wars. Pedlars, usually Italian or French, supplied English traders or sold their wares directly. The Vice Society was horrified at the enthusiasm for obscene snuff-boxes on the part of undergraduates at Oxford and Cambridge, no less than at the success with which some of these objects were sold at the very gates of academies for young ladies. Thomas Wirgman occupied a place unique in legal history as the only defendant ever convicted of 'publishing' an obscene tooth-pick case, 'containing on the inside lid thereof one obscene, filthy, and indecent picture representing the naked persons of a man and woman in an indecent, filthy, and obscene situation, attitude and practice'.[5]

The area of narrow thoroughfares north of the Strand was later to disappear with the building of Aldwych and Kingsway. Until then, Wych Street, Holywell Street and their neighbours were the home of traders in secondhand goods and old clothes shops but were best known as the citadel of a trade in pornography, carried on by those whose names appeared regularly in the indictments of the courts: William Dugdale, Edward Duncombe, John Duncombe, George Cannon, Edward Dyer and their competitors.

The usual method of bringing individual shopkeepers to justice was entrapment by the Vice Society, as one of its agents reported in 1845. One minute he was the knowing connoisseur of bedroom scenes, nudging the shopkeeper to show him something 'warmer'. The next instant he was the concerned and affronted citizen, appalled by the words or images that had blasted his sight.

> I went to the shop two or three times before the day when the sale took place, and bought several innocent publications. On the day in question, the prisoner [Alfred Carlile] showed me a French print in the window, which I had asked to see. I asked him if he had anything more curious, and he at length invited me to go into the back shop. He then showed me several indecent prints. I asked him the price, and selected two which I produce. These form the subject of the present indictment.[6]

A man who operated on the scale of William Dugdale was a target criminal and merited a police raid that turned Holywell Street into a battleground. His books were seized in large quantities, eight hundred copies during one raid in 1851 and three thousand in another search five years later. On 8 September 1851, a party of constables under Inspector Lewis of the Thames Police (who had the powers of a Customs and Excise officer to search and seize) set off for Holywell Street. They were accompanied by strong-arm men whom the Vice Society had hired, 'porters' as they were euphemistically termed. As soon as the posse reached Holywell Street, Dugdale's look-out rushed inside and warned him. The doors were slammed and bolted, being constructed to resist just such an assault. Other inhabitants of the street closed in and began to threaten the police and the Vice Society. Taking their cue from *Paul Pry*, they regarded the Vice Society as 'miscreants in white chokers' who 'croak for the safety of Christian England', and they hated the police as the cynical takers of bribes.

For ten minutes the besiegers tried to break in without success. Then Dugdale opened the door, recognized Sergeant Chadwick of Metropolitan Police 'F' Division, and said, 'Now, Chadwick, you may come in.' Instead of cheering on the forces of decency, the inhabitants of Holywell Street set about the stalwarts of the Vice Society, while the police tried to raid the premises. A large number of prints had been burnt in the previous ten minutes but the police took away 882 books, 870 prints, 110 catalogues and 9 lb of letterpress, as well as lithographic stones and copperplate. Dugdale was later sentenced at Middlesex Sessions to two years' imprisonment.[7]

This privileged world of shops and printing presses was far removed from that of the street-traders who hawked such merchandise in the open air. There was constant hostility between the two groups. The street-traders swore that certain policemen were in the pay of Dugdale and his kind, rewarded for harassing the street-sellers and letting the shops trade 'without being molested'. One street-trader, describing the way in which he was constantly threatened and moved on by constables, asked 'Why should he be considered a greater offender than a shop-keeper, and be knocked about by the police?'

By way of revenge on his more comfortable competitors, the street-trader would stand at a little distance from the shop, waiting for a passer-by to begin studying the sealed packets displayed in the window. He would then approach the potential customer and confide 'that he could sell for 6d. what was charged 5s., or 2s. 6d., or whatever price he had seen announced "in that very neighbourhood"'. The sealed packet which he offered appeared identical to those in the window.

As so often in what Mayhew called the 'Sham Indecent Street-Trade', the purchaser would get home, open the packet and find an old anti-Corn Law pamphlet, or a missionary tract, or even an old newspaper. The trick would only work in the open air. It was far too dangerous to sell the packets in public houses, for example, where purchasers would tear them open at once, something which people were 'ashamed to do in the public street'.[8]

There were also pious frauds, represented by such titles as *The Dreadful Disclosures of Maria Monk*, whose cover promised rampant lesbianism and a hint of bizarre chastisement. A perennial seller, it survived in shrink-wrapped editions for more than a century after Mayhew's time. Though it was the genuine article, the purchaser was seldom pleased to discover that it had been issued by the Presbyterian Tract Society in 1833 and that its earnest propagandizing was not blemished for a single line by anything remotely improper or suggestive, unless an innuendo against Catholicism.

Most customers of the bookshops and the street-sellers came from the educated middle class. Yet there was also a street-trade in near-pornography among the costers and street-folk themselves. Books were bought to be read out to those costers who were illiterate by one who was not. One such reader quoted to Henry Mayhew a passage from a favourite story of the costers and their women, a drama containing a curious piece of furniture popularized elsewhere by the Marquis de Sade.

> With glowing cheeks, flashing eyes, and palpitating bosom, Venetia Trelawney rushed back into the refreshment-room, where she threw herself into one of the arm-chairs already noticed. But scarcely had she thus sunk down upon the flocculent cushion, when a sharp click, as of mechanism giving way, met her ears; and at the same instant her wrists were caught in manacles which sprang out of the arms of the treacherous chair, while two steel bands started from the richly-carved back and grasped her shoulders. A shriek burst from her lips – she struggled violently, but all to no purpose; for she was a captive – and powerless! We should observe that the manacles and steel bands which had thus fastened upon her, were covered with velvet, so that they inflicted no positive injury upon her, nor even produced the slightest abrasion of her fair and polished skin.

The reading was interrupted by shouts from the audience. 'Aye! that's the way the harristocrats hooks it! There's nothing o' that sort among us. The rich has all that barrikin to themselves. . . . Yes, that's the bloody way the taxes goes in.' By contrast, a reading of political comment from *Lloyd's Weekly* was greeted with bewilderment. 'I can't tumble to that barrikin, it's a jawbreaker.'[9]

Between this entertainment of the illiterate and the erotic fantasies of the 'harristocrats', a succession of newspapers and magazines appealed to both. These were not a new phenomenon. The first of them, the *Rambler's Magazine: or, The Annals of Gallantry*, retailing adultery and court scandal, had begun in 1783 and was followed by the *Bon Ton Magazine*, edited by Jack Mitford, and a series of other periodicals in the 1790s. Renton Nicholson was acquitted in 1838 as editor of the *Town*, a scandal sheet and a retailer of stories that were bawdy rather than erotic. At the same time, Nicholson also edited a High Church newspaper, the *Crown*. He later claimed to have had a good deal of fun in the *Crown*, attacking himself anonymously as a degenerate purveyor of vice in the *Town* – and then responding anonymously by denouncing himself as the canting humbug of the *Crown*.

Within a dozen years of the Obscene Publications Act, there were many more newspapers and readers than there had been in the 1850s. The street-traders were replaced by newsboys but William Dugdale and his successors were still busily running off periodicals for the working man. *Paul Pry* had gone to its reward but was succeeded by *Peter Spy*. This in its turn was replaced by the *Ferret*, 'An Inquisitive, Quizzical, Satirical, and Theatrical Censor of the Age', which was none the less still 'Conducted by Peter Spy'.

In January 1870, Inspector James Brennan of the Metropolitan Police was given the job of cleaning up Holywell Street once again. He sent plain-clothes officers to several booksellers with instructions to pose as customers and seek out pornography. Five shops were closed down as a result. Then Brennan turned his attention to the street trade. His men began rounding up newsboys, most of them in their late teens or early twenties, who had been selling the first two numbers of the *Ferret*. There had been complaints from concerned members of the public who had seen the magazine displayed for sale with other periodicals and news-papers at street corners and entrances to railway stations. The greatest offence was caused by the picture on the cover of the second issue, *In a Music-Hall Canteen*. It showed a top-hatted gentleman in a music-hall promenade bar with three ballet-girls in short skirts and high-heeled boots. One girl was facing him with her hands on his shoulders. Another was drawing up her skirt as if to adjust a garter. Since music-hall prom-enade bars, like the Alhambra, were known as places where men picked up prostitutes, the objection to the picture was presumably that it depicted something of the kind.

At the Mansion House police court on 28 January it was alleged that the newsboys were buying the magazine for less than a halfpenny and selling it for a penny, some of them making four shillings a day. Their supplier was Charles Grieves, alias Charles Young, a bookseller of Russell Court and for many years William Dugdale's printer. The police had no need to prove obscenity, since the newsboys' conduct contra-vened the Metropolitan Police Act of 1839. They were fined two shillings and sixpence each with four days in prison if they failed to pay. On 16 February, Charles Grieves went to hard labour for a year.[10]

As a rule, however, the principal trade in pornography was little con-cerned with penny papers but with a sophisticated and well-organized production of novels and magazines for the affluent. Ironically, it was during the 1860s that the Victorian trade in pornography seemed to thrive, a decade in which Lord Campbell's Act and the renewed vigilance of the Society for the Suppression of Vice might have been

The Ferret: *the cover of the second issue which caused the prosecution of newsboys and publisher*

expected to have the greatest effect. These measures, however, encountered the more rebellious culture among a second generation of
Victorians, including a new Bohemia on the fringe of the Pre-Raphaelite
movement. Some of its members were not beyond contributing a
volume or two to the undergrowth of literature, and such books as
Dugdale's were by no means confined to the grimy and ill-kept streets
with which they had usually been associated. When Swinburne's *Poems
and Ballads* (1866) was withdrawn by Macmillan, after *The Times* reviewer
suggested a prosecution for obscenity, the book was quickly reprinted by
John Camden Hotten of Piccadilly.

Despite his fashionable address, Hotten was generally regarded as a
rogue who lived by pirating the copyright of American authors and by
publishing books of his own that were less pornographic or erotic than
grotesque. These included *Lady Bumtickler's Revels* and *Madame Birchini's
Dance*, the former a two-act flagellation opera. To deflect the attention
of the police and the Vice Society, Hotten insisted that these and other
items had been reprinted from originals found in the library of the late
Henry Thomas Buckle, author of *The History of Civilisation in England*
(1857–61), and he issued them collectively as 'The Library Illustrative of
Social Progress'.

In an age of psychopathology many of Hotten's curiosities would
have been categorized as sado-masochistic. There seems little doubt
that he hoped for dramas of the sort from Swinburne, with persuasion
by the genteel blackmailer of the Pre-Raphaelite movement, Charles
Augustus Howell. Among Swinburne's subversive whimsies were such
pieces as *La Fille du policeman* and *La Soeur de la reine*, in which Queen
Victoria has a twin sister who becomes a Haymarket prostitute. The
Queen's own 'unfortunate lapse from virtue' is the work of the elderly
Wordsworth, in which he seduces her by the smouldering sensuality of
his reading of *The Excursion*. After that, Victoria's sexual appetites
require all the energies of Lord John Russell and 'Sir Peel' to assuage
them. Such pieces were circulated privately but Hotten wisely judged
that they would bring him trouble if issued in print.[11]

Among other authors of such material, Henry Spencer Ashbee in his
Index Librorum Prohibitorum identified the creator of *The Romance of
Chastisement: or, Revelations of the School and Bedroom* as Lieutenant St
George H. Stock of the Queen's Royal Regiment. Hotten, though in
possession of the manuscript which had already been issued in part-

form in Dublin, declined to publish it as a book. Lieutenant Stock transferred his labours to Hartcupp & Co. who published English-language erotica in Brussels, until the British Ambassador protested to the Belgian authorities. Hartcupp's books were seized and destroyed in July 1876.

The majority of Victorian pornography showed the middle class writing for the middle class. Among Hotten's best-selling authors was James Glass Bertram who as 'The Reverend William Cooper' wrote *A History of the Rod*, which was never in danger of prosecution, and as 'Margaret Anson' was author of the clandestinely sold novel *The Merry Order of St Bridget*, which continues to be reprinted in paperback more than a century later. In what might be called his real life, James Glass Bertram was a marine economist and author of *The Harvest of the Sea. A Contribution to the Natural and Economic History of the British Food Fishes* (1865).

A writer of curiosities in the same style was George Augustus Sala, the portly friend of Swinburne, a journalist for *Household Words* in St Petersburg at the end of the Crimean War and correspondent of the *Daily Telegraph* in the Confederacy during the American Civil War. Like Swinburne, he belonged to the more Bohemian and bibulous fringes of Pre-Raphaelite culture. Sala was the chronicler of London high life and low life in *Twice Around the Clock* (1858) and of Paris reborn after the Franco-Prussian War in *Paris Herself Again* (1878). He boasted that the *Daily Telegraph* 'treated him like a prince and paid him like an ambassador'. It was not poverty but a certain relish for moral subversion which moved him to write the greater part of *The Mysteries of Verbena House: or, Miss Bellasis Birched for Thieving* (1882), described by Ashbee as 'one of the best books of its kind, and a truthful picture of what is passing around us'. The setting is an academy for young ladies in Brighton, where theft, drunkenness and the circulation of obscene books appear to be the norm. The moral tone is finely sardonic and the Reverend Arthur Calvedon, spiritual adviser to the establishment, is not only permitted to attend the scenes of retribution but is provided with a spy-hole when necessary and afterwards consummates his excitement with the proprietress, Miss Sinclair.

No less paradoxical was the career of Reginald, 'Reggie', Bacchus in the 1890s, an Oxford graduate and author of uplifting stories for religious newspapers in England who also penned the 'Nemesis Hunt' novels which were published in association with Charles Carrington in

Paris. They included *The Confessions of Nemesis Hunt* (1902), *Pleasure Bound 'Afloat'* (1908), *Maudie* (1909) and *Pleasure Bound 'Ashore'* (1909). Bacchus was a translator of French fiction into English and may have been responsible for the English versions of such novels as *Dolly Morton* (1899), originally written in French by the right-wing poet of Action Française, Hugues Rebell, the pseudonym of Georges Joseph Grassal.

Bacchus became the husband of the young actress Isa Bowman, who had first played Lewis Carroll's 'Alice' on the stage and was one of those child friends who shared the Reverend Charles Dodgson's Eastbourne holidays and seaside lodgings. During the early 1890s, she and Bacchus were part of a circle, including Oscar Wilde and Ernest Dowson, whose centre was a Sheffield solicitor and publisher of expensive erotica, Leonard Smithers.

Among such authors, one man stands out from the shadows with distinctive clarity as a figure of the literary *demi-monde* of the 1860s, a contemporary of Swinburne, Rossetti and George Meredith, who might almost have been a character in his own fiction. Captain Edward Sellon (1818–66) had gone to India as a cadet at sixteen and returned to England ten years later with his subaltern's rank and nothing to live on. Like many of his kind, he had engaged in casual encounters with Indian prostitutes, whose beauty and skill were beyond anything he discovered in London. As a man of honour he was also a duellist. In England, he made a marriage that was alternately passionate and cantankerous but which did not last.

After this idyll of courtship, honeymoon and country life, Sellon drifted from one affair to another in the London that Mayhew described. He saw his own family ruined by his mother's dishonest solicitors and tried to support himself by driving the mail coach between Cambridge and London, using an assumed name to protect the prestige of his own. After two years, the growing popularity of rail travel put him out of business. Ever the officer and gentleman, he opened fencing-rooms in London, where the swordsmen of the future could be trained. But swordsmen were out of fashion and that venture also failed. It was in his forties that he began to write novels for William Dugdale.

Sellon's fiction was aimed at a readership brought up on the syllabus of the Victorian public school. His output soon included *The New Epicurean* (1865), *Phoebe Kissagen* (1866), *The Adventures of a Schoolboy* (1866), *The New Lady's Tickler* (1866), and what was recognized as his own autobiography, posthumously published, *The Ups and Downs of Life. A Fragment* (1867). He was also the translator of Boccaccio and author of *Annotations on the Sacred Writings of the Hindus* (1865). He provided a rowdy decade with elegant pornography, embodying the erotic ambitions of a gentler world. *The New Epicurean* was a wistful dream of 'pleasure without riot, and refined voluptuous enjoyment without alloy'. The scene of its pleasures was to be 'a suburban villa, situate in extensive grounds, embosomed in lofty trees, and surrounded with high walls'. Time stood still, so that it seemed to be always summer in pornotopia. The gardens were designed to prevent even the servants glimpsing their employer. Within the house was a *salle d'amour*, as Sellon describes it, 'its fittings and furniture entirely *en Louis Quinze*'.

> The grounds I had laid out in the true English style, with umbrageous walks, alcoves, grottoes, fountains, and every adjunct that could add to their rustic beauty. In the open space facing the secret apartment before alluded to was spread out a fine lawn, embossed with beds of the choicest flowers, and in the centre, from a bouquet of maiden's blush roses appeared a statue of Venus, in white marble; and at the end of every shady valley was a terminal figure of the god of gardens in his various forms; either bearded like the antique head of the Indian Bacchus; or soft and feminine, as we see the lovely Antinous; or Hermaphroditic – the form of a lovely girl with puerile attributes. In the fountains swam gold and silver fish, whilst rare crystals and spars glittered amidst mother o' pearl at the bottom of the basins.[12]

Sellon calls it his 'happy valley', an echo of a more famous description in Samuel Johnson's *Rasselas* more than a hundred years before. Behind the sexual opportunism of the Indian Army officer down on his luck lingers a wraith of his classical education and a memory of pastoral convention in the poetry of Milton and his admirers. In its ornate images, however, Sellon's artificial paradise also anticipates the decadence of the 1890s, or the interior decoration devised by the jaded Des Esseintes as the hero of Huysmans' *À Rebours* (1884). Ashbee described Sellon's novel as showing 'an ultra lasciviousness, and a cynicism worthy of the Marquis de Sade (barring cruelty, which is never practised)'. Since the story was set in the age of *Les Liaisons dangereuses*, such qualities were not inappropriate.

Yet Sellon's race was almost run, as he fashioned these narratives to the demands of the ruffianly William Dugdale's customers. In a letter of 4 March 1866, this 'pleasure-seeking scamp', as Ashbee called him, described his last journey abroad. It seems that the letter was written to William Dudgale as an appeal for money.

Captain Sellon had been engaged to act as companion to a Mr Scarsdale on a tour of Egypt. While waiting alone in Scarsdale's brougham near Wandsworth Road railway station, smoking one cigar after another, he was unexpectedly joined by 'the most beautiful young lady I ever beheld'. She was being taken on the journey to provide Scarsdale's pleasures. When Sellon teased her as a 'mere baby' and used the familiar Victorian taunt, 'Does your mother know you're out?' she gave him a box on the ear and exclaimed, 'Baby indeed! Do you know, sir, I am fifteen?' She claimed to be the daughter of a merchant with offices in the City of London and a house in Clapham. Sellon teased her again and their first hasty copulation took place before Scarsdale reached the carriage. The initial part of the journey was by rail and steamer to Dover, Calais and Vienna. At the last stop before Vienna, the other passengers left the compartment and Scarsdale went to sleep. Pulling the girl on to his lap, Sellon made love to her a second time, 'her stern towards me', during which exercise Scarsdale woke up.

> I made a desperate effort to throw her on the opposite seat, but it was no go he had seen us. A row of course ensued and we pitched into one another with hearty good will. He called me a rascal for tampering with his fiancée, I called him a scoundrel for seducing so young a girl! and we arrived at Vienna! 'Damn it!' said I as I got out of the train with my lip cut and nose bleeding, 'here's a cursed bit of business.'

Sellon had £15 in his pocket and decided to stay in Vienna as long as the money lasted. He managed to meet the girl once more at the Volksgarten where 'we had a farewell poke and arranged for a rendezvous in England'. He returned to London and informed Dugdale, 'Here I am having spent all my money.'

Despite the tone of bluff self-reliance, Sellon at forty-eight was at the end of his tether. A few weeks later, on a spring day in April 1866, he went to Webb's Hotel, Piccadilly, whose site was later that of the Criterion in Piccadilly Circus. He wrote a poem of farewell to a woman who had lately befriended him when his money ran out, its concluding verse being self-explanatory.

> For I am in the cold earth laid,
> In the tomb of blood I've made.

Mine eyes are glassy, cold and dim,
Adieu my love, and think of him
                    No more.
      Vivat Lingam.
      Non Resurgam.

He enclosed the verses in a letter to a friend, to be forwarded to the woman for whom they were written. In the hired room of the hotel, an officer and a gentleman to the last, he took his pistol and shot himself. 'Here then', wrote Ashbee, 'is the melancholy career, terminating in suicide at the early age of 48 years, of a man by no means devoid of talent, and undoubtedly capable of better things.'[13]

*

Sellon was not, like James Glass Bertram or George Augustus Sala, a man well known for other forms of writing who produced a volume or two of erotic curiosities in addition. Erotica or pornography was nearly all his output. It would have surprised him to be accorded literary appreciation as much as it would have amused him to be cited as an ideal husband. He was an author of the literary underworld for whose works Lord Campbell's Act might have been designed. Unfortunately, the flaws in that design were already evident in the 1860s. Even the Lord Chancellor had warned Campbell at first that 'no legislation is necessary' and that he had better leave the law 'as it stands'.

During the debate on the new statute, Campbell had insisted that he had 'not the most distant contemplation' of interfering with great art nor with serious literature, not even with Dumas's *La Dame aux camélias*, much as he disapproved of the novel. The new law was to be directed exclusively at 'works written for the single purpose of corrupting the morals of youth, and of a nature calculated to shock the common feelings of decency in any well-regulated mind'. When the bill became law, however, it was at once out of the hands of Lord Campbell and the legislature, the assurances of protecting art and literature worthless before the ink was dry on the royal assent.[14]

Dugdale and his competitors published as never before, while the Vice Society lamented the triumph of 'Stereoscopic Gems' and the perversion of the art of photography. The first major case under the new law was not against a pornographer but the prosecution in 1867–8 of a Wolverhampton bookseller who had sold a publication by the Protestant

Electoral Union. The Union abhorred pornography quite as much as Lord Campbell, and Catholicism a good deal more. *The Confessional Unmasked* was a selection from the works of Roman Catholic theologians, chosen to reveal the abuse of auricular confession by wayward priests. The book had been openly sold without threat of prosecution since 1836. Its contents were naturally meat and drink to the Protestant Electoral Union, which existed to 'restore and maintain the Protestant Constitution of the Empire as established by the Revolution of 1688'.

Perhaps it was unfortunate that the Union had naïvely bought the plates for printing a new edition of the book from the pornographer William Strange, whom Campbell had sent to prison in 1857. In this case, not only did the evangelical bookseller lose his appeal against conviction. A Protestant activist, George Mackay, gave a series of lectures from a newly expurgated version of the text and was sent to prison for fifteen months. In 1871, the Secretary of the Protestant Electoral Union was also successfully prosecuted for publishing an account of Mackay's trial, including the indictment which contained the objectionable passages from the book. Lord Campbell's assurances had proved worthless.

In 1877, Charles Bradlaugh and Annie Besant were prosecuted for publishing Charles Knowlton's *The Fruits of Philosophy*, a guide to birth control for the working class. The Solicitor-General argued that unless the pleasures of intercourse were tempered by the fear of pregnancy, there would be an end of chastity and decency; that the book was obscene; and that, unless prevented, it would circulate through all classes at sixpence a copy. Though the philanthropic motives of Bradlaugh and Besant, whom *The Times* called 'this well-intentioned pair', set them free on bail, they had at first received sentences of fines and imprisonment. In 1889, a most reputable and long-established London publisher, Henry Vizetelly, who had issued the Mermaid Series of Elizabethan and Jacobean dramatists and had introduced English readers to Dostoevsky, found himself in prison for having published in English translation the novels of Maupassant, Zola and the French Catholic novelist Paul Bourget.[15]

Whatever Lord Campbell's intention, the executive and judiciary had chosen to ignore it. From 1886 they were urged on in their course by the National Vigilance Association, which first began the case against French novels in English translation. As the nation approached the century's end the new prudery, which insisted that whatever might offend women or children had better be kept out of literature and off the stage, was reinforced by the example of such legal proceedings. Where the law alone could not enforce prudery, the publisher, the bookseller and the librarian had it in their power to do so. The result was, as the libertarians described it, to produce sanitized fiction that described a fatuous world to which moral and social correctness aspired, rather than the world and society which existed in reality. The products of this approved writing, wrote George Moore, defending Vizetelly, were 'a motley and monstrous progeny, a callow, a whining, a puking brood of bastard bantlings, a race of Aztecs that disgrace the intelligence of the English nation'. In such a climate, the unexpurgated text of Zola's *La Terre* was more than any English publisher dared to risk issuing until 1954.[16]

If publishers of fiction that had won critical respect faced such hazards, it was not surprising that those who dealt in erotica or pornography began to pack their bags. Charles Carrington, whose literary career began in London as a seller of books from barrows, became the most celebrated publisher of English-language pornography in Paris between 1890 and 1914. Born of a Portuguese family as Paul Ferdinando, he had spent his youth working as errand-boy, van-driver and lavatory attendant before turning to the book trade. He began by issuing unexpurgated editions of the comedies of Aristophanes but rapidly moved on to fiction that was written for him.

Carrington was followed to Paris by H. S. Nichols, publisher of Sir Richard Burton's translation of the *Arabian Nights*. Nichols, who had been in partnership with Leonard Smithers, absconded while on bail. Among others who left abruptly for France at the same time were the photographer Henry Hayler and a bookseller, Henry Ashford. All these fugitives opened shops in Paris and began a postal trade with English customers, though Nichols soon moved on to New York. Scotland Yard sought expulsion orders on these expatriate booksellers. Though the French authorities occasionally agreed to expel the culprits, the orders were seldom served.

Less fortunate than these exiles were men like Edward Avery, who had been a bookseller in London for twenty-five years and a law-abiding citizen. By what the police called 'a certain ruse', he was persuaded to sell an allegedly obscene book to a plain-clothes officer. Other material was found when his shop was searched, including 'beautifully carved ivory models showing persons in the act of coition'. He went to prison for four months.[17]

More dramatic was the fate of Dr Sinclair Roland, alias Roland De Villiers, alias George Ferdinand Springmuhl von Weissenfeld, whom Scotland Yard had concluded on the basis of his surname was probably 'a person of German extraction'. He was the publisher at the 'University Press' in Watford of *Sexual Inversion* by Havelock Ellis and J. A. Symonds. The police first prosecuted a bookseller, George Bedborough, in 1898 on the grounds that the book was 'grossly obscene', though purporting to be 'of a classical or medical character'. Bedborough led the police to Weissenfeld, or rather to a house in Kent where his printing press and books were found. It was not until January 1902 that he was tracked to Edenfield, his home in a residential area of Cambridge. Two Scotland Yard inspectors, Arrow and Badcock, tracked him there, ordered their men to surround the house, and raided it during the night. There was no sign of Weissenfeld. Detective Inspector John Sweeney of Scotland Yard described the sequel.

> At length a secret panel was discovered revealing a passage just large enough to hold one man. At the risk of his life Sergeant Badcock entered stealthily into the dark passage, and flung himself upon a man he found there. Dragged into the light, de Villiers faced his pursuers, a haggard fugitive at bay. Fortunately in the struggle a loaded revolver had been knocked out of his hands, and all his courage fled when the handcuffs were put on. . . . A few minutes later he seemed to develop sudden symptoms of excitement. He called for water. One of the servants of the house ran and filled a glass which was standing on the drawing-room table. De Villiers swallowed a few drops of water which seemed as if it was choking him. A few gasps followed, and he fell dead.

Sweeney wondered whether it was 'unrelated' that Villiers, alias Weissenfeld, used to wear a gold seal-ring with a few grains of poison hidden behind the seal, a poison which he boasted 'would kill a man and leave no trace behind'. In his own case, however, the coroner's jury attributed death to apoplexy.[18]

When Parliament turned its attention to the problem of English pornography that was produced abroad, the proceedings mingled moral outrage and absurdity in more or less equal quantities. The matter was dealt with by the Joint Select Committee on Lotteries and

Indecent Advertisements in 1908, where the principal witness was Chief Inspector Edward Drew of Scotland Yard. Drew revealed that plain-clothes officers were under orders to take accommodation addresses in London, in order to send for indecent publications from Paris. Unfortunately, when the material arrived there was no one who could be prosecuted except the innocent landlady.

Drew also had trouble with the Chef du Sûreté, Gustave Hamard, who explained to the Assistant Commissioner at Scotland Yard that no French law was broken so long as material was sent in sealed envelopes. Worse still was the response when Drew complained to the French authorities that the trade in photographs of naked women 'showing hair on their private parts, would be deemed here to be obscene'. He sent a bundle of these photographs to Paris as proof. The Chef du Sûreté replied that the removal of pubic hair in such photographs was a pecu-liarly English quirk, not shared on the Continent. 'I have the honour to inform you that the photographs forwarded are not considered as obscene in France.'[19]

For the benefit of the parliamentary committee, Inspector Drew also revealed that the underground trade included postcards which appeared quite innocent until they were partly covered by a finger. If the finger was put in the right place they became instantly obscene. The committee chairman asked if some of these postcards could be passed round among the members, so that they might try their hand – or finger – at producing the obscene effects. At first they had no success. 'When certain parts of the photograph are covered up with the finger,' Drew insisted, 'it discloses what is certainly a very obscene photograph.' Since the members were still a little puzzled over the trick of turning an inno-cent photograph into an obscene one, Drew came to their assistance with a demonstration, 'exhibiting the same to the Committee', as the minutes recorded.[20]

At a safe distance from this particular Whitehall farce, Charles Carrington had found premises in the Rue du Faubourg-Montmartre, a narrow commercial street off the boulevards of central Paris. Having first published English translations of literature of the ancient world now banned from general circulation, he had turned his attention to modern writing.

Carrington's list was made up of curious learning, such as Forberg's *Manual of Classical Erotology* (1899), and elegantly written pornographic

'When certain parts are covered up with the finger, it discloses what is certainly a very obscene photograph.' Chief Inspector Edward Drew

fiction. *Dolly Morton* (1899) was a prototype of the 'plantation novel', which mingled sex with sadism under the sub-tropical skies of Virginia. *Woman and her Master* (1904) offered a lurid fable of well-bred Englishwomen as captives in the Mahdi's harem after the fall of Khartoum, though mitigating none of the more general horrors of war. The attraction of some of Carrington's other publications lay principally in their titles. *Raped on the Railway: A True Story of a Lady Who Was First Ravished and then Chastised upon the Scotch Express* (1894) outraged the new woman and appalled Scots the world over by making the pride of the London and North-Western Railway sound like a whisky dray.

Flossie: A Venus of Fifteen (1900) was said to be a work of Swinburne's old age. Though Swinburne corresponded with Carrington and privately wrote schoolboy flagellation epics, there is nothing in this novel that suggests his work. Flossie talks and acts like a female counterpart of P. G. Wodehouse's Bertie Wooster in a world of energetic copulation. Despite the promise of her immaturity in the title, she sounds like

Wooster's contemporary. Another enduring Carrington favourite was *Two Flappers in Paris*, a romance of two heroines from finishing school trying out French vices with the assistance of 'Uncle Jack'. In another vein, his reprinting of *The Yellow Room: or, Alice Darvell's Subjection* (1891) belongs to that more furtive class of reading which James Joyce devised for Leopold and Molly Bloom.

Among his curiosities, the first part of 'Walter's' anonymous diary *My Secret Life*, describing the writer's early years, was published by Carrington in 1901 as *The Dawn of Sensuality*. In the following year, he offered a complete edition of the diary for sale. Carrington also became the publisher of Oscar Wilde after the playwright's conviction and imprisonment in 1895. Yet most of what we know about him comes from such sources as the Parliamentary Joint Select Committee on Lotteries and Indecent Advertisements. 'During the past fourteen years,' Chief Inspector Drew told the committee, 'he has been a source of considerable annoyance to the police here, by the persistent manner in which he has been carrying on his business through the post in the shape of sending catalogues and books of a very obscene and vulgar nature.' The report reveals that Carrington's books were being smuggled into England and that gentlemen of rank, who should have known better, were having them sent to their West End clubs.[21]

Carrington's premises in the Rue du Faubourg-Montmartre eventually masqueraded as a scientific and technical bookstore. He operated openly from 'Ye Olde Paris Booke Shoppe', as he called it. This second shop was at 11 Rue de Châteaudun, convenient for the large number of travellers to and from England who found themselves at the Gare St Lazare. His plain-covered novels, sometimes masquerading as 'Social Studies of the Century' or private publications of the 'Society of Bibliophiles' in London and New York, slipped easily into the capacious pockets of late Victorian and Edwardian overcoats or jackets and hence passed the scrutiny of Customs and Excise undetected.

Carrington was the best-known of the founders of a fugitive book-trade which continued in Paris for half a century, until a more liberal European view of indecency in literature prevailed in England through the Obscene Publications Act 1959. His own career ended with the outbreak of war in 1914, though his books continued to find their way to the Western Front where they contributed to the morale of the British Expeditionary Force. Sir Maurice Bowra recalled with affection his commanding officer who, when the German bombardments began, would summon his men round him and, like a father with his children, would read to them until the shelling stopped from Carrington's edition of Edward Sellon, *The New Lady's Tickler: or, The Adventures of Lady Lovesport and the Audacious Harry*, first published surreptitiously by William Dugdale in London in 1866.[22]

*

To talk of the literature of this erotic underworld as though it were all of a single type or of equal merit would be misleading. A good deal of it in the years following the Obscene Publications Act mocked the moral and social conventions of the day in the kind of *jeux d'esprit* exemplified by Hotten's publication, *Lady Bumtickler's Revels*. In another vein was *Surburban Souls*, published by Carrington in 1901 and written by the lexicographer John Stephen Farmer. An account of obsessional jealousy in a Paris stockbroker's affair with a girl of nineteen who seems part-daughter, part-mistress, it would stand comparison with a good deal of openly published fiction in the late Victorian period. Though it scarcely rivals Zola and Proust, it belongs to the same world.

So far as there was a unity in such literature, it depended on the evidence that pornography like satire is deliberately subversive. It is particularly subversive of its natural enemies. Swinburne, condemned in drawing-room and deanery for the subject-matter of *Poems and Ballads*, created a court for Queen Victoria populated by such grotesques as the Duchess of Fuckingstone, Miss Sarah Butterbottom, the Marchioness of Mausprick and Miss Polly Poke. In another sphere, Dr J. L. Milton had endeavoured to instil chastity in the middle-class young by his *Pathology and Treatment of Spermatorrhoea*, which had gone through twelve editions by 1887. The principle of this gothic ailment was that every orgasm drains away spinal fluid, dooming the victim to a life of imbecility and an early grave. When Milton first published this helpful information, it was saluted by *Harlequin: Prince Cherrytop and the Good Fairy Fairfuck* (1879), a burlesque pantomime whose authors included George Augustus Sala. In one of its scenes, the chorus sang derisively,

> Pity us courtiers, who, moanin' and groanin'
> Are forced willy nilly to imitate Onan,
> Daily and monthly it's surely undoing us,

> Seminal weakness will certainly ruin us.
> Spermatorrhoea,
> That's what we fear,
> We shall all perish from Spermatorrhoea!

While on the subject of moral discipline, the pantomime found a moment to salute England's attachment to corporal punishment as a cornerstone of school and family.

> *Lord.* Good morning, Lady Clara, you I see,
> Are waiting for the King as well as me.
> *Lady.* 'As well as I,' is grammar, Sir, I ween,
> Beside, I wait not for the King but Queen.
> *Lord.* I stand corrected. 'Tis the only way
> That I can stand, excuse the jest, this day.[23]

However sexually alluring or morally repellent erotic writing may seem at the time of its publication, its politics distinguish it in retrospect. In late Victorian England, pornography, if that was what the genre was to be called, took part with enthusiasm in an ideological battle. On behalf of subversion, its authors identified the prevailing forms of moral or social orthodoxy and sharpened their wits. So, for example, if the philosophy of 'Spare the rod and spoil the child' were to be cited, Prince Cherrytop was there to remind its exponents that this maxim was not some biblical injunction, as they had usually assumed. It came from the second part of Samuel Butler's *Hudibras* (1664) and was a sly suggestion for stimulating the jaded libido.

> Love is a boy by poets styled;
> Then spare the rod, and spoil the child.

The child, in this context, was not an errant son or daughter but the god Cupid.

Pornography remained for the most part the preserve of an educated class. An emphasis on the family values of that class was never more sardonically plain than in *Letters from a Friend in Paris* (1874) with its intricate and incestuous couplings, as moral opinion in reality moved towards the formal criminalization of incest. In *Teleny: or, The Reverse of the Medal* (1893) both Camille Des Grieux and his mother are seduced by Teleny. In a 'wicked uncle' novel like *The Yellow Room: or, Alice Darvell's Subjection*, the code of the middle-class nursery is adapted to the fantasies of the brothel. In such publications of Hotten's as *Madam Birchini's Dance* or *Fashionable Lectures* the extent to which moral custom is to be derided requires the whores to dress up as the mothers of their clients.

Did education depend for its success on the tradition of flogging schoolchildren? Hotten replied with *Lady Bumtickler's Revels. A Comic Opera in Two Acts* and George Augustus Sala with *The Mysteries of Verbena House*, under the derisive pseudonym 'Etoniensis'. Sala's Reverend Arthur Calvedon preaches morality at one moment and goggles delightedly through his spy-hole at another. Social progress was mocked as readily as moral conservatism. While the rights of women were increasingly advocated and established, Charles Carrington's publications showed how much more fulfilled the emancipated female would be in the Mahdi's harem and how much more appreciated, if she were black, in the world of *Dolly Morton* and plantation slavery. Was the age of consent raised to sixteen? It seemed all the more important to make plain in the title of her adventures that Flossie was a 'Venus of Fifteen'.

The derisive undertone of pornography was not confined to England. Perhaps it was the relative independence of French women in marriage that led the erotica of Paris and Brussels to elaborate the character of the lesbian heroine. In its turn, the matriarchal culture of the United States inspired, by way of vengeance, a peculiarly American fetishism of bondage, whose female grotesques were unable to move a limb or utter a word. A German insistence on the childhood hygiene of douches and syringes found its reflection in adult pornography. Perhaps, in a retrospective view, it would have been surprising if such forms of writing and illustration had not occurred as a response to the orthodoxies of self-righteousness.

There were, of course, more rebels than pornographers. As George Moore discovered in the case of his own novel, *A Modern Lover* (1883), it was easier every day for the unwary writer to be regarded as indecent, in a culture where the sole criterion of taste was the sensibility of the young unmarried woman. 'It is certain that never in any age or country have writers been asked to write under such restricted conditions; if the same test by which modern writers are judged were to be applied to their forefathers, three-fourths of the contents of our libraries would have to be condemned as immoral publications.'[24]

In the case of Zola, Maupassant, Gautier, Boccaccio and their kind, lawyers and librarians, publishers and critics, now endeavoured to enforce such rules of taste upon writing. Those who hold the rules of the press in their hands are apt to expect compliance, however reluctantly conceded. One form of literature, at least, had simply stepped outside the rules and beyond the law. Dugdale, Hotten, Sala, Carrington and their kind, though they would have thanked no one for suggesting it, were creators of such restrictions as Moore described. If working-class criminals were sometimes known as the poor who fought back, the underworld of literature carried out a fighting retreat by a dissident middle-class Bohemia. In doing so under the onslaught of a prevailing political or moral orthodoxy, the divisions of taste and conviction which it revealed were quite as instructive in their way as anything in Henry Mayhew or Dr Acton.

CHAPTER 6

Entertainments: Town and Turf

WHEN MAYHEW interviewed his coster girl on the causes of promiscuity among her kind, she had no doubt as to where the most pernicious influences were to be found.

> The first step to ruin is them places of 'penny gaffs', for they hears things there as oughtn't to be said to young gals. Besides, the lads is very insiniv-ating, and after leaving them places will give a gal a drop of beer, and make her half tipsy, and then they makes their arrangements.[1]

Penny gaffs were the forerunners of the music-hall, a good deal less respectable than the sing-songs at Evans' Supper Rooms or at the new and enlarged public houses like the Canterbury Arms in Westminster Bridge Road and the London Pavilion in Piccadilly. The penny gaff seemed to be beyond all regulation and all control.

By the Licensing Act of 1737, amended in 1843, all performances in the legitimate theatre were subject to pre-censorship by the Lord Chamberlain and he was to forbid them 'whenever he shall be of the opinion that it is fitting for the preservation of good manners, decorum, or the public peace so to do'. The penny gaffs, however, formed a theatrical underworld, indifferent to such restrictions. They consisted of large shops in working-class areas of London which had been gutted to serve as primitive theatres. The walls were bare and the makeshift stage was a platform at one end, part of the upper floor sometimes being retained as a balcony.

In 1850 the most unlikely gaff was the former Enon Chapel in Clement's Lane off the Strand. This had been built in 1823 by a

Nonconformist minister as a speculative undertaking business, before the Burial Act of 1850 put a stop to the insanitary practice of cramming the pauper dead into shallow city graves. Within twenty years of its construction, 12,000 bodies lay under the wooden floor. In 1842, after the death of the ecclesiastical entrepreneur, it became a dancing-saloon which advertised the novelty of 'Dancing on the Dead. – Admission Three pence. No lady or gentleman admitted unless wearing shoes and stockings.' By 1850, the human remains had been removed to Norwood Cemetery, the floor was cemented over, and the former chapel offered clowns and pantomimes 'gaff fashion'. Within a little while, however, the authorities discovered that not all the bodies had been removed. Indeed, the Nonconformist entrepreneur and his coffin had been cemented into the floor under the stage on which clowns and dancing-girls appeared. The performers and their properties left for an alternative venue, a large shed in the Mile End Road, shortly before the Enon Chapel gaff was raided by the police.

The structure of a chapel was ideal for such entertainment but a large shop or warehouse might be adapted with a little ingenuity. During the 1850s, there was a flourishing gaff in a broad street near Smithfield and the jingling of music could be heard at some distance. Gas-light streamed out into the thick night air, lighting up the faces of the crowd in the road outside. Where the front of the shop had been altered, there were now crudely designed paintings of the comic singers in 'humorous attitudes'. A band was perched on a table against the wall, playing dancing tunes.

The front of the shop formed a foyer and the crowd extended up the stairs to a gallery. Overhead, the ceiling of the makeshift auditorium had been painted sky-blue with whitewash clouds. The audience at such a gaff was young. Mayhew's observations put its members at between eight and twenty years old, the girls in cotton-velvet polkas with dowdy feathers in crushed bonnets. A boy coming out of an earlier performance was asked if there was any 'flash dancing' by the girls who appeared on the stage. He winked and said, 'Lots! Show their legs and all, prime!'

Mayhew described the scene as the audience already in the gaff left when the earlier performance ended.

> The performance inside was concluded and the audience came pouring out through the canvas door. . . . Above three-fourths of them were women and girls. . . . Forward they came, bringing an overpowering stench with them,

laughing and yelling as they pushed their way through the waiting-room. One woman, carrying a sickly child with a bulging forehead, was reeling drunk, the saliva running down her mouth as she stared about her with a heavy fixed eye. Two boys were pushing her from side to side, while the poor infant slept, breathing heavily, as if stupefied, through the din. Lads jumping on girls' shoulders, and girls laughing hysterically from being tickled by the youth behind them, every one shouting and jumping, presented a mad scene of frightful enjoyment.

The performance consisted of singing and dancing, the comic songs coming from draymen and the dancing from girls who were often no more than children. A girl of fourteen, as lightly dressed as any ballet-dancer, moved with more energy than skill. The comic singer in his battered hat and huge bowed cravat was received with 'thunderous applause'. Having shouted at the audience to 'hold their jaws', he sang a song, 'the whole point of which consisted in the mere utterance of some filthy word at the end of each stanza. . . . The lads stamped their feet with delight; the girls screamed with enjoyment.'

Mayhew was one of the most unshockable men of his age, his tone studiously neutral in investigating the lower depths of society. Yet even he was stunned that such performances as those of the penny gaff could be staged publicly in Victorian London.

> A ballet began between a man dressed up as a woman, and a country clown. The most disgusting attitudes were struck, the most immoral attitudes represented, without one dissenting voice. . . . Here were two ruffians degrading themselves each time they stirred a limb, and forcing into the brains of the childish audience before them thoughts that must embitter a lifetime, and descend from father to child like some bodily infirmity.[2]

The songs of the penny gaffs were not allowed to perish after their performance. In about 1850 a number of them were published surreptitiously by W. West in such collections as *The Rambler's Flash Songster*, *The Flash Chaunter* and *The Cuckold's Nest of Choice Songs*. The *double entrendre* of which Mayhew complained was a staple of such numbers as 'The Slashing Costermonger' and his donkey.

> I'm quite a sporting karacter
>   I wisits flashy places,
> Last year, my old voman washed my ass,
>   An' I vent to Ascot races.

A Judge and Jury Show

> I got jist by the royal booth,
>   And there – it is no farce, sirs,
> The king, he often bowed at me,
>   While the queen looked at my ass, sirs.[3]

The king might be a literary figment but there was no doubt as to the identity of the queen, at whose inclusion in the verse the coster audiences stamped and roared approval.

West claimed that his songs made their way to the Coal Hole in the Strand and then to the Cyder Cellars, Maiden Lane, to which 'Baron' Renton Nicholson had transferred his Judge and Jury Show in 1858. Though it was in some respects a rival to the penny gaffs, there was rather more sophistication about the Judge and Jury Show. The 'Chief Baron' in wig and gown, presiding over the drinking and singing with waitresses in diaphanous pink underwear, staged a bawdy re-enactment of the more scandalous courtroom passages of the day's actions for adultery or for 'criminal conversation' with other men's wives.

Nicholson's title reflected the legal hierarchy of the day. There was, as yet, no court of appeal in the legal system. The common form of appeal was to the Court of Exchequer Chamber, presided over by the

Lord Chief Baron. Nicholson constituted himself the supreme arbiter of racy humour just as George Robey, at the end of Victoria's reign, sustained his reputation under the title of 'The Prime Minister of Mirth'.

The Judge and Jury Show had first opened at the Garrick's Head in Bow Street during March 1841, when Nicholson was recovering from his brush with the law over his scandal-sheet the *Town*. Proceedings began each evening with the entry of a gowned crier holding a staff of office announcing to the drinkers and diners the arrival of the 'Lord Chief Baron'. Nicholson, in his robes, bowed to the 'bar', took his seat on the 'bench' and called for a cigar and a glass of brandy and water. An unwary eyewitness, J. Ewing Ritchie, described in shocked cadences what followed.

> A jury was selected; the prosecutor opened his case, which, to suit the depraved taste of his patrons, was invariably one of seduction or crim. con. Witnesses were examined and cross-examined, the females being men dressed up in women's clothes, and everything was done that could be to pander to the lowest propensities of depraved humanity. . . . After the defense came the summing up which men about town told you was a model of wit, but in which the wit bore but a small proportion to the obscenity. The jury were complimented on their intelligent and lascivious appearance, all the filthy particulars which had been noted were referred to in Dog Latin, and poetical quotations were plentifully thrown in; and by twelve, amidst the plaudits of the audience, the affair, so far as the Judge and Jury Club was concerned, was over.[4]

In 1846, after a spell in the Queen's Bench Prison for debt, Nicholson had decided that the one thing lacking in his court was an interlude by living female statues, teenage girls in flesh-coloured tights. They would perform songs behind a curtain and then be revealed in *poses plastiques* before the customers, not moving but standing about in elegant attitudes. This appeared to be as far as the performance could go without attracting the attention of the magistrates and the police.

The growing popularity of the Judge and Jury Show led to its going 'on tour' to Birmingham, Manchester, Newcastle and Glasgow. On Derby Day and at Epsom Races, as well as at Ascot and Hampton Court, 'Lord Nicholson' erected his 'giant pavilion of canvas, containing the good things of this life for the refreshment of the inward man of the sporting community'. 'PAY THE LORD CHIEF BARON A VISIT' was the

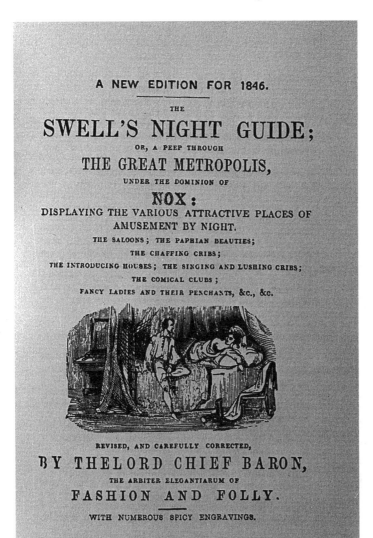

Renton Nicholson's guide to London night-life

invitation on his banner, over a verse of his own, written as 'the first judge that ever sold beef on a race-course'.

> Could Blackstone's shade, in visage pallid,
> Observe the Baron mixing salad;
> Or Eldon's wraith, in shrouded grief,

Just twig his lordship slicing beef;
They'd yearn for plate of boil'd or roast,
And instantly *give up the ghost!*[5]

Renton Nicholson's fame grew as even the legitimate courts before which he frequently appeared seemed to take his self-bestowed title in good part. When cross-examined by Mr Serjeant Byles as a witness in *Bickley* v. *Tasker*, he was asked if he appeared at the Garrick's Head as 'Baron of the Exchequer'. 'Very barren of exchequer, sir, I am sorry to say,' Nicholson retorted among 'Roars of laughter, in which the Chief Justice, Sir John Jervis, joined.' Jervis added that he recognized Nicholson as 'a very old client of mine'. A bystander in court was heard to say, 'Really it appears to me very unbecoming on the part of the Chief Justice to be bandying words with that publican.'[6]

By then, Nicholson's day was almost done and he died in 1861 at the age of fifty-two. Despite his appearances in court and his periods of imprisonment, his Judge and Jury Show added an element of social and political burlesque to the plainer humour of the penny gaff in the constitution of the new music-hall. As a racing man and the editor of a boxing magazine, he also anticipated John Corlett of the *Sporting Times* in forming a link between the turf, the ring and the variety stage.

When the penny gaffs and the supper rooms with their musical entertainments were replaced by the great music-halls of London and the provinces, the original premises were put to other purposes. Stereoscopic photography, with its illusion of views in three dimensions, was soon adapted to erotic purposes. In the later Victorian period, cameras were improved to require far briefer exposure times than the thirty to sixty seconds of the 1850s. A more rapid sequence of photographs could be taken, providing an early form of 'moving picture'. As with the penny gaffs, large shops in Southwark and other working-class areas were gutted to provide rows of machines that were first called 'mutoscopes'. Some of the moving images, the police conceded, might be innocent but most of the rows of primitive 'What-the Butler-Saw' displays were not.

A number of stereoscopic machines, which were also on view, however, are of a very highly objectionable character, consisting of photographs of women undressing, showing their underclothing, and sitting in certain postures in a highly suggestive manner, also there are some paintings of perfectly nude women. . . . Upon each machine is exposed to public view a

The story of the 'Lord Chief Baron'

placard on which is printed a seductive title such as 'How shocking!' 'Naughty! Naughty! Naughty!' 'Very Spicy!' 'Don't Miss This!' etc., as well as in some cases crude paintings of men and women partly undressed.[7]

*

Even those who had never entered a penny gaff could scarcely escape the street entertainments of men like the running-patterer, a wanderer who sold his pamphlets by chanting the contents of each and gathering a crowd about him. Like a running-stationer, he carried his pack on his back, moving promptly from one pitch to another, a source of knowledge to the literate and illiterate alike. Though it was estimated that between eighty and a hundred patterers worked the streets of the capital at mid-century, living in common lodging-houses, some of these were not London men but travelled the country from end to end. Most of their publications celebrated love or death, in the form of murderers brought to justice or trials for adultery and criminal conversation, but sometimes there was a tract on a contemporary political scandal.

One patterer described how he had run away from his parents at the age of sixteen and had been in the trade for twenty years. At first he had done well, particularly during the notoriety of William Corder who was hanged in 1828 for murdering Maria Marten in the Old Red Barn. In the town of Bury, where Corder met his fate, the juvenile patterer had found short-lived fortune with the *Last Dying Speech and Full Confession of William Corder*. 'I worked that there down in the very town where he was executed. I got a whole hatful of halfpence at that.' The pamphlets went so fast that there was no need to tempt wholesale purchasers with a discount. 'Why, I wouldn't give 'em seven for sixpence – no, that I wouldn't.'[8]

Those who gathered round him as he chanted his wares at the side of the street demanded murder or, at least, public scandal. The patterer recalled with affection some of his best pamphlets of the past, notably the account of the Chigwell Row Murder.

> That's a trump to the present day. Why I'd go out now, sir, with a dozen of Chigwell-rows, and earn my supper in half an hour off of 'em. The murder of Sarah Holmes at Lincoln is good, too – that there has been worked for the last five year successively every winter. Poor Sarah Holmes! Bless her! she has saved me from walking the streets all night many a time. Some of the best of these have been in work twenty years – the Scarborough Murder has full twenty years. It's called 'THE SCARBOROUGH TRAGEDY'. I've worked it myself. It's about a noble and rich young naval officer seducing a poor clergyman's daughter. She is confined in a ditch, and destroys the child. She is taken up for it, tried, and executed. This has a great run. It sells all round the country places, and would sell now if they had it out. Mostly all our customers is female. They are the chief dependence we have.[9]

As the years passed, the patterer's fortunes had declined, principally because the murders and scandals of early Victorian England followed in such quick succession that the public tired of each before the stock could be sold, its attention already taken by the next tragedy, as Rush killed the sale of the Wilson murders. Worse still, the opening of Madame Tussaud's waxworks with its Chamber of Horrors had drawn off part of the readership.

Why, there was that Wilson Gleeson, as great a villain as ever lived – went and murdered a whole family at noon-day – but Rush coopered him – and likewise that girl at Bristol – made it no draw to any one. Daniel Good, though, was a first-rater; and would have been better if it hadn't been for that there Madam Toosow. You see, she went down to Roehampton, and guv £2, for the werry clogs as he used to wash his master's carriage in; so, in course, when the harristocracy could go and see the real things – the werry identical clogs – in the Chamber of 'Orrors, why the people wouldn't look at our authentic portraits of the fiend in human form.[10]

This patterer, with his tray of pamphlets round his neck, was living off a current best-seller which revealed the secret life and misfortunes of the public hangman, William Calcraft. In an age of well-attended public executions, which remained one of the great spectacles of national life until their abolition in 1868, the secrets of the hangman as a private person were as eagerly read as those of any film star or footballer a century later. *A Voice from the Gaol: or, The Horrors of the Condemned Cell, Being the Life of the Present Hangman William Calcraft* was the patterer's best hope, as he tried to draw a crowd of customers by intoning his mournful litany.

Let us look at William Calcraft . . . in his earliest days. He was born about the year 1801, of humble but industrious parents, at a little village in Essex. . . . But alas for the poor farmer's boy, he never had the opportunity of going to that school to be taught how to 'shun the broad way leading to destruction'. To seek a chance fortune he travelled up to London where his ignorance and forlorn condition shortly enabled the fell demon which ever haunts the footsteps of the wretched, to mark him for her own. . . . Hence his nervous system is fast breaking down, every day rendering him less able to endure the excruciating and agonizing torments he is hourly suffering, he is haunted by remorse heaped upon remorse, every fresh victim he is required to strangle being so much additional fuel thrown upon that mental flame which is scorching him.[11]

The running-patterer represented a more ambitious street culture than some of his competitors. Yet entertainment was plentiful in the thoroughfares of Victorian London with their strolling actors, whistling men and dancing boys. Some of the spectacles were as traditional as Punch and Judy, the Fantoccini Man with his marionettes, or the travelling acrobats. Others were new, like the exhibition known as the Chinese Shades, a shadow-play performed by stretching calico over a

Punch and Judy frame and setting a lamp behind it. Others attracted their audience by the apparent danger and risk of what they were doing. Among these was the Salamander or Street Fire-King, who appeared at his pitch in stage-armour with a red lion painted on his breastplate. A good deal of the attraction in such performances as his lay in the possibility that the bystanders might see the entertainer suffer pain or harm, as elsewhere they watched men and women put to death by Calcraft, outside Newgate Gaol on Monday mornings. The Salamander spent his days eating fire but not without casual injury. He began by eating the lighted link, or wick, of an ordinary kind which could be purchased at oil-shops. 'There's no trick in it, only confidence,' he insisted as he revealed the art of his profession.

> It won't burn you in the inside, but if the pitch falls on the outside, of course it will hurt you. If you hold your breath the moment the lighted piece is put in your mouth, the flame goes out on the instant. Then we squench the flame with spittle. As we takes a bit of link in the mouth, we tucks it on one side of the cheek, as a monkey do with nuts in his pouch. . . . Sometimes, when I makes a slip, and don't put it in careful, it makes your moustache fiz up. I must also mind how I opens my mouth, 'cos the tar sticks to the lip wherever it touches, and pains sadly.

The medicinal or nutritional qualities of a link were not to be over-looked.

> I don't spit out my bits of link; I always swallow them. I never did spit 'em out, for they are very wholesome, and keeps you from having any sickness. Whilst I'm getting the next trick ready I chews them up and eats them. It tastes rather roughish, but not nasty when you're accustomed to it. It's only like having a mouthful of dust, and very wholesome.

Some of the other tricks, like eating burning sulphur with a fork, were less agreeable. The Fire-King had, by practice and self-control, con-quered the urge to vomit at the taste of it. Yet the taste remained on his palate and he was liable to fits of retching in the morning until he had eaten his breakfast. This was 'the only inconvenience I feel from swal-lowing the sulphur for that there feat'. He showed no resentment at the choice of life to which he had been driven, no indignation at being obliged to demean or injure himself for the amusement of the crowd. However, as a costermonger remarked while he watched the Fire-King's performance, 'I say, old boy, your game ain't all brandy.'[12]

Far worse injuries than these were suffered by men and women in order to provide entertainment. As Serjeant William Ballantine noted in 1882, acrobats and their kind were brought up in their profession from infancy and 'the means used to render their limbs serviceable to the purposes of their wretched trade is to distort their proper movements, which can only be done by subjecting them to infinite torture'. In July 1863, Queen Victoria herself wrote to the Mayor of Birmingham following the death of a young woman known as the Female Blondin, from her feat in crossing the Thames on a tightrope. During an open-air festival at Aston Park, she had walked a tightrope, high above the heads of the spectators, carrying a chair. For the sequel, her head was 'enveloped in a sack so as to completely blind her' and she began to walk back. After what Ballantine called a few faltering steps, either from nervousness or accident, she fell to the ground and was killed instantly. Victoria accused those who had organized the event of having 'sacrificed' the girl's life to the 'demoralising taste' of the onlookers and, worse still, of having decided 'to continue the festivities, the hilarities, and the sports of the occasion' after her death.[13]

*

Though the dancing-girls of the penny gaffs might show their legs and the draymens' songs were bawdy, there was a good humour in such entertainments that was absent from the indoor sports which involved injury or death to animals. Bull-baiting became illegal in 1835 but it took place at London's Agricultural Hall as late as 1870, though the participants were fined. Cock-fighting was banned in 1849 and continued none the less. It was also common for costers to keep fighting-dogs, bull-terriers being the favourite breed. As with cock-fighting, large sums of money were staked on the outcome of an illegal dog-fight and the training of an animal was carried out with care. Among other preliminaries, its ears were cropped in a 'sporting trim' so that opponents would have little chance to get a grip there with their teeth. A young fighting-dog in training was often matched at first against a tame dog – a 'taste dog,' as it was called – in order that it should learn to kill. Parts of the taste dog's body were shaved, so that the young fighting-dog should see where to bite. Though taste dogs were expendable, it was not intended that the trained dogs should fight to the death but nor was it necessarily prevented.

Fighting-dogs would sell at £5 to £25 each if they were bulldogs and a little less if they were bull-terriers. In early Victorian England, while the middle class attended church, the 'Fancy', as followers of human and canine contests were called in the fighting world, went to matches at dog-pits in Westminster and elsewhere on Sunday mornings. Even when the sport was outlawed, the Sunday game continued. 'There's not any public dog-fights,' said one enthusiast in the 1850s, 'and very seldom any in a pit at a public-house, but there's a good deal of it, I know, *at the private houses of the nobs.*'[14]

If dog-fighting became the secret indulgence of wealthier sportsmen, the use of dogs against rats remained a popular sport of the costers and their class. There were public advertisements for the matches, to be held at certain public houses in London which boasted a pit and a good supply of rats, usually caught in the sewers.

RATTING FOR THE MILLION!

———————

A SPORTING GENTLEMAN, Who is a Staunch
Supporter of the destruction of these VERMIN
WILL GIVE A
GOLD REPEATER
WATCH,
TO BE KILLED FOR BY
DOGS *Under 3 3/4lbs. Wt.*
15 *RATS EACH!*
TO COME OFF AT JEMMY MASSEY'S,
KING'S HEAD
COMPTON ST., SOHO,
On Tuesday, May 20, 1851.

———————

To be killed in a Large Wire Pit. A Chalk
Circle to be drawn in the centre for the Second.
Any man touching Dog or Rats, or acting in any
way unfair his dog will be disqualified.

———————

TO GO TO SCALE AT Half past 7 KILLING TO
COMMENCE At Half past 8 PRECISELY[15]

At a public house in Bunhill Row, between two hundred and five hundred rats were killed every week in such matches. At Easter or public holidays, five hundred rats might be killed in an evening. The arena for this sport was usually constructed in the crowded upper room of a public house, where a white-painted and brightly lit ring about six feet across was set up, its wooden walls rising to elbow height. The hat-rack was hung with such notices as:

EVERY MAN HAS HIS FANCY.
RATTING SPORTS IN REALITY.

Admission, up the wooden staircase from the bar below, was priced between sixpence and a shilling. Spectators, holding pots of beer or glasses of gin and hot water, were packed round the wooden rim of the pit or stood upon tables behind. The dingy wallpaper was hung with sporting prints and with glass cases of stuffed dogs who had been champions in their day. Most of the followers of rat-killing had come to the match to back their favourites. Betting was often heavy and it was not uncommon, on such evenings, to hear of wagers like 'the Dog Billy being backed for £100 to kill so many rats in so many minutes'.

In preliminary bouts, a dog would be put into the ring with a dozen rats, while in the grand match of the evening it might face fifty. A time-keeper with a stop-watch checked the rate at which the animal killed the rats, while an umpire ruled in doubtful cases as to whether a rat was alive or dead.

When the fifty animals had been flung into the pit, they gathered themselves together into a mound which reached one third up the sides, and which reminded one of the heap of hair-sweepings in a barber's shop after a heavy day's cutting. These were all sewer and water-ditch rats, and the smell that rose from them was like that from a hot drain. . . . When all the arrangements had been made the 'second' and the dog jumped into the pit, and after 'letting him see 'em a bit', the terrier was let loose. The moment the dog was 'free', he became quiet in a most business-like manner, and rushed at the rats, burying his nose in the mound till he brought out one in his mouth. In a short time a dozen rats with wetted necks were lying bleeding on the floor, and the white paint of the pit became grained with blood. In a little time the terrier had a rat hanging to his nose, which despite his tossing, still held on. He dashed up against the sides, leaving a patch of blood as if a strawberry had been smashed there. 'He doesn't squeal, that's one good thing,' said one of the lookers-on.

When the man with the stop-watch called 'Time!' the dog was lifted out and the dead rats were counted. The spectators went back to their drinking until the next bout was announced. There were also 'private parties' among those whose Sunday-morning amusement was to organize rat-killing in their own rooms. This was expensive, however. Rat-catchers supplied rats to shops which sold birds and other animals. By the time they reached the customer, each rat might cost as much as 6d.[16]

*

By contrast with the stench and blood of a night at a London ratting contest, Victoria's rural England offered an apparently wholesome contrast in its fairs and race meetings, and in its necessary killing of vermin in the form of open-air sports. There was entertainment in the country no less than in the town. The freshness and excitement of a new season was signalled for Kenneth Grahame, as a child in the 1860s, by the approach of a showman's convoy. 'In a hedgeless country of high downland, on a road that came flowing down, a long white ribbon, straight as it were out of the eastern sky, we would watch, each succeeding spring, for the first appearance of these fairy cruisers of the road.' On a closer view, however, it might be doubted whether the entertainment offered to the villages and market towns by the fairy cruisers was more elevating than the raucous verses of the penny gaffs.[17]

> Of old, freaks were the mainstay of every show. The first fair of importance that I ever attended – I was ten years old at the time – was that of St Giles's at Oxford, and I seem to recollect that giants, dwarfs, fat ladies, mermaids, six-legged calves and distorted nature of every variety formed the backbone of the show.[18]

Freaks were popular and simultaneously disturbing, if seeing was believing. However, the truth about the fat lady, Madame Aurelia, was a reassurance to Grahame as a sympathetic child.

> Madame Aurelia's bulk entirely forbade her travelling by train, and a special two-horse van had therefore to be kept at her disposal, yet one could not help feeling uneasily, as one gazed in awe, that there was something wanting. A day or two later, having taken my place in a third-class compartment of a local train, I was greatly pleased when Madame Aurelia – in mufti of course – hopped in as lightly as a bird. Illusion, as the showman knows, is nearly everything.[19]

Even Madame Aurelia could scarcely compete with such aberrations as the Pig-Faced Lady and the Pipe-Smoking Oyster.

The travelling freak-van of old had its contents concealed behind a painted canvas, covering the whole front and depicting the object within under conditions and in surroundings hardly quite realizable, one was tempted to think, within the limitations of a caravan. There mermaids combed their hair on rocks or swam lazily about in warm tropic seas; there boa-constrictors wound themselves round the bodies of paralyzed Indian maidens, in the depth of the Amazonian jungles. . . .[20]

Darwinian science paled as a topic of controversy before Madam Gomez, the tallest woman in the world, thanks to high heels and cork raisers in her shoes. Stepping back on to a concealed dais, she could safely invite the tallest man in the crowd of onlookers to walk under her arm. Tamee Ahmee and Orio Rio were savage cannibal pigmies of the Dark Continent who held Somerset folk in awe. The truth was that the showman James Sanger had acquired them as two 'rather intelligent mulatto children, their mother being a negress and their father an Irishman'. The children were nine and ten years old. 'Feathers, beads and carefully applied paint gave them the necessary savage appearance.' By some lapse of security at Taunton, the two were revealed as impostors. The magistrates intervened, the showfolk fled, and the 'cannibal pigmies' were removed to the Bristol workhouse.[21]

Freaks were no less popular in London, when given the opportunity to appear there. The Hyde Park Fair, which celebrated Victoria's accession, had been graced by Fat Men, Spotted Boys, Fair Circassians, the Hottentot Venus, Miss Scott the Two-Headed Lady, Yorkshire Jack the Living Skeleton, learned pigs and fortune-telling ponies. Most remarkable of the collection was Miss Stevens, the Pig-Faced Lady, in reality a performing bear. The bear's face and paws were partly shaved to give an impression of white skin, while its paws were laced into padded gloves. The animal was strapped into a chair with a table in front of it, and a boy with a stick was concealed to prod it when answers to questions were required, so that the bear grunted in apparent reply. The bear was asked if she was eighteen, whether it was true that she had been born at Preston in Lancashire, whether she was in good health and happy, and whether she was inclined to marry. At each question, a prod of the stick prompted a grunt of assent. When the performance was over, the showman would rush to the front of the caravan as the sight-seers came out and would shout to the next group of passers-by, 'Hear what they say! Hear what they all say about Madame Stevens, the wonderful pig-faced lady!' At Camberwell Fair, however, the authorities intervened and put a stop to some of the freaks, including the Pig-Faced Lady.[22]

Crime and battle became the natural subject-matter of many of the peep-shows. James Sanger had walked to the fairgrounds of Regency England with a peep-show of the Battle of Trafalgar – at which he had fought and about which he could 'patter' – strapped to his back. Twenty years later, his infant son, 'Lord' George Sanger, was to stand before a peep-show of *Murder in the Red Barn*, whose popularity required twenty-six glass apertures so that twenty-six customers could watch simultaneously as the pictures were pulled up into view and the patterer provided a commentary.

> 'Walk up!' I would pipe, 'Walk up and see the only correct views of the ter-rible murder of Maria Marten. They are historically accurate and true to life, depicting the death of Maria at the hands of the villain Corder in the famous Red Barn. You will see how the ghost of Maria appeared to her mother on three successive nights at the bedside, leading to the discovery of the body and the arrest of Corder at Eveley Grove House, Brentford, seven miles from London.'[23]

The story of the murder of Maria Marten and the execution of William Corder remained a classic entertainment of the Victorian period, in print, on the stage as *Murder in the Old Red Barn* and in the fair-ground peep-shows. However, showmen also took notice of topicality. When the Sanger family were at Wantage in Berkshire for the last big fair of the year, the Statute on 18 October, there was a murder at the Red Lion public house. Several field-labourers, one with a reaping-hook, came into the bar. This last man called for a pint of beer and when the landlady brought it he threw the money on the floor. As she bent down to pick up the coins, he cut so far through her neck with the reaping-hook that he almost decapitated her. The Sanger family made hasty alterations to the Red Barn peep-show, cutting out and rearranging the figures, and adding a good deal of red paint. At the fair, their patter described it as 'the authentic representation of the terrible murder at the "Red Lion", as described by an eye-witness of the dreadful deed'.[24]

One reason for local hostility to showmen in early Victorian England was that tricks done by their animals 'were considered, so great was the superstition amongst the ignorant country folk at that day, to be due to supernatural agencies'. George Sanger recalled an old and bent farm labourer warning the spectators, 'Them be witch-taught, them be! Them be witch-taught I tell 'ee! I knows, for I 'ave a-had to work in a place where a charmer abided and small creeturs had to do as she were a-minded they should.' It was, the labourer insisted, a proof of witch-craft in an age of photography and express trains. In 1871, Francis Kilvert found it 'almost incredible', though true, that a country parish-ioner should still bake a toad in a ball of clay, in the ancient belief that during the process it would scratch the name of a thief upon the clay. In Devon, in 1844, Cecil Torr noted from his father's diary, 'Witch-craft a common belief to this day in Lustleigh, and prevalent even among the better-informed classes.' What was evident to their masters about such country dwellers was plainer still to men like Sanger whose customers they were.

> Witches and warlocks were very real beings to them, and Satan was sup-posed to take an active personal interest in the business of blighting crops, spoiling brews of beer or cider, turning milk sour, laming and killing cattle. . . . No wonder, then, that the showman and the conjurer were occa-sionally, to their loss and sorrow, credited with being genuinely in league with the Evil One.[25]

The Mayor of Warminster, for other reasons, regarded showmen as being 'little better than emissaries of the Evil One'. On the advice of his clerk, he declined to recognize their caravans as houses, which made them amenable to arrest as 'rogues and vagabonds' for the crime of 'sleeping out'. They were brought before him next morning in the magistrates' court. When charged, James Sanger produced the little waterproof bag which he wore round his neck and took a parchment from it. This was a royal commission from George IV in recognition of James Sanger's ten years of service in the Royal Navy and his presence at Trafalgar on HMS *Victory*, where he had seen Nelson fall to the deck mortally wounded. The parchment confirmed Sanger's pension of £10 a year and authorized him 'to carry on any trade, craft or profession'. It also gave him travelling rights and threatened with penalties those who impeded him. The Mayor of Warminster capitulated with bad grace. 'You ought to go to gaol, both of you, but this time you may go away.'[26]

A standing objection by magistrates to the presence of such fairs was the amount of violence that accompanied them. Sometimes this was a matter of rivalry between the showmen themselves, as when Hilton's convoy tried to overtake Wombwell's during a night journey to Henley Fair. The incident occurred on the Oxford road, just outside Reading. One of Hilton's men knocked one of Wombwell's drivers off his seat with a tent-pole. A fight began when the Fat Man attacked the Living Skeleton with a door-hook, while the Living Skeleton fought back with a peg-mallet and there was a general *mêlée*. The roaring of animals and shouts of men startled the horses pulling Wombwell's elephant-van. The horses dragged the van off the road, overturning and smashing it, so that the elephants escaped. The fight continued until it was time to take the injured to hospital in Reading, while the elephants were rounded up and walked into the town.[27]

On other occasions, the showmen and their families were the subjects of attack by local inhabitants. At worst, these assaults involved destruction of property, arson and attempted murder.

On 10 August 1839, Lansdown Fair was held on a broad hill-top north of Bath. It was a mile or two from the crescents and terraces of the city, which had once epitomized Regency elegance but had been in decline for almost twenty years. Tents, booths and sideshows were erected in a wide ring upon open turf. At its centre were the droves of sheep, cattle and horses, whose sale drew countryfolk from the entire district. All day the booths were patronized by farmers and graziers who had come to the livestock auctions. At nightfall, the panorama of drinking-booths, gingerbread stalls and sideshows glimmered with candlelight or with flares of rag and tallow.

By 10 p.m. the showmen had begun to dismantle their stalls and sideshows. As they did so, a gang of 'roughs' appeared in force from the Bath road and began to smash up the nearest booths and stalls. Destruction, not robbery, seemed to be the purpose. The mob was led by a woman, 'a red-headed virago', known locally as 'Carrotty Kate'. She was described by George Sanger, whose father suffered at her hands, as 'a big brutal animal, caring nothing for magistrates or gaol, and had long been the terror of every respectable person in Bath and its neighbourhood'.

Finding the drinking-booths, the crowd looted them, beat the owners, and spread out across the fairground. There was too much drink to be carried away but the remaining bottles were smashed and casks staved in, their taps left running so that liquor gushed out on to the ground.

Elsewhere, the torn canvas and broken wood of the booths were set alight. Show-fronts, which represented the livelihood of their creators, were broken into fragments. Some of the showmen told their wives and children to run away into the darkness and lie hidden in the fields of uncut hay. 'Everywhere was riot, ruin, and destruction.' James Sanger loaded his blunderbuss, promising that he would have 'at least one good shot at the wreckers' before he and his caravan were overrun.

The attack continued through most of the short summer night before the mob turned back to the city. The showmen were bruised and bleeding but about thirty of them, armed with improvised cudgels, rode after their assailants on wagon-horses. Having taken the last of the wreckers by surprise, they returned with a dozen prisoners, hands tied behind them, including Carrotty Kate and those whom they recognized as leaders of the assault.

The men who had been taken were tied in 'a living chain' and dragged backwards and forwards through a broad deep pond, the water covering their heads at the centre. Tent-ropes improvised a chain and about forty showmen engaged in this macabre tug-of-war. Their intention was to stop just short of drowning the rioters. After several of the men lost consciousness, the living chain, still tied by tent-ropes, was left 'to drain'.

A little while afterwards, the tethered men were pulled through a taunting crowd to the wagons. One of them shouted, 'Are you a-going to kill us? Ain't you done enough?'

'Not half enough!' replied the showmen.

Another of the captives began to scream 'Murder! Murder!' only to be answered by one of the bystanders: 'Shut it! Save your breath for the next scene. You'll want it then!'

Two by two, the culprits were tied against the large wagon-wheels and flogged by four showmen with riding whips until each had received two dozen lashes. The rural idyll of the day was lost in the horror of men screaming and then stumbling away down the hillside, half naked and covered in blood, while an old woman whose stall had been wrecked shrieked in fury at the leniency of the punishment: 'Make it three dozen! Make it three dozen for all my beautiful chaney ornaments they smashed, the vagebones!'

The proprietor of the waxwork booth turned to the last prisoner, Carrotty Kate. 'We're not going to drag 'ee through the pond, bad as you wants washin', nor use the horse-whips to 'ee, but you're a-going to be made to smart all the same.'

The face of the 'virago' was 'chalky white against the mass of red hair' as six of the women held her over a trestle and she was thrashed by two young women with canes 'until they were tired'. The worst news was not yet known. Most of the Bath mob had come from Bull Paunch Alley and its neighbourhood of slums by the river. As they reached the city, they split up into groups. One of the groups encountered a party of policemen who had now heard of the riot on Lansdown and set upon the suspects, using wooden staves with 'deadly effect'. Several of the slum-dwellers were arrested and sent to transportation for their attack on the showmen. One hit a policeman with an iron bar and crippled him. Convicted of wounding with intent to kill, which remained a capital offence, he was hanged. Such was the reality behind the apparent tranquillity of a formerly prosperous Georgian city and the simple pleasures of a country fair.[28]

*

By the 1890s, popular journalism offered a cultural fusion of entertainment and sport. The world of horse-racing and boxing, bookmakers and tipsters, was also that of Romano's bar in the Strand, of clubs like the Pelican in Gerrard Street, of such papers as John Corlett's *Sporting Times* and Robert Standish Siever's *Winning Post*, as well as of theatrical managers, Gaiety Girls and stage-door rendezvous.

Even in the most censorious decades of the Victorian period, the sporting world preserved a more easy-going morality than its contemporaries. Many of its activities, whether prize-fighting or dog-matches, skirted the law which had banned them. Since Parliament had prohibited off-course cash betting in 1853, a good deal of money had been placed illegally. The bookie's runner succeeded the betting-shops and the more casual services offered by tobacconists and cigar divans in mid-Victorian London.

Away from the prize-ring or the turf, sporting papers like the *Winning Post* contained items that no family newspaper would touch and their columns were known for advertisements offering erotic photographs or 'stereoscopic gems' of the kind that had got *Paul Pry* into trouble. Siever, as editor of the *Winning Post*, was brought before a parliamentary committee to answer for the indecency of a limerick which had appeared

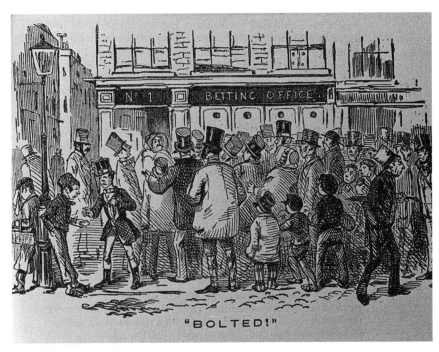

'Bolted!' Frauds of this sort in 1852 led to prohibitions on off-course betting

in the 'Christmas Annual' of his paper. He read it out confidently to his accusers, thereby ensuring that it should be printed in their parliamentary report.

> There was a young lady of France,
> Who decided to give it a chance.
> In the arms of her beau she let herself go,
> And now all her sisters are aunts.

Turning the argument against them, Siever assured the Members of Parliament that 'If you wish to say she let herself go and did something wrong, I say there is a vulgarity there, but it does not suggest that. It suggests that she let herself go, that she was married and did what she liked.' The parliamentarians saw nothing about marriage in the limerick and Siever at length conceded that it was not a poem 'which a clergyman would take for a text', but then 'if you take up some of our religious papers, they are, if you wish to think so, absolutely blasphemous'. The matter was not pursued, perhaps because Siever had a regular column entitled 'Celebrities in Glass Houses', which occasionally led to a writ for libel but usually earned respect from those who might otherwise find themselves the subject of his pen.[29]

That the journalists and followers of the sporting world lived apart from the prudery of late-century was evident to men like Arthur Binstead, 'Pitcher', when he joined the staff of the *Pink 'Un* – as John Corlett's *Sporting Times* was universally known – and was sent to Newcastle-on-Tyne to cover the Northumberland Plate and other events in the race meeting at Gosforth Park. The hotel was occupied as usual by racing correspondents but among the other guests on the night before the Northumberland Plate was 'a smart young fellow, who travelled for a big Manchester firm'. He was talking earnestly to a maid at the office window of the hotel, 'the prettiest girl in the whole of Newcastle'. She was telling him the 'precise location' of her bedroom, even promising to kick over the corner of the mat outside, so that he should not mistake it. A price for his admission to her room and bed had evidently been agreed. Binstead and the other journalists went into Newcastle, drank heavily and returned at 1 a.m. Next morning there was a disturbance, as a group including the hotel landlord, his assistants, a number of the guests, and the commercial traveller in his pyjamas gathered outside the maid's room. The commercial traveller and the maid had agreed that she should be paid £5 for the night. In his confusion that morning, he had given her £50 and now he wanted it back.

In such company and in a hotel for racing men, the landlord took it as a matter of course that a guest might hire any of the maids for £5. His anger was therefore directed against the maid herself, not for spending the night with the commercial traveller but for overcharging him. To the maid, however, £50 was certainly more than she had ever possessed at any one time in her life and more than she was ever likely to possess again. It was at least a year's wages.

'You will give this gentleman back his banknote,' said the landlord firmly, when the bedroom door was at last opened. The maid, however, had decided that her face was her fortune. She was now dressed in her own clothes and carrying her luggage.

'Oh, dear no, nothing of the kind! A gift is a gift. Send for forty constables, if you like, but beware how any of you lay a hand on me!'

Binstead watched her departure as 'the shadows of her taper boot heels, elongated by the wet pavement, disappeared round the corner'.

Taking pity on the commercial traveller, he gave him the name of the horse Barcaldine as a sure thing for the Gosforth meeting. The salesman put £20 on the horse with the 'Nanty Poloney Ironclad Firm' at the far end of the course. Barcaldine romped home. When the novice went to collect his winnings, however, the firm had vanished and he found only its stand, built of old champagne crates, stripped of everything but a leather cloth with the firm's emblem on it. There were also a number of very angry punters. The commercial traveller snatched up the leather cloth as evidence and walked off.

> Next day his body was found floating in the turgid waters of the Tyne, with his right hand still gripping the leathern sign. But it was not a case of suicide. A party of 'Geordies' who had been welshed by the 'Ironclads' had over-taken the man of cotton, on his trudge back to Newcastle, and recognising the 'trademark' he was carrying, and taking him for a member of the Nanty Poloney Syndicate, had – done the rest.

Binstead's account of the tragedy summed up almost every misgiving which the Nonconformist or evangelical middle class of the 1880s and 1890s felt about the sporting world, its lax sexual morals, its violence and its dishonesty. Even those who lent it some respectability were apt to lack that respectability in their private lives.[30]

Almost at the century's end, the death in 1899 of one of the great figures of the sporting scene, John Sholto Douglas, Marquess of Queensberry, seemed an outstanding example of this. He had brought the barbarity of bare-knuckle contests under the civilizing influence of the Queensberry Rules of boxing. As a committee member of the sportsmen's Pelican Club and well-wisher to the National Sporting Club he was admired. Yet he had also dissipated £400,000 of his family fortune in forty years, as much as 150 working men would earn in the course of their lives.

Queensberry attracted publicity on such occasions as when he appeared in 1895 at Marlborough Street police court after brawling in Piccadilly with his son and heir, whom he described without remorse as 'this squirming skunk Percy'. When his wife was expecting visitors for the weekend at their country home, Queensberry arrived with a 'mistress', hastily acquired, and a gang of followers, driving Lady Queensberry and her guests from the house. When Lord Rosebery, as Gladstone's Foreign Secretary, arranged a peerage and preferment for one of Queensberry's other sons, Queensberry's hatred of the Liberal government drove him, horsewhip in hand, to Homburg to thrash the Foreign Secretary at an international meeting. It required the intervention of the Prince of Wales to send the sporting Marquess packing. If he was not to blame for the conduct of a third son, Lord Alfred Douglas, he certainly precipitated the greatest scandal of the 1890s and an action for criminal libel by writing to Oscar Wilde, posing as what Queensberry misspelt as 'a somdomite'. When respectability pursed its lips and looked for a paradigm of sporting life, Queensberry came conveniently to mind.[31]

Yet the sporting underworld and its adjuncts co-existed with that new morally correct culture in which, as its opponents complained, literature was to be written with daughters of eighteen in mind. If there was a literary genre which bridged the division, it was not Robert Standish Siever nor the *Pink 'Un* but the fiction of such best-selling novelists as Nat Gould (1857–1919), whose 130 titles included *The Double Event*, *The Magpie Jacket* and *Racecourse and Battlefield*, the last of which purged sport of vice in a military tale of the turf, the promise of 'A Strong Man's Love' and the charge of the 21st Lancers at Omdurman in Kitchener's reconquest of the Sudan.

*

Those who had been brought up to suppose that racing was the sport of kings were apt to wonder whether throughout much of the Victorian period it was not far more often a sport for cheats. As a pastime, however, it levelled society more than most. Epsom and the Derby belonged as much to the costers and the Cremorne, to 'Baron' Renton Nicholson and 'Lord' George Sanger, as to royalty and aristocracy. *Pace* Karl Marx, it was perhaps sport rather than religion which was to prove the opium of the people. The coster with his donkey-cart at Epsom or Ascot might feel for a few hours that he was nearly as good as the Prince of Wales.

Dishonesty in bookmaking and betting was taken for granted. 'Notice to burglars', read the sign above the safe in the Fleet Street office of the *Sporting Times*, 'There is nothing in this safe. We go racing.' In the 1840s and 1850s racecourses were also known for subsidiary forms of gambling, their practitioners dishonest to a man, the 'tog-tables' being among the most popular. These were tables a dozen feet long and three

Robert Standish Siever,
editor of the Winning Post

feet wide, covered by painted squares, each of which was numbered and some of which were marked with prizes from £1 to £100. The players stood round the table and chose their squares, while an attractive and attractively dressed young woman rolled twelve dice from a wooden box and scooped them together with a flat piece of wood resembling a sickle. Her art was in the rolling and the scooping. The numbers on the dice were then added up to determine the winning square. Handsome prizes were won by the 'bonnets', as the proprietor's stooges were called. None was carried off by members of the public. Yet the lure of a net-work bag displaying newly minted silver crowns and half-crowns, another heavy with gold sovereigns, seldom failed to draw the unwary to the game.[32]

A succession of court cases involving dishonesty on the turf also came to public attention. As late as 1889, there was a court spectacular when Sir George Chetwynd, a former Steward of the Jockey Club, sued Lord Durham for £20,000 in libel damages, after Durham alleged that Charley Wood, Chetwynd's jockey, had pulled horses at Lewes and at Alexandra Park to enable his employer to win large bets on other runners. Chetwynd won his case but with only a farthing's damages. Despite such instances, the turf appeared more honest or immeasurably better regulated by the 1890s. The early Victorian period, by contrast, had been littered with scandals of dishonesty in the major fixtures of the racing calendar. On behalf of the Jockey Club, Lord George Bentinck had campaigned to put a stop to these frauds.

There had been some disagreement as to what was and what was not cheating. Squire Osbaldeston in 1835 decided that the handicapping system had become unfair and corrupt. To level the score, he bought a horse in Ireland, pulled the horse in a trial so that its competitor was seen to win easily, and then won the race itself at a canter. He was hissed by the ladies in the stand and was called to fight a duel by Lord George Bentinck. Osbaldeston had put all the money he could on the race, backing himself to win, and had taken odds of 2–1 against himself from Bentinck for the sum of £200. Far worse scandals had become public. The Derby of 1832 had been won by St Giles, owned by a famous prize-fighter and Member of Parliament, John Gully, because every other horse in the race had been pulled or 'made safe' by agreement among the owners. Osbaldeston might have thought that pulling his horse in a trial was a legitimate *ruse de guerre* but too many other incidents were calculated swindles. John Gully was reputed to have won £50,000 on St Giles and a further £35,000 by similar means when Margrave won the St Leger.

Even those who defended the tactic of pulling horses could scarcely approve of doping. It was not always easy to tell when this had happened, though the favourite for the St Leger of 1834, whom 'Nimrod', alias C. J. Apperley, thought the finest race-horse since the legendary Eclipse, was certainly doped and was beaten before the race was half over.

Systematic fraud by a gang or a syndicate who did not scruple at disguising one horse as another was too common. When Bloomsbury won the 1839 Derby at odds of 40–1, Lord George Bentinck swore that the horse was over the age for the race and, in any case, that it was not Bloomsbury. He could not prove the allegation in this instance but a far greater scandal five years later showed just how such a fraud might be perpetrated.

By the time of the Derby in 1844, two gangs of conspirators appeared to be working independently to win by a cheat. The race was for three-year-olds and, beyond question, one of the horses entered was a four-year-old with a far better chance of winning than the rather indifferent collection of three-year-olds in this particular fixture. The other suspect horse was almost certainly a five-year-old but, as Lord George Bentinck discovered, its age was never to be proved. Moreover, the best of the three-year-olds, Ratan, was mysteriously poisoned in his stable shortly before the race was run.

Stranger still, at the start of the race, the two suspect horses, Leander and Running Rein, were reduced to one when Running Rein kicked and disabled Leander. Whether this was accident or design was never established nor, indeed, was it clear at this stage whether Leander and Running Rein were horses entered by the same or rival conspiracies.

Running Rein was an easy winner but so many rumours had followed the poisoning of Ratan and the disabling of Leander that the winner passed the finishing post amidst howls and jeers from the crowd. The man who gave conclusive substance to the accusations was a farmer, Mr Worley. He had come to see the Derby. When confronted by Running Rein, he immediately identified the horse as Maccabeus, a runner at Newmarket the previous year. Maccabeus had been kept on Mr Worley's farm in Northamptonshire, he and the horse knew one another, and the entire racing world knew that Maccabeus was certainly four – not three – years old.

The Stewards of the Jockey Club and Colonel Peel, owner of Orlando in second place, obtained an injunction in the Court of Queen's Bench to prevent the stakeholders of the prize money for the race from paying it over to the owners of Running Rein. The Jockey Club also declared all bets 'off'. This was followed by the yet more sinister news that the owner of Ratan had dropped dead and by the inevitable rumour that he, as well as his horse, had been poisoned. Mr Crockford had, in truth, died of natural causes.

The owners of Running Rein, fearing prosecution, pre-empted this by bringing a civil action to recover the stake, which had already been given to Colonel Peel. It was not disputed that the owners had backed their horse for large sums of money but so they might have done if it was legitimately entered in the race. Their case was not strengthened, however, when it was admitted that Leander had died and Running Rein had disappeared. Lord George Bentinck found Leander's grave but, when the horse was exhumed, its lower jaw was missing, as if in a deliberate attempt to conceal its age.

In the Court of Exchequer Chamber, Baron Alderson ordered the plaintiffs to produce their horse, Running Rein, and was told that someone had taken it away. 'Then that is horse-stealing,' he announced, 'a case for the Central Criminal Court; and if I am called upon to try the parties implicated, and they are convicted, I shall have no hesitation in sentencing them to a long term of penal servitude.' The truth was that Running Rein had been removed from its stable with the assistance of Francis Ignatius Coyle, described by John Corlett as 'probably the most unutterable of all the unutterable scoundrels who ever disgraced the Turf'. Coyle rode to the stables on a hack to speak to the trainer. Afterwards, he left his hack behind and rode away on Running Rein.

After hasty consultation, the plaintiffs withdrew their action and Orlando remained the winner of the 1844 Derby. Yet Baron Alderson's final comment was one that the turf and the Jockey Club were increasingly to heed.

> Since the opening of this case, a most atrocious conspiracy has been proved to have been practised. Partly, the defendant has only himself to blame for this. If gentlemen would make it a rule to associate only with gentlemen, and race only with gentlemen, such practices would be impossible. But if gentlemen will condescend to race with blackguards they must expect to be cheated.[33]

The memory of such frauds died hard. Even when Fred Archer, the greatest of Victorian jockeys, won the Derby on the Duke of Westminster's horse Bend Or in 1880, it was alleged that the horse had been changed for Tadcaster, who was therefore the legitimate winner. There was no truth in this and the matter was quickly investigated and settled. Meantime, Admiral Rous had succeeded Lord George Bentinck as arbiter of conduct on the turf, ensuring that the Jockey Club kept firm control of the sport, if not of those who followed it. There were still dishonest bookmakers, though many saw themselves as the prey of more sinister presences in the sporting underworld. In the 1890s they complained of new protection rackets by which they were threatened. The Jockey Club endeavoured to initiate a police force to deal with this but proved no match for gangs whose criminality extended far beyond the racecourse.

*

If racing enjoyed the prestige of association with royalty and aristocracy, the belief in the moral superiority of an Englishman's fists to the knives and weapons of cowardly foreigners lent support to prize-fighting and boxing. Prize-fights of the early nineteenth century had an appeal for all classes, not least for patrician romantics like Lord Byron and for the Prince Regent's court. By the time of Victoria's accession, prize-fighting was in decline yet the legends of its golden age persisted sufficiently to make national dramas of the contests that were still clandestinely arranged. A sequence of legal judgments from 1825 to 1882 outlawed the prize-ring. Yet the sport drew tens of thousands to see, for example, Bendigo challenge Caunt in a Buckinghamshire field in 1845 or Tom Sayers fight the American, John Heenan, at Farnborough in 1860. The reputation of the sport was one of stupefying brutality matched by superhuman pluck, its reality a mixture of bare-knuckle boxing and wrestling with few restraints.

These bare-knuckle fights might last for as long as a hundred rounds or more than three hours, by virtue of a rule which enabled a man to be knocked down repeatedly and still continue. If knocked down, he was dragged to his corner and allowed thirty seconds to 'toe the mark' or 'come up to scratch' again. If necessary, his second and his bottle-holder would bring him to the centre of the ring, where he might go down again at the next punch and earn a further thirty-second respite. There was also a break of thirty seconds between the rounds, which might sometimes be as long as fifteen minutes each.

The 'Fancy' expected to see the man they had backed fight until he conquered or dropped to the ground senseless. Three years after Victoria's birth, the essayist William Hazlitt had written a definitive account of a bloody finale when Tom Hickman, 'The Gasman', went down under an onslaught from Bill Neate. The fight had been staged on a low hill outside Hungerford, the ring surrounded by covered carts, gigs and carriages, where the Fancy had come to see 'two men smashed to the ground, smeared with gore, stunned senseless, the breath beaten out of their bodies'. After more than a dozen rounds, the Gasman was beaten but still struggling.

> Neate just then made a tremendous lunge at him, and hit him full in the face. It was doubtful whether he would fall backwards or forwards; he hung suspended for a second or two, and then fell back, throwing his hands in the air, and with his face lifted up to the sky. I never saw anything more terrific than his aspect when he fell. All traces of life, of natural expression, were gone from him. His face was like a human skull, a death's head, spouting blood. The eyes were filled with blood, the nose streamed with blood, the mouth gaped blood. He was not like an actual man, but like a preternatural spectral appearance, or like one of the figures in Dante's *Inferno*.

Yet the Gasman scrambled up and, in this condition, fought on for several more rounds until he fell unconscious for more than thirty seconds and so lost the contest. The spectacle might have disgusted and puzzled middle-class gentility. Hazlitt, however, caught the mood which sustained the prize-ring for so long. Tom Hickman had fought until what seemed, almost literally, his last breath. To Hazlitt, he was a hero rather than a fool. 'Ye who despise the Fancy, do something to shew as much *pluck*, or as much self-possession as this, before you assume a superiority which you have never given a single proof of by any one action in the whole course of your lives!'[34]

Nothing that Hazlitt could write would confer respectability on the prize-ring in the remaining forty years of its public life. Indeed, one of those who travelled with him in the Bath coach that day, the promoter and trainer John Thurtell, was to gain national fame when he was hanged two years later for the brutal and premeditated murder of William Weare. Thurtell was not alone in fixing the results of contests in the prize-ring, though this did little to save him from ruin, the result of arson compounded by gambling debts. But Thurtell died game before the crowds. As the hangman pinioned him, his sole anxiety was to hear the result of the day's championship fight before he was 'turned off'.

More to the point, those who were to read such accounts as Hazlitt's might wonder how it was that men were not killed in these bare-knuckle contests. The answer was, of course, that they might well be killed, some of them in unlikely circumstances. One death resulted from a matter of personal honour at Eton. Charles Wood, who was seventeen, and Ashley Cooper, two years his junior, settled their quarrel when they fought bare-knuckled for sixty rounds and more than two hours. Cooper, though sustained during the match by a pint of brandy, was carried off senseless and died the next day. Charles Wood and one of his seconds were indicted for manslaughter but no witness could be found to testify against them and so they were acquitted. Sentences might, in any case, be little more than nominal. Edward Turner, who killed his opponent in 1816, had been one of the rare cases where manslaughter was proved, but after an 'earnest recommendation of mercy' from the jury he was sentenced to no more than two months' imprisonment. While in Newgate, he was treated by the governor as a celebrity and allowed to receive visitors freely, amongst them 'many titled patrons of pugilism'.

To face death in the ring was the ultimate test of a man's pluck. The 'Fancy' thought no less of the sport when McKay was killed in 1830 by Simon Byrne, and Byrne himself died three years later after a fight with 'Deaf' Burke, as James Burke was known. The fight at St Albans had lasted for ninety-eight rounds, which had taken three hours and sixteen minutes. Byrne was carried from the ring and died three days later, whereupon Burke and the four seconds were charged with manslaughter. At Hertford Assizes, however, Mr Justice Parke directed the jury to acquit all five defendants.

The first years of Victoria's reign brought one civilizing measure in the form of the New Rules of the Prize Ring in 1838. The size of the ring was specified, as was the use of turf, the role of seconds and umpires, and the outlawing of head-butting. Perhaps most important to the spectators, if a contest was undecided all bets were to become void.

By the time that Ben Caunt met 'Bendigo', alias William Thompson, leader of 'The Nottingham Lambs', in September 1845, the prize-ring remained well-supported, despite the efforts of magistrates and police. Bendigo had lost the championship belt to Caunt in 1841 and took this chance to win it back. The presence of the two famous fighters in the neighbourhood of Newport Pagnell alerted the Buckinghamshire police and magistrates to the imminence of a contest but the choice of the site was delayed by the organizers until the last moment.

Thousands of spectators had come by train from London and other cities to Wolverton railway station to see the fight. These crowds followed the 'Fancy' to open land at Lillington Lovel, where the ring was set up. Caunt and Bendigo fought bare-knuckled and stripped to the waist, in knee breeches, faces and fists 'pickled' to harden them. Spectators in the 'inner ring' of onlookers were within reach of the contestants, hitting both Bendigo and Caunt in the course of the fight. Bendigo's supporters, 'The Nottingham Lambs', seemed better organized in aiming blows with their cudgels at Caunt every time he came near the corner where they had gathered. There were numerous alleged fouls on both sides but order and fair play were impossible to enforce in a gladiatorial contest of this kind. However, in the ninety-third round of continuous injury the referee awarded the match to Bendigo, after the challenger claimed that Caunt had struck his genitals.

Some of the most important prize-fights were decided by a foul. William Perry, 'The Tipton Slasher', fought Tom Paddock three times for the championship. The contest was decided in a match at Woking in 1850. Perry was walking away to his corner with his back to his opponent when Paddock ran after him and dealt him a powerful blow behind the ear. This finished Perry but cost Paddock the fight. The Tipton Slasher became champion by default but in the following year lost by a foul when he hit Harry Broome a mighty blow as Broome fell to his knees. It was judged that he was already kneeling when the injury was inflicted.

The last epic fight in 1860 was the most famous of all. It was a match between Tom Sayers, who had begun fighting as 'Brighton Tom' in 1849, winning the championship belt in 1857, and the American John C. Heenan, 'The Benicia Boy'. The venue near Farnborough and the date were a secret that was apparently known to the entire country. However, at the prospect of confronting a hostile crowd of thousands gathered for the spectacle, the authorities preferred to turn a blind eye. As Bernard Darwin described it, 'respectable citizens left their houses at one o'clock in the morning to find their way to London Bridge; every policeman on his beat knew where they were going and wished that he was going too'. One reason for the intensity of public interest was that the more slightly built Sayers was regarded as England's David confronting the bulk of an American Goliath. The two men fought till they could scarcely have continued longer. It was his courage rather than a realistic appreciation of the outcome which convinced Englishmen that Sayers would have won, given ten minutes longer. William Ballantine described the contest, which was 'the talk in every club-room', in less heroic terms.

> It was perfectly fair in intention; both men were thoroughly honourable and their pluck undeniable. Amongst the glories obtained by Sayers was a broken arm. The American nearly lost the sight of one of his eyes, whilst the bodies of both were mauled and battered out of human shape. Two hours and upwards did this disgusting proceeding last, when the victory seemed tending towards one of the combatants, and then the ferocity of the mob broke down the barriers of the ring, a tumult occurred, and which of these two heroes was the victor was never determined.[35]

Trickery was no less common in the prize-ring than on the racecourse, though it might sometimes recoil upon the tricksters, as in an earlier fight between Barney Aaron, 'The Star of the East', and Marsh Bateman on the eve of Bath races in 1828. Aaron was a professional prize-fighter who hired a boxing booth and placarded the town with offers to fight any local contender for a purse of £40. Marsh Bateman, the local champion, accepted the challenge. Several of Aaron's accomplices were in the crowd, placing bets. At first, it seemed that Bateman had far the better of the fight and Aaron, as was his usual tactic in this fraud, allowed himself to get the worst of it during the opening rounds. His accomplices backed him steadily at odds of 2–1, rising to 5–1 while the match continued in Bateman's favour.

At a signal to Aaron that the bets were down, he staged an astonishing recovery in the eighth round, only to find that Bateman weathered the ordeal and came back at him. To the alarm of his seconds, Aaron took numerous blows to the head and was soon bleeding from both ears. By the thirty-fourth round, the two men were exhausted but local sentiment rallied to Bateman. As their man seemed about to fall, the Bathonians cut the ropes, overran the ring and broke up the fight. In consequence, not a single bet was paid, the stakeholders withheld the prize, and for once in his career Barney Aaron made nothing from his performance.

By 1866, the committee of the Pugilists' Benevolent Association had adopted the Queensberry Rules, drawn up by the Marquess with the aid of Arthur Chambers, a professional lightweight boxer. From now on, there were to be no more than twenty rounds, limited to three minutes each, and there was to be a minute between each round. Gloves, which had been used in some contests for half a century, were to be compulsory and there was to be no 'wrestling or hugging'. A man who was knocked down was allowed ten seconds to get up without assistance. If he was hanging on the ropes 'in a helpless state' with his toes off the ground, he was considered to be down. He was also down when on one knee. Skill was to be rewarded by points for attack, 'direct or clean hits with the knuckle part of the glove on any part of the front or sides of the head or body above the belt'. Points for defence were to be given for 'guarding, slipping, ducking, or getting away'. The referee was also to stop the contest 'if, in his opinion, a man is unfit to continue'.

Though Queensberry was not a member of the National Sporting Club when it was founded in 1891, having resigned from all his London clubs, the Pelican Club and its successors did much to institutionalize the Queensberry Rules by offering a venue and patronage for fighters before an audience of the well-heeled and influential.

Illegal prize-fighting continued as a clandestine sport after the 1860s, despite the popularity of the Queensberry Rules and the founding in 1866 of the Amateur Athletic Club which helped to enforce them. The secret prize-matches were little reported and no longer the national events that Bendigo v. Caunt and Sayers v. Heenan had been. As Arthur Binstead and J. B. Booth of the *Sporting Times* recalled, Jem Smith fought Jack Davies in a Sussex wood before carefully selected spectators. Smith became a latter-day champion of the outlawed prizering and fought his Birmingham challenger, Greenfield, on an island in the Seine. Promoters of these fights, notably George Alexander Baird, the 'Squire', had taken the precaution of arranging a number of matches on the far side of the English Channel. Though they were beyond the reach of the English law, they found scant sympathy on the Continent.

The last contest of its kind generated a good deal of unwanted publicity after Smith fought Frank Slavin in the grounds of a château at Bruges on 23 December 1889. As Booth described it, 'Smith's party

John Corlett, editor of the Sporting Times *or*
Pink 'Un

turned up accompanied by thirty or forty of the roughest villains that
ever disgraced creation. They swarmed round the ropes forming the
ring, and with bludgeons, knuckledusters, and even knives, attacked
Slavin whenever he came within reach.' That, at least, had something
in common with the ordeal of Caunt and Bendigo. Yet, to some
bystanders, as Binstead remarked, it was Smith himself who was 'the
most unmitigated blackguard that ever trod the earth'. As the violence
became more general, the police were sent for and the Mayor of Bruges
appealed to Brussels for military assistance. The party was arrested and
the principals were sent to prison. Whatever Byronic glamour the prize-
ring had preserved was lost in the sequel to this incident.[36]

*

The culture of sport in the life of the common people by the end of the Victorian period was marked by an increase in betting, which troubled evangelists and policemen alike. One police inspector remarked in 1903 that 'Betting is increasing out of all proportion to other forms of vice.' No doubt this reflected a parallel increase in the disposable income of a more affluent working class and of many small shopkeepers who enjoyed its custom. Charles Booth, surveying the East End of London, certainly judged that the growth in betting was a sign of better times. '"Gambling," say the clergy (and by this betting is chiefly meant) "presses drink hard as the greatest evil of the day . . . all gamble more than they drink . . . newspapers, knowledge of arithmetic, more holidays, all encourage it."' The public-school ethic of sport as manly and morally improving exercise, celebrated at the century's end by the poetry of Henry Newbolt or boys' magazines like the *Captain*, was unrepresentative of a far greater area of society.

However acute the alarm of the police or the clergy, other voices suggested a more fatalistic assessment of gambling as a social evil. 'You must change the people a bit before they'll stop betting; police orders won't do it. . . . Impossible to stop it without changing the character of the working man, which in twenty-one years shows no change. . . . Betting goes on, and always will. . . . What is a fine of £5 to a bookmaker? He pays it and goes on again.' There had, of course, been changes in the pattern of illegal betting. Betting men were usually known to the police, so that publicans were now reluctant to act as illegal bookmakers for fear of losing their licences. Tobacconists, newsagents and barbers became the new intermediaries. A great deal of illegal betting was also done in the streets, especially during the 'dinner-hour' at midday. The bookies' runners knew perfectly well that the magistrates could only impose a fine of £5. The bookmakers thought this was worth it because the press report of a case would act as an advertisement for their firm. As the law stood, the men who appeared in court were the runners rather than their employers. 'What's the good of carrying me off?' said one man as he was arrested. 'You know well enough that it's not me, but my guv'nor who pays.'

Charles Booth described the scene in an East End street as the pink pages of the *Sporting Times* were delivered after a classic of the turf, when 'All must bet. Women as well as men. Bookies stand about and meet men as they come to and from their work. The police take no notice.'

Derby Night at the Cremorne

See the sudden life in a street after a great race has been run and the news-paper is out: note the eagerness with which the papers are read. Boys on bicycles with reams of pink paper in a cloth bag on their back, scorching through the streets, tossing bundles to little boys waiting for them at street corners. Off rush the little boys shouting at the tops of their voices, doors and factory gates open, men and boys tumble out in their eagerness to read the latest 'speshul' and mark the winner. Every day the sporting papers have a vast circulation; they are found in every public-house and every coffee-shop. They are read and the news and the tips given are discussed before the bets are placed. . . .The more money there is to spend, the more betting is done. . . . Men, women, and children are all at it.

It was by no means clear that this represented a moral decline since the 1850s when costers had played cards for money in beer shops or placed bets on which dog might kill another, or on how many rat-necks it might bite through in four minutes. A marked difference, however, was that the bookie's runner, and the barber or tobacconist as his agent, belonged to a culture professionalized by such institutions as the *Pink 'Un* and the *Winning Post*, the National Sporting Club and the Queensberry

Rules. To the reports of race meetings and boxing matches, the sporting press also added tips for tomorrow, talk of the Tivoli and the Gaiety,
a glimpse of Romano's, saucy limericks and a promise of stereoscopic
gems. *Bell's Life in London* had served something of the same purpose for
undergraduates at Oxford or Cambridge and the middle-class young at
mid-century. Fifty years later, the *Pink 'Un* and its rivals had democra-
tized the process.

As Crockford or Aldridge had claimed the West End with casinos for
the affluent, the East End now boasted houses where gaming was
indulged no less earnestly. Charles Booth visited such a club at the turn
of the century, arriving at one o'clock in the morning, as the rooms were
beginning to fill.

> Entry from the street was through a curtain into a passage, where there was
> a porter, then through a door into a large dancing room; piano at one end,
> bar at the other, seats and small tables round the sides; about eight women
> and several young men clerks, and a few middle-aged tradesmen there. The
> women were of the 'unfortunate' class, but behaving very respectably. A
> lady at the piano strummed waltzes and there was some dancing. An intro-
> duction to the manager – a short thick-set man, professional in the boxing
> line – was followed by soda and whiskey and cigarettes and talk, in which
> the histories of the ladies present were retailed.
>
> Then we proceeded upstairs to the gambling-room, where we found
> about sixty young and middle-aged men round a table playing *chemin-de-fer*,
> and betting with one another whether the banker or punter would win.
> While we were there, there was never more than £6 on the table at once.
> No sum staked was under a shilling, or, so far as we saw, over twenty shillings.
> The majority of the young men were markedly Jewish. The older men
> might have been artisans or shopkeepers, probably both were represented.
> At one side of the room was the tape machine, on the information from
> which at race times there is a good deal of betting during the day. There was
> no excitement at all about the gaming, and not the slightest interest shown
> at our entry. No drinks were served upstairs.

Such establishments were raided by the police from time to time,
'perhaps closed, but are opened again, or make a fresh start in some
way'. One proprietor was overheard saying to his friends as he left the
court after being fined, that 'the club would be open for play as usual
that evening'.[37]

Booth's description has a modernity about it that looks beyond the end of the Victorian period. Such clubs were later to be a cliché of film and fiction. With little alteration, the scene Booth recorded in his *Life and Labour of the People in London* might have served as background to the crime writing of Peter Cheyney in the 1930s and 1940s, to the novels of Patrick Hamilton in the same decades, or even to the pages of Raymond Chandler.

CHAPTER 7

'Misapplied genius'

THAT A figure of propriety, a member of an impeccable profession, should also be a professional criminal contradicted the moral assumptions of Victorian England. No less preposterous was the possibility that such men might share the same bank as members of royalty and nobility. Criminals, in the popular imagination, still came exclusively from the ranks of the poor and the uneducated. Yet major criminals invested substantial sums of money in crime, as they might have done in a legitimate business speculation. If they escaped suspicion because they looked like successful Victorian businessmen, this was because they *were* successful Victorian businessmen. Some of the most spectacular crimes at mid-century were committed by men who did not look like criminals, who had no urgent need of money, and whose ingenuity or sophistication was a match for Scotland Yard.

No panorama of the Victorian underworld would be complete without some account of what Sir Harry Poland, QC, counsel for the Crown in the Bank of England forgery case of 1873, described as 'misapplied genius'. In the form which it took, it appeared to be characteristic of the nineteenth century. As early as 1814, the Stock Exchange had fallen victim to the so-called De Beranger frauds, when a British staff officer from the Continent arrived in a post-chaise at the Marsh Gate, on Westminster Bridge Road, with the news that Napoleon had been defeated and killed by the allied armies in France. Two officers in French uniform followed him. Funds on the stock market rose steadily, substantial profits being made by those who sold before it was discovered that Napoleon was still alive, undefeated, and that the war was not at an end. The funds then fell as fast as they had risen.[1]

The crimes of the disaffected Victorian middle class were on a scale that the burglars who talked to John Binny would never have contemplated. They were the work of men who were no less professional in their attention to forgery or safe-breaking than they might have been as bankers or railway promoters. Moreover, forgers, safe-breakers and confidence-tricksters worked quietly and without violence, their ingenuity making their predecessors seem simpletons and their successors brutal. The flawed hero of the Romantic Age was almost a pattern for the flawed genius of the professional thief.

While some of these men dedicated their talents to removing two hundredweight of bullion from a mail-train or £100,000 from the Bank of England, other mid-Victorians were content with more modest schemes that had an almost perfect simplicity. Henry Mayhew recorded the activities of a man whom he called 'Nicholas A'.

An Irish jeweller, by the name of J. Wise, received a visit from a gallant young officer, lately wounded on active service and carrying his right arm in a sling. The young hero held his rank in a fashionable regiment and was attended by his liveried footman. A glance at him suggested that he was not short of money. Once in the jeweller's shop, he was surprised and pleased to see that its owner's name was 'Wise'.

'Well, that is my name too,' he said.

'Indeed, sir?' said the jeweller eagerly. 'Of the English family, I suppose?'

'Yes, sir. East Kent.'

'Oh, indeed! Related to the ladies of Leeds Castle, I presume?'

'I have the honour to be their brother.'

'James is your name?' asked the jeweller. 'James or John?'

'Neither, sir. It is Jacob.'

'Oh, indeed! A very ancient name.'

After a pleasant discussion of the Wise family and the charms of Leeds Castle, the two men proceeded to business. The young officer had come to hire some silver plate for a reception which he and his wife were giving at the Corn Exchange Tavern. Plate to the value of £150 was selected. At this point, the visitor discovered that he had left his pocket-book at home. Despite the jeweller's protestations, he insisted that he would settle the bill in advance. He could not think of removing a single item from the premises until the deposit of £150 was paid. The footman must return home and fetch the money, while the young officer remained and chatted to Mr Wise. There was one embarrassment, however, in that the young man could not use his injured hand to write. Mr Wise obliged him and wrote the demand at his dictation. 'My dear, do not be surprised at this. I want £150, or all the money you can send by the bearer. I will explain at dinner-time. J. Wise.'

'Now, footman,' said the young man to his servant, 'take this to your mistress and be quick.'

The footman was not quick. Apologizing for the delay, the young officer went to look for him. By five o'clock that afternoon neither master nor servant had returned. Mr Wise locked up his shop and went home. He was met at the door of his suburban villa by his wife, who wondered what had made him so late. She also inquired why he had sent home for so much money.

'But I sent for no money!' said Mr Wise, presumably seeing the trap close upon him.

'How can you say so? Here is your own writing on the note. "My dear, do not be surprised at this. I want £150, or all the money you can send by the bearer." And here is your own name, "J. Wise".'

As Mayhew recorded, 'Every means within the range of constabulary vigilance was taken to capture the offender, but Nicholas and his servant got clear off.' Indeed, Nicholas was already equipped with a forged parliamentary authority for imposing a tax on geese. Armed with this, he collected the tax from unsuspecting farmers for several weeks before their suspicions were aroused. He was last heard of at the age of sixty-two, living with a prostitute in Portsmouth on the five shillings a week his family paid him to stay away from them.[2]

*

Few criminal conspiracies of the Victorian age approached the professionalism of what was variously called 'The Great Bullion Robbery' or 'The Train Robbery' of 1855. The crime that had been planned was by no means unflawed. Its success depended on improvisation This, in turn, grew almost entirely from the absolute self-confidence and mental agility of Edward Agar.

Edward Agar was thirty-seven when he returned to England in the summer of 1853 after ten speculative and lucrative years in America and

Australia. Among his first stock exchange investments was a middle-class fortune of £3,000 in Consols. A year later, he was living with a mistress fourteen years his junior in Cambridge Villas, Shepherd's Bush. With his domestic comforts and servants, his silk hat and frock-coat, he seemed a quiet man of substance who fitted easily into this affluent suburb. Like his neighbours, he managed stock market investments with prudence and foresight. Those neighbours might have been amused by anyone who suggested that Edward Agar had been a professional thief since the age of eighteen. He did not look like a thief, any more than they. He did not behave like one. What need had he of theft? Thieves, as the court reports of the morning and evening press assured them, were pickpockets, housebreakers and their kind. The new arrival in Cambridge Villas was certainly none of those.

Agar was a specialist. By detailed study and preparation, he was to bring the art of safe-breaking to near-perfection. He had never been caught and, even in an age of casual brutality, he had never contemplated violence. In his other conduct, he was a man of honour to a degree that might have brought a tear of sentimental approval to the eye of contemporary moralists. The judge who condemned him at last did so with the words, 'He remained true.' Such was the entrepreneur of Cambridge Villas.[3]

Among his accomplices was an equally unlikely figure. 'Barrister Saward', as he was known to his clients, was twenty years older than Agar with a substantial criminal law practice as a Queen's Bench defence counsel at the law courts of Westminster Hall and in the Central Criminal Court. The world had yet to discover that Saward had also lived as a professional criminal for almost forty years, that this member of the Inner Temple was the reality behind an elusive yet notorious forger hunted by the police as 'Jem the Penman'. Indeed, the notion of a gold robbery being planned by a successful man of business and a well-known barrister within the Inns of Court scarcely fitted the thought patterns of police or public at mid-century.

A taste for gambling brought Saward into contact with William Pierce, an impoverished 'sporting gentleman', who was employed as a clerk at Clipson's betting-office in King Street, Covent Garden. Pierce was thirty-seven years old, a large-faced and rather clumsy man with a taste for loud waistcoats and fancy trousers. With some understatement, he was described as 'imperfectly educated'. The turf was his true schooling.

AGAR, THE APPROVER, OR QUEEN'S EVIDENCE.
(Under sentence of transportation for life.)

*Edward Agar, leader of the Great Bullion Robbery
of 1855, in convict crop*

He boasted of having made £1,000 and more by backing Saucebox
when the horse won the 1855 St Leger. Yet in 1854 he was so hard pressed
that he had to pawn his boots.

Until 1850 Pierce had been a ticket-printer employed by the South-
Eastern Railway, which got wind of his private life as a 'sporting
gentleman' and dismissed him from what it regarded as an office of
trust. But this down-at-heel dandy continued drinking at the Green
Man in Tooley Street and in the beer shops round London Bridge

station, where the railway clerks came for their ale and billiards. In conversation, he heard a story of gold or valuables being sent by train and boat to Paris, from the City of London bullion merchants. It did not happen every day but it happened often enough to be interesting. Pierce checked this story and found that it was true. Gold was regularly shipped from London to the Bank of France, hundredweights at a time. William Pierce, in his simple greed, saw it as the chance of a lifetime.

The South-Eastern Railway Company had been authorized to operate by Act of Parliament in 1836. A site for its terminus was chosen at London Bridge, conveniently close to the commercial and financial district of the City of London. The four platforms were covered by a great glass canopy supported on iron girders, from which hung two rows of iron-framed lamps. Down the brick-built sides of this platform area ran the paired romanesque arches of London brick, which led to offices and amenities.

In June 1843 the building of the railway had reached Folkestone, and the first regular service to Boulogne was begun by the new paddle-steamers of the railway company. The line was then extended to Dover, from which the Ostend ferry sailed. This progress was matched by the Compagnie Chemin de Fer du Nord, operating from the Gare du Nord in Paris. By the 1850s, trains left London Bridge for Paris every day at 8 a.m., 11.30 a.m. and 4.30 p.m. There was an overnight mail-train at 8.30 p.m. and a tidal ferry service. The time of the tidal ferry varied according to high tide at Folkestone, when the steamer could be brought further in to embark heavy cargo.[4]

John Chubb had provided the South-Eastern line with three copies of an impressive 'railway safe' in inch-thick steel plate. Each had the appearance of a three-foot cube with a door formed by the hinged lid, which swung back on a heavy guard-chain. High on the front wall were keyholes to twin locks, whose interior mechanism was some twelve by eighteen inches in area and about six inches deep. A burglar had nothing to work upon but the keyhole with its protective internal barrel and its steel curtain at the mouth.[5]

The weight of gold inside the railway safe might be as much as a quarter of a ton. The coins and ingots were already packed in bullion merchants' chests. At Folkestone, the safe could even be lifted aboard the steamer, if that should prove necessary, while the vessel was berthed close to cranes and gantries at high water. As a rule it went down on the evening mail-train at 8.30 and the bullion boxes alone travelled on the ship under constant guard.

To guarantee security, the railway company ensured that no man could get his hands on both keys to the safe, copies being held by separate officials of the company at London Bridge and Folkestone.

By observation and gossip Agar and Pierce pieced together the routine of the gold shipments. Guarded bullion vans pulled up at the office of the London Bridge station-master, James Sellings. Until that moment, even Sellings was not allowed to know whether gold was being shipped on a particular day. The bullion chests were escorted by the railway police to the station-master's office, where each iron-bound chest was weighed. Then the chests were taken under escort to the luggage van of the ferry-train. The white railway safe with its black bands of reinforcing steel stood in the van, lettered on the front, 'S. E. Ry. LONDON TO DOVER.' Though all three safes were opened and closed by the same keys, only one safe was in use. Once the three bullion boxes had been installed inside it, the heavy steel lid was lowered and the two locks closed by two officials, each with his separate key.

A fully loaded bullion box contained about a hundredweight of gold and required two men to carry it. Three bullion merchants of the City of London were involved in the shipments, Abell, Spielmann and Bult. Not only were the chests locked, each bore a bullion merchant's individual wax seal which would be broken as the box was opened. To lay hands on the stamps of firms like Abell, Spielmann and Bult would, to begin with, involve breaking into their vaults.

Security at Folkestone was a match for London Bridge. Passengers' luggage for the cross-channel steamer went down a chute from the harbour pier to the deck below. The railway safe remained under guard until such time as the bullion boxes were taken out for checking and shipment. One key was held by the superintendent of the railway at Folkestone, another under lock and key in a cupboard of the office on the harbour pier. The bullion chests were taken out, their seals examined, and each chest weighed and checked against its weight in London. Only then was the bullion allowed to leave for Boulogne.

The gold was in the care of the captain and the mate of the steamer. At Boulogne it passed into the custody of the Messageries Impériales, who checked the bullion boxes and their weights again before the onward journey to the Gare du Nord and the Bank of France, from where the boxes were collected by the Paris merchants. Pierce reported all this to Saward, who passed the details to Agar. Even for a professional safe-breaker, a robbery of gold bullion under such circumstances was a daunting challenge. The price of failure might well be fourteen years' transportation to a penal colony.

'I said that I believed it would be impossible to do,' Agar reported.[6]

*

It was not Pierce but Agar's young mistress, Fanny Poland Kay, who persuaded her cracksman that the robbery might be possible after all. Fanny Kay a stolid well-built young woman of twenty-three, had been a barmaid at Tonbridge station. In the course of her duties, according to Serjeant Parry at the Central Criminal Court, she had 'fallen from the position which a virtuous woman always occupies in this country'.[7]

Among other employees known to her was James Burgess, a guard on the South-Eastern since the line to Folkestone had opened in 1843. Burgess was neither criminal nor feckless but a responsible married man who practised thrift and invested the proceeds, purchasing Turkish Government Bonds when the Crimean War news was bad for the Allies, and selling them again as the British and French gained the upper hand against Russia in 1855. Yet Pierce also knew Burgess well and saw how he might exploit the sense of grievance among such railwaymen at the way in which their wages had gone down rather than up with the passing of the railway boom. Percy Cruikshank was to draw Burgess's portrait two years later. The face is hard and expressionless, the mouth thin and a little crooked, the eyes holding a slight suggestion of scorn in them. Despite his years of service, it is not the picture of a conscientious and contented man.

The last of the conspirators was the least likely. William George Tester was only twenty-four in 1854, a young man of education, soft-faced with a curly beard, a wistful expression, and a monocle on a black cord, hanging level with his lowest waistcoat button. In any gallery of Victorian criminal types he would have looked absurdly out of place. In 1855 he was appointed to the traffic department at London Bridge, as assistant to the superintendent. Yet his eye was already on better things and he was briefly to hold a senior position with a Swedish railway company. Neither Burgess nor Tester would be asked to take part in the safe-breaking itself. They would merely pass on information or close their eyes to what was done. Both became accomplices.

If Agar had the promise of allies, he also faced a notable antagonist. As the bullion shipments to Paris began, the directors of the South-Eastern Railway Company appointed a new secretary. He was Samuel Smiles, four years older than Agar, and soon to be the most celebrated model of the self-made man in all Victorian England. Smiles held a medical degree and had written on physical education and on the great engineers. As a journalist, he had edited the radical *Leeds Times*. Despite the Dickensian absurdity of his name, there was nothing frivolous about this future author of such bestsellers as *Self-Help* (1859), *Character* (1871), *Thrift* (1875) and *Duty* (1887). Never were stern moral values more powerfully and attractively embodied.

As Mr Smiles explained, no man was too poor to be a capitalist. The worker who resolved never to spend more than ninepence in every shilling of his wages would save five shillings in every pound and ten pounds in every forty. By forgoing so little, he would become master of so much. Smiles confessed that he himself had not always practised what he preached. In childhood he had robbed his own money-box and squandered the pennies. As he wrote later and contritely, 'I thought the principal use of money was to be spent.'[8]

Mr Smiles belonged to that enlightened class of employers who had lately introduced improved conditions for its clerical workers. At the risk of corrupting them by sloth and late rising, managers and proprietors allowed their workers to arrive at their desks as late as 7 a.m. and to leave for home as early as 6 p.m. Because of what was called 'these near-Utopian conditions', employers would expect 'a great rise in the output of work'. So there would no longer be a meal-break in the eleven-hour day. During a stipulated half-hour, the staff were permitted to eat, so long as they did not cease working. Calls of nature, as the delicate phrase had it, might be answered with permission, an area of a nearby garden being provided for the purpose. In some cases, where these pampered workers wished to be coddled by having heat in the office during winter, they were allowed to bring in their own coal.

Despite his initial pessimism, Edward Agar at length decided that Mr Smiles should become the victim of self-help on a scale which he could never have envisaged.

To being with, Agar needed the two keys to the railway safe in his hands for a few minutes, so that he might take impressions in a tin of green wax, from which he could cut duplicates. Making duplicate keys to a sophisticated lock was not easy. They would seldom work the first time and would require filing down more finely. Having obtained the co-operation of Burgess and Tester, Agar thought this might be possible. Yet since the two keys to the safe were held separately under conditions of secrecy and security, it was hard to see how there could even be a beginning.

The harbour pier at Folkestone appeared to be the weakest link in the shipment of the bullion and Agar went down there in the spring of 1854. The arrival and departure of the steamers for Boulogne was a moment of drama for the holidaymakers in the warm spring weather. Under cover of this interest, he studied the procedure followed by the police with the railway safe. One key seemed to be kept securely in the railway office on the pier but, at least, could be located. The other remained in the hands of the railway superintendent. When there was no bullion shipment to France, the safe remained in the luggage van of the train and travelled backwards and forwards to London. Sometimes it carried packets that were going no further than Folkestone. When that happened, it might only be locked by one key, so that the railway officials at Folkestone pier could open it and deliver the packets to their customers without needing to bother the superintendent of the railway for a second key.

Every means of Agar getting his hands on both keys seemed to be frustrated. Then, in the autumn of 1854, the robbers' plan was saved by a stroke of fortune. One of the Folkestone keys to the safe went missing. Even if it fell into Agar's hands, he knew that it would be useless without the key to the second lock on the safe, which was probably unobtainable. Yet he saw at last how the missing key might open the game.

As he expected, the railway company responded in panic to the loss of what it called the 'mislaid key'. Tester told Pierce that Samuel Smiles and the directors had resolved that 'the safes were to go back to Chubbs'. There was to be 'a recombination of the locks, an alteration of the tumblers, and the fitting of new keys'. Given the value of the shipments, nothing less would do. The superintendent of traffic was given the job of liaising with Chubb. He in turn delegated the writing of letters to his senior clerk, William Tester.[9]

Some weeks later, Tester received a letter from Chubb, announcing a date for the return of the safes with their new keys. However briefly, those keys would be in his hands. Agar hired a room at the Green Man in Tooley Street, a few minutes' walk from the station. Tester was to bring him the keys so that impressions could be made. Five minutes would be long enough. Alone in a hired bedroom of the public house, Agar would press the keys into two tins of green wax. The impressions would give him a sufficiently accurate pattern.

Tester arrived with the keys at the bar of the Green Man where Agar waited. The young man was at first so fearful that he refused to part with them. He asked Agar whether it would not be possible to take the impressions there and then in one of the open booths of the bar. Pierce and Agar argued with him, pointing out the greater risk of taking wax impressions in a public bar. At length Tester agreed. Agar went upstairs and made the impressions. Only when it was too late did he discover that instead of one copy of each key, Tester in his nervousness had brought two of the same.

There was no hope of getting the London Bridge keys again, since these were now securely held by separate officials. The only other known copy of the second key would be kept at Folkestone. Agar set about making yet another key to open the railway office on the harbour pier. He went down to the port and stayed at the Royal Pavilion Hotel, overlooking the pier. The lock on the office door was substantial but primitive with a narrow opening and a spindle, over which the hollow of the key fitted like a glove over a finger. Round this spindle were eight iron sliders, pressed forward towards the mouth of the lock by a powerful spring. Each slider had a tiny knob whose position corresponded with a notch in the central spindle. The correct key would be cut so that it would push each slider back to the point where the knobs and notches were in line. Then the key would turn, moving the knobs into the notches. The bolt would be set free and the door would open. Without the right key, the knobs would merely press against the central spindle and the lock would remain fast.

Agar made his key to the office by 'smoking' the lock. A man of his skill and practice could deal quickly with so simple a lock. When the officials left the building and went to the incoming steamer, they were away for five or ten minutes. They were supposed to man the office at all times but, as one of them admitted in evidence, they saw no harm in leaving it 'unattended' but with the door securely locked while they met the ferry. Had anyone noticed Agar in the dim light of an oil lamp, he would have appeared to be a gentleman in a travelling cloak, shifting about impatiently as he waited for the office to open again. He took two slender half-cylinders of metal, resembling the halves of a very slim pencil split lengthwise. They had been held in the flame of a candle or a lamp until they were black with carbon. He slid first one and then the other into the lock so that between them they covered the central spindle. Then, with the delicacy of long practice, he turned them slowly against the enclosing metal barrel until he felt them rub against the eight notches of the sliders.

When the two halves of the metal probe were drawn out, the carbon which covered them was lightly scratched by contact with the eight little knobs, four on each side. Though it might not be perfect in every detail, this made up a map of the inside of the lock. A key could be cut, tested quite easily in the lock when Agar was standing outside with the coast clear, and the blank filed down where necessary.

Once he was sure of being able to open the office door, Agar sent himself a box of three hundred gold sovereigns, by the South-Eastern Railway, to Folkestone. It was to be collected from the railway office on the harbour pier. He went down to Folkestone and again stayed ostentatiously at the Royal Pavilion Hotel. He had set off for Folkestone on Friday, arranging that the cash-box of gold coins would travel down at a weekend, when there was no bullion shipment to Paris.

Agar went to the railway office at Folkestone harbour pier on a quiet Sunday afternoon. The safe would travel as far as Folkestone and then back to London. If his information from Burgess and Tester was correct, it would be locked only by one key at London Bridge and would require only the key at the harbour pier to unlock it, since it contained no bullion for the cross-channel ferry. John Chapman, who was alone in charge of the office on the harbour pier that afternoon, consulted his documents and saw that Agar's box of sovereigns had come down from London Bridge in the safe that morning.

Chapman looked at the frock-coated and silk-hatted figure, the very emblem of prosperity and success. There was nothing in the office for a visitor to steal, even if he had seemed likely to do so. Chapman took a key from his pocket, went to a wall-cupboard and used this key to unlock it. From inside he took another key, which fitted the second lock of the safe. He went out to open the safe, leaving the cupboard key in its lock.

William Pierce, not shown here in his disguise of railway uniform, brings Agar the second key at Folkestone harbour pier

When Chapman returned, the smartly and expensively dressed visitor was still standing patiently at the counter. Agar opened his box and examined the gold coins for Chapman's benefit, then he returned to the Royal Pavilion Hotel. In his pocket, a flat tin of green wax contained an impression of the comparatively simple key which opened the little cupboard in the harbour pier office, where the second key to the railway safe was kept.

A few weeks later, Agar returned to Folkestone with Pierce. They went to the harbour pier, Pierce dressed in railway uniform, at a time when the safe was not travelling and its key would not be in use. While the two clerks from the office attended the steamer's arrival in the lamplit gloom, Pierce in his borrowed railway uniform entered the office using Agar's key. It was a matter of a few more seconds to cross the room and try the wall-cupboard with the other key which Agar had filed. Scarcely half a minute after going in, Pierce was back again with the second key to the railway safe. By the light of the office window, Agar pressed both sides of the key into the green wax of a shallow tin. As always, he wiped the key clean, so that no future examination of it would show traces of the green wax. Pierce took it, returned it to its cupboard, which he then locked, came out and closed the office door.

There was no trace of the two men by the time the officials returned from the steamer.

*

After such meticulous preparation Agar cut two keys to the safe from his wax impressions, trimming and filing the blanks until they seemed exact replicas. The next step was to try them on the railway safe when it was travelling empty in the luggage van and when no one was paying much attention to it. This must be done on those evenings when Burgess was guard of the mail-train. After seven or eight trips in the luggage van of the train, during April and May 1855, Agar felt both keys move freely and was able to open the safe.

In the next few days, he and Pierce went separately across Hungerford Suspension Bridge to the shot tower on the south bank of the Thames. They bought and carried away two hundredweight of lead shot. Agar then went to a shop on the corner of Drury Lane and Great Queen Street, where he ordered courier bags of drab leather, a type worn by bank messengers or confidential couriers, strapped tight to the body, high up under a travelling coat or cloak. He also bought several carpet bags for the larger packets of lead shot. If one of the bullion chests as well as the safe could be opened quickly on the spot, there was now a means of carrying off even more gold. It would require William Tester to be waiting at Redhill, the earliest stop after London Bridge, so that he could take the first of the heavy bags and be on his way back to London even before the remaining chests had been opened. He might be home in Lewisham while the mail-train was still on its way to Folkestone. Tester was a nervous young man but such a plan offered him a near-perfect alibi.

In May 1855, Agar decided that he and Pierce must be ready to commit the crime every evening from now on. They would rob the railway safe on the first night that it happened to hold a full cargo of bullion. When Burgess knew that the gold had arrived from the bullion vaults in sufficient quantity, he would walk out into the forecourt of London Bridge station and mop his brow with his handkerchief. Agar and Pierce would be watching in a cab near the station approach. By then, Tester would also know of the gold shipment and would be on his way to Redhill.

On 15 May, as Agar watched the forecourt, he saw Burgess come out

While Burgess looks on, Agar opens the first of the bullion chests in the luggage van of the mail-train

in his cap and uniform. Burgess looked in his direction, took out a handkerchief and wiped his face. Agar and Pierce bought first-class tickets for Dover.

Pierce took his seat in a first-class carriage of the mail-train, while the carpet bags of lead shot were taken to the luggage van. Agar, as he later said, 'watched for my opportunity' to board the train, strolling along the platform, as if waiting for someone who was travelling with him. It was almost half-past eight. Burgess walked the length of the train, ringing his handbell to signal its departure. As the train was about to leave, Agar stepped forward like a man wanting to speak to the guard. Burgess looked about, making sure that no one was watching the luggage van at that moment, and gave Agar the signal to board. Agar jumped into the guard's compartment, which formed part of the luggage van, just as the train began to move. Even if anyone had seen him, he would appear like an innocent passenger who had almost missed the train but was taken aboard by the guard. As the mail-train pulled out across the arches above Tooley Street, Agar was secure until the first stop at Redhill. In the carpet bags, apart from lead shot, were the tools of his trade. He had pincers and hammer, box-wood wedges and a pair of scales.

London Bridge to Redhill was a journey of about thirty-five minutes. The safe was opened at once by the duplicate keys, though a clerk,

Thomas Ledger, later suggested – to the discomfiture of the railway company – that the second lock had not been used. Agar had filed a pair of iron pincers fine enough to get a grip on the rivets holding the iron bands to the bullion boxes. When the bands were raised, the lock lost its reinforcement. A row of box-wood wedges was then placed along the crack dividing the lid from the lower part of the chest at its front. The wedges were hammered into place in such a way that the bolt of the lock might be jarred free from the lid. Yet this was to be done with sufficient delicacy to ensure that the lock would still appear intact on casual inspection at Folkestone.

Before Redhill, the first bullion chest had been opened, its rows of gold bars removed, weighed, stored in a large leather bag and replaced by an exact weight of lead shot in small bags. Once again with the care of a craftsman, Agar shut the wooden chest and closed the lock. He hammered down the iron bands and then drove each rivet back into its place. There was little sign that the bands had ever been interfered with. On the following day, the chest would be opened in Paris. The lock would be examined and signs of damage might be found, but it would do until then.

Finally, Agar took out a taper, dies and a stick of red wax, which he melted over the oil lamp. Replacing the wax seals had appeared an impossible trick and Burgess had no idea how Agar could have got dies that were kept locked in the three vaults of Abell, Spielmann and Bult. But these were ordinary dies, bought at an ironmonger's in Tooley Street. Agar's reasoning was simple and perfect. Those who examined the seals at Folkestone or Boulogne would see that they were in place. How closely would they scrutinize them by oil-light? If they seemed different on that night, the railway police might assume that the bullion merchants had more than one die. Even if the seals became suspect, Agar knew the psychology of Victorian petty officialdom. The police and railway authorities boasted that the safe was burglarproof. The bullion boxes would look undamaged, their weights tallying exactly with those noted at London Bridge. The safe and its contents had been under constant guard. In such circumstances, no minor official at Folkestone would start breaking open bullion boxes in the middle of the night on his own authority.

As the engine lost speed on the approach to Redhill, Agar crouched down in a corner of the guard's compartment with Burgess's overall concealing him. The door of the luggage van was opened at the platform and the robber from his hiding place heard Tester's voice, saying to Burgess, 'Where is it?'[10]

Burgess handed Tester a black travelling bag with the first consignment of gold bars, weighing over a quarter of a hundredweight. Pierce left the first-class carriage in which he had been travelling. He walked briskly down the platform, looked round to make sure there was no one watching him, and jumped aboard the luggage van. Abell & Co.'s bullion chest had yielded well over a hundredweight in gold bars. Tester had taken more than a quarter of this.

As the train pulled out towards Tonbridge, the two other chests from Spielmann and Bult were brought out and examined. Spielmann's chest contained hundreds of United States gold 'eagles', coins worth five dollars each. These were better than bullion. They could be exchanged easily and untraceably without bothering James Townshend Saward as a fence. Agar weighed them against an equivalent in packets of lead shot. The gold eagles went into the courier bags and the lead shot into the bullion chest.

Apart from the coins and the gold carried off by Tester, the robbers already had about three-quarters of a hundredweight in bullion from the first chest. The third bullion chest revealed rows of yellow bullion bars beyond anything they had expected. Agar had reckoned on gold to about two and a half hundredweight. Long before they had emptied the third bullion chest, the lead shot was exhausted. Agar insisted that they must not take an ounce of gold which they could not replace by shot. When Pierce continued to argue, Agar reminded him that the weights would be checked at Folkestone harbour while they were still on the train, wearing courier bags stuffed with gold coins and while the bullion was still in the luggage van in carpet bags known to belong to them, bags which also contained the tools that had been used to commit the robbery.

Between Tonbridge and Folkestone, Agar swept the floor of the luggage van to remove any traces of splinters from the bullion chests or flakes of wax from the bullion merchants' broken seals. It was about half-past ten when the mail-train pulled into Folkestone harbour station. In the oil-light, Burgess gave a signal that the coast was clear for the two robbers to leave the van. Encumbered by the weight of the coins in their courier bags, they walked down the length of the train towards the first-class carriages.

At Dover, Agar and Pierce went back to the luggage van to collect their carpet bags. Each of them now had to carry almost a hundred-weight, part of it strapped round the torso in courier bags and the rest divided into carpet bags in either hand. Agar led the way across the road to the Dover Castle Hotel. He went into the coffee-room and ordered supper. While they waited for the meal to be prepared, he went alone for a walk. The keys which he had made for the railway safe were thrown out into the dark waters of the English Channel. They were followed by the hammer, pincers and box-wood wedges, as well as the wax, the dies and the taper.

The two men finished their supper at leisure and stayed in the coffee-room of the hotel until after one o'clock. Then they set off for the London train, approaching the station as if from the quay where the boats from Ostend and Calais docked. Agar's final touch of artistry was to provide Pierce and himself with return halves of tickets from Ostend to London Bridge via Dover. Had there been any alarm following the robbery, the tickets offered apparent proof that he and Pierce had been on the high seas all the time that the 8.30 mail-train was travelling between London Bridge and Folkestone.

At the entrance to the station, Agar put down his carpet bags and presented the tickets from Ostend to London Bridge. The inspector looked at the tickets. Then he looked at the carpet bags closely, without handing the tickets back. He informed the two travellers that they would not be allowed to proceed to London Bridge.

Neither Agar nor Pierce had the least idea of what had gone wrong. They stood in the station lamplight with bags of stolen coins strapped round their bodies and bars of bullion in the thin covering of the carpet bags. The inspector explained that their luggage lacked the chalked cipher which certified that it had been examined by Her Majesty's Customs and Excise. All items from the Ostend boat must pass through the customs house. It was his duty to escort them back there, so that the bags could be opened and the contents scrutinized.

It was Agar who laughed and said, 'I don't think the waterguard would thank us for putting them to the same trouble twice. We came over on the boat from Ostend last night and have been staying in the town.'

The inspector turned to one of his colleagues and asked a question. Better to put passengers through the customs twice than to be repri-manded for letting them through unchecked. Agar and Pierce stood like criminals awaiting a verdict. The inspector turned back, took their tickets and waved them through. Their luck had held so finely that at first they could not understand how. It was their good fortune that the steamer from Ostend that evening was delayed. It had not yet docked. There was no question of their just having come over that night. With the suspicion removed, they could pass on their way with luggage unopened. Yet their Ostend alibi had almost trapped them.[11]

In the first-class carriage of the London train, they drank brandy and water from a soda-water bottle in a mood of relief and hysterical frivolity. In the early daylight, they reached London Bridge. A uniformed policeman, Constable Dickinson of the railway police, approached the first-class carriage and opened the door. Once again the two robbers waited for the worst. But Dickinson had merely opened the door out of courtesy. He asked them whether they would like assistance with their obviously bulky luggage. Even Edward Agar had never anticipated the pleasure of having a policeman to carry the stolen gold for him.

When a cab pulled up, Agar gave loud instructions to the driver to take them to the Great Western Railway terminus at Paddington. As they were crossing London Bridge, he tapped the roof of the hansom and told the driver that it was Euston station they wanted. At Euston, they paid off the cab and hired another to take them to Pierce's house in Crown Terrace off the Hampstead Road.

A few hours later, as soon as the business day began, Agar and Pierce pulled up outside Massey's, a money-changer's shop at the corner of Leadenhall Street and St Mary Axe. Pierce emerged from the shop with £213 10s. in untraceable sovereigns. The next stop was the Haymarket premises of Rudolf Prommel. Pierce came out with a cheque for £203 6s. 8d. in exchange for a further two hundred gold eagles. He now had in his pocket enough money to buy a surburban villa.[12]

'At this time, I was not in want of money,' Edward Agar said, 'but Pierce was, he having been obliged to pledge his things to obtain the means of support.'

On the far side of the English Channel, the bullion chests were checked at Boulogne. James Golder, the mate of the steamer, thought that one of them looked damaged. A porter noticed a crack through which it was possible to see a money-bag inside. Since no one at Folkestone had thought this significant, there seemed no reason for concern at Boulogne. James Major, agent for the Messageries

Impériales, travelled from Boulogne with the gold and witnessed another weighing of the chests on their arrival in Paris. On the next morning, 17 May, a representative of Everard and Co. was summoned, as the recipient of the bullion chest sent by Abell and Co. from London. James Major was present when this and other chests were opened. Monsieur Everard produced his key for Abell's bullion chest and handed it to one of the officials. It opened easily. Its contents consisted of lead shot in neatly tied packets.

The bad news was telegraphed to England. More than a hundred-weight of the gold bullion, belonging to Abell and Co., had been insured through the South-Eastern Railway. Abell demanded compensation. 'The railway company resisted my claim', he said sourly, 'on the ground that the robbery had been committed in France.' The South-Eastern Railway and the Chemin de Fer du Nord fought one another, as the best means of saving face and money alike. Each, for its own part, denied the bullion merchant's claims. Collectively, they asserted that the crime was an impossibility.[13]

*

Contemporary estimates for the melting point of gold varied somewhat and, in any case, depended on the source and composition of the metal. It was put at between 1,200 to 1,420 degrees centigrade, with a general agreement that 1,240 degrees was a good working hypothesis. Whatever the necessary temperature, it was hotter than anything else that Cambridge Villas had ever known.

Agar informed Fanny Kay and the maidservant that he and Pierce had decided to go into the business of leather-apron manufacture. It would be necessary to take the stones out round the hearth of the back bedroom and replace them with fire-bricks. Fanny was not to worry about the furnace heat which would be generated. That was normal when one manufactured leather aprons.

Then the two men set about their task of melting down the gold bullion. There was near-tragedy. In the fierce light of the furnace, Agar was using the tongs to remove a crucible of molten gold. He picked it up and drew it forward over the iron mould. As he was about to tilt it, the crucible broke and molten gold spat across the floorboards, setting fire to them. He and Pierce beat out the flames but not until after the floorboards had been charred. They had avoided the worst but there

The furnace in a back bedroom of Cambridge Villas, Shepherd's Bush,
as Agar and Pierce melt and re-cast the bullion

remained a fair chance that they might burn down Cambridge Villas
before the job was over.

Yet the melting down of the gold was finished without further
damage. Agar disposed of almost all the recast gold bullion, principally
through the agency of James Townshend Saward. The money was then
distributed equally between himself, Pierce, Burgess and Tester. William
Pierce leased a betting-office near Covent Garden. To those surprised
by his new affluence, he made his boast of winning a fortune by backing
Saucebox, which had just won the St Leger at long odds.

Nothing would turn Fanny Kay, now brought home drunk in a
wheelbarrow, into a model of Victorian womanhood. Despite the birth
of a child, she and Agar became irreconcilable. It was agreed that he
should leave Cambridge Villas. He arranged for the remains of the gold
to be brought to Pierce's new villa at Kilburn and hidden there. In the
next few months, Saward would buy the rest and dispose of it. Of the
other two conspirators, Burgess had already given fourteen years' exem-
plary service as a guard on the South-Eastern. He was duly exonerated
by the inquiry into the robbery and returned to his duties. Tester had
several impartial witnesses, including servants of the South-Eastern
Railway, who could swear that he was never on the mail-train, let alone

Agar sells the gold to James Townshend Saward, 'Jem the Penman',
at a public house in the Balls Pond Road

the cross-channel steamer, on the night of the robbery. They had seen him at London Bridge station while the train was still on its way to Folkestone from Redhill.

There was nothing flashy or risky about the manner in which the four men invested their wealth and played the market. Burgess chose Turkish bonds again as the campaign in the Crimea turned in the Allies' favour. He increased his holding in Reid's Brewery, a household name in mid-Victorian England. Tester preferred Spanish Active Bonds, which Agar bought on the stock market for him. Even Pierce invested £2,000 in Turkish bonds as the gold was disposed of, using the rest to buy 'leases, deeds, and securities of different sorts'. A year was to pass, during which Scotland Yard's 'detective police' got nowhere. The South-Eastern Railway Company, under Mr Smiles and his directors, continued to blame the robbery on the negligence of the Chemin de Fer du Nord and refused to pay insurance claims.

As he separated from Fanny Kay, Agar met a friend of Pierce's from the sporting underworld, a pimp called William Humphreys. He took a fancy to one of Humphreys' girls, nineteen-year-old Emily Campbell, and Humphreys behaved as if he had just lost the love of his life. Agar saw the chance of overcoming this hostility when Humphreys said that he needed a short-term loan of £235. Agar made the loan and soon afterwards Humphreys sent a message asking him to come to a house in Bedford Row, Bloomsbury, on an August morning in 1855, to receive back his £235.

When he approached the house, Agar saw one of Humphreys' bullies, who went by the convenient name of Smith. Smith came towards him with a look of exaggerated concern, though he was holding a large bag of coins in his hand. He came close and said in an agitated manner, 'Bill sent me to tell you not to come in. There's a screw loose.'

Agar took the bag of coins, which he assumed would be £235 in sovereigns, and hesitated. He saw two men coming up behind Smith. Smith whispered, 'Run! You'd better run!'

Agar turned and ran. Smith shouted, 'Stop, thief! Stop, thief!'[14]

Agar ran with the second two men in pursuit. One of them laid hold of him, then the other. They were 'private-clothes' policemen under the command of Inspector Frederick Williamson of Scotland Yard. The bag of coins was pulled open and he saw not sovereigns but farthings. They were not worth five shillings. He then heard details of an absurd charge involving people he did not know and a forgery he had never committed. The case was remanded for trial at the Central Criminal Court.

Agar protested his innocence but his evidence was not believed. Against him there appeared witnesses paid by Humphreys, including the helpful Smith and a perjured attorney. It was Humphreys' savage vengeance for the loss of Emily Campbell. The sentence for forgery was still life imprisonment and until 1832 had been death by hanging. Agar was to be held in Pentonville prison until he was taken to the convict hulks at Portland Harbour. From there he would make his last journey to the penal inferno of Port Jackson or Parramatta in Australia. As a precaution, in the event of his arrest, he had previously arranged that Pierce should hold his share of the proceeds from the robbery on behalf of Fanny Kay and their child.[15]

On 2 April he wrote a final letter from Pentonville to Fanny Kay. He asked her to use a little of the money which Pierce held for her in order to buy their child a silver cup as a memento of his father and an atlas, so that she might later be able to show the child where its father was. Though he must surely have wondered whether he could not save himself or win some mitigation by betraying the truth of the bullion robbery, he endured months of privation while awaiting the sailing of the transport and kept silent.

Yet even before Agar left Portland harbour for the far side of the world, Pierce had cheated Fanny Kay, turned her out of the house and left mother and child destitute. By this time, however, even if Fanny Kay knew nothing about the specific crime of the bullion robbery, she had gathered details of some plan carried out against the South-Eastern Railway. In desperation she went to Newgate Gaol and asked to see the governor, Mr Weatherhead. As a result, Edward Agar heard of Pierce's treachery.

From that moment, the other bullion robbers were doomed. Mr Rees, solicitor to the railway company, began conducting his own search at Cambridge Villas. He ordered his men to remove the grate in the back bedroom. When it was lifted out, he found that there were three fire-bricks still embedded in the wall. The area around them, leading into the chimney, 'bore evident marks of having been subjected to great heat'. The floorboards between the grate and the window were 'very much burnt'. Whatever particles of gold might have fallen there had been painstakingly removed before Agar's departure. However, Mr Rees had the floorboards taken up and found underneath 'a number of small bits of gold which had evidently run through the floor'.

The trial of William Pierce, James Burgess and William Tester opened at the Central Criminal Court in January 1857 with Edward Agar giving Queen's evidence against them. All three men pleaded not guilty and denied the truth of his story. Agar was a self-confessed pro-fessional criminal who had not made an honest living since the age of eighteen. 'I have been more or less engaged in the commission of crime ever since,' he told the court candidly. Now he was serving a life sentence and had every reason to tell a string of lies that might win a reduction of his sentence.[16]

Despite such suggestions by the defence, the evidence against the three accused men appeared conclusive and it took the jury only ten minutes to return verdicts. Pierce, Burgess and Tester were all found guilty. Ironically, Pierce was not an employee of the railway company and so could only be charged with simple larceny. Sir Samuel Martin, the trial judge, regretted this but declined to 'strain' the law against him. Burgess and Tester were sentenced to be 'severally transported beyond

Queen's evidence: Agar testifies against the three other robbers at the Old Bailey in January 1857

the seas for the term of fourteen years'. Pierce went to prison for two years, three separate months of it in solitary confinement on bread and gruel. The sentence of life imprisonment on Agar still stood. But the judge had been moved by Agar's chivalry and disgusted by Pierce's conduct towards Fanny Kay. As he told Pierce, 'It is a worse offence, I declare, than the act of which you have just been found guilty. I would rather have been concerned in stealing the gold than in the robbery of that wretched woman – call her harlot, if you will – and her child. A greater villain than you are, I believe, does not exist.'

At this point, the press reported, the entire court broke into 'a loud burst of applause'.[17]

Edward Agar was an enigma to the judge.

> The man Agar is a man who is as bad, I dare say, as bad can be. But that he is a man of most extraordinary ability no person who heard him examined can for a moment deny. . . . It is obvious, as I have said, that he is a man of extraordinary talent; that he gave to this, and perhaps to many other robber-ies, an amount of care and perseverance one-tenth of which devoted to honest pursuits must have raised him to a respectable station in life, and, considering the commercial activity of this country in the last twenty years, would probably have enabled him to realize a large fortune.

Indeed, before Sir Samuel Martin finished, a mantle of romantic moral heroism appeared to descend on the doomed robber. Agar was now 'a slave for life – separate from all he holds most dear. . . . No doubt he deserves all that they have said, but let it be said in his favour that he remained true to you, that he said not a word about this robbery until he heard of Pierce's base conduct.'[18]

There was a concluding legal irony. Anyone who had read the newspapers, let alone sat in court, now knew that Agar was the criminal genius behind the bullion robbery. But he had not been charged with it or convicted of it, having turned Queen's evidence. In law, he was innocent of the theft. Mr Smiles and the South-Eastern Railway Company had not the least right to the loot found in the possession of Pierce and entrusted to him by Agar.

Counsel for the Crown seemed dumbstruck by this. Where, in that case, was all the money from the bullion robbery to go? Sir Samuel Martin, seized by the romance of Agar's sacrifice, announced that it was to be 'handed over to Fanny Kay'. In a split second, by judicial decree, this unlikely young woman acquired the proceeds of the most celebrated robbery of the age. On 17 January, having lectured its readers on the new breed of professional middle-class criminals revealed by the case, *The Times* turned to the ruling by Martin. 'By this decision, Agar's wish will be realized, and the woman Fanny Kay will become possessed of a sum which will enable her to lead an easy, and, if so inclined, a reputable life.'[19]

*

One man, closely involved in the disposal of the stolen gold, escaped arrest and suspicion as the others went to their fates. James Townshend Saward, the forger, was spared by Agar and the law alike. With his Inner Temple chambers and a substantial practice in criminal law as a defence counsel, he remained for a little while longer a familiar figure to the police and the underworld as 'Barrister Saward'. By this time, as he himself later revealed, 'I had made several thousand pounds a year by various sorts of crime. These sums I generally paid into my account at Coutts Bank. I had had an account with them for some time.'

Of all crimes among the professional class, forgery was traditionally the most lucrative and the most perilous. It struck at the heart of commerce and confidence, often bringing into doubt the good name of the

Crown. Even Dr William Dodd of Clare College, Cambridge, a famous preacher, royal chaplain and composer of sentimental verses, died for it on the gallows at Tyburn in 1777, despite a hot bath and a surgeon waiting to revive him when he was cut down. When the Victorian period began, the penalty remained transportation to a penal colony for life.

Saward recruited his lieutenants from grateful clients who had avoided prison by his forensic skill. He built up a network of accomplices in such a way that other offenders did not even know his name. They would have to be caught before danger threatened him. By the early 1850s Saward's current protégé was a Shoreditch safe-breaker, Henry Atwell. As a forger, Saward used safe-breakers to enter commercial premises, open the safe and steal blank cheques, leaving no trace of their visit. He would then go to some lengths to get the signature of his victim on a legal document or letter – even upon a genuine cheque. Using this, he was able to inscribe a near-perfect imitation on the blank cheques. J. B. Doe, a large ironmongery firm in Brick Lane, Ash and Co., ironmerchants of Upper Thames Street, and Dobree and Sons of Tokenhouse Yard were among the firms whose safes were opened and closed again by Atwell. Through other connections, principally a man named William Salt Hardwicke, Saward could also cash forged cheques in London drawn on a bank in Hobart, Tasmania. Australia was a world away and months passed before anything was found amiss.

The cashing of forged cheques involved James Anderson of Whitechapel, former gentleman's valet and hotel waiter. Anderson posed as an employer of casual workers and recruited respectable dupes. The existence of substantial 'surplus labour', as the unemployed were termed, helped to ensure a co-operative work-force. Anderson would employ a man for a day. They would meet only in public, usually at Gregory's Hotel, Cheapside, or the Magpie in Bishopsgate Street, Farringdon Market, or the Eastern Counties railway station in Shoreditch, subsequently known as Liverpool Street station.

Among his day's errands, the dupe would take a cheque to the bank and get it changed for cash. One of Saward's men would shadow him as he took the forgery to the bank. If there was any sign of trouble from the cashier, the shadow would give the alarm to his accomplices. The dupe could offer little information, even if the police interrogated him, having no idea who the criminals were. If he was tempted to make off with the proceeds of the cheque, he would come face to face with Anderson or one of the shadows.

Years had passed without the police getting any closer to 'Jem the Penman', who was now in his fifties. Having once been content to forge cheques for £50 or £100, he now felt the need to provide more handsomely for his old age. Not even the most security-conscious were safe from him. Most embarrassingly for the victim, he managed to defraud the famous safemakers Bramah & Co. of several hundred pounds early in 1856 by stealing their blank order-form for a cheque-book, forging the order and cashing three cheques at Barclays Bank in quick succession. After that, he grew more ambitious. Cheques for £500 and £1,000 were tried. There were two refusals by the cashiers and the hired dupes were left to explain as best they could.

Barrister Saward also found the means of cashing forged cheques for considerable amounts by defrauding solicitors. Alfred Turner of Red Lion Square had his pocket picked to order in a London street in March 1856 and his firm's blank cheques thus passed into Saward's hands. However, solicitors' cheques were generally made out with greater than usual care because the sums of money were often very large. The forgers would therefore need a signed cheque from Alfred Turner as their model. Saward set about defrauding Turner's partnership by financing the project like a good Victorian capitalist.

He sent Henry Atwell, under the name of 'Hunter', to Turner's offices with a bogus IOU for £30 which had apparently been long due for payment by 'Mr Hart', who lived at James Anderson's address in Shoreditch. Anderson, alias Hart, took the money owing to Turner's offices in response to the solicitor's demand. A few days later, Atwell followed him, hoping for a cheque from Alfred Turner. He was paid in cash. Jem the Penman was philosophical. 'Mr Saward said that could not be helped for once.' Atwell tried again with a bogus IOU for £100. The larger the sum, the more likely that the collected debt would be paid by the solicitor as a cheque. This time he was successful. Saward borrowed Alfred Turner's cheque for long enough to make his copies before it was cashed.

It was not long before Turner and his firm were astonished and alarmed to find that hundreds of pounds at a time were now being withdrawn from their bank account without their authority. The forged cheques were presented to their bankers, Gosling and Co., and the money was paid out in £50 notes. The numbers of these notes were recorded by the bank and the currency was, in theory, traceable. But Saward had little to learn about laundering money. By the time that the £50 notes were tracked down they were in Hamburg, having been changed by a long succession of holders whose identity was unknown and who had vanished across Europe or over the North Sea to England.

It might seem curious that Saward should have needed so much money. He lived, as Dickens described Scrooge, 'solitary as an oyster' in his Inner Temple chambers. But his pastime was gambling, a weakness of lawyers at a time when George Augustus Sala swore that more money was staked on such races as the Derby and the Oaks by Her Majesty's judges than by any other group of men. Moreover, Saward had little talent as a gamester. Yet just as the risk of detection quickened his blood, so did the thrill of winning and losing. He lost considerable sums in places where hazard and other games of dice challenged the old supremacy of cards. He left a small fortune in the patrician St James's Street rooms of Crockford's, in the lamplit dens of rookeries like the Seven Dials and the Holy Land, and at private gaming parties.

By the age of fifty-six, he was at the peak of his long criminal career, a man who wanted one more triumph. In the course of picking pockets in London, a cheque drawn on Laytons Bank in Yarmouth came into the hands of Hardwicke and Atwell. Saward already knew the names of four firms of solicitors – three in Yarmouth and one in Norwich – who banked with Laytons. He soon discovered others. A provincial bank presented fewer difficulties to a forger than its larger competitors in London, money sometimes being drawn simply by a letter from the depositor. The plan was to hit four firms of solicitors at once so that none would have time to warn the others. They included the partner-ship of Reynolds and Palmer in Yarmouth, as well as those of Prestons and Chamberlains in the same town. The victims in Norwich were to be Miller and Son. As before, the firms were asked by Saward's accomplices to collect 'debts' owed by men in London. The money was paid and the firms wrote cheques to their clients. The 'clients' then copied the genuine cheques on the blank forms for very large sums and cashed them.

Saward at last overreached himself by a swindle of this sort on Barclays Bank and their Yarmouth agent Gurneys for a still larger sum. Atwell and Hardwicke went down to Yarmouth and toured the solicitors, employing each firm to obtain payment for an IOU from a man in London. Though each IOU had a different name, all the demands were received and answered by Saward, using a false name and an accommodation address. He sent the money in payment of each debt to the solicitors with an accompanying letter in which he complained bitterly of the harshness of his creditors. His style was practised and convincing. Meantime, he had kept the letters from the four firms of lawyers as models for the proposed forgeries.

It was important that Hardwicke should be able to put on a show of wealth and prosperity at Yarmouth. Most of all, he needed to be seen drawing large sums of money from a bank, as though the supply was inexhaustible. Hardwicke and his friends habitually scattered false names about them as a first line of defence. On 11 September 1856, he went into Barclays Bank in London with £250 supplied by Saward to finance the last big hit. Avoiding his own name as a matter of habit, Hardwicke paid the money in as 'Mr Whitney'. It was to be forwarded to the 'corresponding' bank in Yarmouth. When Mr Whitney was known as a man who could draw such a sum on Barclays, there would be no questions asked about cheques made out to him by reputable firms of solicitors.

Though the plan to defraud four law firms at once was more ambitious, Saward's final triumph was not intrinsically more dangerous than any of his earlier successes. He played his own part perfectly, while Hardwicke and the cracksman Atwell returned to Yarmouth. On their arrival, Hardwicke went to the bank to draw some of the money. He went in confidently and introduced himself as James Ralph, forgetting in an absent-minded moment that he had put the money under the name of Mr Whitney. The clerk received the inquiry politely, checked the details and, just as politely, said that the bank had never heard of Mr Ralph. Hardwicke tried to repair the damage by saying that of course Mr Whitney had paid the money in but that it was for the use of Mr Ralph. The clerk replied just as courteously that the bank had no instruction nor information to that effect.

Hardwicke left the bank in something of a panic and communicated the bad news to Saward. Saward sent his accomplice James Anderson to Barclays in London under the name of 'Mr Roberts'. Anderson informed the bank that he could support the fact of Mr Whitney having placed the money there for the use of James Ralph. Unfortunately, Mr

Whitney had now left for a tour of the Rhine and would not be back for a couple of weeks. Morris, the clerk at Barclays, insisted that only Mr Whitney could put the matter right. If he were to come in upon his return and confirm that the money was to be paid to James Ralph at Yarmouth, Barclays would convey that instruction to their agents.

From that moment, all the conspirators but Saward lost their heads. He wrote to his accomplices, 'I can see through a brick wall sometimes – I see through one now. Be guided by me.' Hardwicke and Atwell remained in lodgings at Yarmouth for a day or two more. Saward decided that it was imperative for 'Mr Whitney' to return from his tour of the Rhine as quickly as possible, visit Barclays Bank and explain that the £250 was intended for the credit of James Ralph. On 15 September, the day on which Anderson had made his fruitless journey to Barclays as 'Mr Roberts', Saward wrote to Hardwicke in Yarmouth. 'I expected today to have rectified your unfortunate mistake,' he told Hardwicke, and then gave him the bad news that Barclays wished 'Mr Whitney' to go to their head office and 'explain the matter'. A whiff of criminality was rising up around the incident and the visit of 'Mr Roberts' on 15 September had only intensified it.

Saward instructed Hardwicke, as James Ralph, to go to the bank in Yarmouth and ask to see the paying-in note – 'mind, you must see it'. He was to say that he had written to Mr Whitney and that he would call again in a day or two. Hardwicke was then to come straight from Yarmouth to London, as Mr Whitney returning from his tour of the Rhine. He must write a new paying-in note, specifying that the money should be paid to James Ralph at Yarmouth. Then he could go down to Yarmouth and collect it. The cleaning out of four firms of solicitors was postponed.

The whole episode of 'Mr Whitney' and 'James Ralph' had not so far lasted more than a week. But the banks now discovered that the handwriting of the two men appeared identical, as did their physical descriptions. Though it was not criminal for a man to send himself money under another name, it might be a cover for crime. John Moss of the City of London police was given charge of the case. Confidential warnings to firms of solicitors revealed that several had been asked to collect IOUs and that the debtors' letters now proved to be in the same writing, sent from a public house in Great Queen Street, London.

The police visited the suspects' lodgings in Yarmouth and discovered that 'James Ralph' was known to them as William Salt Hardwicke, who had served a sentence of seven years in a penal colony. They took Hardwicke and Atwell into custody. Among Hardwicke's papers, they found letters from four firms of local solicitors, demanding payment of bogus IOUs. The search spread to London and to Hardwicke's rooms in Nelson Square, an alley running off Blackfriars Road just south of the river. He had taken no precautions in the event of a search. Evidence of fraud practised on the Australian banks was found and charges were brought against both Hardwicke and Atwell for obtaining £1,000 by forgery in the previous June.

Saward's letter written to Hardwicke on 15 September did not arrive in Yarmouth until after the police had visited the lodgings. It was 'opened and read' by them, revealing all Saward's instructions. There was no address to identify its origin and it was signed only by 'Your faithful friend, J.' 'J' was evidently at the centre of the conspiracy but was not yet identified with the shadowy presence of 'Jem the Penman'. Saward had no idea of the arrests until he went to visit Mrs Dixon, Hardwicke's cousin who knew him as 'Mr Sharp'. She told him that the police had searched Hardwicke's rooms in Nelson Square.

The investigation had penetrated the Penman's carefully layered anonymity and had almost reached his chambers at 4, Inner Court. He told Mrs Dixon to burn any letters that might have come for her cousin and to burn any more that arrived in future. If the police came asking questions, she should say that a lady had called and taken Hardwicke's correspondence away.

At the trial of Hardwicke and Atwell for the earlier £1,000 forgery, both men received sentences of transportation for life. It was put to them that they could scarcely hope for leniency while their accomplices remained at large. Atwell tried to save as much of his skin as possible by informing on Saward and Anderson. Saward left the Inner Temple for the last time. After nearly forty years as a professional criminal, the 'Barrister' was forced into hiding.

John Moss was on plain-clothes duty on Boxing Day 1856. He had gone to Oxford Street with Constable Huggett after a tip-off that Saward was hiding in a coffee shop under the name of 'Hopkins'. Moss went in and asked the proprietor if Mr Hopkins was around. The keeper of the shop said obligingly that Mr Hopkins had just gone out to the public house in Oxford Market.

Moss sent Huggett to check this story, while he kept watch on the coffee shop. A door at the back of the shop opened, 'very gently'. Moss ran back through the coffee shop and burst into the room before the door could be locked against him. He found an elderly man alone.

'Mr Hopkins, I have been looking for you.'

'My name is not Hopkins,' said the old man.

'No,' said Moss, 'I believe it is Saward.'

'You are entirely mistaken,' the old man said, 'I know nothing at all about him.'

Presently, Huggett returned and was told by Moss to do his duty.

'I must apprehend you for forgery – for forging a bill of £1,000 upon Messrs. Heywood and Co., and with also being concerned with Anderson, Hardwicke, and Atwell.

'I don't know any such persons,' the old man replied.

He then confided that he wished to use the water-closet, a tribute to the modern plumbing of the coffee house.

'You may go,' Huggett said, 'but before you do you must be searched.'

The search produced two blank cheques on the St James's branch of the London and Westminster Bank. According to both officers, as they drove down Oxford Street through the cold December afternoon, the man in their custody said, 'I suppose I need not hold out any longer. My name is Jem Saward.'

Anderson had already been arrested. With the capture of Saward, all four members of the conspiracy were accounted for. But those who heard the case must have reflected that effectiveness counted for nothing without the sudden betrayals and self-interest, the irrational greed and hatred, which characterized certain members of the gang.

Saward was tried for the crimes of Jem the Penman at the Central Criminal Court on 5 March 1857 with his accomplice James Anderson. Henry Atwell and William Hardwicke testified against him. When he failed to brief counsel, Baron Pollock informed him that the case would go ahead anyway. Saward swore that a brief had been prepared but he had been 'unable to retain counsel'. It was the simple brief of an 'entirely innocent' man. Pollock refused an adjournment and the case went ahead without defence counsel. At the end of the Crown's evidence, Saward and Anderson declined to make any defence. It took the jury five minutes to bring in verdicts of guilty against both. Baron Pollock remarked that Saward, as a barrister, was a member of 'an

*The Bank of England Forgeries,
1873: Austin Bidwell*

honourable profession', and regretted that such 'ingenuity, skill and talent has received so perverted and mistaken a direction'. The men were sentenced to transportation for life.[20]

*

Jem Saward had resembled a Dickensian creation, not out of place among the legal grotesques of *Bleak House* and not unlike Fagin as the controller of petty criminals. Yet within twenty years of his downfall, the craft of forgery had become more sophisticated and ambitious than he could have imagined. Its practice crossed frontiers and oceans to confront the greatest of financial institutions. Even Jem the Penman never contemplated taking on the wealthiest bank in the world. Yet within the first two months of 1873, the phrase 'safe as the Bank of England' acquired an ironic ring. Before February was over, the Old Lady of Threadneedle Street had been robbed of £100,000 without even noticing. Though precise monetary equivalents are apt to be misleading, the loss was about thirty million pounds in modern terms.

The robbery was carried out by four young Americans, George Bidwell who was in his thirties and three accomplices in their late twenties: the other men were his brother Austin Bidwell, George Macdonnell and Edwin Noyes, alias Edwin Noyes Hills. It was afterwards alleged by Allan Pinkerton that they were working to the plan of Walter Sheridan or George Engles, two masterminds of the New York underworld. The crime certainly required initial finance, which Engles was thought to have provided.

The Bidwell brothers and their accomplices exploited the use of bills of exchange, which had existed in varying forms for at least three thousand years. In an age before rapid communication they remained essential to international trade. A merchant, in the nineteenth century as surely as in the seventeenth, would go to his bank before setting off and purchase one or more of these bills of exchange. He was then able to go to a bank in the country to which he travelled and draw money to the limit on the bill. The bill would then be returned to the issuing bank who would redeem it at the end of a three-month period from its purchase. Conditional bills might warrant a query but unconditional bills were more readily accepted. George Macdonnell could forge either.

A bill of exchange was rather like a private banknote. The authorities were alert to any attempt to forge such a bill but the same danger existed with nineteenth-century banknotes in general. Indeed, a bill of exchange appeared more secure than a banknote. It was not automatically transferable from one person to another, as a banknote was. A criminal would also require a substantial sum of money to buy one in the first place. When it was presented, the receiving banks were careful, if not downright suspicious. The Bank of England would not recognize such a bill from a businessman who did not have an account with it, which would require recommendation or references. Even when received, the bill must pass as a matter of routine before the eyes of a committee of scrutiny in Threadneedle Street. The bank's experts were said to be able to smell 'bad paper' at a considerable distance.

The two Bidwell brothers and George Macdonnell appeared in England in April 1872, evidently three young men doing a grand tour of Europe. George Bidwell had already defrauded banks in Bordeaux, Marseille and Lyon of some £6,000, using a genuine letter of credit from the London and Westminster Bank with false letters of credit from the North Wales Bank, forged for him by George Engles. The Bidwells had earlier tricked their way through Wall Street, while Macdonnell joined them as a middle-class rebel who had been educated at Harvard. Though they travelled a good deal in Europe before the following spring, George Bidwell's tour of France, which he unblushingly called 'as brilliant a "solo" operation as has been recorded in the annals of crime', was sufficiently profitable to finance the scheme to rob the Bank of England.[21]

As a result of his solo venture, George Bidwell's face was now too well known for him to take the lead. It was his brother Austin who was to open an account with the Bank of England under the name of 'F. A. Warren', posing as an entrepreneur who was financing the building of American-style railway Pullman cars in England. His story was that he hoped to have the cars ready in time for travellers to a proposed International Exhibition in Vienna. His business required him to pay large sums to the account of C. J. Horton at the Continental Bank in the City of London. Austin Bidwell was now both 'C. J. Horton' and F. A. Warren.

The Continental Bank was happy to receive 'Horton's' money. To open an account with the Bank of England as 'Warren', however, he needed a recommendation. Since 1855, the bank had had a Western Branch in Burlington Gardens, parallel with Piccadilly behind the Burlington Arcade and the Royal Academy. The head office of the bank in the City of London was the great temple of finance and commerce. Its Western Branch had been opened to gather private customers from the fashionable squares and streets of St James's and Mayfair. The operations of the Western Branch were so limited otherwise that, as Austin Bidwell discovered, it was not authorized to deal with bills of exchange in any form.

He lost little time in finding a recommendation. One of the streets running north from Burlington Gardens was Savile Row with its exclusive tailors and their expensive shops. Bidwell was sure that some of them must have accounts at the Western Branch, which was within a couple of minutes' walk. On 17 April 1872, from his vantage as a window-shopper near the Burlington Arcade, he saw the master tailor and military clothier Edward Hamilton Green emerge from the Western Branch and return to his shop at 35 Savile Row. A few days later, 'F. A. Warren' called at the shop and ordered a range of expensive suits. Austin Bidwell, alias Warren, was an open-handed customer and was soon on good terms with Edward Green. Bidwell confided a few weeks later, as he paid a substantial bill in cash, that he was carrying a good deal of money and was uneasy about leaving it at his lodgings.

Would it be possible for him to deposit it in the safe of the shop? Mr Green agreed, until he saw that the amount was about £2,000. It was impossible for him to take responsibility for so large a sum. He advised Bidwell to deposit it at once in a bank. His own bank was close at hand and he offered to introduce Bidwell to the manager. A few hours later, Bidwell had an account with the Bank of England's Western Branch.

For six months, he deposited and withdrew money and bought and sold bonds. His account was impressively active, even if most of the money did not stay in it for long. In November 1872, he asked the manager, Colonel Francis, to accept a few genuine bills of exchange for relatively small amounts. Francis explained that the Western Bank was not authorized to deal with such matters but agreed to ask the Head Office in Threadneedle Street if they would help his customer. The Head Office did so and, before long, the acceptance of Austin Bidwell's genuine bills through the Western Branch was routine. The account of a man who was to have the exclusive manufacture of Pullman cars for British and European railways was an important acquisition, even for the Bank of England.

While travelling in Europe that autumn and winter, Bidwell bought blank forms for bills of exchange in various languages, as well as a selection of pens, inks and stamps. Macdonnell set off to find engravers in Paris and elsewhere who could produce blocks for printing bank bills without understanding their exact significance in another language or the purpose to which they might be put in England. By December 1872, Austin Bidwell and Macdonnell were back in London at the Grosvenor Hotel near Victoria station, where Macdonnell worked night and day, as it seemed, copying the handwritten portions of genuine bills on to the forgeries.

The manufacture of the Pullman cars was supposed to take place in Birmingham, in the heart of industrial England. On 28 December 1872, George Bidwell posted from Birmingham ten genuine bills of exchange of European banks to the Western Branch of the Bank of England with a letter from 'Mr Warren'. The total value of the bills was £4,307 and they were accepted by the bank.

Austin Bidwell travelled to Paris and bought from Rothschilds Bank a bill for £4,500 at three months' notice. He also bought from a stationers in the nearby Rue Lafitte blank bill-forms on blue paper, identical to those used by Rothschilds. On 17 January 1873, the Bank of England changed the genuine Rothschilds bill. Six days later it changed three more, apparently identical, for £4,250. They were the first of George Macdonnell's forgeries and passed the bank's scrutiny without question. The name of Rothschild enhanced their pedigree, not least because Lionel Rothschild was a director of the Bank of England. It would need a bold scrutineer to suggest that the bills of his family's financial house were suspect. The conspirators had chosen their first target with that in mind.

They then arranged that a series of genuine debts to be paid by 'Mr Warren' should fall due, so that the bank would not be surprised by the arrival of more bills of exchange to cover the amounts. The majority of bills were still posted to the bank by George Bidwell from Birmingham to match Austin Bidwell's story as 'Mr Warren'. On 25 January, eight more bills of exchange, two of them from Rothschilds, arrived and were accepted for £9,350. All were forgeries. They were followed by a third batch for £11,072 which also passed scrutiny.

Speed was increasingly important, since the forgeries would be detected as soon as the three-month bills had to be redeemed by the issuing banks at the end of March. The extent of the robbery during January and February 1873 was shown by the bills exchanged and the money withdrawn: 21 January, £4,250; 25 January, £9,350; 3 February, £11,072; 10 February, £4,642; 13 February, £14,696; 21 February, £14,686; 25 February, £19,253; 27 February, £26,265. The total of the robbery amounted to £100,405 7s. 3d.

Apart from their skill in defrauding the bank, the four young men were pioneers of money-laundering, a term not generally current until Al Capone used a chain of laundries as a means of putting the proceeds of crime into legitimate circulation. In 1873, however, the money from the bills of exchange went first into the account of 'C. J. Horton' at the Continental Bank, in the form of Bank of England notes. These were then withdrawn, taken to the Head Office of the Bank of England in Threadneedle Street, where the Bidwells were not known, and exchanged for gold sovereigns. The sovereigns were used to buy Bank of England notes, under any names they chose, and the notes might be used to buy whatever bonds or other securities they pleased.

They had never believed that it would be so easy. 'It appears', said George Bidwell, 'as if the bank managers had heaped a mountain of gold out in the street, and had put up a notice, "Please do not touch this", and then left it unguarded with the guileless confidingness of an Arcadian.'[22]

Edward Noyes had now joined them in England as the clerk of 'C. J. Horton'. The intention of the Bidwells and their two accomplices was to continue in business until 25 March. They would then have about a week to get clear of England and disappear to Europe or America with the proceeds of one of the biggest robberies in history, the whole of it transferred into gold coins and untraceable negotiable bonds. By the end of February, they already had such a stack of bonds that there was no room to keep them. They began to parcel them up and post the paper to hotels and safe deposits in New York to await their arrival.

The final packet of forged bills of exchange reached the Western Branch of the Bank of England on 28 February. Colonel Francis handed them to his discount clerk, who returned presently and pointed out that one of the issuing banks had omitted to put the 'sighting date' on two bills for £1,000 each. It was a reputable London bank, B. W. Blydenstein & Co. Colonel Francis sent a messenger with the bills to the banking house in Great St Helen's to have the dates filled in. Next day, Saturday 1 March, he received a short note in reply. 'We have no record of these bills and can only assume they are forgeries.'

These was no explosion of anger in Burlington Gardens or Threadneedle Street, merely the intense silence of dismay and disbelief. Had not George Macdonnell forgotten to date the forged bills, how much longer might the Bank of England have been duped?

The robbery was discovered on a Saturday. That day, the four conspirators knew that the game was up. Edward Noyes had been identified as a man whose employer 'C. J. Horton' had an account at the Continental Bank in London. When Noyes went to collect foreign currency from the bank on Saturday morning he was recognized and arrested. George Bidwell was waiting at Garraway's coffee house and saw Noyes marched away between two policemen. By Monday morning, the plight of the Bank of England was headline news and rewards were offered for the capture of the remaining three criminals.

The Bidwell brothers and Macdonnell escaped for the time being and two of the fugitives managed to leave England before the net tightened. Austin Bidwell was arrested in Cuba on 20 March. There was a controversy over the legality of his detention, let alone of his extradition to England in the absence of any treaty. It was only when the Bank of

*The Bank of England Forgeries, 1873: the hearing of charges
before the Lord Mayor*

England's lawyers in New York brought proceedings against him for £100,000 that Judge Faucher of the United States Supreme Court ruled in favour of the legality of Bidwell's arrest. The Secretary of State in Washington then gave authority for the fugitive to be handed over to the British police but Bidwell frustrated this for several days when he escaped from the military prison in Havana by jumping from a balcony into a crowd beneath. He was recaptured a few days later and by the end of May was back in London, in Newgate Gaol.

Macdonnell was arrested as he arrived by ship in New York. By June, he too was lodged in Newgate Gaol. George Bidwell fled first to Ireland, then to Edinburgh, where he was tracked down and arrested on 2 April.

The Old Bailey trial opened on 18 August 1873 and was a match for the crime itself. It was discovered that three Newgate warders had been bribed to assist in the escape of the prisoners. There were allegations of guns being smuggled to them through the agency of a third Bidwell brother who was present during the hearing. The courtroom was cleared and searched. Mr Justice Archibald was said to be the first judge

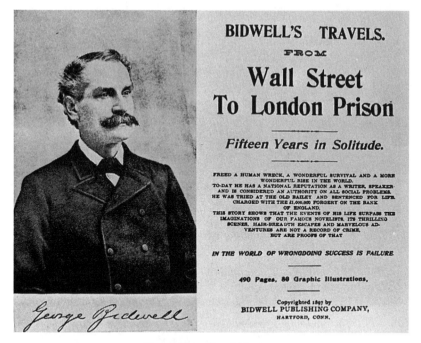

George Bidwell and his story

in English legal history to sit through proceedings with a gun under his ceremonial robes.

It made little difference to the outcome. The four defendants were convicted and sentenced to penal servitude for life, retribution for a crime that had 'given a severe blow to the confidence which has so long been maintained in this country'. In the event, George Bidwell was released in 1887 on the grounds of ill-health, his brother in 1890, and Noyes and Macdonnell in 1891, after serving eighteen years' imprisonment.[23]

The simple ingenuity of Mayhew's Nicholas or the forgeries of Jem the Penman and the Bidwells represented the professionalism of crime. Yet even Saward's talent drew upon those of pickpockets and safebreakers. The battle of skills was between safemaking firms like Chubb or Milner and the ingenuity of professional cracksmen. The new industrial age had produced security devices that would have been beyond the imagination of an eighteenth-century criminal. The greatest pioneers, in this respect, were the members of the Chubb family, locksmiths and safemakers to Prince Albert, the Duke of Wellington and the Bank of England.

The first patent for a security lock was issued to Robert Barron in 1778, another to the more famous Joseph Bramah in 1784. Yet it was not until after the Napoleonic Wars that locks of this kind became at all common. The more sophisticated types dated from 1818, when Charles Chubb, ships' ironmonger of Portsea, and Jeremiah Chubb his brother patented a Detector Lock. The family set up its first factory at Wolverhampton and was granted a royal licence by George IV in 1823. The firm had its London headquarters in St Paul's Churchyard from 1820 and opened a second shop in Old Broad Street.

There was a good deal of competition, which took the form of lock-smiths offering to pick a rival's lock in public to show its inferiority to their own. As early as 1832, Thomas Hart claimed that he had succeeded in picking one of Chubb's Patent Improved Detector Locks. Like Edward Agar at Folkestone harbour pier in 1854, he did this by 'smoking the lock', inserting carbon-covered probes in the keyhole to discover the location of the levers, and making a key to match these. This was considered to be unsporting and not the action of a gentleman. Charles Chubb refused, in any case, to believe that Hart had done it. He fixed one of his locks to the door of a hotel, closed it, and offered £10 to anyone who could open it. No one managed to do so.

His successor, John Chubb, was a cautious man who did not believe that his locks were always burglarproof. The greatest danger, he wrote in 1845 in the *Banker's Magazine*, was of thieves seducing 'female dom-estics' and getting their hands on the keys. Safes were not even proof against the skill of one man working alone. There was a lock-picking contest at the Great Exhibition of 1851, where an American lock-smith, A. C. Hobbs, publicly opened one of Chubb's locks. John Chubb grumbled that Hobbs was working under 'favourable conditions', whereas a cracksman would not be.

Chubb's 1851 design had a defect in that it allowed a burglar to get two fine steel picks into the lock and work them simultaneously. Chubb redesigned his locks. There was now to be a steel barrel surrounding the groove for the key, reducing the space in which a safe-breaker could manipulate his pick and denying him access to the other workings of the lock. There was also a steel 'curtain' at the opening of the lock, tailored closely to the shape of the key. To work two picks within this narrow aperture seemed impossible.

Charles Chaplin, a bullion carrier responsible for bringing gold from the City of London vaults and the Bank of England to London Bridge station, made a further suggestion to Chubb. It ought to be possible to design a key in two parts. The handle of the key could be detached after use, leaving part of the key in the barrel of the lock, thus blocking the cracksman's access to the levers. But this was countered by the objection that if the burglar could find a means of turning the remaining part of the key, he could open the lock.

The criminal underworld, no less than the safemakers, had benefited from the tools of the Industrial Revolution. One of its most effective devices was the 'Jack-in-the-Box'. This consisted of a heavy brass stock, a large upper barrel and a smaller lower one. The device was clamped to the frame of a door or a chest by a powerful steel screw whose length would be driven into the lock from the smaller barrel. The upper part of the stock contained a heavy screw, which could be wound by a lever through its head, forcing the screw into a lock or exerting an almost irresistible force between a door and its frame. If the structure did not give way the lock would, since the Jack-in-the-Box could exert a force of three tons.[24]

If Edward Agar was the supreme cracksman of the 1850s, his successor in the 1860s was Thomas Caseley. He and his accomplices launched an attack on the safes of the City of London, taking £4,000 from Threadneedle Street, £10,000 from Lombard Street, and £1,000 from the Strand in a few months. One of the premises that seemed secure from his attentions was that of the jeweller John Walker at 63 Cornhill, the so-called Cornhill Vaults. When the shop was closed, Mr Walker kept his stock of jewellery and a considerable quantity of gold in the latest 'Quadruple Patent' Milner safe, which the makers ill-advisedly advertised as 'thief-proof'.

Mr Walker's diamond rings, bracelets, gold watches, cash and gold were easily negotiable. However, the safe stood in a strong-room whose wall was reinforced by iron plates. Where it fronted the street, there was a slit in the iron so that every policeman on the beat, and anyone else who cared to, might look into the room at any time. Public display seemed to be the best security. The gas burned day and night, while mirrors ensured that no part of the room was free from surveillance. It was difficult to see what more Mr Walker could have done and he was understandably outraged when, on a Monday morning, 6 February 1865, he entered the strong-room and found that his 'thief-proof' Milner Quadruple Patent safe had been opened. On Saturday it had held jewellery and gold to the value of £6,000, now it held none.

From the damage done to his premises and those adjoining, Mr Walker saw how the robbery had been carried out. The thieves had chosen a weekend, so that they might work from Saturday evening, after the shops along Cornhill had closed, until the small hours of Monday morning. They had entered the building on Saturday while it was still open and had gone up to some offices on the floor above, where they hid and were locked in when the premises closed. These first-floor offices ran over the Cornhill Vaults and over an adjoining tailor's shop. Thomas Caseley and his accomplices had cut a hole in the floor of the offices, fixed a pair of iron tongs across it, dropped a rope ladder from these and climbed down into the tailor's shop. The wall between the tailor's shop and the jeweller's strong-room defeated them, being iron-plated. Instead, they found an area in the basement of the tailor's shop from which it was possible to drill through the floor above them, and come up into Mr Walker's back room.

By this time they had a look-out in Cornhill who would signal if a policeman or any other interested passer-by approached the slit that gave a view of the safe. Caseley had bought a secondhand Milner safe to practise on and knew the extent of the task that confronted him. So long as the coast was clear, he and his accomplices came out from the shelter of the back room and worked on the safe. As soon as a signal was given, they snatched up their tools and ducked back behind a partition.

Most safes of this sort were impossible to open because time was of the essence. However, almost any safe could be broken open if the assault went on long enough. Caseley had the whole of Saturday night and all of Sunday, if that were necessary. As he later confessed, his practice with a Milner safe had enabled him to open it in seven hours, but it could only be done by using a five-foot iron bar, whose sections were folded up so that they could be carried without causing suspicion.

The robbery was not subtle but it was lengthy. The first iron wedges were slim and were driven by hammers into the narrow gap between the door and the wall of the safe merely to widen it a little. When this had been done, larger wedges were used and the gap was widened further, though Milner's lock still held fast. Hour after hour, Caseley and his accomplice swung their hammers and drove the iron wedges deeper. Gradually, the wall of the safe was forced away from the lock. At last they used the 'alderman', the bar that Caseley boasted would open any safe once the 'citizens' had widened the gap sufficiently. The wall of the safe was forced out further still by the five-foot iron bar and the lock was sprung open.

It was not intended to repair the damage, as Edward Agar had done with the bullion chests. The safe was emptied and Caseley with his companions made their way back to the tailor's shop, up the rope ladder to the offices above, and out of the building. They closed the door of the safe as best they could and, to the casual surveillance of the passing policeman in the street, it appeared to be in place.

Thomas Caseley would not have been caught on this occasion but for the sexual jealousy of a woman who felt betrayed by a member of the gang. Edward Agar's experience was repeated as one man was betrayed and then, in turn, betrayed another. Caseley was sentenced to fourteen years' penal servitude but his court appearances were not over. John Walker sued Milners for having supplied him with a thief-proof safe, which had shown itself to be nothing of the kind. Milners argued that it was Mr Walker's negligence in leaving his premises unattended from Saturday until Monday which had made the robbery possible. Thomas Caseley was brought from prison to act as an expert witness. At the end of his evidence, the Lord Chief Justice remarked grimly, 'It is a pity you did not turn your talents to better account.' In a laconic farewell to freedom, Caseley replied, 'It is a pity the police did not let me.'[25]

By the 1870s, English safe-breakers, according to George Chubb and the Deputy Chief Constable of Manchester, were still using jacks, jemmies, crowbars and wrenches, many of them made to order in Birmingham by a man well known to the police but against whom there was no 'actual proof' of criminal activities. There had been a number of such makers in London, Birmingham, Manchester and Sheffield, according to John Binny, in the 1850s. 'Some burglars keep a set of fine tools of considerable value,' he added. The new specialities of the 1870s included diamond drills at £200 each, which were used to destroy the lock of a safe. Among the regular customers of the

Birmingham craftsman was a gang who were caught at a jeweller's shop in Manchester in 1874. They had carried out fourteen successful robberies in Birmingham the previous year. In some cases the Birmingham safes had had steel over the keyhole. A blow-pipe was used to soften it, fuelled by use of a rubber tube leading to the bracket of a gas-light. The robbers themselves worked by the light of a small oil-lamp and used cotton wads to deaden the sound of their hammers, chisels and wedges.[26]

Until the introduction of dynamite in 1867, the cracksman's skill lay in his fingers. Even after this date, dynamite was not commonly used by English safe-breakers for many years. The major jewel robbery of the 1920s was still carried out by cutting open the side of the safe with a ring-saw, powered by the steering-wheel of a car.

Yet despite the engineering skills of the cracksman, a good many safes were opened by the simple techniques of the confidence trickster. Indeed, John Chubb had been the first to acknowledge that bur-glarproof safes and unbreakable locks might induce an unwise sense of security. 'Some people, it is true, expect perfect impossibilities and imagine that having obtained a secure lock they have done all that is necessary. This is a great mistake. No lock whatever will guard against culpable negligence.' More than one victim might have heeded his words.[27] A prosperous Victorian strolling home one evening through an affluent residential neighbourhood was surprised to see two men arguing. One was a well-dressed professional man and the other was his coachman or servant. The well-dressed man was evidently a doctor called out on an urgent case, to judge by the way he was berating the other for having left behind the master's keys, including the key to his instrument-case.

As the stroller drew level, the doctor turned to him, apologized, pro-duced the medical instrument-case and explained his predicament. His patient was in immediate need of treatment but he could not open his instrument-case. The lock was simple enough and a common type of key would fit it. Was it possible that the stroller had such a key on his ring? At the thought of a dying patient denied medical help, the new arrival willingly produced his keys. There was a certain amount of obscure fiddling and turning. The doctor turned back with repeated thanks, the instrument-case now open. The stroller had no idea that he had been selected as a target long before. In the darkness, he had not seen the tin of wax. A few days or a few weeks later, he went to his safe and found it empty.

Despite the ingenuity which had removed hundredweights of gold bullion from the mail-train or £100,000 from the Bank of England, some of the true professionalism among Victorian criminals depended on the simplicity of the doctor's dilemma or the plausibility of Nicholas 'Wise' in the shop of a Dublin jeweller.

Retribution

Brixton Prison: female convicts sewing outside their cells during the silent hour

CHAPTER 8

Lagged for Life

In 1836, Henry Williams lay in the condemned cell of Newgate Gaol, awaiting execution in a few days' time. Williams was not a violent man, he had killed or injured no one, but he had been convicted of burglary which, at the time, remained a hanging matter. The law allowed so few exceptions in crimes against property that, three years earlier, a boy of nine had been sentenced to death for the offence of putting his hand through a shop window and stealing 'fifteen pieces of paint worth twopence'. He was not executed, yet there were so many capital crimes and so many criminals to be dispatched that the prison authorities could not find officers to watch each condemned felon day and night until his appointment with Jack Ketch. It was enough to lock a man like Henry Williams in a place from which there was no escape and leave him to his thoughts.

From the cell where he was kept, Williams was allowed to exercise in a little 'airing-yard' outside. There was nothing to prevent him from walking into it alone, since it offered no hope of freedom. One or two men had tried to climb its walls, as a last resort, but none had succeeded. The sheer granite of the walls was more than fifty feet high, for the most part ice-smooth. At about fifty feet above the ground, just short of the top, there was also a revolving *chevaux de frise*, iron spikes set in timber, which moved at the slightest touch. It was razor-sharp and so close to the wall that no climber could pass under it, between the blades and the granite surface. An iron railing ran round underneath the *chevaux de frise* to support it but the only hand-hold was on the points of the railing's sharpened spikes.

Newgate Gaol: the condemned cell

Even though his gaolers permitted Williams to exercise unsupervised in the yard, as though it were an extension of the death cell, it seemed impossible that he could escape by that route. They and he knew that men who had attempted to scale the walls of the airing-yard had achieved nothing beyond inflicting injury on themselves, a misfortune which was not allowed to prevent or delay their executions. Nine years earlier, John Williams – who was no relation – had made a futile attempt to cheat the noose on the very morning of his execution by climbing the wall of the yard. In his fear of the gallows, he did better than most, and had climbed high by the time the guards saw him. Then he lost his hold on the smooth granite and fell back into the airing-yard, where he lay with his legs badly gashed. An obliging surgeon patched him up so that he could be carried or supported to the gallows, and the hangman was not kept waiting.

Henry Williams surveyed the airing-yard and noticed that in one corner of the wall, not far below the *chevaux de frise*, an iron gravity-cistern had been installed. Indeed, those who had watched John Williams struggling towards it were dismayed only by the thought that he proposed to cheat the hangman by drowning himself in Newgate's drinking-water. However, in the course of the cistern's installation the stonework had been roughened at one corner of the yard. Henry Williams chose his moment when the guards were changing shifts and when it would be several minutes before he was under observation again.

As the *Chronicles of Newgate* described it, he slipped out into the airing-yard, as if to take exercise, and stood barefoot in the corner below the cistern. To anyone who noticed him, it would seem absurd that a man should choose to escape barefoot. As it happened, Williams knew that it was the only way in which it could be done. He kept his back to one side of the corner with his hands behind him. Then, with a sudden burst of agility, 'he used his bare feet like claws on the other side of the wall-angle'. Bare feet moulded themselves to roughened granite as boots never would. By this means he got as high as the cistern, braced himself in the angle and used his hands to get hold of the tank. He was now at a dizzy height above the yard. He pulled himself up to the top of the cistern and managed to find a grip on the spiked iron railing running below the *chevaux de frise* and supporting it. He could get no further up the wall, the space between the granite surface and the blades of the *chevaux de frise* being far too narrow. Nor could he hold the *chevaux de frise* itself. Apart from the damage that would be done to him by its razor-edged blades, it would revolve downwards, throwing him fifty feet to his death on the stone paving of the yard below.

Williams hung from the iron railing, while its spikes lacerated his hands. With death at his heels, however, he seems to have closed his mind to the pain as he worked his way round three sides of the yard, dangling from the rail. At last he came to a point where he was eight or nine feet from the flat roof of the condemned cells. In the most danger-ous moment of his escape, he launched himself outwards, falling and clutching until he had hold of the roof-ledge. Having struggled up on the roof, he then worked his way from building to building, jumping the narrow gaps, until he was beyond the precincts of the gaol and some-where above the first houses and industrial premises of Newgate Street.

By now he was covered in blood and had thrown away his coat. Barefoot, wearing only shirt and trousers, he found himself on the flat leads of a house roof, where a woman was hanging out her washing. Williams hid behind a chimney stack until the woman went back down an attic ladder into the building. He followed her, reassured her as she stared in terror at the bloody sight he presented, and told her his story. At once she offered to help him get down through the building and out into the street. He then made his way from London to Hampshire with sixteen pence in his pocket, first stopping for a pint of beer in Southwark.

Though caught after another robbery, Henry Williams was a legend in his day. Yet he had an advantage that was not known to his captors, who thought him a mere burglar. In childhood, he had been put to work as a sweep's boy. The trick of climbing by using his hands behind him and his bare feet on the opposite surface was one that he had known since boyhood. Having had enough of that trade, however, he had waited until the day when his master put him up a forty-foot factory chimney. Working his way to the top, he climbed down the outer surface of the far side and was never seen by his master again.[1]

Escapes from the security of a condemned cell were rare at any time, yet the ease with which some men found their way out of Newgate was a symptom of the rottenness of the system in the 1830s. In 1831, for example, Ikey Solomons of Islington was facing a capital charge of receiving stolen goods. While in Newgate, he applied for a writ of habeas corpus so that he might be released on bail. There was never the least chance of success but his application required his attendance at the law courts in Westminster. He was taken there by coach, in the custody of two Newgate turnkeys. While waiting for the application to be heard, he suggested that he should take the two officers to a nearby public house where they might 'refresh', since the party could not be expected to go all day without food or drink. From the public house they returned to the court where his application for bail was briskly refused and he was ordered back to prison to confront his fate. On the way there, he per-suaded the turnkeys to stop at another public house. As they left, Mrs Solomons entered the coach and had a 'fit'. Solomons suggested that they should make a detour down Petticoat Lane, where his wife might be entrusted to her friends. By this time one turnkey was 'stupidly drunk' and the other was most anxious to get rid of Mrs Solomons. They stopped at the house door to let her out, whereupon Solomons leapt after her, dashed through the door, and slammed and locked it behind him. He was next heard of in Copenhagen and afterwards in New York.

Newgate, though destined to be closed in 1880 and demolished to make way for the new Central Criminal Court, was extensively modern-ized in 1858–60. This, however, did not prevent escapes. A sailor by the name of Krapps escaped one night because the wooden panels of his cell door had not been sheeted with iron, and because the authorities had so little confidence in the watchman patrolling the prison after dark that they preferred to leave the outer gates of the cell-block open for him rather than entrust him with the keys. Krapps got into the corridor and, hence, into the yard. He made his way to the women's side, where sheets had been left out to dry. Taking the sheets and the washing-line to fashion a rope, he then looked for the step ladder which was used by the gas-lighter to reach the prison lamps when they were lit at dusk and extinguished at dawn. Though this ladder was too short for his purposes, Krapps doubled its length by cutting the cord and opening out the two sections into one. It was now tall enough for him to get over a *chevaux de frise*, on to a wall, along the roof of the cook-house, and down into the street using his improvised rope.

When Krapps slid down into Newgate Street it was almost daylight and the roadway was filling with market-carts. As the drivers and traders watched him come down from the prison roof, not a single person raised the alarm on behalf of law and order. Instead he found himself congratulated and offered sanctuary. The prison authorities knew nothing of his disappearance until the police informed them that a rope improvised from sheets was hanging from the cook-house roof. Krapps was never recaptured.

The last attempt at an escape from Newgate occurred less than a year before the prison closed. A prisoner who had been ordered up on to the roof by a warder, to flush water down a chute, failed to reappear. He had crossed the roofs to a party wall, dividing the prison from Tyler's Manufactory. Though he never managed to get down to the street, he was encouraged by the cheers and helpful signals of men who were working on a building across the road. No one gave him away. A similar lack of public co-operation with the authorities was evident when, in 1849, a convict escaped through a public house at 1 Newgate Street, and in 1853 when three men, Bell, Brown and Barry, passed unchallenged even though in prison uniform. Bell returned his uniform by parcel post to the Governor of Newgate, with a polite note explaining that he would have no further use for it. Unfortunately, this confidence was misplaced. He was in bed when the police raided his home and was arrested while hiding in the bedroom cupboard.[2]

*

As the Victorian period began, the great London prisons seemed little altered since John Howard's condemnation of them as a prison reformer in the 1770s. In 1774, Jack Rann, 'Sixteen-Stringed Jack', so called because he wore fancy breeches with eight strings on each knee, was allowed by the prison authorities to divert his thoughts on the night before his execution in a celebration that brought him wine, women and song. He had 'seven girls to dine with him', as well as other cronies, and on the following morning was said to have surveyed the gallows 'with confidence'. Even in the 1830s, the likelihood of being hanged for the most trivial crimes still turned villains into stoics. The philosophers of the underworld boasted that there was nothing in hanging but 'a wry neck, and a pair of wet breeches', a variant of the gallows wisdom that 'a man will piss when he cannot whistle'.

The bravado of the desperate man facing the noose was popularized among the mid-Victorians by the murderer Sam Hall, who ''ates yer – one and all' and whose death-cell ballad was not performed in politer entertainments.

> Oh, the parson he did come, he did come!
> Yes, the parson he did come, he did come!
> And he looked so bloomin' glum
> And he talked of Kingdom-Come!
> He can kiss my bloody bum,
> Blast his eyes!

Drunkenness and debauchery remained common in prison life. In 1776 the penologist Dr William Smith had thought it scandalous that, for example, there were 'no less than 30 gin-shops at one time' in the King's Bench Prison. In these, there was a weekly sale of 'two hogsheads or 120 gallons of gin, which they call by various names, as vinegar, gossip, crank, mexico, skyblue, etc.' When Newgate was at last inspected in 1835–6, little had changed, the inspectors reporting that they had seen prisoners 'giddy drunk, not able to sit upon forms'. Some inmates, those who were sober enough to do so, passed the time in playing cards, dice, skittles, billiards, fives or tennis. The wardsmen, prisoners who were trusted to impose order on others, had more effective power than the gaolers but could do little to stop rioting or fighting.[3]

Male prisoners in Newgate might get access to any female prisoner on the pretext that she was a relative. A woman on a capital charge was, of course, best advised to get pregnant while held in prison before her

Millbank Penitentiary, seen across the Thames by moonlight

trial. She could then 'plead her belly' if convicted, and so escape or postpone execution. Indeed, the Governor of Newgate was in the habit of choosing the more presentable female inmates as servants in his house and had kept back a pretty young girl from transportation to a penal colony in order that she might be available to him.

Children, as well as men and women, were among the prisoners. The boy who had been reprieved from the gallows at the age of nine was by no means the youngest. In 1863, Henry Mayhew talked to a warder at Millbank who remembered 'a little boy six years and a half old sentenced to transportation; and the sentence carried into effect, too, though the poor child couldn't speak plain'. Though they were no longer used in the 1860s, Millbank still possessed 'little baby handcuffs, as small in compass as a girl's bracelet, and about twenty times as heavy'.[4]

The conditions of prison inmates at the beginning of the Victorian period varied from the barbaric, in which lunatics who ought to have been sent to asylums were locked up at Newgate instead, to the luxurious, when comforts were provided for those prisoners whom the governor permitted to live in his own house, their meals prepared and brought in from restaurants like the nearby London Coffee-House. Some of the prisoners in the governor's house were also attended by their own valets, who lived with the governor's servants and were swiftly attracted to the young girl saved from transportation. 'There was revelling and roystering as usual, with high-life below stairs,' wrote Arthur Griffiths, an inspector of prisons. 'The governor sent down wine on festive occasions, of which no doubt the prisoner housemaid had her share.'[5]

When the inspectors appointed by Parliament reported in 1836, it seemed incredible to most of those who read their account that they could be talking about a prison system which had survived into the dawn of the new age. One paragraph in the report, describing the fate of the first-time felon, was to determine the reforms of prison and punishment for the Victorian criminal.

> Instead of seclusion and meditation, his time is passed in the midst of a body of criminals of every class and degree, in riot, debauchery, and gaming, vaunting his own adventures, or listening to those of others; communicating his own skill and aptitude in crime, or acquiring the lessons of greater adepts. He has access to newspapers, and of course prefers that description which are expressly prepared for his own class, and which abound in vulgar adventure in criminal enterprise, and in the histories of the police, the gaol, and the scaffold. He is allowed intercourse with prostitutes who, in nine cases out of ten, have originally conduced to his ruin; and his connection with them is confirmed by that devotion and generosity towards their paramours in adversity for which these otherwise degraded women are remarkable. Having thus passed his time, he returns a greater adept in crime, with a wider acquaintance among criminals, and, what perhaps is even more injurious to him, is generally known to all the worst men in the country; not only without the inclination, but almost without the ability of returning to an honest life.[6]

The report, a salutary shock to Parliament and the nation, required the abolition of prisons as they had been and the construction of a system dedicated to moral regeneration, no matter what the expense might be.

*

By the 1840s, crime was seen primarily as a contagion whose virulence was a match for cholera, the contemporary 'plague from Bengal'.

Neither the misfortunes of birth nor the squalor of living conditions could be a sufficient explanation of delinquency. To prevent contagion, whether through cholera or crime, there was no means but quarantine and, indeed, the new system was referred to as 'criminal quarantine'. In support of its aim, the great prisons of London and England's new cities were to be built, or in a few cases rebuilt. The speed with which this happened told its own story. The new house of correction at Tothill Fields, Westminster, was built in 1836. Pentonville Prison was constructed north of King's Cross in 1840–2 as an institution where those men sentenced to transportation would serve a period of probation before being shipped to a convict settlement in Australia. Work began on the new Surrey House of Correction at Wandsworth in 1849. In the same year, the foundation stone was laid for the City House of Correction at Holloway. Brixton, a female convict prison, was built in 1853. A number of prisons, including Newgate, Clerkenwell, Horsemonger Lane Gaol in Lambeth, and Millbank – the last built to a design by Jeremy Bentham in 1821 – pre-dated the Victorian boom in prison building but were improved as necessary.[7]

Where there had been overcrowding, there was to be solitude. Where there had been fraternization between convicts, there would be the silent movement of masked figures in their 'scotch caps', known only by their prison numbers, like wanderers in a landscape of the damned. Indeed, 'revealing the features' was to become an offence punishable by solitary confinement within a pitch-dark cell on bread and water. Less than five years after the young Queen's accession, the days of meals from the London Coffee-House and prisoners with their own valets had gone for ever.

Other changes made new prisons necessary. In 1853, transportation was abolished for convicts sentenced to less than fourteen years, and a new system of penal servitude introduced. As Henry Mayhew wrote, 'it is unworthy of a wise and great nation to make a moral dustbin of its colonies'. During the 1860s, transportation was discontinued and 'our felon population increases among us as fast as fungi in a rank and foetid atmosphere'. In London, each prison had a specific role. Some held men or women sentenced to imprisonment, or transportation, for more than two years. Men went to Pentonville, Millbank or the hulks at Woolwich, women also to Millbank or to Brixton. Those sentenced to shorter terms went to Holloway or Wandsworth, or to Coldbath Fields

if adult males and Tothill Fields if adult females or boys. Those awaiting trial were held at Clerkenwell, Newgate and Horsemonger Lane.[8]

In 1842 Sir James Graham, as Home Secretary, described Pentonville
as a new type of prison where a man sentenced to transportation would
serve his months of probation before being shipped to a convict settlement. 'But from the day of his entrance into prison . . . I extinguish the
hope of return to his family and friends.'[9]

> At the end of eighteen months, when a just estimate can be formed of the
> effect produced by the discipline on his character, he will be sent to Van
> Dieman's land; there, if he behave well, at once to receive a ticket-of-leave,
> which is equivalent to freedom, with a certainty of abundant maintenance,
> the fruit of industry.
>
> If, however, he behave indifferently, he will, on being transported to Van
> Dieman's Land, receive a probationary pass, which will secure to him only
> a limited portion of his earnings, and impose certain galling restraints on
> his personal liberty.
>
> If, on the other hand, he behave ill, and the discipline of the prison be
> ineffectual, he will be transported to Tasman's Peninsula, there to work in a
> probationary gang, without wages, and deprived of liberty – an abject
> convict.[10]

Behind the rhetoric of wholesome discipline lay such stories as James
Tucker's in his documentary novel *Ralph Rashleigh*, of prisoners in labour
camps under the brutal command of those who had once been convicts
themselves, abused, flogged, hanged for attempts at escape, forced to
work naked at the lime-burners, the corrosive powder searing the
wounds of flogging. 'You're like a motherless cub,' was the greeting to a
new arrival, 'all your sorrows to come.'[11]

The 'criminal quarantine' of Pentonville and similar prisons, with
which these sentences began, consisted of a separate system and a silent
system. The separate system prevented the spread of contagion by pro-
hibiting prisoners from associating. It was defined by Sir Joshua Jebb,
the Surveyor-General of Prisons, as a regime 'in which each individual
prisoner is confined in a cell, which becomes his workshop by day and
his bed-room by night, so as to be effectually prevented from holding
communication with, or even being seen sufficiently to be recognized by
other prisoners'.[12]

When prisoners left their cells for exercise, chapel or some other
reason, recognition was prevented at Pentonville, as at Wandsworth, by

Convicts exercising at Pentonville Prison

the imposition of the brown scotch cap, whose large peak came down to the chin like a mask, with holes for the eyes, 'like phosphoric lights shining through the sockets of a skull'. At communal exercise in the prison yard, men in tunics and trousers walked silently, identified only by numbers sewn on their uniforms.

> This gives to the prisoners a half-spectral look . . . the costume of the men seems like the outward vestment to some wandering soul rather than that of a human being; for the eyes glistening through the apertures in the mask give one the notion of a spirit peeping out behind it, so that there is something positively terrible in the idea that these are men whose crimes have caused their very features to be hidden from the world.

The swarm of identically clad prisoners in their brown uniforms and masks leaving their cells for the exercise yard made them look to Mayhew like 'so many bees pouring from the countless cells of a hive'.[13]

After the ten years of such innovations, there were general objections to the separate system. Confinement to a cell in this manner was said to cause physical ill-health, usually dyspepsia and constipation, which was not surprising. Moreover, prisoners were liable to mental distress, especially during the earlier part of separate confinement. In the 1840s, following the introduction of the system at Pentonville in 1842, the incidence of mental breakdown or 'insanity' in the prison was four times the level found by Home Office inspections of the country's prisons as a whole.

Jebb defended the humanity of the new regime, protesting at attempts to equate separate confinement with solitary confinement. A man kept in his cell was not allowed to communicate with other prisoners but he might speak to warders or instructors as often 'as is compatible with judicious economy'. Moreover, in solitary confinement he would be allowed only bread and water, which was not the case with the separate system. Even if he should be sent to solitary confinement, this punishment had now been softened by a good-natured Home Office so that a man could not be kept on bread and water for longer than a month or for more than three months in any one year. Joseph Kingsmill, chaplain of Pentonville, also came to the defence of the separate system, by which 'the propagation of crime is impossible – the continuity of vicious habits is broken off – the mind is driven to reflection, and conscience resumes her sway'.[14]

A second ingredient of the new discipline was the silent system which applied on those occasions when it was necessary for prisoners to leave their cells. They were forbidden from communicating with one another 'by word, sign, or gesture'. This seemed to complement the separate system, since the thousand prisoners at Pentonville were bound to be in one another's company at exercise, in the chapel, or when put to hard labour on the row of tread-wheels. Unfortunately, as the Inspectors of Prisons admitted, it was almost impossible to enforce a silent system in these circumstances without an inordinate number of warders. As its critics pointed out, the silent system was scarcely compatible with the separate system, since the latter would work only if men had no occasion to leave their cells. Once a man was out of his cell and put to labour, silence was impossible to enforce. While prisoners were in rows of twenty-four on the tread-wheels, for example, it was the easiest thing in the world for them to communicate with each other.

> Although there is a turnkey stationed in each tread-wheel yard, and two monitors, or wardsmen, selected from the prisoners, stand constantly by, the men on the wheel can, and do, speak to each other. They ask one another

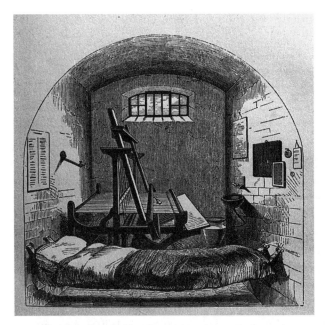

A cell in Pentonville Prison under the separate system

how long they are sentenced for, and when they are going out; and answers are given by laying two or three fingers on the wheel to signify so many months, or by pointing to some of the many inscriptions carved on the tread-wheel as to the terms of imprisonment suffered by former prisoners, or else they turn their hands to express unlockings or days.

The chaplain of Pentonville also complained that the labour of picking oakum, which required men to lower their heads, 'gives ample opportunity of carrying on a conversation without much chance of discovery'.[15]

The failure of such systems was evident by the 1860s. Since they had been introduced early in the 1840s, crime had risen by a fifth and the number of convicts who reoffended had not been reduced by months of solitude. Perhaps the most discouraging evidence related to the proportion of prisoners who had reoffended in the first dozen years of the new system. In 1841 reoffenders made up 25.6 per cent of all those committed to prison. In 1853 they still accounted for 25.4 per cent, the average for the period being 25.3 per cent. Such figures might not be conclusive but they scarcely encouraged faith in the moral innovations of the 1840s.

Like the flower-girl who broke the Lord Mayor's lamps at the Mansion House, there were a number of prisoners who committed crimes in order to find their way back to the food and shelter which such houses of correction as Tothills Fields or Holloway offered them. Out of ten boys questioned at random in Tothill Fields, five had been convicted of 'heaving stones', one of 'heaving clay', one of 'heaving an oyster-shell through a street-lamp'. One had threatened to stab another boy, one had stolen a bell from a garden, and one was said by a woman to have hit her baby. The boy who had heaved clay had been in prison fourteen times for similar offences, two others had been in four times and one three times. The last of these had thrown the oyster-shell to break a street-lamp and, according to a warder, 'very probably committed the offence merely to get another month's shelter'. An added inducement to such crimes was that the boys at Tothill Fields were allowed a bath once a month.[16]

In such circumstances, even isolation and silence might have seemed a price worth paying to many of the mid-Victorian poor. By the 1860s, moreover, the time spent alone in a cell under the separate system was reduced from eighteen months to nine months and then abolished. It was even suggested by such reformers as Mayhew and John Binny that separation was 'wicked' and that more good might be done by supervised association. Convicts were now allowed to receive occasional visits from their friends. A man who 'may have conducted himself in a satisfactory manner' for six months, as the Home Office described it, would be allowed one visit and the privilege of wearing a badge, in the form of a red stripe. If his conduct continued to be satisfactory for a further three months, he was allowed a second badge and a second visit. At the other extreme, the notice which hung in each cell warned its inmate that 'Convicts deemed to be incorrigible, will be specially dealt with.'[17]

One of the Newgate turnkeys was sure that by offering certain privileges for good conduct, the power of the gaolers over their prisoners was greater than it had ever been in the days of thumb-screws, gags and branding. 'At present, you see, we cut off the right of receiving and sending letters, as well as stop the visits of their friends; and a man feels those things much more than any torture he could be put to.' Such sentiments put an end to the separate system and broke the absolute rule of silence. Punishment, however, was still the guarantee of stability and order.[18]

*

'There are few persons who can hold out against short commons,' said the Pentonville prison cook philosophically, 'the belly can tame every man.' Most Victorian criminals who served their sentences in such gaols as Pentonville or Wandsworth knew the truth of this. Despite the reputations of these places, floggings or corporal punishment of any kind had become rare. In 1862, the Governor of Holloway remarked that no prisoner had been flogged there for ten years, except those who had been sentenced to such punishments by the magistrates in police court proceedings. Taming the belly was far easier and more effective, especially when a diet of bread and water was combined with detention in a cell devoid of all light.[19]

Even a full prison diet might have seemed a deterrent to crime. At Millbank, in the mid-Victorian period, breakfast consisted of three-quarters of a pint of cocoa and eight ounces of bread. Dinner at midday was five ounces of meat, a pound of potatoes and six ounces of bread. Supper was made up of a pint of oatmeal gruel and eight ounces of bread. The punishment diet reduced this nourishment to a pound of bread a day. Hospital diets, however, might include a pint of soup and even a pint of porter. The diet was similar elsewhere, though at Coldbath Fields the prisoners received only soup for their main meal on three days of the week and, if they were sentenced to two months or less, their dinner on five days of the week was simply soup or gruel. 'The meat and soup for dinner are given as a species of medicine, which the short-term men, who carry to jail a body healthy with recent liberty and a mind supported by the knowledge of a speedy liberation, are not supposed to require.'

Once again, men who were sick might have their diets supplemented on the recommendation of the medical officer, perhaps being allowed cocoa instead of gruel for supper, or jelly, fish and chicken if they were in the infirmary. It was an invitation to some men to feign illness but they were generally made to regret it. 'If the doctor suspects a man to be scheming,' said a Pentonville warder confidentially, 'he puts him on low diet; and that soon brings him to, especially when he's kept off his meat and potatoes.' A suspected malingerer might also be put to hard labour on the crank until he decided that he was fit again.[20]

A peculiarly Victorian innovation, intended for prisoners serving shorter sentences but used everywhere, was the concept of useless labour, of which the crank was an example. A man who was set to work making shoes or hammocks might feel some sense of purpose or achievement. Yet the tread-wheel, the crank and shot-drill had been designed to deprive the convict of any feeling except that he was being punished.

Shot-drill lasted for an hour and a quarter every afternoon. Men older than forty-five were excused the drill because of the danger to their health. The younger prisoners were paraded round three sides of a square, the men three yards apart, facing inwards to the warder who gave the commands. At one end of each of the three lines of men was a pyramid of cannon balls. At the word of command, the first man took a cannon ball from the pyramid, carried it and put it down by his neighbour, who then stooped to pick it up and put it down by the next man, while the first man fetched another from the pyramid. The three lines drilled by numbers as the pyramids of iron shot dwindled at one end of each line and increased at the other. When all the cannon balls had been passed down the lines, the process was reversed, and reversed again until the hour and a quarter was at an end. Henry Mayhew was allowed to witness an afternoon's drill and was alarmed at the appearance of some of the convicts.

> One, a boy of seventeen, became more and more pink in the face, while his ears grew red. The warder was constantly shouting out, 'Move a little quicker, you boy, there!'
> The men grew hot, and breathed hard. Some who at the beginning had been yellow as goose-skin, had bright spots appear, almost like dabs of rouge, on their prominent cheek-bones. . . . When all were evidently very tired, a rest of a few seconds was allowed. Then the men pulled out their handkerchiefs and wiped their faces, others who had kept their waistcoats on, took them off, and passed their fingers round their shirt collars, as if the linen were clinging to the flesh, whilst the youth of seventeen rubbed his shirt sleeve over his wet hair as a cat uses a paw in cleaning itself.

When the drill continued and the men grew more weary, some of them began to drop the shot rather than put it down, which earned them a reprimand and the danger, if they disobeyed further, of moving

A cell with a prisoner at 'crank-labour' in the Surrey House of Correction, Wandsworth

towards the class of 'incorrigibles'. However, as one of the warders watching the drill remarked, 'It tries them worse taking up, because there's nothing to lay hold of, and the hands get hot and slippery with the perspiration, so that the ball is greasy like. The work makes the shoulders very stiff too.'[21]

The crank remained the medical officer's way of dealing with malingerers. A man who complained of an imaginary or ill-defined ailment 'such as pains in the back or chest', and who was disbelieved, would not be excused work but put to crank-labour in his cell until he volunteered to go back to his prison trade. A day's labour involved turning the crank-handle ten thousand times. In appearance, the crank resembled a Victorian knife-cleaner, a narrow iron drum on a stand, a handle at one side. When the handle was turned, a series of scoops inside gathered sand from the bottom of the drum and, as they rose to the top, tipped it down again. A glass-covered dial-plate at the front of the drum counted the number of times the crank-handle had been

Tread-wheel and oakum shed at the City Prison, Holloway

turned. The dial ensured that a prisoner could be punished in this way without requiring a warder to supervise his ordeal.

> Sometimes a man has been known to smash the glass in front of the dial-plate and alter the hands; but such cases are of rare occurrence. As may be easily conceived, this labour is very distressing and severe; but it is seldom used, except as a punishment, or, rather, as a test of feigned sickness. A man can make, if he work with ordinary speed, about twenty revolutions a minute, and this, at 1,200 the hour, would make his task of 10,000 turns last eight hours and twenty minutes.[22]

The futility of the crank and the despair of its victims were not quite matched by the tread-wheel, where twelve or twenty-four men were punished simultaneously rather than in solitude and might at least exchange messages when neither the warders nor the wardsmen were looking. However, anyone who supposed that the tread-wheel fan at Coldbath Fields was a useful piece of machinery driven by the prisoners' labour was soon disillusioned. It was an ingenious piece of Victorian engineering whose sole purpose was to increase resistance, reduce ventilation, and so make it harder for the men on the tread-wheel to turn it. Only at Holloway was the tread-wheel put to a useful purpose, that of drawing water from a well for the prison supply. To accomplish this, the men were put on the wheel for four and a half hours a day and, in their rest-periods, were made to pick oakum.[23]

The tread-wheel itself consisted of twenty-four steps round a central horizontal cylinder which revolved twice a minute. Its length was divided into compartments two feet wide, each containing a man undergoing the punishment. As the cylinder turned, it appeared as if the man were climbing an endless flight of stairs, though, as one of the warders explained, it was more arduous than climbing stairs. 'You see the men can get no firm tread like, from the steps always sinking away from under their feet, and *that* makes it very tiring. Again, the compartments are small, and the air becomes very hot, so that the heat at the end of the quarter of an hour renders it difficult to breathe.'

The regulation labour on the tread-wheel consisted of fifteen periods of quarter of an hour every day. After each of these, the men came down 'with their faces wet with perspiration and flushed with exercise'. The Governor of Coldbath Fields remarked with some pride that he was obliged to limit the amount of water the men were allowed to drink, since they would otherwise drink to excess in order to 'disorder' their stomachs and escape the tread-wheel. They were also known to swallow salt water to make themselves sick, eat soap to cause diarrhoea, or inflict wounds that could be presented as sores to escape the punishment on medical grounds. The futility of the labour led to the prisoners calling it 'grinding the wind'; and because it also rubbed off skin between the legs, it was less politely known as the 'cockchafer'.[24]

*

When Mayhew visited Pentonville, almost twenty years after it had opened, he was impressed by the 'Dutch-like cleanliness' and the size and comfort of individual cells. The prison landings radiated from a central point like the spokes of a half-wheel, 'like a bunch of Burlington Arcades, that had been fitted up in the style of the opera box lobbies, with an infinity of little doors'. Yet what remained most vividly in his mind was the departure of convicts for the hulks in the darkness before dawn, each man manacled to the chain which linked the file. Transportation might be dying but England's floating prisons remained. The Home Office, following the restriction of transportation in 1853, had laid down that 'All convicts under sentence of penal servitude will be subjected to a period of separate confinement followed by labour on public works.'[25]

Convicts were transferred from Pentonville and Millbank to work at the Woolwich Arsenal, the Portland quarries or the dockyard at Portsmouth. Detachments left Pentonville for Portsmouth before dawn, chained in lines of ten or twelve, each group in an omnibus bound for Waterloo station and thence by train to their destination. Despite what lay ahead of them in the convict hulks, 'every cheek was puckered with smiles at the sense that they were bidding adieu to the place of their long isolation from the world'.[26]

The practice of turning old warships into floating prisons dated from the American War of Independence, which deprived the British government of convict settlements to which a variety of criminals had been dispatched. Though new penal colonies had been created in Australia, the old hulks off Woolwich, providing convict labour for the Arsenal, were still the most familiar evidence of the system to Londoners. Their continued existence in 1860 was commemorated by Dickens in *Great Expectations* and more prosaically by Mayhew from the high ground of the churchyard by Woolwich dockyard.

> From the elevated churchyard, crowded with graves, the sharp outlines of which are rounded by the waving of the uncut grass, the first view of the river, with the flat Essex marshes beyond, is obtained. Here, immediately opposite the yard, rises the bulky form of the great *Warrior* hulk, which, the authorities declare, can hardly hold together. Painted black and white, and with her naked and puny-looking spars degraded to the rank of clothes-props for the convicts, she stands in curious contrast to the light steamers that dance by her, and to the little sloops laden with war stores, and bound for Sheerness or Portsmouth, that glide like summer flies upon the surface of the stream, almost under her stern. . . . The *Defence* and *Unité*, moored head to head with the bulky hammock-houses reared upon their decks, their barred port-holes, and their rows of convicts' linen swinging from between the stunted poles which now serve them as masts, have a sombre look.

The *Unité* was a hospital ship for the hulks and a little further down the river was the *Sulphur*, used as a washing ship. A boatload of Royal Marines with rifles upright were rowed round the convict fleet at anchor.[27]

There was no separate or silent system on the hulks. At night, the men were confined almost unsupervised to their prison wards on the lower

The Defence *hulk and the* Unité *convict hospital ship, off Woolwich*

decks, each a communal cage slung with hammocks. 'The state of morality under such circumstances may be easily conceived,' wrote Mayhew, 'crimes impossible to mention being commonly perpetrated.' When the shirts of the prisoners were hung out to air upon the rigging, they were so infested with vermin that the linen appeared to have been sprinkled with black pepper. The decks were washed with acrid chloride of lime in an unsuccessful attempt to kill contagion. When cholera reached the hulks, men died in such numbers that coffins were ferried ashore six at a time. The chaplain, fearing for his own health, refused to accompany them ashore but stood on the poop of the hulk a mile from the churchyard. There he read the burial service and dropped a hand-kerchief at 'ashes to ashes and dust to dust' as a signal to those on shore that they should lower the coffins into the grave.[28]

The squalor of the hospital ship, which received 354 admissions from 608 prisoners in 1841, was described after an inspection eight years later, in terms suggesting that conditions had got worse rather than better.

In the hospital ship, the *Unité*, the great majority of the patients were infested with vermin; and their persons, in many instances, particularly their feet, begrimed with dirt. No regular supply of body-linen had been issued; so much so, that many men had been five weeks without a change; and all

Convicts returning to the hulks from their labour in the Woolwich Arsenal

record had been lost of the time when the blankets had been washed; and the number of sheets was so insufficient, that the expedient had been resorted to of only a single sheet at a time, to save appearances. Neither towels nor combs were provided for the prisoners' use, and the unwholesome odour from the imperfect and neglected state of the water-closets was almost insupportable. On the admission of new cases into hospital, patients were directed to leave their beds and go into hammocks, and the new cases were turned into the vacated beds, without changing the sheets.[29]

In the routine of the hulks, the men on the lower decks were woken by the bell at 5.30 a.m. and escorted with rolled hammocks to one of the square hammock-houses that had been built on the upper deck. Breakfast consisted of a piece of bread from the laundry basket and cocoa bailed from a bucket. Working parties were ferried ashore to the Arsenal to begin work at 7.30 a.m., breaking granite, stacking timber, building mortar batteries in the marshes, cleaning sheds and shells, clearing drains, digging gravel, discharging mud or repairing roads. Warders whose carbines were fitted with bayonets looked on, though a man might sometimes escape while ashore with the assistance of a dockyard worker. At 11.30, the parties were returned to the hulks for their midday meal, each man being routinely searched. This main meal of the day on the hulks consisted of a potato and a ladleful of boiled meat, often rotten.

Labour from 1 to 5 p.m. was followed by a final meal of bread and cocoa. Hammocks were collected and slung, and the prisoners left to their own thoughts and to sleep as the tide gurgled along the wallowing hull. The worst Victorian slums, the debtors' prisons and Newgate itself can scarcely have brought more despair to their inhabitants than the passing of years upon the hulks.

*

Men constituted about four-fifths of the prison population in the 1850s so that, for example, the daily average of prisoners in England and Wales for 1853 was 13,609 men and 3,082 women. Rival figures for the year as a whole showed that a quarter of criminal offences were committed by women and that this had risen from a fifth over a period of twenty years. Prostitution, though widely practised, was not widely prosecuted and, in many views, was not regarded as a crime without some aggravating circumstance. Where crimes were committed, women were proportionately less likely to murder, rob or destroy property but more likely to be embezzlers, thieves or receivers of stolen goods. In coining, forgery, perjury and keeping disorderly houses, they retained their fifth share of criminality. The explanations for a growth in crime by women ranged from the decline of chastity to their employment in unfeminine occupations in those areas where mining or fabric manufacture were prevalent.

After the rigours of Pentonville or the squalor of the hulks, it would have taken little for women to be treated more humanely than men in the Victorian prison system. The vast majority of the staff at Brixton, from the superintendent downwards, were female. The inmates, according to the Directors of Prisons, consisted of 'the many who are good, and the few who are bad'. The bad were not, of course, subjected to such punishments as the crank or the tread-wheel and many of them made the best of the system of transportation. By the time that Brixton was opened as a female convict prison in 1853, transportation was restricted to those with sentences of at least fourteen years. However, many women had thought transportation a promising adventure, knowing that their initial months of imprisonment in England were 'only a necessary step towards all but absolute freedom in a colony'.[30]

The worst behaviour among these female convicts occurred after transportation was restricted and those who had hoped to be sent to Australia found that they were to serve their sentences in England. Worse still, they were to be released in England and sent back to the lives from which, in some cases, imprisonment had rescued them. 'A few of these had, according to their own statement, even pleaded guilty for the purpose of being sent abroad; but when they became aware that they were eventually to be discharged in this country after a protracted penal detention, disappointment rendered them thoroughly reckless.' Once in Australia, they would have been free to marry, settle down and live their lives in a new world. Deprived of this hope, as Mayhew described it,

> they actually courted punishment; and their delight and occupation con-
> sisted in doing as much mischief as they could. They constantly destroyed
> their clothes, tore up their bedding, and smashed their windows. They fre-
> quently threatened the officers with violence, though it must be stated, at the
> same time, they seldom proceeded to put their threats in force; and when
> they did so, some among them – and generally those who were most obnox-
> ious to discipline – invariably took the officers' part to protect them from
> personal injury.[31]

The Directors of Prisons reported that 1,209 punishments were awarded to the 600 prisoners at Brixton in 1854, more than a third of these being reprimands or admonishments. Most of the other offenders were confined to cells, withdrawn from association with other prisoners or deprived of a meal; 288 were sent to the refractory cells, half on a full diet and half on bread and water; 31 were put in handcuffs and one in a straitjacket, these being imposed for offences of violence, self-inflicted or on others. Unlike male prisons, there was no systematic punishment of the kind that shot-drill represented and for which no offence in prison need be committed. Prisoners were, however, divided into three classes and might be promoted or 'degraded' according to conduct.

The cells in which the women were separately confined differed little from those at Pentonville, each resembling a whitewashed cellar with a chimney and gas-jet, shelves, a small table and stool, a clothes-box and a hammock slung from wall to wall. There was no view of the outside world, the only window being a long-light near the ceiling.

A civilizing difference between such prisons as Pentonville and Brixton was the existence of a convict nursery for children born to women who were serving their sentences. However, Home Office regulations forbad women whose children were already born from bringing them to Brixton, the woman being committed to prison and the child to the Union workhouse. Even when a child was born at Brixton and admitted to the nursery, it seemed unlikely that it would be kept there beyond four years of age. There had been one child who had been kept longer at Millbank but, being as much a prisoner as its mother, it then emerged knowing nothing of the world and without the least idea of the difference between a horse and a cat.

Even Mayhew's image of 'little babes there, clinging to their convict mothers' skirts, or playing with their rag-dolls in the convict nursery' was tarnished at the first reflection. If these children escaped the workhouse, they were still destined to be released from prison into a world where they knew only their mothers, who in turn knew little beyond crime or prostitution. 'Is it not most likely that, in after life, those who drew their first breath inside the prison walls will come to breathe their last gasp there also?' Brixton showed a good deal more humanity than the hulks but, perhaps, not much more hope. There were still girls imprisoned in Millbank scarcely ten years older than the children in the nursery. While the days of children aged six or nine in prison were now a living memory, girls of fifteen remained adult prisoners in the 1860s.[32]

Despite the poignancy of the prison children, only thirty of the six hundred women in Brixton during its first year had children in the nursery. While they worked at dresses for their infants, other convicts laboured at the troughs of the laundry, their bare, reddened arms scrubbing the sodden flannels against a wooden grooved board. At other times the women sat outside their cells and were supervised at needlework. Some of this was done for the outside contractors of the slop-shops, thus reducing further the wages of those for whom Hood, Kingsley, Mayhew and their kind had campaigned.

> No wonder, thought we, that honest women cannot live by the labour of shirt-making, when such as these, who have neither rent, nor food, nor clothing to find are their competitors. . . .
>
> From eleven till twelve, the women located in the wings pursue their needlework in silence, and seated at their doors; and then it is a most peculiar sight to see the two hundred female convicts ranged along the sides of

Convict dress at Pentonville and Millbank

the arcade, and in each of the three long balconies that run one above the other round the entire building, so that, look which way you will, on this side or on that, you behold nothing but long lines of convict women, each dressed alike, in their clean white caps, and dark, claret-brown gowns, and all with their work upon their knees, stitching away in the most startling silence, as if they were so many automata – the only noise, indeed, that is heard at such a time being the occasional tapping of one of the matrons' hammers upon the metal stove, as she cries, 'Silence there! Keep silence, women!' to some prisoners she detects whispering at the other end of the ward.

All the shirts for Portland, Pentonville and Millbank were made at Brixton, as well as those for slop-shops. The women's prison caps and other clothes were also made by the less skilled, while one woman was allowed to cut a dress out for a matron. Another was working at open embroidery – 'She's in for life!' – and another at a crochet collar so fine that it seemed carved from ivory.[33]

For all its defects, the system at Brixton offered to some of its inmates a chance to work at something more rewarding than the tread-wheel or shot-drill and a regime which inspired observers like Mayhew and Binny with hope for the development of prisons in the future.

> Indeed, we left the establishment with a high sense of the kindness and care that the female authorities exhibited towards the poor creatures under their charge, and it is our duty to add, that all at Brixton was done more gently and feelingly, and yet not less effectually, than at other prisons – the feminine qualities shining as eminently in the character of the warders as in that of nurses.[34]

*

For all the improvements of the prison system, however, the longing of the law's captives for the freedom of the outer world was little diminished. Even the rigours of the separate and the silent systems could not entirely quench a last flicker of hope that escape might still be possible from the new fortresses of Victorian justice. The regime at Pentonville, the closely guarded processions of masked men with numbers sewn to their uniforms, might have daunted the most determined fugitive. The prisoners exercised only under the barked orders of warders, following the 'rope-walk' of the airing-yard in drilled silence, each man holding the rope in his right hand as he followed a permitted path. Even in the prison chapel, each man was locked in his separate 'pew', a wooden stall above which only his head was seen and whose wooden partition divided him from the men on either side, ranged, as it seemed, in so many pigeon-holes. Looking down on this collection of some two hundred and fifty heads, even the chaplain on his perch appeared more like a prison guard than a minister of God.

The more obvious methods of escape usually failed. One man at Millbank melted his pewter cocoa mug over his gas-light and moulded it into roughly made keys which might, according to the governor, 'have opened every door in the prison'. The keys were cut from a pattern, obtained by using a piece of soap in the lock. Unfortunately, metal as soft as pewter and moulded in this way was apt to bend or break off in

*Pentonville Prison chapel under the separate system, showing pews of the kind
from which Hackett made his escape*

the lock when it was turned. Other men found that, where there were
bolts on the outside of a door, an escaper might use a jointed metal rod,
'like the handle of a lady's parasol, which could be doubled up'. In this
form it was pushed through a keyhole and one half allowed to fall
against the surface of the door on the far side. If this could be brought
into contact with the bolt, it might be possible to push it back. Yet the
successful escapers of this later generation were quiet men whose
methods owed more to thought than to technology.[35]

Among the prisoners at morning chapel in Pentonville was a man
whose name was, not inappropriately, Hackett. He rose and knelt in his
high-walled little stall, sang and prayed, in unison with the rest. At
prayer, all the heads of the prisoners vanished below the level of the
wooden walls of the pews as they knelt and bowed forward, only the
chaplain on his roost perhaps glimpsing the worshippers. One Sunday
morning, as the prayers ended, Hackett's head did not reappear. In a
few moments, the warders had opened his pew but Hackett was not
there. During the periods of prayer in recent weeks, he had been
working patiently at the bare boards which formed the floor of his indi-

vidual pew. The tall wooden walls of the separate stalls in which each prisoner sat gave him a perfect cover for what he was doing. On this last morning, he had lifted one of the boards clear and disappeared under the chapel floor. That was as far as he might have got but, on his visits to the exercise yard, the chapel and other parts of the prison, Hackett had quietly examined the structure of the building while the guards roared and barked. He calculated that it was possible to get under the chapel to a point where a narrow opening had been cut in the wall of the main building for ventilation. It was a tight fit but he thought he could get through it. Once outside it, he was free, in an escape that did more to damage the reputation of the new prison system than any amount of moral protest. If his neighbours in the prison chapel stalls suspected what he was doing, they thought it a point of honour to keep the information to themselves.[36]

'Lagged for life' was a phrase to chill many of those whose good fortune, rather than conduct, had saved them or their kin from criminal convictions. The rigours of Pentonville and the brutality of the hulks attracted the sympathy of Victoria's underclass towards those who stood in danger of such confinement, no less than towards those who were trying to escape from it. No one gave Hackett away. Not one man nor woman in the Newgate Street crowd betrayed Krapps as he shinned down from the cook-house roof. The last fugitive from the prison in 1879 was encouraged and cheered by the workmen who watched him from their building site. In 1853, Bell, Brown and Barry passed unchallenged – and unreported – through the neighbourhood in their prison uniforms. It seemed that little had changed in the response of ordinary men and women since Henry Williams was assisted to escape the hangman in 1836.

The same people who cheered on the escapers were often prepared to do their best in preventing men and women from being taken to prison in the first place. The experiences of Inspector James Brennan, for example, showed something of the attitude of slum-dwellers in this matter. For some time, at the end of the 1850s, he had been on the trail of a man by the name of Morris, suspected of coining. The first raid on a house near Westminster went badly wrong because, as Brennan ran to the upper floors, a trap slammed down over the well of the stairs. It was armed with rows of three-inch iron spikes, which struck his hat but not his head. While he tried without success to force the trap open, the wanted man got out through the attic, ran along the roofs of adjoining houses, and jumped twenty-five feet on to a shed below. Though badly injured, he was rescued by sympathetic neighbours, taken to Birmingham, and treated in hospital. Not one of them thought of informing the police.

Worse still, for Scotland Yard, Morris returned to London two years later. Brennan tracked him to Kent Street in the Borough. Accompanied by several other officers, the inspector burst in one winter's night and found Morris sitting on the floor contentedly making half-crowns. At the sight of Brennan, he jumped through an open window and landed on top of a policeman who had been left on duty in the yard below. Scrambling up, Morris ran off through the dark winter streets in his shirt, with Brennan and others in pursuit. The pursuers saw him run through a doorway into some gardens and then in through the back door of a house. As he followed, Brennan did not know that there was a step down into the house. He missed his footing and fell across a bed with a child in it. Getting up, he explained to the parents who he was and why he was there, then raced after his prey.

> Mr Brennan tripped up the coiner as he was endeavouring to escape, and threw him on the floor, secured him and put him into a cab, where a low mob which had meantime gathered in this disreputable neighbourhood, tried to rescue the coiner from the hands of the officers. They threw brickbats, stones and other missiles to rescue the prisoner.

Despite the instinctive sympathy of the crowd for Morris and the feeling that anyone in trouble with the police deserved assistance, the coiner was taken in handcuffs to Horsemonger Lane Gaol. After his trial at the Old Bailey, he was sentenced to thirty years' transportation for coining and for 'assaulting the officers in the execution of their duty'. To the crowd who had witnessed his arrest, he was a martyr, a man who had tried to make money in the most literal and harmless manner.[37]

Even when a suspect was arrested, the police might lack evidence or witnesses in the most straightforward of cases. Interference with witnesses by professional criminals was already a cause of frustration in the early Victorian period, not least because the witnesses seemed content to be bought off and none of their neighbours thought the worse of them for it. In the 1850s, for example, there was a burglary at Acutt's linen drapery in Westminster Road, discovered when a policeman on the beat heard a man give a signal from the shop doorway at four o'clock in the morning. Thinking that the thieves must be on the premises, the officer had 'sprung his rattle' and brought several other constables to his assistance. Inside the shop they found silks and satins bundled up ready for removal. There were two burglars in the building, men who had got in by climbing over some closets, scaling the rear boundary by a drain-pipe and walking along a high wall nine inches wide. They had then removed the skylight at the back of the roof and let themselves down into the shop by a rope ladder.

When the police arrived, the burglars retreated to the roof, running along it and jumping from one house to another, a gap of eight feet at a height of fifty feet above the ground. No policeman was prepared to risk such a challenge. The inspector in charge left two private-clothes officers on surveillance and withdrew. It seemed that the burglars might have got clear but, as it happened, they could go no further along the roofs and had hidden behind a chimney stack. Next morning the occu-pant of one of the houses, Mr Fitzgerald, was washing in his back yard as the two men slid quietly down a drainpipe behind him. One of them made the mistake of jumping on him, rather than getting clear, and Fitzgerald yelled, 'Murder!' and 'Police!' At this point, the private-clothes men rushed into the yard and arrested the two fugitives.

There was some dismay at the trial when Mr Fitzgerald swore that he could not positively identify the two defendants as the men he had seen. By that time, it transpired, he had been well-bribed by one of the gang's women to lose his memory of the entire incident. The two burglars were acquitted, though they were arrested, convicted, and transported for subsequent crimes.[38]

In response to the unreliability of such witnesses, Scotland Yard introduced systems of identification so that known criminals might be more easily watched by uniformed or private-clothes detectives before they committed further crimes. Officers from every district were rou-tinely brought to see men and women on trial for major crimes and memorize their appearances. By the 1880s, with improvements in the camera, it had become the practice to photograph suspects when arrested. Even so, the first attempts to photograph criminals for police files were frustrated by the subjects pulling faces and trying to twist their heads aside, until held firmly in place for the camera by a pair of con-stabulary hands.

Police photography of reluctant subjects after arrest in the 1880s

The routine recognition of thieves was used in such campaigns as that to combat burglaries by the use of skeleton keys. Detection in this area had been made more difficult by the subversive methods of the criminals. The usual approach was to corrupt a servant in the house, usually a maid who would be 'courted' by a plausible young man. Access to her master's keys and the making of copies meant that the house could be opened at any time. As a rule, burglars who used this method were opportunists rather than strategists and were content to take whatever might come to hand, if only such day-to-day items as Inverness capes and umbrellas.

By the mid-Victorian period, despite the unhelpfulness of many citizens who protected their criminal neighbours, the compilation of files containing descriptions and photographs began to pay dividends. A number of arrests were made simply when a known thief was recognized by a policeman as he entered a house or when a 'visitor' was seen entering a house without a cape or umbrella and coming out with both. On other occasions, police officers watched suspects for any sign of articles that might have been reported stolen. In 1862, there was a robbery in the West End by the use of skeleton keys, a theft discovered when the butler found that all his master's clothes and linen, his dressing-case, gold watch and chain had gone. The police officer who had charge of the investigation was given a tip by an informant which led him to a public house in the Tottenham Court Road on a Saturday night. He noticed 'a middle-aged, intelligent man, like a respectable mechanic, conversing with a person at the bar over a pint of half and half'. The man was wearing a choker which corresponded closely in its appearance to one of the many items taken in the robbery.

Late that night, the private-clothes detective followed the man to his lodgings. On Sunday morning, he raided the house with two other officers and found the suspect in bed with his woman. The house was searched and a handkerchief was found, marked with the crest of the nobleman who had been robbed. As the woman got out of bed, it seemed that she had concealed something under her petticoats. Though she denied this, she was searched by a police matron and a second handkerchief with the same crest was discovered. The man arrested was identified as entering the house and went to penal servitude for seven years, another inmate of the hulks.[39]

During the 1860s, however, there was to be a significant change. It was not prisons and their inmates but the men sending them there who became subject to public scrutiny. However fiercely the separate and silent systems might be criticized by middle-class philanthropists, however strong the horror and fascination which the convict hulks inspired, cynicism over the honesty of the police and the reliability of the system of justice had so far been largely confined to criminals and the class which bred them. Much as the costers might hate the police who interfered with trade, sure though they were that individual constables took bribes from brothels or individual prostitutes, there seemed no reason to regard policemen of rank and experience as systematically corrupt. In the 1860s, however, the well-known senior barrister Serjeant William Ballantine and newspapers like the *Daily Telegraph* began to suggest that the courts dispensed injustice and that the police gave perjured evidence. By the 1870s, it was plain that the most important branch of Scotland Yard, far from being the sworn antagonist of the underworld, was part of that underworld. Documents which would have put major criminals in prison for years were systematically burnt by senior members of Scotland Yard on their office fires. The uncomplicated moral zeal of 'lagging', of prison and punishment, seemed to dissolve in a reality of ineptitude and corruption.

CHAPTER 9

Justice Denied

If Galley was wrongly convicted, he certainly assisted very much in his own conviction by the irregular and improper life he led. . . . It is something like contributary negligence on his part. . . . He might or might not have been innocent of the crime of which he was accused; but if he was charged with it, it was because he belonged to the classes amongst whom they looked for crime.

In dismissing demands in 1879 for a pardon on behalf of Edmund Galley, whose alibi for a crime of murder was first established and ignored forty years earlier, Sir Robert Lowe as Home Secretary described a war against the underworld that was collective rather than individual. A man or woman of the criminal class was not to complain if wrongly convicted from time to time. However objectionable to any principle of justice, it was a view that won support. The fear that men and women who were innocent might be convicted, condemned and hanged was not one which had troubled the crowds outside Newgate a dozen years earlier as they waited all night for the excitement of seeing 'a man die in his shoes'. The merrymakers were lost in the shouts from the back of the crowd of 'Hats off!' and 'Down in front!' from those whose view was obstructed as the condemned man or woman was led to the trap. At such moments it mattered little that, if an innocent defendant were to be hanged for murder, the true killer would still be at large and able to kill again.

It was a truism, not confined to the Victorian period, that the poor, the uneducated, the alien in culture, class or race, but most of all those with other criminal convictions were most likely to be wrongly convicted and unjustly punished. Capital punishment also removed the principal witness in any further inquiry. Execution followed sentence with particular speed and decision in the earlier nineteenth century. In March 1835, for example, a Suffolk farm worker, Edward Poole Chalker, was convicted on a Friday evening at Bury St Edmunds of murdering a gamekeeper. At this time, execution usually followed within forty-eight hours, though a further day's delay was allowed where necessary to avoid putting men and women to death on a Sunday. Chalker was hanged on the Monday, still maintaining his innocence. Seven years later, an English soldier on his deathbed in India confessed to the crime.

Sometimes, as in Chalker's case, the innocence of those who had been condemned was later established when the true perpetrator of the crime was tracked down or made a confession. In 1876, William Habron, a gardener with convictions for disorderly behaviour, was convicted of shooting dead a policeman, Nicholas Cock, who had previously arrested him on a charge of drunkenness. 'Damn and bugger the bobby,' he was heard to say in a public house before the trial for drunkenness. 'If he gets the day, we'll finish him and we'll see an end to that bugger.' No weapon was found at the scene of the murder and there was little beyond Habron's threats in a public bar to incriminate him. He denied murdering the policeman, but was tried, convicted and sentenced to death none the less.

Because he was only just eighteen, Habron's sentence was commuted to life imprisonment. Two years later, in 1878, he was pardoned when the far more notorious Charles Peace was about to go to the gallows for shooting dead a man with whose wife he had been having an affair. Peace, a burglar who carried a gun as a matter of habit, confessed that he had also been the killer of Nicholas Cock. He was certainly known to have shot another policeman since Cock had been killed. The day before murdering his rival in love, Peace had travelled to London and attended the trial of young William Habron, so that he might see the man who was intended to hang in his place and hear the death sentence passed.

The Victorian period saw a number of instances in which another person confessed to a crime of murder some time after the defendant had been convicted and sentenced. In 1892, in a famous case that had already aroused a good deal of feeling on both sides, W. T. Stead was to re-open the argument over the guilt of Florence Maybrick, three years after her conviction for having murdered her husband by poison. In this instance, a man on his deathbed in South Africa had confessed to being part of a conspiracy to throw suspicion upon her.

Wrongful convictions of petty offenders on major charges were also caused by mistaken identity and uncorroborated circumstantial evidence. If the defendant was lucky, a trial judge might feel sufficiently uneasy to intervene in a doubtful case. Sir Henry Hawkins, Baron Brampton (1817–1907), recalled his experience when presiding over a hearing in which five men as co-defendants faced two trials. Four seemed to be old hands at poaching, while the fifth and youngest was one of their associates. On the first day they were convicted of grievously wounding a gamekeeper during a night's poaching. The evidence against the youngest depended on his cap being found near the scene of the attack and on the gamekeeper's identification of an assailant who struck suddenly and in the dark. The young man pleaded his innocence but was convicted with the others. Hawkins' doubts about the verdict were so strong that when the five men were tried for a second offence, he did not appoint counsel for the young man but undertook to watch the case himself. In the course of questioning, the other men admitted that the youth had not been present and that one of them had borrowed his cap. The young man, whom Hawkins had sentenced to a long term of penal servitude the day before on the first charge, received a pardon.[1]

Very few judges felt it necessary to be as scrupulous as Hawkins on this occasion. In a fraud trial of 1844, an attorney, William Henry Barber, was convicted before Sir John Gurney on charges of forging wills and impersonation, despite evidence that he had acted professionally and in good faith for apparently honest clients. He was sentenced to transportation for life, though ultimately pardoned and compensated. He died soon after his return, 'his tall form gaunt and haggard, and the sufferings he had undergone stamped upon his features'. Charles Wilkins, in his speech as Barber's counsel, addressed Gurney as the trial judge who had done his utmost to ensure Barber's fate. 'There exist upon the bench [those] who have the character of convicting judges. I do not envy their reputation in this world or their fate hereafter.'[2]

By 1860, however, there were misgivings among barristers and judges alike which led to Serjeant William Ballantine's insistence on 'the necessity of a Court of Appeal'. Ballantine appeared in many of the most famous mid-Victorian cases and saw injustice at first hand. Without such a court, men were not equal before the law, in his view. The rich defendant who was convicted had a means of appeal and escape which was denied to the poor.

> Cases may, by a well-known process, be moved into the Court of Queen's Bench, and there, although supposed to be tried by the highest officer of the law, and with the assistance of a special jury, a verdict of guilty is not necessarily final, it may be appealed against. As the process of removal is expensive, it may not unfairly be alleged that in some cases there exists one law for the poor, another for the wealthy. The verdict against the defendant unremoved would be final.[3]

The most sinister miscarriage of justice was that caused by police perjury or negligence. One of the worst scandals of the mid-Victorian period, because it challenged the integrity of the police in a murder case, occurred in 1864. On Boxing Day afternoon in the previous year, there had been a fight in the bar of the Golden Anchor public house at West Saffron Hill, Clerkenwell, near an area known as 'Little Italy'. Alfred Rebbeck, the potman of the Golden Anchor, noticed that knives were being flourished by several of the customers. A little while later, Rebbeck himself had been stabbed and Michael Harrington, a seaman, was lying on the floor of the bagatelle room, bleeding to death from a knife-wound in the stomach. Serafino Pellizzioni, one of the Italians present at about the time of the murder, had been seized and was being held down over the body of the dying man when a policeman arrived. Not surprisingly, the captive had Harrington's blood on him. Though Pellizzioni claimed that he had not entered the bagatelle room until just after Harrington was stabbed, having been with a party of Italians at the Three Tuns, Harrington identified him as the assailant before he died, though he did so under sedation.

Pellizzioni's story was that he had only come to the Golden Anchor from the Three Tuns to pacify those Italians who he was told were involved in a disturbance there. He had entered within seconds of the crime being committed, had been seized, and was then held down over Harrington's body. By chance there was also a policeman on the premises, though in another room. This officer was Detective 'Flash Charley' Fawell, as he was known locally. When Fawell was questioned, however, he was unable to explain why it was that Pellizzioni had been seized and thrown down at once after Harrington was stabbed, yet there was no sign of a knife or any other weapon. Such a weapon was never even alluded to by the prosecution at his trial. If Pellizzioni was the murderer, how had he committed the crime?

Pellizzioni was sentenced to death by Baron Martin, who remarked that he had 'never known more direct or conclusive evidence in any case'. However, the condemned man had had the good fortune to be defended by William Ballantine, the advocate of law reform and, specifically, of the establishment of a court of appeal. Ballantine was convinced that in Pellizzioni's case there had been 'very gross' perjury – almost certainly on the part of police witnesses – and refused to let the matter drop.

Serafino Pellizzioni, who had worked as a picture-framer, was of good previous character, though a number of his associates were not. Even more important than his good character was the intervention of the press. Doubts as to the conviction were aired in the columns of the *Daily Telegraph*. It seemed that everyone in the neighbourhood knew the true killer to be Gregorio Mogni, who soon confessed to having stabbed Harrington in self-defence during a tavern fight. Pellizzioni's friends thereupon brought a successful private prosecution for manslaughter against Mogni, who was convicted and sentenced to five years' imprisonment. Until 1898, the defendant in a murder trial was not permitted to give evidence. However, Pellizzioni was able to tell his own story as a witness in Mogni's trial. As a result of that trial and its predecessor, two men had now been sentenced for killing Harrington, though it was impossible that they could both be guilty.

The Crown might have pardoned Pellizzioni. Instead, unnerved by accusations of perjury against its servants, it further charged Pellizzioni with wounding Rebbeck, as if to occupy his attention while he awaited execution. He was tried on the wounding charge and acquitted. Moreover, it was now discovered that the police had long been in possession of the murder weapon and that it had been found too far away from the scene of the crime for Pellizzioni to have dropped it there. After a further delay, Pellizzioni received a pardon. There had seldom been so strong a rebuke to the police as William Ballantine's in this case.

> Their duties are extremely trying and calculated frequently to cause anger and irritation, feelings which almost invariably induce those possessed by them to exaggerate if not to invent . . . Everybody knows that 'an experienced and intelligent officer has, with his accustomed acuteness', secured

the murderer, &c.; and in this case the police did not like publishing the fact that they had committed a flagrant blunder, and so an innocent man was very nearly being executed.[4]

Striking still harder at the integrity of the Metropolitan Police, Ballantine publicized an undated case of the decade in which two young men 'of perfect respectability' were walking home through St John's Wood one night, in an area where there had been a number of burglaries. They were seized by three policemen and charged with attempting to break into a house.

> The three officers declared that they had watched them, and caught them in the act, and had actually taken from them the implements of burglary. It is obvious that, if the young men told the truth, one of the most wicked cases of conspiracy ever known had been planned by the police, and was carried out by flagrant perjury.

At their trial, the jury believed that the two young men were telling the truth and discharged them. The young men then brought charges of perjury against the three police officers. English law permitted only one defendant to be named on an indictment for perjury and the first police officer was convicted at the Central Criminal Court. The case against the police was of sufficient public importance for the other two indictments to be removed to the Court of Queen's Bench and for sentence on the first officer to be deferred. However, the two young men could not afford to bring further prosecutions in the Court of Queen's Bench and the Crown declined to do so on its own behalf.[5]

By no means all the cases in which an innocent man or woman might be sentenced to death were the result of malice on the part of the police or bias in the courts. The Victorian period saw a considerable advance in science as a weapon against crime, in the examination of gunshot wounds, in the first forms of fingerprinting, but most of all in the detection of poison. Yet reliance upon such techniques of investigation was sometimes premature. When, in 1859, Dr Thomas Smethurst was sentenced to death for poisoning the 'wife' he had bigamously married, the Reinsch Test had provided more than sufficient evidence to show a lethal quantity of arsenic. When the Marsh Test later showed no arsenic at all, there was a further and hasty investigation as Smethurst waited to be hanged. Only then was the source of arsenic discovered to be in the scientific apparatus, whose copper gauze was losing its top coating and releasing arsenic from the undercoat in large quantities into the specimen liquid.

Where scientific analysis was central, it might imply guilt while failing to determine it. Florence Maybrick's trial was a *cause célèbre* in consequence. Mrs Maybrick was an American who in 1881, at the age of twenty-six, had married a Liverpool cotton-broker almost twice her age. James Maybrick was in the habit of taking tonics or aphrodisiacs containing arsenic or strychnine in medicinal doses. A fatal dose was reckoned at two grains, a medicinal dose at one-fifteenth of a grain. After eight years of marriage, Mrs Maybrick began an affair with her husband's friend Alfred Brierley, who posed as 'Mr Maybrick' when they stayed at a London hotel. Florence Maybrick's true husband discovered this in March 1889, when he apparently blacked her eye but after which there was also an uncertain reconciliation.

In April, Mrs Maybrick bought three dozen flypapers from the chemist. She was seen by her servants soaking them in water to extract the arsenic, which she claimed she used for cosmetic purposes. A few days later James Maybrick suffered an attack of vomiting. A fortnight later he was dead. Two days before he died, Mrs Maybrick had taken a bottle of Valentine's Meat Juice from the sick-room and returned it a few minutes later. On analysis it was found to have had arsenic added. The day before his death, one of the nurses heard Maybrick say three times to his wife, 'Oh, Bunny, Bunny, how could you do it? I did not think it of you!' The coroner's jury found that he had died of arsenic and that Mrs Maybrick had administered the poison to him.

The evidence was apparently damning until the autopsy revealed only a tenth of a grain of arsenic in Maybrick's body, rather large for medicinal purposes but not a fatal dose in itself. Defence and prosecution agreed that he had died of gastro-enteritis. The question now was whether that had been precipitated by arsenic, and to that question there was no conclusive answer. One doctor attending him had called him 'a chronic dyspeptic', while Maybrick himself had taken arsenic and strychnine in tonic form for that reason. Yet it seemed that someone had added enough arsenic to various jars, pans, and bottles of food and medicine in the Maybrick household to kill fifty people.

The trial judge, Sir James Fitzjames Stephen, had presided over the case of Israel Lipski who was convicted and hanged after a controversial summing-up. In the Maybrick hearing, he earned criticism for

telling the grand jury at the outset that Mrs Maybrick's adultery provided a motive for murder. Though it was not the best time to make such
an observation, the truth of it was self-evident to most contemporaries.
A further objection to his conduct of the case was that his summing-
up appeared rambling and unbalanced, showing already the mental
deterioration which led to insanity two years later. Yet Mrs Maybrick,
rather than her judge, did most of the damage to her case, some of it
by asking to make a statement at the close of evidence for the defence.
In this statement from the dock, on which she could not be cross-
examined, she repeated that arsenic from the flypapers was for cosmetic
purposes and that, though she added white powder to the meat juice, it
was at Maybrick's request and she did not know it was arsenic. Her
statement was as ill-advised as her counsel, Sir Charles Russell, feared.

Florence Maybrick was found guilty and sentenced to death. Yet the
forensic evidence pointed to attempted murder rather than murder. She
was reprieved in terms which gave her the benefit of the doubt and
which also gave the lie to any claim that she was a martyr to contemporary prejudice as a faithless wife. As Henry Matthews, the Home
Secretary, wrote, 'although the evidence leads clearly to the conclusion
that the prisoner administered and attempted to administer arsenic to
her husband with intent to murder, yet it does not wholly exclude a
reasonable doubt whether his death was in fact caused by the
administration of arsenic'.

A not dissimilar murder case was tried in 1896–7 before the British
Consular Court at Yokohama, where the consul exercised jurisdiction
over the British community as in other treaty ports. Walter Carew, the
Secretary of the Yokohama Club, died in mysterious circumstances. A
heavy drinker, he had also suffered from malaria, venereal disease and
a consequent stricture. For some years he had taken arsenic as a tonic,
in the form of Flower's Solution of Arsenic. His wife, Edith Carew, had
formed an attachment to a young man, Henry Vansittart Dickinson, a
clerk at the Hongkong and Shanghai Bank in Yokohama. The question
was whether Mrs Carew had poisoned her husband. The post-mortem
revealed about a third of a grain of arsenic in the body, not a fatal dose
in itself but enough to suggest that there had been a fatal dose at some
time, if only because it was five times the size of a medicinal dose. Edith
Carew was convicted and sentenced to death, the hanging to be carried
out in the British naval prison at Yokohama. Before that could happen,

Crowds waiting to witness an execution outside Newgate Gaol

she was reprieved by the British Ambassador in Tokyo, by virtue of an amnesty issued to prisoners in Japan by the Mikado. She was brought back to England and served a life sentence in Aylesbury Prison.

*

The holiday crowds who attended public executions, until such festivals were abolished in 1868, sought what Robert Browning in his poem 'Ned Bratts' called 'amusement steeped in fire'. A Gloucester hangman, for example, would please the crowds after the trap dropped by spinning the dangling corpse, slapping it on the back, shaking hands with it, and pretending to exchange banter. Not only did the onlookers applaud, they did so with the sense of being morally and legally justified in their enjoyment as witnesses of legal retribution. Even the entertainment of watching men and women flogged or exposed to insult and injury in the pillory had survived almost until their own time.

Yet there was a slow change during the Victorian period from the self-righteous 'Old Red Barn Murder' morality of 'Be sure your sins will find you out' to the belief that it was better for a hundred guilty men to go free than for an innocent man to be wrongly condemned. It was less easy, however, to change the view expressed by Sir Robert Lowe that the known criminal who was wrongly convicted of a major crime was in part to blame.

In the 1860s, it was not a lone pamphleteer but the *Daily Telegraph* which called the conviction of Serafino Pellizzioni into question. Twenty years beyond that, it became relatively common for sections of the press to challenge the decisions of courts, juries or Home Office officials. Their opponents deplored what *The Law Times* called 'trial by newspaper'. The *Saturday Review* denounced 'the practice of endeavouring to re-try convicted criminals'. The targets of these criticisms included W. T. Stead's *Pall Mall Gazette* and the *Review of Reviews*, as well as the *Commonweal*, a socialist weekly to which William Morris contributed.

The new mood was reflected rather than inspired by the appearance in 1887 of Sherlock Holmes, part of whose appeal lay in establishing the innocence of the obvious suspect in such stories as 'The Boscombe Valley Mystery', 'The Norwood Builder' or 'The Sussex Vampire'. When, in the second of these, Inspector Lestrade announces that the guilt of Holmes' client is 'definitely established', nothing is more certain than that the man's innocence will be proved. Sir Arthur Conan Doyle, no less than his famous creation, was later to devote his energies and money to fighting on behalf of the wrongly accused and improperly convicted. Yet the popular influence of Sherlock Holmes, as one of the half-dozen most famous creations in modern literature, would be hard to overestimate. His scepticism and dislike of authority, his instinctive response to the helpless, were a match for the contemporary journalism which questioned in an increasing number of cases whether justice had been done.

W. T. Stead was by temperament a natural combatant in the battle over the 're-trial' of cases in the late 1880s. The crime which brought this issue before the public, replete with slum life, poverty and racial ill-feeling, was the murder of Miriam Angel in 1887. The reputation of the Home Secretary and that of one of the most eminent jurists of the age, Sir James Fitzjames Stephen, became Stead's targets. If he failed to prove the innocence of the accused, Israel Lipski, he inspired a degree of disrespect for judicial and executive authority that would have been unthinkable twenty or thirty years earlier.

On 28 June 1887, the body of Miriam Angel was found in a Stepney lodging-house off Commercial Road. There was yellow staining round her mouth and froth on her lips, which proved to be nitric acid. Under her bed was a young man of twenty-two who lived in the same house, Israel Lipski. He was semi-conscious and had identical yellow staining round his mouth.

Israeli Lipski was a Polish Jew who spoke little English. He claimed he had been set upon by two men on the first-floor landing. They demanded money and, not receiving any, forced a piece of wood in his mouth and poured nitric acid down his throat, saying they had already killed Miriam Angel. Thinking him dead, they pushed him under the bed in her room.

Miriam Angel had died of suffocation, not nitric acid. It was alleged that Lipski came up the stairs, where an internal window looked into her room. Perhaps there was a chink in the curtain or perhaps the light in the room was strong. Though Miriam Angel was covered by bedclothes when found, perhaps she was not when Lipski saw her. It was assumed by the prosecution that he could not resist the temptation which she presented. He entered the room and seized her. When she resisted, he struck her, forced acid down her throat and held her face in the pillow until she suffocated.

There was no scientific evidence that sexual intercourse had taken place. Though Lipski was identified as a man who had bought nitric acid, intruders in the lodging-house might have laid hands on it as easily as he. Was it credible that he would swallow it himself? If Lipski had not had intercourse with the girl, why murder her? The contradictions were investigated by the improbably named team of Detective Inspector Final and Detective Sergeant Thick. Yet it was Mr Justice Stephen who caused controversy by insisting in his charge to the jury that 'passion was the motive for the crime' and that it was the work of one man. In this summary, he swept away Lipski's defence before the jury began to consider its verdict.

Martin L. Friedland wrote in a major study of the case in 1984, 'Was Lipski properly convicted? I believe that he was not. The judge's charge was grossly unfair in stressing the "lust" theory and effectively took the case out of the hands of the jury. An appeal court today would, I think, quash the conviction.'

Against the accusation that he had been unfairly tried was Lipski's confession the day before he was hanged. He claimed he had intended to rob Miriam Angel but found no money. He had already bought nitric acid in order to commit suicide. This confession was made after constant visits by Rabbi Singer, who no doubt acted with good intentions. But the confession was odd. It was soon challenged in the *Pall Mall Gazette* by one who knew Lipski. On the morning that Lipski bought the nitric acid, he was starting a business: not the time when a man commits suicide. Moreover, the confession got the time of the murder wrong by two or three hours. Finally, according to Lipski's confession, he slipped into the room to take what he could before Miriam Angel woke. Why, then, did he lock the door and make it harder to get away?

Such questions were unwelcome to the Home Office. On the streets, latent prejudice had become overt anti-semitism during the trial hearing. Fights broke out between those who thought the defendant was guilty and those convinced he was not. When the black flag was hoisted at Newgate to indicate that the execution had taken place, the crowd which had formed one side in the street fights gathered at the prison to raise three cheers.

In the face of the last-minute confession, Stead allowed that the jury had come to a correct verdict but that they had done so on the wrong evidence. William Morris and Belfort Bax in the *Commonweal* argued that the confession was forced from Lipski by 'cajolery or even threats'. When he confessed, having repeatedly denied his guilt, Lipski had lost all hope of reprieve. Was he persuaded that confession might somehow help his people, his family or himself? Did he confess to shield someone or in the hope of a last-minute pardon? It was certain he had nothing to lose by confessing on the last day. As Morris and Bax put it, 'those who have never believed in his guilt have no need to do so now'. He went to his death leaving, in some people, a feeling that he had not had a fair trial and that the whole truth had never been told.

Israel Lipski, like Serafino Pellizzioni, was a recent immigrant to whom England was a strange land. They both lived in a society which, however admirable their own lives, was regarded as a nursery of crime. Florence Maybrick was an adulteress and, indeed, by Bracebridge Hemyng's moral definition, a prostitute. Had these three defendants, therefore, received less than justice? To some sections of the press, Henry Matthews, as Home Secretary, or Sir James Fitzjames Stephen, as trial judge, became targets of obloquy. Yet the fate of the inarticulate, of outsiders or defendants with a criminal past bred a new race of champions. Sir Edward Marshall Hall and Patrick Hastings made names for themselves as defenders in court, while Sir Arthur Conan Doyle employed his energy and wealth to support individual campaigns for justice.

Among those who deplored this development was Victoria's son and successor, King Edward VII, as he wrote to Herbert Gladstone when the latter was Home Secretary. 'The tendency nowadays to regard a criminal as a martyr, and to raise an agitation on sentimental grounds in order to put pressure on the Home Secretary, is one which may eventually prove very inconvenient, if concessions are too readily made.'[6]

With hindsight, a good deal of argument and ill-feeling might have been avoided by incorporating a Court of Criminal Appeal in the other major reforms of the legal system during the 1870s. The case which prompted Edward VII's displeasure had its roots in the controversies of those earlier decades and was one of several that brought such an appeal court into being. This particular defendant was one of many Victorians who had been fathered out of wedlock by the middle class and then abandoned to their working-class mothers. Most lived quiet but respectable lives, some took to crime, but few were ever heard of by the nation at large.

Horace George Rayner's mother had been a shop-girl and he claimed that his father was her employer, William Whiteley, the 'Universal Provider', proprietor of one of London's most famous stores, Whiteley's of Bayswater. It was said of Whiteley that he combined commercial instinct with Bible-reading and philandering in more or less equal portions. It was also said that he was a canting hypocrite. Horace Rayner was destitute, thrown out of work while his wife was pregnant. He entered Whiteley's store on 24 January 1907 and confronted its proprietor. He explained who he was and asked for help. Mr Whiteley told him to go to the Salvation Army.

In the course of the argument, Rayner shouted, 'Then you are a dead man, Mr Whiteley!' He drew a gun from his pocket and shot Whiteley dead, then turned the gun on himself and fired a bullet into his own head. He did not die but shot out his right eye, apparently because his hand was shaking and his aim was bad. Two months later he appeared at the Central Criminal Court, where his counsel offered a defence of temporary insanity. Rayner had carried the gun only to commit suicide, if Whiteley refused help.

This defence was destroyed by the discovery of a note in his pocket, written before the Bayswater encounter: 'William Whiteley is my father. He has brought upon himself and me a double fatality by reason of his own refusal of a request perfectly reasonable. R. I. P.' The jury found Rayner guilty and Lord Chief Justice Alverstone sentenced him to death with the customary promise of a judge who intended to advise the Home Secretary against a reprieve. 'I cannot hold out to you the slightest hope that the sentence of the law will not be carried into effect.'

Horace Rayner was content to die, indeed he twice more tried to commit suicide, once by cutting his wrists and once by setting fire to his prison bedding. Yet the revelation of William Whiteley's conduct and character rallied public opinion behind the young man. Within a couple of days, a petition for his reprieve gathered 179,000 signatures and the response obliged his solicitor to open special offices for the collection of letters and protests. The government ignored Lord Chief Justice Alverstone's advice and announced a reprieve. King Edward VII, who privately voiced his support for Alverstone, signed the document, informing the Home Secretary that 'The murder of Mr Whiteley appeared to be a very cold-blooded one, incident on a failure to obtain blackmail, and this circumstance seems to have been somewhat lost sight of in the agitation which has taken place.'[7]

Encouraged by a press whose popular readership far exceeded that at the time of Pellizzioni's case in the 1860s, the crusaders in the case of Horace Rayner showed a populist power which the government found hard to ignore. Tens of thousands of men and women were now prepared to save a murderer from the gallows rather than celebrate a death. In these circumstances, Parliament passed the Court of Appeal Act 1907, setting up a further check between the dock and the gallows. Other reforms were overdue. Not until 1908 did Parliament abolish the death sentence for youths under sixteen, later raised to a minimum age of eighteen. Women were far less likely than men to be hanged after conviction and none was executed for fourteen years following the new legislation. In 1922, infanticide when committed by a woman was taken out of the category of murder.

*

So far as one man caught the public eye in defending those who suffered injustice because of their criminal associations or mere suspicion of criminality, it was Sir Arthur Conan Doyle. With the fame of Sherlock Holmes behind him, he confronted the authorities after the convictions of George Edalji in 1903 and Oscar Slater in 1909. No one who has dealt with the Home Office on such matters would be unsympathetic to Conan Doyle's comment on his experiences.

> The sad fact is that officialdom in England stands solid together, and that when you are forced to attack it you need not expect justice, but rather that you are up against an avowed Trade Union, the members of which are not going to act the blackleg to each other, and which subordinates the public interest to a false idea of loyalty.

As Conan Doyle wrote years afterwards, 'I can hardly think with patience of this case.'

'This case' involved George Edalji, a young man of mixed race, the son of an English mother and an Indian father. His father, Shapurji Edalji, was a Christian who had come to England, was ordained, and in 1875 became Vicar of Great Wyrley, in the Staffordshire mining district south of Cannock. George was born two years later. In 1888, the family received a number of anonymous threats which proved to be from a maidservant. From 1892 to 1895, several local families, including the Edaljis, were subject to further abusive letters, not the work of the maidservant, some of which included death-threats. The Edaljis also became the victims of hoaxes and bogus announcements in the press. Missing objects were found in their garden and even in the house. Letters purporting to be written by – and about – Shapurji Edalji were sent to other clergy, including one which accused him of rape and adultery. When a key from Walsall Grammar School was found in the house, the Chief Constable of Staffordshire, Captain G. A. Anson, informed Shapurji Edalji that the police considered his son responsible for the letters and the thefts. There was no evidence for this but it was certainly true that the letters then stopped.[8]

In 1903, by which time George Edalji went daily to work as a solicitor in Birmingham, there were serious attacks on horses, cattle and sheep round Great Wyrley. It was rumoured that Edalji was responsible for these nocturnal atrocities, allegedly proof of pagan worship. He was accused in anonymous letters of being in a gang of such criminals. The police, having decided that he was the author of the earlier letters, searched the vicarage and found a pair of muddy boots, a coat and trousers that were damp and had two small bloodstains on them, as well as four dirty razors with stains which proved to be rust. Not only were the two bloodstains – the size of small coins – on the cuff of the jacket far less than the perpetrator would have had on his clothes but, though the jacket was damp, the bloodstains were dry and could not have been recent. There were certainly horsehairs on his jacket but in an age before motor transport this was commonplace. None the less, the young man was tried at Stafford Assizes and sent to prison for seven years. At the trial, a handwriting expert, T. H. Gurrin, identified the latest anonymous letters as being in Edalji's handwriting. Unfortunately, Gurrin's expertise had already assisted in the more famous wrongful conviction and imprisonment of Adolf Beck in 1896 on charges of larceny and false pretences.

Gurrin's blunder in the Beck case was discovered in 1904, a year after the Cannock trial. There was also a petition on George Edalji's behalf with ten thousand signatures, including those of many lawyers. Worse still, the maiming of animals at Great Wyrley went on. The Home Office remained unmoved by representations but then, three years into the seven-year sentence, it released Edalji without explanation.

Conan Doyle now learnt of the case. He established that Edalji's clothes offered no evidence against him at all. Mud on his boots was not from the field where the crime had been committed. Conan Doyle traced the cattle-maiming to three brothers named Sharp, one of whom was quickly sent to South Africa by his family. Careful comparison showed that the letters accusing Edalji were not in his own writing, as Gurrin swore, but in that of Rodney Sharp, a backward and difficult product of Walsall Grammar School.

One thing, above all, convinced Conan Doyle of George Edalji's innocence the moment he saw him. It was plain that the young man had 'not only a high degree of myopia, but marked astigmatism'. He was unable to recognize those he knew from a distance of more than six feet. Yet he was said, on a moonless night, to have traversed a couple of miles of rough ground and climbed innumerable fences and obstacles to reach his prey.[9]

Conan Doyle's findings were published in the *Daily Telegraph* during January 1907 with permission for anyone to reprint them. The Home Office, whose three-man inquiry included a second cousin of Captain Anson, accepted the views of the Chief Constable of Staffordshire, endorsing the guilt of Edalji and the innocence of Rodney Sharp. The Law Society, however, exonerated Edalji and reinstated him as a solicitor. Readers of the *Daily Telegraph* raised £300 for him, which he gave to the man who had financed his defence at the trial.

George Edalji was an innocent man, whose race and appearance caused him to be regarded by the police as a criminal long before the offence for which he was sent to prison. Conan Doyle's greater battle was on behalf of a man who seemed perfectly to fit Sir Robert Lowe's theory of 'contributory negligence'. Anyone asked to draw, from imagination, a portrait of a criminal from the lower depths of the underworld, might well have produced a likeness of Oscar Slater. If he was not the man who murdered Marion Gilchrist, he seemed to the police the sort of man who might have done it, a pimp and a frequenter of billiard-parlours and the twilight world of clubs and gambling, on both sides of the Atlantic. As surely as Israel Lipski, his race and origins were against him, for he was also a Jew and had been born in Germany. Yet his underworld habitat, rather than any crime that he committed, was to cost him nineteen years of his life.

On a December night in 1908, at about 7 p.m., the octogenarian Marion Gilchrist was murdered in her Glasgow flat by blows to her head. The disturbance brought a neighbour to her door, opened from outside by her servant Helen Lambie, who was returning from an errand. The intruder came out of the flat, passing behind Helen Lambie, who never saw his face. The neighbour, Arthur Adams, glimpsed him as he rushed down the stairs. In the dark street, a girl of fourteen, Mary Barrowman, was bumped into by a man as he hurried past. Marion Gilchrist's diamond brooch was missing and a box of documents had been ransacked.

Oscar Slater became a suspect the day after the murder, when he was reported as offering a diamond brooch for sale at the Sloper Club, India Street. It was soon discovered that Miss Gilchrist's brooch had three rows of diamonds and Slater's only one, but police interest in him quickened as the type of man they were seeking. Before they found him, Slater left for New York on a pre-arranged journey, now seen as a flight from justice. He concealed neither his name nor his destination. Application was made for his extradition from the United States and Slater returned without contesting this.

Before his return, the three eyewitnesses had been taken to New

York to identify the suspect. Arthur Adams could only say that Slater resembled the man he had glimpsed but that he could not identify him as the suspect. The two girls were confronted by Slater in handcuffs and asked, 'Is that the man?' – a procedure which in England might have invalidated their evidence. Moreover, Helen Lambie had not seen his face and could identify him only by his walk. After the trial she was alleged to have said that the murderer appeared to belong to a superior social class to Slater. Mary Barrowman agreed that she could identify Slater from the two or three seconds in which he bumped into her in the darkened street. Many years later, she insisted that Slater was merely 'very like the man' she had seen but that, as a girl of fourteen, the procurator fiscal had bullied her into saying that the man was definitely Slater.

Mary Barrowman and Helen Lambie also identified a discarded leather jacket as the one the suspect was wearing. Since it would have been heavily bloodstained, it was subjected to forensic examination. So was a tack-hammer in Slater's possession, which the police favoured as the murder weapon. No traces of blood were found on either. A number of witnesses had seen a man loitering in the street near Miss Gilchrist's rooms on evenings before the murder. They picked out Slater at an identification parade but all of them had first seen or been shown his photograph. He stood in a line of nine plain-clothes policemen from the local division, and two railway officials, none bearing any resemblance to him. Such was the extent of the evidence against him.

For the defence, Andrée Antoine, who was Slater's young mistress, and their servant both testified that he was at home at 7 p.m., when the murder was committed. He had certainly been seen at a billiard-hall in Renfield Street at 6.30, in clothes other than those the suspect wore. It was not impossible that he could have hurried half a mile home, changed his clothes, gone straight out again, walked to Miss Gilchrist's flat and committed the murder by 7 p.m., but nor was it likely. Duncan MacBrayne, a greengrocer of Sauchiehall Street, made a statement to the police that he had met Slater near the latter's home at 8.15. Slater was not dressed as the other witnesses remembered the murderer being dressed and he had behaved normally. MacBrayne's evidence was never called nor revealed to the defence, though it was known to the Crown and the trial judge. Similarly, Detective Lieutenant Trench later revealed that Helen Lambie had made a first statement on the night of the murder, identifying the killer by name as someone other than Slater. Trench had received the statement and passed it to the High Court. It was never seen again and officialdom denied all knowledge of its existence.

Sir Edward Marshall Hall later remarked that in England such a case would have been dismissed at the magistrates court. Slater was, none the less, convicted. In Scottish law a majority verdict was possible and, of his fifteen jurors, nine found him guilty, one not guilty and five not proven. It was small comfort to know that if two more jurors had voted 'not proven', he would have gone free. The Scots poet and man of letters Andrew Lang read the trial transcript and remarked that 'a cat would scarcely be whipped for stealing cream' on such evidence as the Crown had brought.[10]

Though there was no Court of Criminal Appeal in Scotland for almost twenty years more, public disquiet secured Slater's reprieve a few days before the date of his execution. The sentence was commuted to penal servitude for life. In 1912, following a campaign for his freedom, a commissioner was appointed to examine the case. Detective Lieutenant Trench was invited by the Secretary for Scotland to submit evidence. He did so. He was then dismissed from the police force for having communicated information to an unauthorized person – the commissioner himself.

In a more ominous development, Trench and a solicitor, Conan Doyle's informant David Cook, were arrested on a charge of receiving stolen property a year before. Trench had recovered stolen jewellery with Cook's assistance, but received it only in the sense that it passed through his hands on its way back to the lawful owners. The case against the two men was withdrawn from the jury when it came to court.

Oscar Slater served nineteen years of his sentence before a special Act of Parliament referred his case to the new Court of Appeal in Scotland. The verdict was set aside and he received £6,000 compensation for what the Home Secretary called his 'wrongful conviction'. He was, however, left to pay £1,500, the cost of his appeal, a bill underwritten by Conan Doyle.

In dealing with a minor figure of the underworld like Oscar Slater, the law was checked by the scrutiny of such men as Conan Doyle, Andrew Lang and Marshall Hall. The defendant escaped the gallows by a narrow margin. Yet a man of his kind might as easily be hanged by a narrow margin, if those who sought his death were ruthless in their application of the rules.

No Conan Doyle or Marshall Hall came to save such men as John Williams, a professional burglar accused of shooting dead a policeman as he escaped from a house near South Cliff, Eastbourne, on an October evening in 1912. He was never identified by witnesses as the gunman. Though he had a gun, it was never identified as the one used. Though the killer's trilby hat was picked up, it was never proved that Williams owned one. However, his rival in love went to the police and accused him. The investigating officer, Chief Inspector Eli Bower, was described by colleagues as 'A rough diamond, one of the old-time dicks'. Bower 'wasn't too particular' about how he got results, least of all when a policeman had been murdered.[11]

Florence Seymour, the object of Williams' affection, was arrested and threatened with a murder charge herself. She became hysterical or was what the police surgeon called 'in a highly distressed and agitated condition'. In this state she was questioned until midnight and a statement was produced which she later insisted Bower had written. By the time a doctor was called, she had collapsed on the floor.

The Eastbourne police had earlier taken a statement from a witness who saw two men – neither of them Williams – within three hundred yards of the crime on the night it was committed, both of them agitated and talking of the murder in detail, one of them carrying a gun. After Williams was arrested, that statement disappeared and the witness was never interviewed. Florence Seymour alleged that her first statement, not made to Bower, was also missing. Petitions, questions in Parliament and an appeal against the verdict failed to save John Williams, who was hanged at the end of the year.

To Robert Lowe's view of a criminal's 'contributory negligence' in the injustice he might suffer was added a more comfortable doctrine that the authorities might be trusted to know what they were doing. As late as 14 April 1948, Sir David Maxwell Fyfe, a future Home Secretary and Lord Chancellor, rebuked those members of the House of Commons who argued for the abolition of capital punishment. 'As a realist I do not believe that the chances of error in a murder case . . . constitute a factor which we must consider. . . . Of course a jury might go wrong, the Court of Criminal Appeal might go wrong, as might the House of Lords and the Home Secretary; they might all be stricken mad and go wrong. But that is not a possibility which anyone can consider likely.'

Justice in the Victorian period might be frustrated by incompetence or bias. Occasionally, as Ballantine recorded, there was evidence of police perjury. Far worse, in the 1870s, was the discovery that the most important branch of Scotland Yard, in its fight against crime, contained officers who were corrupt on system and who had for some years been in the pay of professional criminals.

CHAPTER 10

The Arrest of Scotland Yard

FAR FROM the great issues of murder and its punishment, costers and petty thieves who smarted under justice dreamt of vengeance on their persecutors. A few, as Mayhew had described, found their opportunity for brief and bloody satisfaction at the expense of an individual policeman. Yet in their most exotic fantasies, they can scarcely have pictured professional villains capable of bringing down the entire structure of criminal investigation. They knew, of course, that policemen on a particular beat might accept money for ensuring that a brothel traded quietly. Some officers were said to threaten prostitutes with the alternatives of handing over their takings or being arrested. As a barrister, William Ballantine had dealt with police perjury and knew that there were officers who would conspire against innocent men in order to improve their record of arrests and convictions. These, however, were individual betrayals of trust. That a major group of detective officers – senior officers of Scotland Yard at that – should be systematically corrupt was surely no more than a tasteless fiction.

During the 1870s, the Victorian press and public suffered a twofold moral reverse. Once again, the underworld produced men whose audacity and enterprise might as easily have made them champions of industry or builders of empire. Far worse was the revelation in 1877 that their success depended largely on an ability to select and corrupt those police officers who had seemed the most honest and experienced. Only by suborning such men could the conspirators ensure the success of their grand designs. That was why the corruption must go to the heart – and head – of Scotland Yard.

A hundred years earlier, public expectations had been more modest. The Bow Street Runners of the mid-eighteenth century were a force recruited by two city magistrates, Henry Fielding the novelist and his half-brother, the 'Blind Justice', Sir John Fielding. Many of the recruits were useful for their knowledge of the criminal world, of which they had once been members. Some were entirely reformed, others less so, but all worked for rewards. However, the necessity of setting a thief to catch a thief was assumed to have been removed by Sir Robert Peel's Metropolitan Police Act of 1829 and the new order of the 1830s. The uniformed figures of the Victorian streets were intended to instil confidence. Their success in doing so was reflected in such famous pantomime songs of the early 1890s as E. W. Rogers' 'If you want to know the time ask a p'liceman'. These men might be figures of fun to the middle class but rarely the objects of moral scorn.

The Metropolitan Police, however hated by Mayhew's costers or patronized by the middle class, had not appeared systematically corrupt. When the contrary was shown to be the case in 1877 during the so-called 'Trial of the Detectives', the extent of the infection caused public dismay. Three of the four most senior officers in the Detective Force of Scotland Yard, under Superintendent Frederick Williamson, were among those who appeared in the dock at the Old Bailey on 24 October that year, charged with conspiracy 'to obstruct, defeat and pervert the due course of public justice'. Two of them, as well as a detective sergeant and a corrupt solicitor, were sentenced to imprisonment with hard labour at the end of the trial.

These were men who undertook the most sensitive duties at Scotland Yard. Chief Detective Inspector Nathaniel Druscovich was fluent in French and Italian and had been engaged upon 'important government business'. Chief Detective Inspector William Palmer had been a bodyguard 'attending upon the Queen' when it was rumoured that there was an Irish Fenian plot to assassinate her. The highest-ranking officer on trial was Senior Chief Inspector George Clarke, second-in-command to Superintendent Williamson. Clarke was acquitted but released only on his own recognizances to answer further counts in the indictment if called to do so. He hastily retired from the police and became the landlord of a public house. There was sympathy for the three detectives who went to prison, as victims of the skill and guile shown by international criminals. Yet, as Baron Pollock remarked in passing sentence, their offences had been of 'peculiar enormity'.

The corruption had come to light as a result of the so-called 'Turf Frauds' of 1876. In September that year a number of wealthy victims in France had been contacted by the 'Society for Insuring Against Losses on the Turf'. To anyone less gullible and greedy the scheme would have seemed about as rational as insuring against the certainty of death. Each dupe was sent what appeared to be a genuine newspaper but which had actually been manufactured for the occasion and run off by an Edinburgh printer. The leading article in *The Sport* for 31 August 1876 protested on behalf of Mr Hugh Montgomery against the conduct of English bookmakers. Mr Montgomery had made so large a fortune by backing horses that the bookmakers – 'vultures', the editorial called them – had combined together to boycott his bets. He might, of course, persuade others to bet for him. Unfortunately, wrote *The Sport*, 'this cannot be done in England, where the rules of the Jockey Club void any bet made in an assumed name'. The author of this nonsense guessed correctly that dupes living abroad would have no idea whether there was such a rule or not. Mr Montgomery, the paper added, proposed to get round the ban by allowing agents abroad to bet for him in England by post.

Those who received the bogus newspaper found that it was accompanied by a letter from Mr Montgomery.

> Your name has been favourably mentioned to me by the Franco-English Society of Publicity, and I consequently repose in you the most esteemed confidence. What I require of you is very simple indeed. I will send you for each race the amount which I desire you to put on the horse which must, in my opinion, win. You will have to forward the money *in your name*, but *on my account*, to the bookmaker, and thus will be able to get the real odds, which on account of my success and great knowledge are denied to me. The bookmaker will, on settling day, send you the amount, added to the stake originally forwarded to him. This you will please remit to me, and on its receipt I will forthwith forward to you a commission of five per cent.

The Comtesse de Goncourt was one of those who received this letter. How could she lose? The cheques sent to her by Mr Montgomery must be genuine, otherwise they would not be accepted by the London bookmakers. If the horse lost, Mr Montgomery would be out of pocket, not she. If it won, she would have 5 per cent of the profit. She agreed to do as he asked.[1]

Mr Montgomery sent a cheque for £200, drawn on the Royal Bank of London, Agar Street, The Strand, with instructions as to the horse to be backed. The money was to be forwarded to Mr Jackson, 'a sworn bookmaker' at an address near Charing Cross. The Comtesse could hardly be expected to know that there was no such thing in England as a sworn bookmaker, a term which merely made the bogus transaction sound more solemn. The horse evidently won, however, since the Comtesse received a cheque from Jackson for the winnings, which she forwarded to Mr Montgomery.

Back came another cheque for her commission and a further £1,000 to be invested on the Great Northern Handicap with a sworn book-maker named Francis. Again the horse won and again the Comtesse received her commission. In these few days, she had become more than eager to invest a little money of her own in the expertise of Mr Montgomery. He demurred at first, unwilling to encourage her to take such a risk, since even her first proposed investment was £1,000. She invested the money anyway on the horse he had also chosen and received a substantial cheque for her winnings. At that point, discretion was dead. Next, with Mr Montgomery's approval, she planned to invest £30,000. Even if she lost, her earlier winnings would pay the sum. 'If you have not the whole amount at hand, see what you can stake and I myself will willingly advance the difference,' wrote Mr Montgomery, showing himself not only an unfailingly shrewd adviser but a true friend. Happily for the victim, this last transaction was never com-pleted.[2]

The whirligig of avarice spun for a week or two and then crashed. It was necessary for the Comtesse de Goncourt to consult her lawyer about raising more funds to complete the £30,000. He inquired into the scheme and soon told her bluntly that there was no such bank as the Royal Bank of London, no such races or horses as those she had invested in, no bookmakers – sworn or otherwise – at the addresses to which she had sent the money. There was no such issue of *The Sport* as she had received and no Mr Hugh Montgomery known to the Jockey Club or on the turf. What made matters worse was that, in her eager-ness to prove her assets, she had sent Mr Montgomery his winnings in drafts on her own account at Crédit Lyonnais. In the brief course of the swindle, which lasted less than four weeks, such greed and stupidity had cost its victims somewhere between £12,000 and £14,000. The drafts on the Crédit Lyonnais were changed at Reinhardt's in London for Bank of England notes, which could be traced, and these were then changed in Glasgow for Bank of Scotland notes which could not.

The hunt began and the headquarters of the 'sworn bookmakers' were discovered at 8 Northumberland Avenue, 'one hundred paces from the rear of Scotland Yard'. By the time that these offices were raided, however, the tenants had long departed. News of the fraud had reached Scotland Yard on 25 September. Thereupon, Chief Detective Inspector Clarke took a blank sheet of blotting-paper and posted it in an envelope which had been self-addressed by William Kurr, a bluff and youthful underworld figure who owned a public house in Islington and two racehorses.

William Kurr left the Northumberland Street office for the last time that afternoon. He saw Chief Detective Inspector Druscovich standing near the entrance of Scotland Yard. The conversation was furtive and brief.

'I am glad I have seen you,' Druscovich said, 'there is a big swindle come in from Paris, £10,000.'

'Is it a racing swindle?' Kurr asked.

'No I don't think it is, something to do with spurious bills of exchange; a solicitor has been to the office.'

'Keep the case in your hands.'

'It is all right. I have got all the papers in my desk.'[3]

George Clarke was Druscovich's superior. He was sixty years old, had served thirty-seven of them as a police officer, and was still the senior detective officer at Scotland Yard in the absence of Superintendent Williamson. The same night, William Kurr called at Clarke's house in Great College Street, Westminster. That month, Kurr had paid Druscovich £25 and Clarke £50 in order 'to tell me when any application is made for [arrest] warrants, or when any complaints come'.

'There is something from France,' Clarke now told him, 'I am frightened and alarmed.'

They discussed the alert from the Sûreté and Kurr asked if it was still safe to exchange bank drafts from France.

'I think it will be all right if you lose no time,' Clarke said. As Kurr left, the Chief Detective Inspector added helplessly, 'Do something.'

Overnight the situation grew worse. Kurr met Druscovich underneath the arches at Charing Cross station the next morning.

William Kurr (left) *and Harry Benson* (right) *appearing as convicts to give Queen's evidence at the trial of Scotland Yard detectives*

'I know I am being piped off,' Druscovich said excitedly, meaning that he was being followed or watched. 'What more are they doing? Have they stopped the notes?'

'I don't know,' Kurr answered.

'I have told you now and you will have to look out for yourself,' Druscovich said, turning and walking away 'very sharply'.[4]

A tidier brain than William Kurr's had contrived a series of swindles, this being the last. That mind also plotted the fall of Scotland Yard. Harry Benson, known as 'Poodle' Benson in the underworld, was Hugh Montgomery, as he was also the Marquess Montmorenci and the Comte de Montagu. His home was Rosebank, a comfortable villa at Shanklin on the Isle of Wight, where he was attended by a housekeeper, a French valet, servants, horses and carriages. He owned a newspaper in the town and mixed in the best society. Benson had been educated in France and England, was a fluent linguist, an accomplished musician and, as he claimed, a composer. He was twenty-eight years old and had known Kurr for two years. His trail of frauds and victims already stretched from Edinburgh to Biarritz and from Charing Cross to Mexico City. His income from crime was at one time £4,000 a week.

Uncharacteristically, in 1872 he was caught during the commission of a relatively minor offence. In the aftermath of the Franco-Prussian War, he walked into the Mansion House and presented himself as the Mayor of Châteaudun. He walked out again with a cheque in his pocket for £1,000, signed by the Lord Mayor of London, in aid of the war-damaged town in France. For the first time, he was caught and was sent to prison for a year. While in Newgate Gaol, he tried to commit suicide by setting fire to his bed. Though he survived, he was afterwards obliged to walk with the aid of a stick. Released in 1873, he turned his remarkable energies to new forms of financial fraud.

While Harry Benson swindled his French dupes from England by means of the Turf Frauds, he was not averse to swindling the English from France. A year before the Turf Frauds, he had launched upon his English public the City of Paris Guaranteed Loan, using offices in the French capital. So great was the need for a sewerage system and the dread of cholera or typhoid in the city that the French government had guaranteed a premium of 15 per cent annually on the investment required so long as the work should last. There was to be repayment of the investment in full at the end of that period.

The English recipients of this offer were supplied with pages, apparently taken from the French financial press, which praised the scheme as an investment without parallel in modern European finance. A statement of the guarantee by the Minister of Finance and a confirmation of the forecasts by the Governor of the Bank of France were also enclosed. The eyes of those who had been content in London with interest of $2\frac{1}{2}$ per cent on Consols sparkled in anticipation. By the time that this farrago of forgery and imposture had been investigated, the greedy and the gullible in England had paid the price of experience. The Sûreté swooped on the offices of the City of Paris Loan, only to find them as empty and deserted as those at 8 Northumberland Avenue were to be.

Before leaving Paris for London, Benson, alias the Marquess Montmorenci, acted as agent for a wealthy American in the purchase of a £13,000 tiara from a Palais Royal jeweller. Benson went to the jeweller and explained that he wanted to buy both a tiara for his wife and an exact replica in artificial diamonds for usual wear. He would give the jeweller a cheque, which weeks later proved to be worthless, on an American bank. He would of course leave the genuine tiara with the jeweller until the cheque was cleared, making do with the replica in the meantime. He then returned to the American purchaser with the replica and a receipt for £13,000 from the jeweller. The dupe, seeing an apparently genuine tiara and a receipt from a jeweller of international standing, never doubted the honesty of the Marquess Montmorenci. He paid his cheque to Benson, who cashed it at once and left hastily for London.

Such had been the prelude to the Society for Insuring Against Losses on the Turf. Deplorable though Benson's activities were, he scaled the heights of his profession. It seemed that most of his victims, including those at Scotland Yard, never stood a chance. His plausibility and proficiency might have sold water to a drowning man.

*

All that stood between Benson and an absolutely secure career in crime was Scotland Yard. The solution to this was to buy the fifteen established Detective Police or, at least, the senior officers. The three Chief Detective Inspectors, all of whom appeared in the Old Bailey dock, were paid £275 a year, Inspector John Meiklejohn £225. When Kurr handed Clarke £50 as a casual present, it was more than two months' salary. Indeed, at that time detective officers still depended on rewards given by the courts to supplement their pay.

Benson used Kurr as a contact, a racing man who met Chief Inspector Palmer and others on the course at Sandown Park and elsewhere. Kurr gave them racing information and backed horses on behalf of Meiklejohn. Yet Meiklejohn swore that at first he knew no more of the young man than that. The first chink in the armour of constabulary virtue was when Meiklejohn's brother in Stirling fell badly into debt. The Detective Inspector turned to his friend Billy Kurr. As he said later, 'I borrowed £500 from him for the relief of my folks.' On Benson's instructions, Kurr kept documentary evidence of this money changing hands. If Kurr should say it was a bribe rather than a loan, it would be hard for Meiklejohn to rebut the assertion. Then, at the Angel, Islington, Kurr loosened the policeman's tongue sufficiently to get him talking about the methods of illegal betting-shop owners and the tactics of the police in their running battle. Confidential information was revealed in front of witnesses.

By November 1874, Meiklejohn's family appeared to be in still greater trouble and the Detective Inspector sold himself to Kurr and Benson without too much compunction. When Kurr had said to him, 'Here is £300, Jack,' Meiklejohn merely answered, 'This won't do.' Kurr gave him £500, more than two years' salary, 'Now you stand a bottle of champagne. . . . Perhaps you will now pay me back that £20 you borrowed of me.' 'You may go and whistle for that' said Meiklejohn, who was about to buy a house in South Lambeth Road with the money he had received.[5]

Kurr had meanwhile launched a fraudulent firm in Edinburgh as 'Philip Garner & Co.' Meiklejohn met him in the Nag's Head, Holloway, and showed him a police bill with his name on it as a wanted man. Meiklejohn later wrote to Kurr about Garner & Co., a letter which delivered him yet more securely into the trickster's hands, 'I can settle that affair for you in Scotland. I suppose that Burke has told you that I shall want 100 quid.' Kurr prudently withdrew to America for six months until the investigation went quiet.[6]

Benson on his own behalf had woven a snare for Chief Inspector Clarke. A man called Walters, posing as Kurr's betting-shop manager, pretended to have important information about a robbery. He insisted, however, that he was in fear of his life as an informer and that he would only talk to Clarke at the latter's house in Great College Street. Clarke wrote him a letter.

> Sir, I shall be glad if you could make it convenient to call at my house in Great College Street, Westminster, from eight to nine p.m. this day. Very important. Don't show this or bring anyone with you. If you cannot come, I will be at Charing Cross Station at twelve noon tomorrow.[7]

Walters took the letter to Benson, who made photographic copies of it, sending one to Clarke and saying that Walters claimed Clarke had been taking bribes from him and that the letter described a meeting for that purpose. Read dispassionately, the letter was open to just that interpretation, and Clarke in his panic had cause to regret almost every phrase of it. Benson pretended to be on Clarke's side and continued to send him letters under the guise of friendship and the brotherhood of freemasonry as 'Dear Sir and Brother'. Benson also kept witnessed copies of these letters, all of which were written in a style to suggest shared secrets and the exchange of money.

A warrant for Kurr's arrest was still out when Benson summoned

Clarke to Rosebank, his Shanklin villa. He informed Clarke that Kurr had the incriminating letter which Clarke had written to Walters and would publish it to the world if he was arrested. It was imperative that Clarke should go to the Treasury Solicitor and get the warrant for Kurr withdrawn. Shaken by this, Clarke went to the Treasury Solicitor and did as Benson had asked.[8]

Chief Detective Inspector Druscovich had meantime stood surety to his brother for a debt of £60. It fell due for repayment and neither brother had the money. Meiklejohn introduced Druscovich to Kurr as 'a perfect gentleman and an owner of racehorses'. Druscovich knew better but agreed to borrow the money. The three men met by arrangement at the Oriental Restaurant at Blackfriars station and the cash was handed over. Druscovich muttered to Meiklejohn that he did not like being seen in such a public place with a man like Kurr who had been so frequently wanted by the police. 'Suppose we ran against old Clarke?'

Meiklejohn enlightened him about Clarke, who was familiarly known as 'Bill'. 'Don't be such a fool. Bill has got them all right at our place, and at the City of London police as well.' It was then said that Clarke was paying Superintendent Bailey of the City Police £15 a week in bribes.[9]

If this was true, corruption had spread so far that, under current police organization, it might be impossible to eradicate. By now the City of Paris Guaranteed Loan had been launched by Benson. Its papers fell into the hands of the Sûreté. Kurr and Meiklejohn forged a telegram from Superintendent Williamson ordering the release of the documents. The Dover police uncovered the same swindle but their telegram was destroyed by the conspirators on its arrival at Scotland Yard. The police in Leeds discovered that proceeds of the fraud were being banked in their city. Their report was burnt by Druscovich on his office fire before Superintendent Williamson had seen it.

Equally grotesque was the black humour in which policemen and criminals shared. While the Turf Frauds were in progress, Meiklejohn entered the office in Northumberland Avenue with a face like doom and said to Benson, 'It is very thick for you, Poodle, there is a warrant out for you, and there is a warrant for Montgomery, Jackson, and Francis.'

'Do not joke, Jack,' Benson said earnestly. 'Is it a fact?'

'No, it is only my fun,' Meiklejohn replied. 'I have just come from Scotland Yard. It is all right.'[10]

Even Druscovich was in high spirits. When he read Benson's letters and the faked City of Paris Loan newspapers in French, he said to Kurr, 'There is no mistake, you have got a clever fellow behind you. Talk about Victor Hugo, I never read such French in my life.'[11]

The conspiracy was made a little more bizarre by the code in which the participants wrote to one another. Druscovich was known as 'The Dustman' or 'The Contractor', Meiklejohn as 'The Countryman', Scotland Yard as 'The Factory', Chief Inspector Clarke as 'The Chieftain', and Her Majesty's Treasury as 'Monkey'.

After the alarm was raised in Paris over the Turf Frauds, humour gave way to apprehension. Druscovich, particularly, grew desperate as the chances of discovery increased. At thirty-six he was the youngest as well as the brightest of the detective officers. Abrahams, a dogged London solicitor acting for the Comtesse de Goncourt, pestered Scotland Yard with inquiries and complaints. When Detective Sergeant Reimers asked Druscovich, as they walked over Vauxhall Bridge together, how he was getting on with the Turf Frauds, Druscovich lost his temper.

'Oh, damn the Turf Swindle! I wish I had never heard of it. But I can tell you that I have documents in my hands which could smash two.'

'Have you told the Governor so?'

'No I have not. Let him find out like I have done.'[12]

In despair, Druscovich went to see Billy Kurr about the dangers of the Turf Frauds investigation.

'I must arrest somebody over this job!'

'Then arrest me, if you like,' Kurr said obligingly. 'Take me round all the places where the bookmakers were, and then you will have performed your duty.'[13]

Kurr knew that it was Harry Benson who had been seen in such places and that no one could identify Kurr alone. However, the arrest would satisfy Superintendent Williamson for the time being.

Disaster was averted a little while longer until, on 4 December 1876, Benson, under the alias of 'Morton', and two accomplices went to Holland and were arrested in Rotterdam on smuggling charges. Soon the Dutch police suspected them of more than smuggling and Benson was held pending extradition to England. Kurr was tipped off in London and sent an inspired telegram to the Rotterdam chief of police.

Find Morton [Benson], and the two men you have in custody, are not those we want. Officer will not be sent over. Liberate them. Letter follows. Signed, Frederick Carter, Scotland Yard.[14]

The trick almost worked. The Dutch police prepared to release Benson but, on second thoughts, decided to await the letter from Scotland Yard, promised by the non-existent Inspector Carter. When the letter failed to arrive, Benson was returned to England in custody. Kurr's own turn came three weeks later. A party of Metropolitan Police, led by Detective Sergeant Littlechild, a future head of the Special Branch, set out for Kurr's house in Canonbury. Three men came out of the house, one of whom was Kurr. He saw Littlechild and turned with a revolver in his hand. 'Don't make a fool of yourself!' Littlechild shouted. 'It means murder!' Billy Kurr hesitated, then slowly lowered the gun.[15]

Benson, Kurr and several minor accomplices were held in Newgate, where their solicitor Edward Froggatt proved able to 'square the screws', as he called it. Benson also smuggled out messages by leaving a scrap of paper that would stick to a warder's shoe as the man walked over it and would then fall off outside the prison to be picked up by a waiting accomplice.

On 13 April 1877, at the Central Criminal Court, Harry Benson was sentenced to fifteen years' penal servitude and Kurr to ten years. 'Harsh though they be,' wrote *The Times*, 'the sentences are no less than is required to express the strong condemnation of practices which threaten to undermine all confidence in the integrity of commercial enterprise.'

At Scotland Yard, Superintendent Williamson was puzzled by the number of papers apparently missing. He wrote to Druscovich.

Henderson of Leeds called upon me yesterday and told me that about six weeks since he wrote me a letter stating that one of the numbered bank notes held by Benson and Kurr had been changed at Leeds. If I had seen it, I must recollect it and should have taken some action upon it. I cannot find it has ever been received at the office. Did you ever see it? Let me know at once.

Druscovich, who had burnt this and other papers from Leeds on his office fire as soon as they arrived, replied, 'Dear Sir, I know nothing of the letter. Nathaniel Druscovich.'[16]

Left: *Superintendent Frederick Williamson.* Right: (left to right) *Inspector Meiklejohn and Chief Inspectors Druscovich and Palmer*

It was not Williamson but Harry Benson who settled the matter by deciding to give the authorities what he picturesquely called 'Flower Show Information' about the Detective Police of Scotland Yard. If he was to go down, those who had taken his money to guarantee his immunity should go down with him. Druscovich, Palmer, Meiklejohn and the solicitor Edward Froggatt were arrested. Chief Detective Inspector Clarke gave evidence against Froggatt at the magistrates court and was himself arrested upon leaving the witness-box.

The Trial of the Detectives in October 1877, with Benson and Kurr as the principal witnesses for the Crown, followed a predictable course. Kurr revealed that he and Benson had bribed the police at Scotland Yard and in America, the warders in Newgate and at Millbank, as well as two Post Office inspectors, Jebb and Goodwin, Superintendent Bailey of the City of London Police 'and a good many more'. It was inevitable that press reporting of the trial should blacken the reputation of the Metropolitan Police still further. The moral standing of the force was not enhanced when, for example, the Defaulters Sheet for the prosecution witness Detective Sergeant William Reimers had to be given in evidence. It showed this conscientious officer to have eight convictions for disobedience, incivility, drunkenness and assault. He had also been suspended from duty and then reduced from Inspector to Sergeant after supplying confidential police information to Ignatius Paul Pollaky, a well-known private inquiry agent. At one point, he had been confronted with an unspecified offence and invited to resign. This was not the image of the Victorian police force which most contemporaries cherished.

At the end of the trial, only Clarke was acquitted, the other defendants being sent to hard labour for two years. George Dilnot, one of the first to examine the proceedings in detail, wrote in 1928, 'Any person studying this case cannot fail to come to the suspicion that many other detectives, both inside and outside Scotland Yard, were in the pay of Kurr and Benson. It is doubtful if the ramifications of this great plot were ever brought to light.' It was certainly true that all but twenty detective officers of the Metropolitan Police were now put on three months' probation.[17]

In 1877, the Home Secretary set up a commission to inquire into 'the state, discipline and organization of the Detective Force of the Metropolitan Police'. As result of this, a Criminal Investigation Department was created, thereafter known as the CID and commanded by Superintendent Williamson. In the light of the growing threat from Sinn Fein in 1884, there was also to be a Special Irish Branch, later known as the Special Branch, commanded in 1884 by Chief Inspector Littlechild who, as a sergeant, had arrested the armed fugitive William Kurr seven years before. It was also Littlechild who had first suggested to Superintendent Williamson that all was not as it should be in the former Detective Police.

A further reform was the institution in 1880 of the office of Director of Public Prosecutions, under the Prosecution of Offenders Act 1879. Appointed by the Home Secretary, the Director was to be independent of both the police and the Treasury. Sir John Maule, QC, Recorder of Leeds, was the first incumbent. No longer would it be possible for Chief Inspector Clarke and his kind to stop a case by strolling across to the Treasury Solicitor's office and asking for a warrant to be torn up. The new Director was the nearest thing that England had yet had to a European Ministry of Justice, with a promise of being independent of politics and the police alike. In policing, no less than in crime, the age of the Victorian amateur had begun to fade into a new professionalism.

CHAPTER 11

Past and Future

THE LIVES of wanderers and street-folk, tradesmen and burglars, whose ancestors had filled the pages of *London Labour and the London Poor*, showed continuity and change in the opening years of a new century. Often, the continuity prevailed. Henry Mayhew would not only have recognized the world of the following description, it might almost have come from his pen.

> You cannot see, as I can see, the dark empty way between the mean houses, the dark empty way lit by a bleary gas-lamp at the corner, you cannot feel the hard chequered pavement under your boots, you cannot mark the dimly lit windows here and there, and the shadows upon the ugly and often crooked blinds of the people cooped within. Nor can you presently pass the beer-house, with its brighter gas and its queer, screening windows, nor get a whiff of foul air and foul language from its door, nor see the crumpled furtive figure – some rascal child – that slinks past us down the steps. We crossed the longer street, up which a clumsy steam-tram, vomiting smoke and sparks, made its clangorous way, and adown which one saw the greasy brilliance of shop fronts and the naphtha flares of hawkers' barrows dripping fire into the night.[1]

The scene suggests the costers' habitat of the 1850s, whose people were more than half a century in the past by the time this cameo of urban life, its final images of market-stalls so close to Mayhew's own, was published in H. G. Wells' *In the Days of the Comet* (1906).

In many other areas, the social and criminal underworld of London survived its famous mid-Victorian chroniclers and the century in which they lived. Wells reflected the poetic quality of Mayhew's London panoramas. In *The Secret Agent* (1904), Joseph Conrad created a locale that John Binny might have known, in Mr Verloc's shop with its 'photographs of more or less undressed dancing girls' in the window and its back-parlour trade in sealed envelopes or soiled volumes in paper covers with promising titles. It was the precise reflection of those Holywell Street shops which William Dugdale and his allies had overseen in the 1850s, as it was of those which led to another Scotland Yard corruption scandal and an Old Bailey trial in the distant future of 1976.[2]

The images of fiction compressed a truth which might take several volumes of social investigation to illustrate. To those who had a more personal and professional contact with poverty or crime, however, the same continuity was evident. To many of them, the Victorian underworld ended rather as it began. G. W. Cornish, a future Scotland Yard superintendent, joined the Metropolitan Police in 1895. He found the society of the East End of London as impenetrable as it had been to his predecessors forty or fifty years earlier. Its customs and rituals, though for different reasons, seemed as remote as those of the furthest continent to the majority of his readers. The more recent criminals were perhaps better organized than their predecessors but had woven themselves just as closely into the fabric of their communities. As an earlier wave of refugees from hunger in Ireland had formed London neighbourhoods, so their successors represented fugitives from political and racial tyranny in eastern Europe. Far in the future, they were to be replaced in their turn by migrants from former colonies.

If there was a single novelty in the criminal class of the 1890s, it was in the greater readiness to combine together in gangs. London's East End was divided between two of the most notorious, the Bessarabians and their rivals the Odessians, who hunted in packs of about forty each. Their single alliance, as Cornish found, was against the police, for whom they showed what he called a racial hatred. Even a member of one gang grievously wounded by his enemies would do nothing to assist the investigation.

Such gangs at the end of the Victorian period lived by racketeering, levying protection on immigrant shopkeepers or on the proprietors of coffee stalls. At the first sign of protest by their victims, the extortioners descended in force, armed with guns, knives and broken bottles. Shops and stalls would be smashed and their owners beaten. There was little that the police could do, since both the predators and their prey were migrants from a Tsarist police-state who instinctively avoided contact with authority. Many of the law-abiding members of the community and the petty criminals would tolerate the activities of the gangs rather than complain to the police. To some this was a matter of honour. Others feared what would happen to them if they were known to have 'betrayed' their persecutors. The Metropolitan Police were 'continually having to let cases drop through lack of evidence'. Lack of evidence, the buying off of witnesses, was nothing new in such areas. The mid-Victorian police had been no less frustrated by it in their dealings with London's burglars.[3]

The extent and mobility of gang warfare or protection rackets might seem new in the 1890s but there was a dispiriting familiarity in the accounts of the communal dwellings of a contemporary criminal class. The description which Cornish gave of such places in 1895 might have been taken from the great documentary literature which had begun to appear half a century before, though in his duties he dealt increasingly with criminals and victims who, literally, spoke a language he could not understand. Crime flourished in the most squalid public houses of the East End, as it had done fifty years earlier. Though many of the criminal rookeries had gone, lodging-houses were still linked together by cellar doors and secret passages in areas which once again earned the policeman's cliché of a 'rabbit warren'. In 1851, the Metropolitan Police had been given the task of supervising such lodging-houses as Mayhew described. By 1894, seven hundred of the worst houses had been closed down but conditions in the remainder improved little until 1902, when the London County Council was granted additional powers to make regulations and by-laws controlling them. Even this seemed to change the nature of the problem rather than remove it. With the passing of the old padding-kens, Cornish thought philosophically that crime had not diminished but was merely dispersed over a still wider area.[4]

Under pressure from new immigration, the native-born criminals of the East End began to move to areas of London just south of the river. These included confidence-tricksters, safe-breakers and 'high-class' thieves, who regarded themselves as the aristocrats of the underworld. Yet the influx from the East End also brought coiners, forgers, race gangs and particularly housebreakers and pickpockets, many of the latter being attracted by the proximity of the West End, a short distance away across the Thames bridges. By the 1920s and 1930s, this new settlement gave rise to further gang warfare between members of the racecourse and protection rackets from Bermondsey and Southwark, including Monkey Benneyworth's Elephant Gang, and their rivals north of the river, among them Darby Sabini's gang from Clerkenwell's 'Little Italy'.

This underworld of the 1890s and the early twentieth century lacked a popular chronicler to rival Dickens or Mayhew, though such fiction as Arthur Morrison's novel *A Child of the Jago* and his stories in *Tales of Mean Streets* enjoyed considerable success. Yet the existence of that under-world in its most outrageous activities was graphically represented in the press by such incidents as the so-called 'Tottenham Outrage' and the 'Siege of Sidney Street', and by such trials of professional criminals as that of Steinie Morrison for the murder of Leon Beron. Between them, these cases had a profound effect on the popular view of the East End as containing a nest of gangsters whose power might extend to areas hitherto unaffected.

The improvement in the East End, in Cornish's experience, came from business and development, and the extension of the Underground which brought to Arthur Morrison's mean streets the restaurants, cinemas and department stores of a more affluent culture. The East End was not after all to be overrun by foreign gangs but by the popular culture of the variety theatre and the Picturedrome, the *palais de danse* and the weekly magazine.[5]

*

Modern crime, so far as it was to be distinguished from the activities of the Victorian underworld, appeared to many contemporaries as a phe-nomenon of the 1920s, the product of a moral schism represented by the First World War. The artefacts of a new age, the motor-car, the tele-phone and the gun, appeared as innovations in their easy availability to robbers and murderers. The war of 1914–18 had certainly left an ample legacy of Webley service revolvers and .455 ammunition. In 1919, one service revolver murdered Kitty Breaks at Blackpool and another killed Bella Wright in the Green Bicycle Case. A car and a gun were central in such crimes of the decade as the vindictive yet impersonal murder of PC Gutteridge by the two ex-convicts Frederick Browne and William Kennedy in 1927.

To a reader of the press in the seven or eight years following the war, the major cases in the criminal courts seemed to testify to this culture of mechanized ruthlessness. In 1921 the confidence-trickster Ernest Dyer shot dead his business partner to prevent the discovery of a fraud and was then killed with his own gun by the policeman who arrested him. In 1922, the murderer of Olive Young was found to be a gun-obsessed lunatic, Ronald True, while in the same year Cecil Maltby shot his mistress with a Winchester rifle and later shot himself. In 1923 a military deserter, Alexander Mason, gunned down a cab-driver. The same year saw the shooting dead of her sexually aberrant husband by Madame Marguerite Fahmy at the Savoy Hotel. In 1924, Jack Goldenberg shot dead the manager of a bank he was robbing. In 1926, John Merrett shot his own mother. In 1927, the so-called 'Shooting in Whistling Copse' might have come from the pen of Conan Doyle. Four years later, in a further defiance of law and order, a policeman was shot by gunmen in Thames Ditton. Mr Justice Humphreys, passing sentence, opened the issue of whether 'the police of this country are to continue to go about their duties unarmed'.

Whatever the readers of the press might think, Scotland Yard recognized the new dimension of violence and attempted to defeat the modern criminal on his own ground by forming twelve officers, armed when necessary, into the quaintly named 'Flying Squad' in 1919. Only seven years earlier, the Countess Sztaray's call to Eastbourne police station, as a police officer was shot dead, had been answered by a single unarmed inspector setting off from the station on a bicycle, the only transport available.

Similar anxieties to those of the 1920s were to be prevalent in the post-war 1940s, as they had been in the post-war 1740s, when Horace Walpole warned Sir Thomas Mann that the return of men from the War of the Austrian Succession obliged Londoners to travel in their city as if going into battle. In the 1920s, however, it could not be denied that training for war coincided in the criminal mind with the malign example of gang rivalry in the United States during a decade of prohibition. Those accused of the murders of Bella Wright and Kitty Breaks in 1919, as well as the murderers Ernest Dyer and Ronald True, Alexander Mason and Jack Goldenberg, Frederick Browne and William Kennedy, had learnt to use guns in the army. Browne and Kennedy had previous convictions for armed robbery, while Kennedy was proud of having been a Sinn Fein gunman as 'The Fair-Haired Sniper' and 'Two-Gun Pat'.

Yet even in this willingness to use firearms, there was a continuity which stretched back into the Victorian period and beyond. Guns, though more freely available after a world war, had long been the means by which victims were dispatched in some of the best-known murder cases. For example, Julian Hall was murdered in 1913; Arthur Walls, a policeman, in 1912; in 1911 another policeman was saved only because Charles Arthur's gun misfired; John Nisbet was shot dead in a 1910 robbery; Mrs Luard was murdered by a firearm in 1908; William Whiteley in 1907; Camille Holland in 1899; another policeman, George Cole, in 1882; Isaac Gold was shot in a train robbery in 1881; Charles Peace shot dead Arthur Dyson in 1879, not before he had also killed one policeman, Nicholas Cock and wounded another, Edward Robinson; Isaac Jermy was murdered by shooting in 1848; and even the celebrated 'Murder in the Old Red Barn' had been committed with a firearm a hundred years before Browne and Kennedy shot PC Gutteridge. By contrast, two of the most famous cases of the 1920s, involving Harold Greenwood and Major Armstrong as defendants, turned upon the use of nothing more novel than a large, old-fashioned dose of arsenic.

The images of American crime, in magazines and on the cinema screen, seemed a new and deplorable incitement to the commission of crime. After the conviction of Yaroslav Charles, leader of the Thames Ditton gunmen, in 1931, Cornish believed that he had been drawn to armed robbery by the stories in American crime magazines found in his rooms. Such influences might be unwholesome but were scarcely new. In 1836, the Inspectors of Prisons had complained to Parliament of the extent to which even the most dangerous criminals in Newgate were given free access to the worst type of newspapers 'which abound in vulgar adventure in criminal enterprise, and in the histories of the police, the gaol, and the scaffold'. In principle, it seemed that little had changed in the reading habits of offenders and the availability of this material between the 1830s and the 1930s.[6]

So far as the integrity of the police was at issue, the new and less stringent post-war morality of the 1920s, which was so eagerly spoken of, might have bred some corruption of authority. There were certainly such scandals as those of 1928–9, involving the taking of bribes and the perversion of the course of public justice to ensure that the newly glamorous 'nightclubs' were not interfered with. Yet such embarrassments must have seemed long familiar to those who had read the newspapers fifty years earlier, during the 'Trial of the Detectives' and the revelations of the 'Turf

Frauds' in 1877. Indeed, the costers of the 1850s, no less than the diarist of *My Secret Life*, had always supposed that policemen took bribes to ensure that vice might trade undisturbed. The scandals of 1928–9 appeared rather less sensational than their Victorian counterparts.

In other areas of endeavour, England's criminals showed an innate conservatism. Safe-breakers travelled by car in the 1920s but they still opened safes by cutting a hole in the side with a ring-saw, very much like old-fashioned peter-cutters seventy years before. Superintendent Cornish's comment in 1935 that the professional Victorian or Edwardian burglar or safe-breaker was restricted in his activities to the distance he could walk or by the short journey he might make, on a bus or a tram, would have caused amusement and reassurance to Edward Agar, Thomas Caseley and their kind. It was precisely this view of crime which had been so helpful to Agar in the bullion robbery of 1855.

The simplest tricks of certain trades died hard. In the 1950s, as surely as in Mayhew's observations on the 1850s, street-corner sharps offered the public a chance to grow rich at the Three-Card Trick or Three-Thimbles-and-a-Pea. Little shops selling postcards in their windows and 'something warmer' in the back room had scarcely changed since the days of William Dugdale. Where Mayhew saw the 'Sham-Indecent' trade, a new age had its 'Sucker-Traps'. Many of these were familiar, even before Mayhew's time.

Victorian England bequeathed to an underworld and an underclass a continuity that was to be largely unbroken for a further forty years. Many of Patrick Hamilton's descriptions of London in his popular trilogy *Twenty Thousand Streets Under the Sky* (1929–35), for example, have almost everything in common with Mayhew. Hamilton's is not merely the grey litter and rumbling trams of the Hampstead Road at dusk, the first glimmer of lights and the last red glow on the clouds. The padding-kens of the 1850s live on in a Soho doss-house of the 1930s, little altered from *London Labour and the London Poor*, a communal ward resounding to the snortings and snorings of 'London's defeated grasping angrily at oblivion'.[7]

The lower depths of urban society and its underworld, which Mayhew and Dickens described and upon which 'Walter' preyed, were to survive in recognizable form until the Second World War. 'Darkest England', as William Booth of the Salvation Army had called it, the 'other England' of the Victorian period, lived long enough to forget the

Gustave Doré, The Devil's Acre, Westminster

Queen whose name was associated with it. The destruction of cities in the Blitz of the early 1940s, the dispersal of their populations in the brave new world of twenty years' rebuilding and the settlement of new immigrant communities obliterated at last the neighbourhoods formed by costers and street-folk, penny gaffs and padding-kens, the haunts of dodgers and the swell mob. Until that point, the century long past remained the predominant force in the present.

Notes

Abbreviations

LL & LP: Henry Mayhew, Bracebridge Hemyng, John Binny and Andrew Halliday, *London Labour and the London Poor*, London: Charles Griffin, 1861–2

Criminal Prisons: Henry Mayhew and John Binny, *The Criminal Prisons of London and Scenes of Prison Life*, London: Griffin, Bohn, and Company, 1862

Report (1): *Report from the Select Committee of the House of Lords on the Law Relating to the Protection of Young Girls; Together with the Proceedings of the Committee, Minutes of Evidence, and Appendix. Ordered by the House of Commons to be Printed*, 1881

Report (2): *Joint Select Committee on Lotteries and Indecent Advertisements: Minutes of Evidence and Appendices, Ordered by the House of Commons to be Printed*, 1908

CHAPTER 1: VICTORIA'S OTHER LONDON

1. *Punch*, XVIII (1850), 93.
2. LL & LP, II, 218–26, 253.
3. *Punch*, XVIII (1850), 93.
4. Charles Cavendish Fulke Greville, *The Greville Memoirs 1814–1860*, ed. Lytton Strachey & Roger Fulford, London: Macmillan & Co., 1938, II, 213–14, 262–3.
5. LL & LP, I, 394.
6. Ibid., IV, 439.
7. Ibid., I, 11.
8. Ibid., I, 21, 42.
9. Ibid., I, 530.
10. Ibid., I, 24.
11. Ibid., I, 40–2.
12. Ibid., I, 47.
13. Ibid., I, 40.
14. Ibid., I, 47.
15. Ibid., I, 14.
16. Ibid., I, 22.
17. Ibid., I, 16.
18. Ibid., I, 28.
19. Ibid., I, 22.
20. *Morning Chronicle*, 1 August 1850.

21. Charles Dickens, 'Shops and their Tenants', in *Sketches by Boz*.

22. Charles Dickens, 'Meditations in Monmouth Street', in *Sketches by Boz*.

23. LL & LP, IV, 224.

24. Charles Kingsley, 'Cheap Clothes and Nasty', in *Alton Locke: Tailor and Poet*, London: Macmillan, 1879, pp.lxxviii–lxxix.

25. LL & LP, II, 280.

26. Ibid., I, 268, 272, 275; Charles Terrot, *The Maiden Tribute: A Study of the White Slave Traffic of the Nineteenth Century*, London: Frederick Muller, 1959, pp.23–4.

27. LL & LP, I, 452; III, 402; III, 414.

28. Ibid., IV, 223–4.

29. Ibid., I, 275.

30. Ibid., I, 266–7.

31. Ibid., I, 267.

32. Ibid., I, 267.

33. Ibid., I, 268.

34. Ibid., I, 232–3.

35. Ibid., I, 265.

36. Ibid., I, 141–2.

37. Ibid., I, 142.

38. Ibid., II, 168.

39. Ibid., II, 167.

40. Ibid., II, 168.

41. Ibid., II, 446.

42. Ibid., II, 449.

43. Ibid., II, 171–2.

44. Ibid., II, 508–9.

45. Criminal Prisons, p.29.

CHAPTER 2: THE DODGERS AND THE SWELL MOB

1. *Fraser's Magazine*, V (1832), 521–2; W. D. Morrison, *Crime and its Causes*, London, 1891, pp.141–2.

2. PRO/SP 36/125/4; *The Yale Edition of Horace Walpole's Correspondence*, ed. W. S. Lewis, New Haven: Yale University Press, 1937–65, XX, 188.

3. LL & LP, IV, 295.

4. Ibid., IV, 300.

5. Ibid., IV, 300.

6. Ibid., IV, 299–300.

7. Ibid., IV, 301.

8. Charles Dickens, 'On Duty with Inspector Field', in *Reprinted Pieces*.

9. Charles Dickens, 'Gin Shops', in *Sketches by Boz*.

10. LL & LP, I, 277.

11. Ibid., I, 268–9.

12. Ibid., IV, 203.

13. Ibid., IV, 406–9.

14. Ibid., IV, 412–13.

15. Ibid., I, 465.

16. Ibid., I, 465.
17. Ibid., IV, 435.
18. Ibid., IV, 437–8.
19. Renton Nicholson, *Rogue's Progress: An Autobiography of 'Lord Chief Baron' Nicholson*, ed. John L. Bradley, London: Longmans, 1966, p.10.
20. LL & LP, IV, 438–9.
21. Ibid., IV, 377.
22. Ibid., IV, 378–9.
23. Ibid., IV, 368.
24. Ibid., I, 389–91.
25. Ibid., IV, 273–4.
26. Ibid., IV, 273.
27. Ibid., IV, 278.
28. Ibid., IV, 372.
29. Ibid., IV, 281–2.
30. Ibid., IV, 303.
31. Ibid., IV, 320.
32. Ibid., I, 457.
33. Ibid., IV, 308.
34. Ibid., IV, 333–4.
35. Ibid., IV, 343.
36. Ibid., IV, 294.
37. Ibid., IV, 336.
38. Ibid., IV, 335.
39. Ibid., IV, 339–40.
40. *Fraser's Magazine*, VI (1832), 464–5.
41. LL & LP, IV, 352–4.

CHAPTER 3: MODERN BABYLON

1. Report (1), p.64.
2. Ibid., p.69.
3. Geoffrey Faber, *Jowett: A Portrait with Background*, London: Faber and Faber, 1957, p.93; 'Walter', *My Secret Life*, London: Arrow Books, 1994–5, III, 256–7.
4. Charles Booth, *Life and Labour of the People in London*, Final Volume, London: Macmillan, 1902, pp.126–7; Albert Fried and Richard M. Elman, ed., *Charles Booth's London*, London: Hutchinson, 1969, pp.128–9; William Acton, *Prostitution: Considered in its Moral, Social and Sanitary Aspects*, ed. Peter Fryer, London: Macgibbon and Kee, 1968, p.73.
5. Sir William Hardman, *A Mid-Victorian Pepys*, ed. S. M. Ellis, London: Cecil Palmer, 1923, pp.88–91.
6. Ronald Pearsall, *The Worm in the Bud*, London: Penguin Books, 1971, p.333.
7. Papers of Edwin Chadwick, Depositions, Box 129.
8. William Acton, *Prostitution: Considered in its Moral, Social and Sanitary Aspects*, p.48.
9. LL & LP, IV, 357.
10. Ibid., IV, 213.
11. Ibid., IV, 223–4.

12. Ibid., IV, 224.
13. Ibid., IV, 357.
14. William Acton, *Prostitution: Considered in its Moral, Social and Sanitary Aspects*, p.61.
15. LL & LP, IV, 252, 253.
16. Ibid., IV, 239.
17. Ibid., IV, 248.
18. Ibid., IV, 247.
19. Ibid., IV, 233.
20. Ibid., IV, 234.
21. Ibid., IV, 229–30.
22. Ibid., IV, 231–2.
23. Ibid., IV, 237.
24. James McLevy, *The Casebook of a Victorian Detective*, ed. George Scott-Moncrieff, Edinburgh: Canongate, 1975, pp.2–8.
25. LL & LP, IV, 215, 359.
26. Donald Thomas, *A Long Time Burning: The History of Literary Censorship in England*, London: Routledge and Kegan Paul, 1969, p.424.
27. Charles Cavendish Fulke Greville, *The Greville Memoirs 1814–1860*, II, 426.
28. *Trials of Oscar Wilde*, ed. H. Montgomery Hyde, London: William Hodge, 1948, p.190.
29. Henry Spencer Ashbee [Pisanus Fraxi], *Index Librorum Prohibitorum*, London, 1877, pp.xlii–xliii.
30. Algernon Charles Swinburne, *The Swinburne Letters*, ed. Cecil Y. Lang, New Haven: Yale University Press, 1959–62, VI, 245.
31. Henry Spencer Ashbee, *Index Librorum Prohibitorum*, p.313.
32. 'Walter', *My Secret Life*, III, 115.
33. John Francis Stanley, Earl Russell, *My Life and Adventures*, London, 1923, p.157.
34. T. J. Wise, *A Bibliography of Writings in Prose and Verse of Algernon Charles Swinburne*, privately printed, 1919–20, I, 220.
35. *The Extraordinary Life and Trial of Madame Rachel*, London: Diprose and Bateman, [1868], *passim*; William Ballantine, *Some Experiences of a Barrister's Life*, London: Richard Bentley, 1882, II, 77–80; Montagu Williams, *Leaves of a Life*, London: Macmillan, 1890, I, 224–49.
36. Daniel Farson, *Jack the Ripper*, London: Michael Joseph, 1972, p.125.
37. Richard von Krafft-Ebing, *Psychopathia Sexualis with Special Reference to the Antipathic Sexual Instinct: Only Authorized English Adaptation of the Twelfth German Edition*, tr. F. J. Rebman, London: William Heinemann, 1914, pp.95–9.
38. *Reminiscences of Sir Henry Hawkins, Baron Brampton*, London: Edward Arnold, 1905, p.287.
39. Arthur Griffiths, *The Chronicles of Newgate*, London: Chapman and Hall, 1884, p.538.
40. W. T. Stead, *Criminal Law Amendment Act: Vigilance Committees and their Work*, London: Pall Mall Gazette, 1885, p.10.
41. Richard von Krafft-Ebing, *Psychopathia Sexualis*, p.553; 'Walter', *My Secret Life*, I, 12.
42. Krafft-Ebing, op. cit., p.499.
43. W. T. Stead, *The Maiden Tribute of Modern Babylon*, London: Pall Mall Gazette, 1885, p.9.
44. Ibid., p.10.
45. Report (1), p.63.
46. Ibid., p.64.

47. *Gentlewoman*, 5 February 1898; *Fortnightly Review*, CL (1941), 282.
48. Charles Terrot, *The Maiden Tribute*, p.69.
49. LL & LP, IV, 269.
50. Report (1), pp.110–12.
51. Ibid., pp.127, 140–1.
52. Ibid., pp.111, 137, 139.
53. Ibid., p.35; *Belgium No. 1 (1880) Correspondence Respecting Immoral Traffic in English Girls in Belgium*, 1881 [Appendix to Report], p.36.
54. *Belgium No. 1 Correspondence (1880)*, p.36.
55. Report (1), p.35.
56. *St James's Gazette*, 22 July 1885; W. T. Stead, *The Maiden Tribute of Modern Babylon*, p.4.
57. *St James's Gazette*, 15 July 1885.
58. Sir William Hardman, *The Hardman Papers*, ed. S. M. Ellis, London: Constable, 1930, p.99.
59. Charles Terrot, *The Maiden Tribute*, p.215.
60. Ibid., pp.93–6.
61. Ibid., p.169.

CHAPTER 4: THE UNKNOWN VICTORIAN

1. Sir William Hardman, *The Letters and Memoirs of Sir William Hardman: Second Series 1863–5*, ed. S. M. Ellis, London: Cecil Palmer, 1925, p.99.
2. 'Walter', *My Secret Life*, I, xiii.
3. Ibid., I, 49.
4. Ibid., I, 45.
5. Ibid., I, 180.
6. Ibid., I, 99.
7. Ibid., I, 392–7, 405.
8. Ibid., I, 407.
9. Ibid., I, 419.
10. Ibid., I, 382–7.
11. Ibid., II, 48.
12. William Acton, *Functions and Disorders of the Reproductive Organs*, 3rd edition, London, 1862, p.101.
13. 'Walter', *My Secret Life*, II, 95; III, 503.
14. Ibid., I, 9, 313.
15. Ibid., III, 457.
16. Ibid., III, 482.

CHAPTER 5: 'MORE DEADLY THAN PRUSSIC ACID'

1. *Parliamentary Debates* (3rd series), CXLV, 102.
2. Cf. PRO KB 28/504/13; 28/509/21; 28/515/13; 28/534/14; 28/547/25; 28/602/1; 28/602/3.
3. *Parliamentary Debates* (3rd series), CXLVI, 327.
4. *Society for the Suppression of Vice: Occasional Report and Appeal*, 1868, p.5.
5. PRO KB 28/443/16.
6. 1 *Cox's Criminal Cases*, 229.

7. *The Times*, 22 June 1877.
8. LL & LP, I, 256.
9. Ibid., I, 27.
10. *The Times*, 29 January 1870; 17 February 1870.
11. Cf. *New Writings by Swinburne*, ed. Cecil Y. Lang, New Haven: Syracuse University Press, 1964.
12. Henry Spencer Ashbee, *Index Librorum Prohibitorum*, pp.314–15.
13. Ibid., pp.379–96.
14. *Parliamentary Debates* (3rd series), CXLV, 102; CXLVI, 329.
15. *The Times*, 22 June 1877.
16. George Moore, *Literature at Nurse: or, Circulating Morals*, London: Vizetelly, 1885, p.18.
17. Report (2), p.40.
18. Ibid., p.41; John Sweeney, *At Scotland Yard*, London: Grant Richards, 1904, p.196.
19. Report (2), p.40.
20. Ibid., p.41.
21. Ibid., p.39.
22. C. M. Bowra, *Memories 1898–1939*, London, Weidenfeld and Nicolson, 1967, p.87.
23. Donald Thomas, *A Long Time Burning*, p.277.
24. George Moore, *Literature at Nurse*, p.19.

CHAPTER 6: ENTERTAINMENTS: TOWN AND TURF

1. LL & LP, I, 47.
2. Ibid., I, 42–4.
3. *The Cuckold's Nest of Choice, Flash, Smutty and Delicious Songs with Rummy Toasts. Adapted for Gentlemen Only*, London: W. West, c.1850.
4. Renton Nicholson, *Rogue's Progress*, p.xi.
5. Ibid., p.246.
6. Ibid., pp.252–3.
7. Report (2), p.44.
8. LL & LP, I, 237.
9. Ibid., I, 236.
10. Ibid., I, 237.
11. Ibid., I, 239.
12. Ibid., III, 124–5.
13. William Ballantine, *Some Experiences of a Barrister's Life*, II, 275–6.
14. LL & LP, II, 64.
15. Ibid., I, 504.
16. Ibid., III, 7–11.
17. 'Lord' George Sanger, *Seventy Years a Showman*, Introduced by Kenneth Grahame, London: J. M. Dent, 1927, p.8.
18. Ibid., p.16.
19. Ibid., p.17.
20. Ibid., p.18.
21. Ibid., pp.39–41.
22. Ibid., 115–16.
23. Ibid., p.49.

24. Ibid., pp.50–2.
25. Ibid., pp.122–3.
26. Ibid., pp.160–1.
27. Ibid., pp.45–6.
28. Ibid., pp.72–83.
29. Report (2), p.89.
30. Arthur M. Binstead and Ernest Wells, *A Pink 'Un and a Pelican*, London: Bliss Sands and Co., 1898, pp.14–21.
31. The Marquess of Queensberry and Percy Colson, *Oscar Wilde and the Black Douglas*, London: Hutchinson, 1949, p.60.
32. J. B. Booth, *Old Pink 'Un Days*, London: Grant Richards, 1924, p.24.
33. J. B. Booth, *'Master' and Men: Pink 'Un Yesterdays*, London: T. Werner Laurie, 1927, pp.35–6; C. L. McCluer Stevens, *Famous Crimes and Criminals*, London: Stanley Paul, 1926, p.168.
34. William Hazlitt, 'The Fight', in *Fugitive Writings*.
35. William Ballantine, *Some Experiences of a Barrister's Life*, II, 273–4; *Early Victorian England: 1830–1865*, ed. G. M. Young, London: Oxford University Press, 1934, I, 281–2.
36. Arthur M. Binstead and Ernest Wells, *A Pink 'Un and a Pelican*, p.95; J. B. Booth, *'Master' and Men*, p.62.
37. Charles Booth, *Life and Labour of the People in London*, Final Volume, pp.56–9; Albert Fried and Richard M. Elman, ed., *Charles Booth's London*, pp.187–9.

CHAPTER 7: 'MISAPPLIED GENIUS'

1. George Dilnot, ed., *The Bank of England Forgery*, London: Geoffrey Bles, 1929, p.11.
2. LL & LP, I, 264–8.
3. George Dilnot, ed., *The Trial of Jim the Penman* [containing the trial of William Pierce, James Burgess, and William George Tester], London: Geoffrey Bles, 1930, p.268.
4. George Measom, *Official Guide to the South-Eastern Railway*, 1853, pp.1–66.
5. Noel Currer-Briggs, *Contemporary Observations on Security from the Chubb Collectanea 1818–1968*, London: Chubb and Son, 1968 [unpaginated].
6. *The Trial of Jim the Penman*, p.157.
7. Ibid., p.233.
8. Asa Briggs, *Victorian People*, London: Penguin Books, 1965, pp.127–8.
9. *The Trial of Jim the Penman*, p.135.
10. Ibid., p.168.
11. Ibid., pp.169–70; Donald Thomas, *Honour Among Thieves*, London: Weidenfeld and Nicolson, 1991, p.80.
12. *The Trial of Jim the Penman*, p.171.
13. Ibid., p.180.
14. Ibid., p.178.
15. Ibid., p.178.
16. Ibid., p.178.
17. Ibid., p.266.
18. Ibid., pp.264, 268.
19. Ibid., p.269.
20. Ibid., pp.11–33; 67–123.

21. *The Bank of England Forgery*, p.31.
22. Ibid., p.53.
23. Ibid., p.273.
24. Noel Currer-Briggs, *Contemporary Observations on Security*.
25. Richard Byrne, *Safecracking*, London: Grafton, 1991, pp.11–16.
26. Ibid., pp.39–41; LL & LP, IV, 344.
27. Noel Currer-Briggs, *Contemporary Observations on Security*.

CHAPTER 8: LAGGED FOR LIFE

1. Arthur Griffiths, *The Chronicles of Newgate*, pp.413, 517–19.
2. Ibid., pp.519–22.
3. William Smith, *State of the Gaols in London, Westminster, and the Borough of Southwark*, London, 1776, p.49.
4. Criminal Prisons, p.246.
5. Arthur Griffiths, *The Chronicles of Newgate*, p.412.
6. Ibid., pp.418–19.
7. Criminal Prisons, p.80.
8. Ibid., p.96.
9. Ibid., p.114.
10. Ibid., p.114.
11. James Tucker, *Ralph Rashleigh*, London: Folio Society, 1976, p.99.
12. Criminal Prisons, p.102.
13. Ibid., p.141.
14. Ibid., pp.102, 103.
15. Ibid., p.101.
16. Ibid., p.411.
17. Ibid., pp.139–40, 335.
18. Ibid., p.139.
19. Ibid., p.132.
20. Ibid., pp.131n, 349.
21. Ibid., pp.308–10.
22. Ibid., pp.307–8.
23. Ibid., pp.307, 570–1.
24. Ibid., pp.303–5.
25. Ibid., pp.119–20.
26. Ibid., p.127.
27. Ibid., pp.197–8.
28. Ibid., pp.199, 200.
29. Ibid., pp.199–200.
30. Ibid., p.176.
31. Ibid., p.181.
32. Ibid., p.190.
33. Ibid., p.195.
34. Ibid., p.196.
35. Ibid., p.243.
36. Ibid., pp.160–1.

37. LL & LP, IV, 379–80.
38. Ibid., IV, 336–7.
39. Ibid., IV, 288.

CHAPTER 9: JUSTICE DENIED

1. *Reminiscences of Sir Henry Hawkins*, pp.289–93.
2. William Ballantine, *Some Reminiscences of a Barrister's Life*, I, 263–4.
3. Ibid., II, 263–4.
4. Ibid., II, 16–23.
5. Ibid., II, 25–7.
6. Fenton Bresler, *Reprieve: A Study of a System*, London: Harrap, 1965, p.70.
7. Ibid., p.70.
8. Pierre Nordin, *Sir Arthur Conan Doyle*, Paris: Didier, 1964, p.138.
9. Ibid., p.135.
10. Peter Hunt, *Oscar Slater: The Great Suspect*, London: Carroll and Nicholson, 1951, p.142.
11. Macdonald Hastings, *The Other Mr Churchill*, London: Harrap, 1963, p.55.

CHAPTER 10: THE ARREST OF SCOTLAND YARD

1. George Dilnot, ed., *The Trial of the Detectives*, London: Geoffrey Bles, 1928, p.28.
2. Ibid., p.29.
3. Ibid., p.29.
4. Ibid., pp.2930.
5. Ibid., pp.100–1.
6. Ibid., p.83.
7. Ibid., p.87.
8. Ibid., pp.121–7.
9. Ibid., p.90.
10. Ibid., p.94.
11. Ibid., p.97.
12. Ibid., p.179.
13. Ibid., p.97.
14. Ibid., p.78.
15. Ibid., p.46.
16. Ibid., p.47.
17. David Ascoli, *The Queen's Peace: The Origins and Development of the Metropolitan Police 1829–1979*, London: Hamish Hamilton, 1979, p.149.

CHAPTER 11: PAST AND FUTURE

1. H. G. Wells, *In the Days of the Comet*, Chapter 3.
2. Joseph Conrad, *The Secret Agent*, Chapter 1.
3. G. W. Cornish, *Cornish of Scotland Yard*, New York: Macmillan, 1935, pp.7–8.
4. Ibid., pp.4–5.
5. Ibid., p.6.
6. Ibid., p.237.
7. *The Midnight Bell*, Chapter LVI, in *Twenty Thousand Streets Under the Sky*.

Index